CONCERTO FOR *Cootie*

American Made Music Series

ADVISORY BOARD

David Evans, General Editor
Barry Jean Ancelet
Edward A. Berlin
Joyce J. Bolden
Rob Bowman
Curtis Ellison
William Ferris
John Edward Hasse
Kip Lornell
Bill Malone
Eddie S. Meadows
Manuel H. Peña
Wayne D. Shirley
Robert Walser

CONCERTO FOR *Cootie*

THE LIFE AND TIMES OF COOTIE WILLIAMS

Steven C. Bowie

UNIVERSITY PRESS OF MISSISSIPPI / JACKSON

Support for this publication was provided by Furthermore grants in publishing, a program of the J. M. Kaplan Fund

The University Press of Mississippi is the scholarly publishing agency of the Mississippi Institutions of Higher Learning: Alcorn State University, Delta State University, Jackson State University, Mississippi State University, Mississippi University for Women, Mississippi Valley State University, University of Mississippi, and University of Southern Mississippi.

www.upress.state.ms.us

The University Press of Mississippi is a member of the Association of University Presses.

Any discriminatory or derogatory language or hate speech regarding race, ethnicity, religion, sex, gender, class, national origin, age, or disability that has been retained or appears in elided form is in no way an endorsement of the use of such language outside a scholarly context.

Copyright © 2025 by University Press of Mississippi
All rights reserved
Manufactured in the United States of America

∞

Publisher: University Press of Mississippi, Jackson, USA
Authorised GPSR Safety Representative: Easy Access System Europe – Mustamäe tee 50, 10621 Tallinn, Estonia, gpsr.requests@easproject.com

Library of Congress Cataloging-in-Publication Data

Names: Bowie, Steven C. author
Title: Concerto for Cootie : the life and times of Cootie Williams / Steven C. Bowie.
Other titles: American made music series
Description: Jackson : University Press of Mississippi, 2025. | Series: American made music series | Includes bibliographical references and index.
Identifiers: LCCN 2025028700 (print) | LCCN 2025028701 (ebook) | ISBN 9781496859433 hardback | ISBN 9781496859440 trade paperback | ISBN 9781496859457 epub | ISBN 9781496859464 epub | ISBN 9781496859471 pdf | ISBN 9781496859488 pdf
Subjects: LCSH: Williams, Cootie | Williams, Cootie—Interviews | Trumpet players—United States—Biography | Jazz musicians—United States—Biography | Trumpet players—United States—Interviews | African American jazz musicians—United States—Interviews | Jazz musicians—United States—Interviews | LCGFT: Biographies | Interviews Classification:
LCC ML419.W528 B69 2025 (print) | LCC ML419.W528 (ebook) | DDC 788.9/2165092—dc23/eng/20250715
LC record available at https://lccn.loc.gov/2025028700
LC ebook record available at https://lccn.loc.gov/2025028701

British Library Cataloging-in-Publication Data available

To Julie, you are my life!

CONTENTS

Introduction 3

Part I—Alabama
1. Mobile Blues. 9
2. Boy Meets Horn 14
3. A "Young" Professional 18
4. Florida 21
5. New York 25

Part II—Duke Ellington (1929)
6. Cotton Club Stomp 35
7. Catherine 40
8. Bugle Call Rag 44
9. The First European Tour 47
10. Williams, Whetsel, and Stewart 52
11. Echoes of Harlem 56
12. Carnegie Hall 61
13. The Second European Tour 62

Part III—Benny Goodman (1940)
14. When Cootie Left the Duke 69
15. Benny Rides Again 77
16. Building a Band 91

Part IV—Cootie Williams, Big Band Leader (1942)
17. Fly Right 103
18. Back to New York 108
19. The Impact of War 113
20. Moe Gale and the Savoy Ballroom 119

21. Trumpet Student 124
22. Closing at the Savoy 128
23. *Film Vodvil* 131
24. A Return to the Studio 137
25. 'Round Midnight 151
26. Personnel Changes 159
27. Capitol Records 164
28. Mainstream Press Attention 172
29. A Change in Management 176
30. A Year of Change 188
31. End of an Era 196

Part V—Cootie Williams, Combo Leader (1947)

32. Things Ain't What They Used to Be 207
33. Gator 212
34. Savoy Ballroom Champion 218
35. The House Band 225
36. Back to the Studios 228
37. The Holy City 234
38. European Triumph 238
39. Back Home 249

Part VI—Duke Ellington (1962)

40. Drifting Right Back 261
41. The Road 269
42. The State Department Tour 273
43. The Bookends 279
44. The Road Manager 288
45. Mortality 291
46. We Love You Madly 295

Part VII—Mercer Ellington (1974)

47. Now More Than Ever 302
48. Continuum 308
49. Unretirement 312
50. The Last Tenure 316
51. The Last Tour 318
52. Passing the Torch 321

Acknowledgments 327
Notes 331

Cootie Williams Discography. 379
The Compositions of Cootie Williams. 415
Awards and Honors 419
Bibliography 421
Index 425

CONCERTO FOR *Cootie*

INTRODUCTION

This book started as a dream. One night in 2010, I dreamt that I was at a bookstand somewhere in Los Angeles. Out of the corner of my eye, I saw Cootie Williams standing next to me. He was attired in the outfit you see him wearing on the cover of the *Cootie Williams in Hi-Fi* album. Cootie was leafing through a book. I asked him what he was reading, and he said, "It's a biography of me." "Who wrote it?" I asked. "You did," he replied.

It turned out to be a very vivid dream because I remembered it past the short amount of time it usually takes for dreams to be forgotten upon waking. As I sat on the edge of the bed pondering the dream, off the top of my head I couldn't recall if there was an existing Cootie Williams biography. Later in the day, I checked online and was surprised and disappointed to find out that there indeed wasn't a full book on him. I took the dream to be a celestial assignment. Fast forward fourteen years and you hold the results of that commission in your hands. The long gestation period was due to limited spare time. There were no sabbaticals, grants, or research assistants. Until the beginning of 2022, I was employed full-time at Northrop Grumman in Palmdale, California. The commute from our home in Pasadena was 150 miles (round trip) and consumed three hours a day. Fortunately, I was able to use a vanpool to do this commute. So on days when it wasn't my turn to drive, some time was available to use my laptop to work on the book and my "Ellington Reflections" podcast.

Perhaps it was a blessing to work on this book in recent times due to the amount of data that is now available remotely online. In researching this book, I went through many databases. Between Newspapers.com, ProQuest Historical Black Newspaper Collection, RIPM Jazz, and other databases, there were over 21,000 references to Cootie Williams to evaluate. These reference hits ranged from mere mentions in personnel listings to full interviews, but each hit had to be examined. (But in those same sources "Duke Ellington" yielded almost 900,000 hits!)

The book you are now reading could have been lost in limbo or delayed for a long time or perhaps permanently lost. On July 13, 2024, I was in the midst of gathering image permission when I suffered a heart arrhythmia episode that left me dead for six minutes with another death episode that lasted two minutes during the ambulance ride to the hospital. The survival rate for heart arrhythmia (which is different from a heart attack) is 5 to 10 percent. I not only survived, I surprised the excellent doctors at USC Arcadia Hospital by coming out of the whole experience with nowhere near the physical and mental damage that is typical under the circumstances. After installation of a pacemaker/defibrillator, I was released from the hospital after an eight-day stay. And after a period of rest and some physical therapy, I was able to resume working on this biography.

Duke Ellington has been the subject of at least a dozen English-language biographies. This doesn't include book studies like Mark Tucker's excellent *Duke Ellington Reader*, Matthew J. Cooper's *Duke Ellington As Pianist: A Study of Styles*, Kurt Dietrich's *Duke's 'Bones: Ellington's Great Trombonists*, *Duke Ellington Studies* (edited by John Howland), and *The Cambridge Companion to Duke Ellington* (edited by Edward Green), to name just a few. Almost every day's activities of Duke Ellington's life has been documented in books like Ken Vail's *Duke's Diary* and Dr. Klaus Stratemann's *Duke Ellington Day by Day and Film by Film*. Those efforts have been expanded on by David Palmquist's massive website, "The Duke Where and When" at www.tdwaw.ca. But only a few of Duke's musicians have received biographical treatment: Ben Webster, Juan Tizol, Johnny Hodges, and Billy Strayhorn. A few, including Rex Stewart, Barney Bigard, and Clark Terry, wrote autobiographies. There's a comprehensive biography of bassist Jimmie Blanton by Matthias Heyman in the pipeline. And that's about it.

Cootie Williams was unique among Ellington musicians because of his high-profile stint with Benny Goodman and his successful term as a big band leader in his own right. None of the other Ellingtonians could claim a similar résumé. In Mr. Williams's seventy-four years on this earth, his story has a lot of territory to cover. But I've read too many biographies that became chronologies; I didn't want to get so bogged down in the day-to-day aspects of his life that the big picture gets obscured by gratuitous detail. I hope I've succeeded in my goal of sorting detail and tedium. Most of the available biographical information on Cootie Williams doesn't dive beyond the surface and consists of a handful of articles and chapters in anthology-style biographies. There are several references that say Cootie was self-taught when actually he had lessons from a young age and continued to take tutelage on his instrument during his years as a professional. His time with Duke Ellington and Benny Goodman gets covered because of those leaders' prominence. But Williams's years as a leader and the time he spent under the baton of Mercer Ellington have received scant coverage.

In the recent book about the pioneering Black musical, 1921's *Shuffle Along*, titled *When Broadway Was Black*, author Caseen Gaines asked "How many other brilliant Black Americans who left a lasting impact on this country, their country, have had their praises left unsung?" James Lester's 1994 biography of Art Tatum was dedicated to "the hundreds of jazz musicians whose lives and contributions also deserve books but will probably never get them." Cootie Williams is one of the many musicians whose compelling life story has been unsung, but now, finally, almost forty years after his death, he is getting some of the attention that he so greatly deserves.

It's not very hard to find glowing testimonials about Cootie Williams. Jazz writer Barry Ulanov wrote in 1956 that "Cootie Williams . . . made the trumpet into a vehicle of personal feeling unmatched in jazz or any other music." Barry Kernfeld's *The New Grove Dictionary of Jazz* entry says, "Williams was a master of swing style trumpet playing, and achieved a range of tone and shading on his instrument that was unsurpassed in his day." Tenor saxophonist Franz Jackson said, "[Cootie Williams] is one of our great trumpet players, a great contributor and a man that I credit for enlarging my understanding of music." Benny Goodman had many great trumpeters pass through his bands, yet he said "Cootie Williams was by far the most versatile man that ever played in the [trumpet] section. He was a fast reader, had the biggest tone and unlimited power. Nobody can play lead like Cootie, and his solos are great."

The Cootie Williams Orchestra was popular during most of its brief five-year existence (1942–1947). During this same time period, Cootie won the trumpet category for several of the leading magazine musical polls. Williams became the first to record Thelonious Monk's haunting jazz standard "'Round Midnight." But he was handicapped by several factors—World War II, the AFM recording ban, and, by the end, the death of big bands in the postwar period. Also, Williams was largely relegated to the Black market and was never able to become a crossover artist like Duke Ellington, Cab Calloway, and Louis Armstrong. As Williams himself observed, "Once you were identified in the white field, then you were established forever."

When he was able to record on his own, Cootie's biggest label association was with Capitol, and unfortunately that was a short-lived partnership. He was released from his contract after only sixteen months. During that time, the label only released thirteen of the twenty-four titles he recorded for them, barely over 50 percent.

It seems to have been forgotten, but Cootie Williams was also involved in various aspects of the African American struggle for civil rights. He wasn't the first Black musician to integrate a white orchestra, but he was certainly one with a high-visibility profile as a member of the Benny Goodman orchestra. He participated in various benefit performances for civil rights and associated causes. He wrote letters (or at least put his name on them) speaking out for the American Negro (to use the parlance of the time) against the Daughters of the American Revolution (DAR) and for the Fair Employment Practices Committee (FEPC).

Eddie Colston (1913–1960), writing for the *Ohio State News*, a Black newspaper, said in 1946: "One of these days some enterprising person may decide to write the great American novel about swing music and its personalities. If that time ever comes, the name of Cootie Williams will certainly be entitled to at least one big chapter." Mr. Colston would have been pleased to see that Cootie merited more than a chapter in a novel; he now is the subject of a full biography.

PART I *Alabama*

MOBILE BLUES

> How old would you be if you didn't know how old you are?
> —LEROY ROBERT "SATCHEL" PAGE

Charles Melvin Williams was born in Mobile, Alabama, the third son born to Isaac "Ike" Williams Sr. and the former Melvina Frost. That is not disputed. What is uncertain is the date of his arrival. Various publications cited his date of birth as early as 1904. Cootie himself reported 1910[1] and 1911 as years of birth. His date of birth was July 10, 24, or 26, depending on the source. Infant Charles had not been included in the 1910 census, which specified that only persons born before April 15, 1910, were to be counted. Given that Williams was at least consistent about being born in the month of July, there is the possibility that he could have been born in July 1910. For convenience, he eventually settled on a date of birth and stuck to it—July 10, 1911, a Monday. The reason for the uncertainty was simple—Williams, like his hero Louis Armstrong, simply didn't know when he entered the world,[2] saying, "[M]ost of the old folks who know have moved or passed on."[3]

In 1911, the presumptive year of Cootie's birth, Mobile billed itself as the "Queen City of the South." The Mobile Commercial Club bragged that the city was "Alabama's only seaport," it was the "Gateway to Panama" and "the shortest route to Panama from the great producing centers of the West." Mobile was the second-largest city in Alabama, with a population of 51,521 per the recent 1910 census. Of this number, 44 percent (22,763) were African American (Negro or "Colored" in the parlance of the time).

Like most of America and particularly the American South, the Black population was relegated to a subservient place in society. Where they lived, ate, worked, and even were buried was limited by custom and law. These limits were especially important in cities where the Black population approached majority status.

In explaining the origin of his nickname, Williams liked to tell the story of seeing a band playing in a park at the age of about six or seven. When asked what he heard, he replied he heard "Cootie, Cootie, Cootie."[4] As a result, his family began calling him "Cootie." But his nickname may have originated earlier, as a toddler or even an infant. "It was my father who used to call me like a little chick when I started walking: 'Cootie, cootie, cootie . . .' The nickname stuck with me, even after I left Mobile with the Alonzo Ross Orchestra."[5] Yet another explanation was provided in a 1945 interview—"Cootie" was what Williams said as a baby instead of "Goo."[6]

There's also the possibility that none of these explanations are true and were just made up to satisfy the curiosity of the press and the public. In a 1940 interview, Cootie confessed that he had no idea where the nickname came from, saying he'd "been called Cootie ever since anybody called him anything" and that not even his father could say where it came from.[7] Regardless of which version of the origin story is true, the nickname stuck. The name "Cootie" is one of those jazz mononyms (like Duke, Satchmo, Dizzy, and Bird) that substitutes perfectly for a first and last name.

Researching African American genealogy is a daunting task. There is scarcity of nineteenth-century records listing Black Americans by name. Prior to the 1870 federal census, only African Americans who happened to be free people of color were listed by name. Until that time, African Americans were only enumerated by sex and age under the name of the enslaver. Due to those limitations, the earliest relatives that could be found on the paternal branch of Cootie's family tree are his great-grandparents, Samuel (1825–?) and Luvenia (or Lucy) (1828–?) Williams. In the 1880 census, Samuel states his parents were born in Mississippi and Luvenia gives her parental birthplace as Georgia. Thus, Cootie's roots in America extend at least to the late eighteenth century.[8] Their son, Stephen (Steve) Williams, Cootie's paternal grandfather, was born in 1847; he died when Cootie was an infant.[9] Given that Samuel, Luvenia, and Steve Williams were born in antebellum Alabama, it is highly likely that they were enslaved until the end of the Civil War.[10]

Samuel, Luvenia, Stephen, and five other sons are enumerated as citizens of Montgomery County in Alabama in the 1870 federal census. It's likely that this is where they lived prior to being emancipated. Over the forty-year period from 1820 to 1860, Montgomery County had the number of reported slaves jump from 2,655 to 23,710—an increase of almost tenfold. Because it was near the country's fertile Black Belt region, Montgomery also became one the South's largest trading centers for slave labor.[11] J. M. Williams of Montgomery County had seventy-one slaves listed under his name in the 1860 federal census and there it is possible that this is where Cootie's ancestors were held in bondage.[12]

Duke Ellington saw the music produced by African Americans as an outgrowth of these harsh times. In 1933, he told the *Irish Times*, "The music of my race is something more than what is adequately termed the American idiom. It is the result of our transportation to American soil and was our reaction in the plantation days to the tyranny we endured. What we dared not say openly we endeavoured to express in music."[13]

In 1976, Cootie Williams sat for a six-hour interview for the Smithsonian Institution's Oral Jazz History Project. The transcript of the interview is 327 pages long. Yet for all of his discussion of his family—parents, grandparents, brothers, and even his wife—Williams does not refer to any of them by name. This lack of detail complicated researching the Williams family. Of his grandparents, Cootie only said, "I don't remember them."[14] "My [paternal] grandfather [Steve Williams][15] was a farmer. He had eighteen children. My father was the smartest."[16] Since it appears that that assessment came from Cootie's father, it seems a little suspect. Cootie's father, Isaac "Ike" Williams, was born on December 24, 1886, in Faunsdale, Alabama (about 140 miles from Mobile), to Steve Williams and his wife, the former Maggie Sam.[17] Faunsdale was a small unincorporated area of Marengo County at the time Isaac was born. Even today, it only has a population of about ninety people.[18]

Cootie's mother, Melvina Frost, was born in 1881[19] in Newbern, Hale County, Alabama, a small town located approximately 155 miles almost directly north of Mobile.[20] The Frost family can be traced back to Cootie's great-grandparents, Granville Frost (1810–?) and the former Mary Huckabee (1815–?). Both were born in Tennessee, but by 1870 they were living in Newbern. Granville Frost was among those African American men who were able to vote for the first time as part of the United States' Reconstruction period that followed the Civil War. On July 19, 1867, accompanied by his oldest son Gilbert, Granville registered to vote for the first time.[21] It's not known if the Frosts were actually able to exercise their right to vote. And if they did vote, it was to be a short-lived opportunity, because the white backlash against Black votership resulted in the disenfranchisement of Black voters for almost a century.

Granville Frost, like many southern African Americans, made his livelihood and supported his family by farming. According to the 1880 census, he rented his farm, most likely from a white man who lived nearby named Caswell Campbell Huckabee (1818–1909). It may have been that Granville's wife, the former Mary Huckabee, was enslaved on the plantation of Caswell Huckabee. Huckabee reported forty-four enslaved souls in the 1850 census.[22]

Granville's plot consisted of sixty acres. On it, he grew twenty acres each of wheat and corn, ten acres each of oats and cotton, and a small number of sweet potatoes. He had a few cows, ten chickens, but no pigs. Granville and Mary worked on the farm with their children and their spouses. Baalam A. Frost, the fourth of five children of Granville and Mary Frost and Cootie's maternal grandfather, was born circa 1852.[23] Of the Frosts, Cootie said, "It was a big family, yeah. A real big family."[24] His mother had twelve siblings, not to mention all the aunts, uncles, and cousins.

Individually, Isaac "Ike" Williams and Melvina Frost eventually migrated south to Mobile. When and how they met is unknown, but they were married in about 1906.[25] Their first son, Isaac Jr., was born on February 24, 1907, and a second son, Elbert, was born in 1908.

Melvina's occupation in the 1910 census was laundress. Ike's profession was listed as laborer in the sawmill. Alabama's plentiful forests generated lots of work in the sawmills and the resulting wood products also generated employment in the port city of Mobile.[26] While sawmill laborer was Ike Williams's "official" occupation, Cootie said, "he did sort of a lot of different things. First he worked for a furrier. He used to go to the country and buy furs from the people in the country. And he used to go out in the country and buy these furs from these people."[27] Williams made sure his profit margin was as large as possible since he paid "little or nothing for them."[28]

Ike Williams could probably be best described as a hustler. As Cootie would say of him, "He was going to get that dollar from some kind of way." "Some kind of way" also included managing a gambling house. Cootie didn't have details about what went on there since he wasn't allowed inside. Cootie only knew where it was located—Davis Avenue, the "main drag" for Black Mobile. The street had been named in honor of Jefferson Davis, an unsubtle reminder of southern sympathies. It would be renamed Dr. Martin Luther King Jr. Avenue in 1986. Cootie recalled, "We called [Davis Avenue] '[T]he Street.'" Ike's gambling establishment was located in the back of a Davis Avenue pool hall. "And, of course, I wasn't allowed in there. I didn't ever get to look at [the inside of] it. I knew where it was situated, but he didn't allow me in the pool room," so Cootie was ignorant about details of the goings-on in the back room—"I don't know what he had in the gambling place." According to Cootie, his father didn't own the pool room, so perhaps he rented space in the back or paid a percentage of his intake to the pool hall's proprietor.[29] As young person, Cootie may not have known the details of what occurred on "The Street," "but I know they used to have a red light district."[30]

Cootie allowed that his father was "very successful" in his gambling enterprise.[31] His success allowed the family to be "fairly well off" in comparison to "most Negro kids in Alabama."[32] The legendary baseball pitcher Leroy "Satchel" Page was born in Mobile five years before Cootie. His early years were decidedly harder than Cootie's. Page said: "in Mobile I was a n----r kid. I went around with the back of my shirt torn, a pair of dirty diapers or raggedy pieces of trousers covering me. Shoes? They was someplace else . . . I found out what it was like to be a Negro in Mobile."[33]

As to his maternal side, Cootie said, "My mother played the organ in church, and the piano, and so we all had to take music. And I was the only one that followed [in] her footsteps, I would say.[34] The rest of them went into other fields."[35] At church, though, Cootie said, "in general I fell asleep on the pews of the church, and I was waked up by slaps."[36] Although the boys played a little piano, Cootie gravitated toward the drums at "[a]bout five or six years old. I loved the drums."[37] Cootie described his mother as a "religious type of woman."[38] The family's religious affiliation is not known. There are many churches in Mobile still active from early in the twentieth century, but none of those churches that responded to author queries had a record of her. Melvina wasn't the disciplinarian in the family; the "whuppings" came from Ike, but Ike never had to give out too many to Cootie. Cootie said, "I was afraid of my father . . . I was about the only one afraid of him." The other boys didn't seem deterred by the thought of these corrections—"[My father] used to whip my youngest brother and I used to cry. And about the next hour, he'd be doing the same thing over again."[39]

The Williams family moved a few times during their time in Mobile. At the time the 1910 census was taken, they resided on Ghent Street in an area of Mobile an area known as Napoleonville. (No address was noted in the survey.) Today the area is known as the Crichton neighborhood. A few years later, they moved to 264 S. Cedar Street,[40] very near the Mobile River. This part of the city is an historically African American area known as Down the Bay.[41] The Mobile city directories show residences on Dearborn and Lafayette Streets for the Williams family after the Cedar Street stay.

BOY MEETS HORN

Cootie's attachment to the drums was short-lived. "[L]ater, in the school band, I wanted to switch [from drums] to trombone. But my arms were too short to reach the lowest position on the slide, so the bandmaster told me, 'You play trumpet.' I said I didn't like the trumpet, so he gave me a whooping, and I played the trumpet."[1]

Cootie also had another version of the story that explained his switch to trumpet: "Well, we was in the [elementary] school band. I had a knack of going around and picking up all the instruments at the time, you know. During rehearsals, everybody went out to play. And I picked up this trumpet and started to play 'Twelfth Street Rag.' The bandmaster heard this thing, and he come running in there, and said, "That's the instrument for you." I said, 'Oh, no. Oh, no. Oh, no. I'm a drummer. I ain't playing that.' And so that's how I started playing the trumpet. I got a whipping [from the bandmaster] and he made me play the trumpet."[2]

Fortunately for young Cootie, his father decided that he should take trumpet lessons from a good friend of his named Charlie Lipscomb (1882–1949). Like Ike Williams, Charles Bridget Lipscomb had deep roots in Alabama.[3] Lipscomb ran a laundry business, which Cootie described as a "cleaning and pressing club." His wife Parico handled the alterations.[4] For a time, Lipscomb ran his "pressing club" out of his personal residence at 450 Bloodgood Street. By the mid-1920s, Charlie and Perico Lipscomb had moved to 608 Walnut Street, with the clothes-cleaning business separate and located on the main stem for Black activity, 650 ½ Davis Avenue. His address put his establishment in back of the McGowan & McCleskey Drugstore.[5]

After school, Cootie delivered clothes for Lipscomb on his bicycle. In exchange, Lipscomb "gave me four dollars a week and my lesson. That was good money. And when business was slow, that's the time he would teach me."[6] Cootie also made money using his bicycle to deliver newspapers.

Cootie's lessons were taught out of the Arban trumpet method book.[7] The full title is *Arban's Complete Conservatory Method for Trumpet*. Written in 1864 by Jean-Baptiste Arban (1825–1889), this comprehensive manual is still widely used today and is referred to as "The Trumpeter's Bible."

Besides his in-store instruction, Cootie was assigned lessons to practice at home. But he wasn't always diligent about doing his homework: "[I]f he would give me a lesson to take home to learn, I would be listening to jazz records, Louis Armstrong records, trying to copy them, and wouldn't pay the lesson no mind. And when I'd come back for him to go over the lesson with me—when he got ready to go over the lesson with me, I wouldn't know none of it. And by the time he started hitting me on my head with his hand [or a]nything he had, I got sick and tired of him bopping me on my head. I said, 'Louis Armstrong and everybody else is going to have to go. I'm going to get this lesson.' And so, I would begin to get the lesson. And that's when I started."[8]

Cootie said Lipscomb "was a terrific trumpeter. He taught me about breathing." Cootie eventually realized that "as long as I came in with those lessons, he didn't bother about what [else] I was doing."[9] Sometimes they would play trumpet duets out of classical books. While there was no jazz allowed during the lessons, Lipscomb himself played jazz with Mobile's Excelsior Band, which was founded in 1883. Still extant, it is believed to be the oldest marching jazz band in the country. For an unknown period of time, Lipscomb was the leader of the band.[10]

Some biographical sketches[11] have described Cootie Williams as a self-taught musician. That is completely untrue. Williams was a diligent student of the trumpet. Even as an adult professional, Cootie even took lessons from the best trumpet teachers in New York City.

Eventually realizing the importance of his lessons and practice, Cootie said that his father soon saw "that the only thing that I wanted was the trumpet and music, see. And that he didn't have to make me study or do anything. Sometimes on Sundays, he would have to take the trumpet from me . . . and lock it up in the closet."[12] Most parents have to coerce or force their children to practice. "But not me. They'd have to stop me."[13]

"When I was large enough to realize what was happening with the trumpet Louis Armstrong was my influence."[14] In another interview, he stated, "He was my idol, the greatest trumpet player that ever lived."[15] Besides hearing him on records, "I used to listen to Louis Armstrong on the radio playing with Fletcher Henderson from the Roseland [Ballroom]. 'Boy,' I used to say to myself, 'if I could only get to New York and hear *him*.'" Cootie's musical taste at that time was very specific—"I didn't listen to singers. I was only interested in trumpets."[16]

"Well, nearly everyone had an idol. And [Armstrong] was my idol." Armstrong's "beat" (swing), and sound were "the greatest thing I ever heard." Cootie was to remain in awe of Armstrong for his entire life.

Cootie said his school made a summer field trip to Chicago. While there, he snuck off one night to hear his idol Louis Armstrong, who at that time was a member of King Oliver's Creole Jazz Band.[17] (Williams didn't give much in the way of specifics, but the summer of 1922, 1923, or 1924 are possible dates. Armstrong joined Oliver in August 1922 and in late September 1924, he went to New York to enlist in Fletcher Henderson's orchestra.[18]) "I stood outside the fence of the Oriental Garden [sic, Lincoln Gardens], I think it was, and listened to Louis in King Oliver's band. When I got back that night, I got a whooping for that. I listened to King Oliver in later years on records, but during that period of time, I only listened to Louis."[19]

Cootie wasn't alone in his zeal for the new sounds of the King Oliver band. The teenaged white musicians of Chicago, too young to be admitted, would gather outside the Lincoln Gardens to soak in what the doorman called their "music lessons." The enthusiasts included Bud Freeman, Jimmy McPartland, and Benny Goodman.[20]

The marriage between Ike and Melvina was not the picture of tranquility. Cootie said his mother "had a hard time with [my father]. He [Ike] told me that. He said he was gone all the time."[21] Running a gambling establishment would have required odd hours, most likely at night.

On September 17, 1917, Melvina Williams gave birth to twin boys, most likely delivered at home, which was customary at the time. Unfortunately, only one of the babies survived. He was given the name Leroy Barney Williams. Melvina developed puerperal septicemia from the complicated birth and died twenty-four days later, on October 4, at the young age of thirty-five.[22] Infant and maternal mortality rates were higher across the board at the beginning of the twentieth century. Without real access to hospitals, the Black population suffered. Sadly, even today, women in Alabama die in childbirth or its complications at a rate that is twice the national average.[23]

Melvina's death meant Isaac Williams was left with three young boys and an infant to raise on his own. Cootie described his brothers: "[T]he oldest one [Isaac Jr.] was seven years older than me. The other one [Elbert] was three years older than me."[24] Actually, Isaac Jr. was four years older than Cootie. Cootie's fuzzy and incorrect description of the age difference between him and his eldest brother may have been because, like Ike Sr., "[Ike Jr.] was gone all the time."

But Cootie said, "[M]y aunt sort of raised us." Cootie didn't say which of his many aunts this could be, but perhaps it was Melvina's younger sister Agnes Frost, since she is shown as living with the family at the time of the

1910 census. Ike Jr. stepped up, too—Cootie said he'd "look out for us after my mother passed [and] helped to raise us too." Elbert was placed with an uncle, Clinton Williams, who lived in Marengo County, Alabama, Ike Sr.'s place of birth.[25] Clinton eventually adopted Elbert.[26]

A "YOUNG" PROFESSIONAL

Visiting the carnival was apparently a regular event for the Williams family. One year, Cootie heard the family band of Willis "Billy" Young (1872–1943) performing there. The three Young children, Lester, Irma, and Lee, all played saxophone in the family band. Young's oldest son Lester particularly impressed Cootie. Lee Young was later to become a drummer, playing and recording with Benny Goodman, Lionel Hampton, and Nat "King" Cole. He became the first Black musician to obtain regular work in the movie studios.[1] All of the members of the Young family played multiple instruments, but their specialty was a five-saxophone section feature.

"Dad, I sure do want to play with them," Cootie told the elder Williams. The next day, Cootie came back and sat in with the band. Afterward, "my father talked with him. [Willis Young] wanted me, after he heard me play."[2] Cootie impressed Willis Young so much that he told Ike Williams that he'd like to take him on the road with the family band. "So, my father said, 'Well, I can't let him go away from home by himself, because he's too young. You'll have to take his older brother.' The one older to me, next to me [meaning Elbert]." The senior Young agreed to the condition. Elbert didn't play an instrument but worked odd jobs at the carnival. This became Cootie Williams's first professional job.[3] According to Lee Young, they were with the Lachman and Carson Show, "that's when the carnival used to have railroad cars and you traveled just as the circus did."[4]

While Cootie remembers being "around ten or twelve years old"[5] when he joined the Young family band on the band road, he was more likely fourteen years old, especially since he recalls Elbert being a seventeen-year-old at the time. While Williams couldn't recall the exact year he played with the Young family band, according to Lester Young biographer Douglas Henry Daniels, it was the spring of 1925.⁶ Cootie wasn't nervous taking on the gig because "[m]y teacher [Charlie Lipscomb] stopped me from being scared. [H]e'd hit me and say, 'Don't you ever get nervous doing nothing in music. Because you can't produce when you get nervous.' And he'd hit me like that. 'Don't you never.' And he broke me out of that habit of being nervous." As a result, Williams claimed that throughout his career, he never suffered from nerves.⁷

Williams reported that Lester Young (1909–1959) was a great player with his own tone and concept, even at that age. "That's what made me want to go with them. . . . Because he was different from anybody I ever heard." At this point in his life, Williams could declare, "He was the greatest thing I'd ever heard in person. And I wanted to learn something about it." In particular, Cootie was impressed with Lester's rhythmic feel, his "beat" and the "different syncopations that he had." Young, later dubbed "the president of the saxophone" (commonly shortened to "Pres" or "Prez") by singer Billie Holiday, would go on to become one of the most influential saxophonists in jazz history.

Cootie wasn't drawn to Lester as a friend and didn't hang out with him. Perhaps due to an awe of Lester's skills, Cootie perceived a five-year age difference between them while actually it was only two years. Instead, he spent most of his time with Lee, Irma, and their father. While Williams reported he didn't learn anything specific from Willis Young, he regarded him as a very talented musician with admirable tone and technique.

The band functioned like the usual circus band—"We played for the acts. And we played—then Lester, then, would go on the stage with his father and his [step]mother and Irma and Lee with the saxophone act and we would stay down there in the pit with the drums and the trumpet and things, to back them up."⁸ (Ben Webster, another future Ellingtonian, spent time with the Young family organization in 1929–1930.⁹ By that time, Williams had joined Ellington. Webster and Williams were bandmates in Ellington's band for almost a year in 1940.)

However musically rewarding the job turned out to be, financially it wasn't good because Willis Young "never did give me no money. He was supposed to send my father the money. . . . Sometimes he'd give me 50 cents. Sometimes. But he'd feed me." But Cootie wasn't there for the money, he was there for the music. "I didn't pay it any mind. I was happy." Cootie was able to make some money by helping in the carnival, doing odd jobs like helping break down the Ferris wheel between cities and other menial-labor jobs.¹⁰

While traveling with the circus, Cootie marked an important rite of passage—the transition to wearing long pants. It was a milestone that meant going from a boy to a young man, done with the playground games. Perhaps the main reason for waiting until adolescence was younger boys tended to tear the knees out of their pants from rough play. Why waste money on clothes that were going to be damaged or that would require patching? Plus there was the expectation that clothes be maintained in good enough condition to be passed down to younger siblings. During Cootie's summer with the carnival, they traveled to many towns, but the only one Cootie was able to remember by name forty years later was East St. Louis and it was only because it was here that Cootie was able to use the savings from his carnival work to buy his first suit with long pants from a local pawn shop.

When the summer season ended and it was time to return home, Ike Williams sent train fare money for his two young sons. However, the enterprising Elbert Williams put Cootie on the train and decided to pocket his fare and "hobo" home instead. Ike wasn't mad because he knew that was how Elbert was. Cootie's described his brother as "wild."[11]

Despite being a gambling man, the elder Williams was very strict with his sons. "My father, when I got big enough to go out and play dances with bands, my father would go with me. And as soon as the dance would be over, he'd bring me back home. I never did get a chance to go out with girls . . . [u]ntil I left home, to go down to Florida. And another thing he was strict on, you had to be in that house before 12:00 o'clock. He wouldn't care if it was the oldest one, or any one of us, we had to be in that house before 12:00 o'clock at night."

In discussing the gigs of his early years, Cootie said, "I worked around Mobile with Holman's jazz band and Johnny Pope's band . . ."[12] Holman was Nathaniel T. Holman (1880–1946), and it was said that "there was no instrument he could not play" and that he was "one of the most talented African American musicians that ever lived in Mobile." His band played for social events like balls and weddings, so they probably didn't play much jazz. Said to consist of sixteen members, it probably was a reading band, which would have further enhanced Williams's musical skills.[13] Perhaps by mentioning "Johnny Pope's band," Cootie meant the Excelsior Band, a band of which his teacher Charlie Lipscomb was also a member. John "Johnny" C. Pope (1883–1972) was the son of the founder of the Excelsior Band, John A. Pope.[14]

Cootie said, "the bands from New Orleans used to come over there and play dances." The bands would play during the day on an open bed truck, and they'd stop and play at different streets to advertise their dance gigs for later that night. Sometimes, Cootie would sit in on these advertising sessions, sometimes from the street and sometimes on the truck. Cootie garnered a reputation as a skilled musician. "After they knew about me, they let me play with them."

4

FLORIDA

One of the bands that would pass through Mobile was the Pensacola Jazz Band. The band's clarinetist was Edmond Hall, perhaps best known today as a member of Louis Armstrong's All-Stars in the 1950s. Hall said the band passed through Mobile and "we had a night off and went to a dance, and I heard a little boy playing the trumpet, and man, he really played it. You know who that was? It was Cootie Williams."[1] Perhaps this encounter resulted in Hall inviting Williams to sit in with the Pensacola Jazz Band on their next working night. Cootie said, "So, Edmond Hall was playing with the Pensacola Jazz Band, and they came to Mobile, and I sat in with them and played. And that's how I got started out."[2] The experience was strictly a guest role—"I didn't replace nobody. I didn't go with the band. I just would sit in with them while they were [in town]. They didn't have no music. They played by ear."[3]

Edmond Hall (1901–1967) left the Pensacola Jazz Band and traveled to Jacksonville, about 350 miles away and located on the east coast of Florida. There, he joined the band of pianist Eagle Eye Shields. Hall told the band about the young trumpeter, and they decided to recruit him. Hall said, "So (Shields) asked me where could he get a trumpet player. That's when I got Cootie Williams from Mobile, Alabama. I'd played with Cootie once before this. As he was in his teens still, his father made me take care of him. I hope I did. We were together a long while."[4]

Ike Williams was approached for permission to move Cootie to Jacksonville. Cootie was still young at this point, about fifteen years old. It may have helped alleviate Ike's workload as a single father of four young boys, but sending a minor child out of state to work in a band was not responsible parenting. Fortunately, there was a solution: "My father's partner in the gambling house business happened to live in Jacksonville, Florida. So, he told them he would have to talk to his partner about it first. To see if the partner would take care of me. So, the partner said yes, that he would look after me. And so that's how I got a chance to leave home. To go down there to play with Eagle Eye Shields. His was the first band I ever played with."[5] Trumpeter Jabbo Smith and trombonist James "Trummy" Young were also members of the Shields band early in their careers. Shields (1897–1946), never recorded and is so obscure that it was difficult to ascertain that his legal name was Calvin Anthony Shields.[6] Shields died in 1946 at the relatively young age of forty-eight. Although he is listed in various official documents as a musician by trade, he also made money by shining shoes and selling cigars.[7]

Ike's partner was named Son Coin.[8] Unlike Ike Williams, Coin wasn't based in a particular gambling establishment; instead he floated around and made his money by gambling "with the biggest gamblers in America. Whenever they would have these big games, he would go and gamble with them."[9] Coin was African American but passed for white. Unfortunately, when his true racial identity was discovered, he was gunned down while sitting on his porch, allegedly by some gamblers who lost money to him. Losing was one thing, but to lose to a Black man was unacceptable. Cootie Williams noted that Coin was married but the couple had no children. (This may have been because there is no guarantee that the offspring of a mixed couple, no matter how light the Black person, might be dark enough to reveal the couple's true racial identity.)

The second trumpet player in the Shields band was Julian Carlo Adderley (1904–1989). His two sons were jazz greats Julian Edwin "Cannonball" (1928–1975) and Nat Adderley (1931–2000). According to Nat, "Pop played lead, Cootie Williams played what Pop said was 'ride'—he said, 'I play lead, Cootie plays "ride.""'[10] (As defined in *The New Grove Dictionary of Jazz*: "To take a ride" is to improvise a solo and a "ride man" is an improvising soloist.[11])

According to Edmond Hall, he joined Alonzo Ross's DeLuxe Syncopators in late 1926 on the condition that Ross take Cootie, too. Hall told Ross, "I got a kid I got to look out for, which is Cootie Williams, so if you can make room for him, we'll join your band. The next couple of days I got a letter from Ross saying (he'd) make room for Cootie. Ross was making a tour of Florida, and when he came through Jacksonville, Cootie and I joined his band."[12] Alonzo Ross (1893–1966), like Shields, was a piano player.

Coy Herndon, a former vaudeville performer, wrote a regular column detailing music and entertainment for the *Chicago Defender* under the banner "Coy Cogitates." His October 23, 1926, column happened to document the arrival of Williams and Hall to the DeLuxe Syncopators, which he dubbed "a hard combination to beat": "I understand Ross has made several changes in his orchestra and new members have been added—Alonzo Ross, pianist and leader; Casker Towie, banjo and sax; Cootie Williams, trumpet; Eddie Cooper, trombone; Earl Evans, sax; Robert Cloud, arranger and sax; Edmund

Alonzo Ross's DeLuxe Syncopators, 1928. Cootie Williams is seated at the far left holding a book or folio. (This is the earliest known photograph of him.) Richard Fulbright is third from the left and Edmond Hall is sixth from the left. Bandleader Alonzo Ross is at the far right.

Hall, sax; Frank Houston, drums, etc.; Richard Fulbright, Sousaphone." This is the earliest known mention of Cootie Williams in the press.[13] Unlike the Shields band, which didn't use sheet music, the Ross band "was a reading band. We had three brass, three reeds and four rhythm, the regular combination then," said Hall.[14]

The band had ambitions; they advertised their services in a January 1927 issue of *The Billboard* with an availability after the end of March. It's unknown if the ad bore fruit, but in April 1927, the band departed on a short tour of Florida after concluding their second season at Miami's Della Robia Garden, a "negro night club," with stops in West Palm Beach, Daytona Beach, and then a return to their home in Jacksonville.[15] They played The Palms in the state capitol of Tallahassee, where the *Chicago Defender* reported that "Ross really has one of the best bunches of Race musicians in every respect that one wants to see or hear."[16] In May, it was reported that the band was in Cuba and was also on a "tour of the principal cities" of this country.[17] However, this Cuban engagement seems doubtful since Williams said his 1928 trip to New York was the first time he had been on a ship. The full extent of the band's touring has been lost to history.

Cootie Williams was able to take his first known professional musician's photograph as a member of the DeLuxe Syncopators. As can be seen in the photograph, Ross's organization dressed well. The *Chicago Defender*'s correspondent noted that the band was "looking like ready money, as they were all dressed alike in cool suits and had the old sports suits . . . That speaks well for the profession."[18] Remember, this was a time when jazz musicians were not well thought of.

The Ross DeLuxe Syncopators recorded for the Victor Talking Machine Company at a tobacco warehouse set up for recording in Savannah, Georgia, on August 22, 1927. Edmond Hall said, "Victor wanted that tune 'Girl of My Dreams' recorded by Blue Steele (a sweet band then popular in the Florida area) and sent a mobile outfit to Savannah to get it. They had scouts out who heard our band. We were asked to Savannah to do some sides and made some records, mostly original tunes."[19] Erroneously, some discographies point to this session as the recording debut of Cootie Williams. While he was a member of the band at the time, Cootie Williams isn't present on this date and Robert "Cookie" Mason substituted for him; Cootie missed what was to be his recording debut due to illness.[20] Most of the composition and arranging work was handled by the group's saxophonist, Robert Cloud. Of the eight songs recorded that day, Cloud wrote five and cowrote a sixth. Cloud was credited with making the band "the pride orchestra of Florida" and "just as big in the South today as Isham Jones, Ben Bernie, Paul Ash and others are in the North."[21]

Two of their recordings from this session attracted national attention in *Variety*: "Ross De Luce Syncopators, a Jacksonville (Fla.) colored organization, has 'canned' a couple of torrid fox-trots, 'Mary Belle' [sic, "Mary Bell"] and 'Lady Mine,' for Victor. Played as only native Ethiops [sic] can play 'em, this couplet, arranged by Robert H. Cloud, is a sizzling dance duo."[22] The recordings of the Alonzo Ross DeLuxe Syncopators were reissued as part of a CD under Cloud's name entitled *Florida Rhythm*, subtitled *The Story of Robert H. Cloud*.[23] The recordings show that the band was a polished organization and swung well in the mode of that time. Cloud (1895–?) never achieved the fame his talents warranted and disappeared into obscurity in the early 1930s.[24]

In mid-October 1927, the DeLuxe Syncopators opened their third season at Miami's Della Robia Garden, which was to be their home until the end of the winter. The *Chicago Defender* noted that the records Ross made in August would be placed in the RCA Victor export catalog, something that usually wasn't done for Black music.[25]

The DeLuxe Syncopators also did weekly radio broadcasts from Miami Beach on station WOID.[26] It was unusual for the time because Williams said, "there wasn't no colored allowed over there on the beach, then. [S]o they used to sneak us over there to the radio station and sneak us back."[27] The radio broadcasts caught the attention of Jay Faggen, owner of Brooklyn's Rosemont Ballroom. "[H]e came down [to Florida] and listened to the band. So he hired the band. You know, two weeks."[28] Hall recalled it differently: "When the records came out the manager of the Roseland heard them and sent for us. He had two places, the Roseland on Broadway and the Rosemount [sic] in Brooklyn. We played at the Rosemount."[29]

NEW YORK

Whether it was because of their recordings or their radio broadcasts, in the winter of 1928 the Alonzo Ross band was booked for an indefinite engagement at New York's Rosemont Ballroom. Sailing from Miami, with a stop in Savannah, the Alonzo Ross DeLuxe Syncopators arrived in New York on March 15, 1928.[1] It was the first time Williams, just short of seventeen years of age, had been on a boat. It was also the first time Williams and Hall had seen snow.[2] This chance to go to New York City was the culmination of Cootie's childhood dream. "[W]hen I used to say my prayers at night, I used to say, "Dear Lord, please hurry up and let me grow up so I can get to New York. I didn't care how I got there. I was coming."[3] When he wasn't on the road, Williams called New York home for the rest of his life.

After disembarking from the ship, the band was shuttled to the Brooklyn residence of a woman who had agreed to house the band during the engagement. The Rosemont Ballroom was also in Brooklyn, located at the intersection of Fulton Street and Flatbush Avenue.[4] They usually booked two bands for their shows, with a visiting band like Alonzo Ross's given the opening slot. The Rosemont also had additional visibility for their acts with daily radio shows on WBBC and WMCA.[5]

The change in climate from sunny Florida to snowy New York proved daunting to some of the musicians as about half the band caught bad colds. (According to historical weather records, the high temperature in Brooklyn was 45 degrees Fahrenheit on March 15, 1928. That same day, the high in Miami was 80 degrees.[6]) Because of ill absentee musicians, Ross opened with a ten-piece band, although fourteen pieces were contracted for. The band opposite the DeLuxe Syncopators was Tommy Morton and his Original Indiana Five. Edmond Hall said, "We got ten men and they only got five, but those guys was really playing. They made us look bad for a while. Ross seemed to be one of the weakest guys in the band, so we got this piano player, Arthur Ford, to played for us and made Ross the leader."[7]

The engagement at the Rosemont was supposed to be indefinite,[8] but management was so displeased they gave the band their two weeks' notice.[9] After their two-week gig, most of the band was ready to return home to Florida, perhaps thinking that staying in New York was too much of a gamble. Per Williams, the Alonzo Ross orchestra was "the biggest [colored] band in the state of Florida. And during that time, it was a cooperative band, making $150 a week during them times."[10] That would be the equivalent of almost $2,600 a week or $135,000 a year in today's dollars. Not a bad income for a teenager! Despite that, Cootie elected to remain in New York, saying, "This is the place I've wanted to be all my life. I'm not thinking about going back to no Florida." Alonzo Ross would continue in music for a few more years, leading a periodically touring band. By the mid-1930s, they were known as the Harlem Babies.[11] But by the 1950s, Ross made his living as a porter on the Atlantic Coast Line Railroad, which was his occupation when he died at age seventy-two in 1966.[12]

Williams and Edmond Hall decided to stay in New York even though they had no employment lined up. Cootie figured he had a fallback plan. "I used to send my father all my money. So I wrote home for some money and my father sent me $50." Williams used the money pay the lady whose house the band was staying in and gave some to the bandsmen.[13] "And after all that was gone, I wrote home for some more money. My father told me he didn't have no more money. My father had lost all my money, his money, everybody's money." Ike Williams had expanded his gambling activities at some point to include horse race betting in New Orleans, about ninety miles from Mobile. "That's how he got broke."[14] Another communication from Ike Williams implored his son to come back to Mobile. "He wrote me a letter and told me he was going to sell the house, the home, if I didn't come home. So I wrote back and told him to sell it, because I wasn't coming back home. So he lost the home, lost the gambling place, lost everything."[15]

So with not much money, they were forced to be resourceful. "Me and Edmond Hall found a place in Brooklyn where there was a baker's shop, where we used to get our breakfast for a dime. [Y]ou used to get rolls and coffee for a dime. [F]or our lunch we used to get soup and bread for 15 cents. [T]hat's what we ate for a long time."[16] Dinner was soup and a roll.[17]

Soon Williams and Hall got a gig playing in a four-piece band with pianist Arthur Ford and drummer Casey Short at the Happyland Ballroom.[18] Hall said, "This Happyland (Ballroom) was what they called a taxi dance hall, use to be all the rage. You paid so much for a ticket, for a girl to dance with you if she chose, or you could sit it out. The band played ten numbers to each set, including one waltz, then took an intermission for two minutes. Of course, the numbers weren't long. Sometimes we'd have to cut 'em real short, down to a chorus, to get the dancers off and get others on. The Happyland was a taxi dance hall, where one paid on a per song basis to dance with women."[19]

Fortunately, the young musicians encountered a helpful soul who asked how they were faring. Cootie told them, "We need a job." They said, "Why don't you all go over to New York?" We said, "We're in New York." (To a New Yorker, Brooklyn isn't New York.) So they said, "No, go over to Manhattan. They have jam sessions over at the Band Box, for different nights. They have trumpet night, saxophone night, piano players' night, trombone night." So we goes [sic] over there, and we find out what night. So I go in there [on] trumpet night."[20]

"All the great musicians used to hang out there—Tommy and Jimmy Dorsey, Bix Beiderbecke. They used to come up after hours and have jam sessions."[21] "I went up there the night of the trumpets." "I was just a kid up from the South and nobody knew me, but I got up and blew everybody out of the joint."[22] Someone suggested that drummer Chick Webb needed to hear this newcomer. It was easy to do since Webb lived in an apartment across the street from the club. "[H]e listened to me play. 'Where you come from, boy?' And I told him the story, after I got through blowing. So he says, 'Well, come on. I'll go over there to get your things.' I said, 'I owe the landlady money. I have to pay the landlady before I can get out.' So he went over, and he paid the landlady up and I moved in with him."[23]

Cootie left his guardian's Happyland band to join Chick Webb's fledgling organization. Hall said, "I was sorry to see him go. From Mobile to New York, I was with him all that time."[24] But soon Hall was able to make his mark at the Band Box during saxophone night and he landed a job with pianist Claude Hopkins at the Roseland Ballroom. Besides exposure, there was another benefit to be found at the Band Box—they had free breakfasts for musicians consisting of sweet rolls and coffee.[25] "And so I used to go and get my breakfast, free breakfast every morning."[26]

On Monday, June 18, 1928, Cootie Williams made his first recording session. It was under the leadership of pianist and composer James P. Johnson (1894–1955) who was one leading exponents of "stride piano." In his autobiography, *Music Is My Mistress*, Ellington referred to himself as "one of the close disciples of the James P. Johnson style."[27] The piano roll of Johnson's early composition "Carolina Shout" was used as learning tool for a young Duke Ellington, who slowed it down to get the fingering. Johnson's best-known song was "Charleston," which defined the Roaring Twenties. Williams was brought into the session as a substitute for Cladys "Jabbo" Smith (1908–1991). Smith was a virtuoso trumpeter who was promoted as a possible rival to Louis Armstrong. But Smith's career suffered because his drinking made him highly unreliable. He was nowhere to be found for this date, so the almost seventeen-year-old Cootie Williams took his place. Due to "contractual involvements" (probably musicians' union rules), Cootie had to pretend to be Jabbo. This meant that even the band addressed him as "Jabbo"![28] In addition to Williams, the band included Charlie Holmes on reeds, who would be a charter member of Cootie's big band, and a second pianist, the great Thomas "Fats" Waller. Two songs were recorded at the date, "Chicago Blues" and "Mournful Tho'ts." "Mournful Tho'ts," composed by James P. Johnson is played briskly and is largely arranged with little solo space. The last minute of the three-minute piece provides the best opportunity for Cootie to emerge from the ensemble. He plays a confident variation on the melody above what sounds like a collectively improvised portion of the performance.

"Chicago Blues" is not a blues. The song, credited to the now forgotten S. Walter Williams, Paul Biese and James Altiere, was recorded by the Bucktown Five in 1924 and featured some hot breaks by their cornetist, Muggsy Spanier. That same year, Fletcher Henderson recorded it for Pathé.[29] The recording has a railroad theme, with chugging train sound effects generated by the saxophones.[30] The Johnson recording of "Chicago Blues" is also train themed. It addition, there's an announcer calling imaginary passengers to board a train on track number seven. Once again, Cootie gets to shine in the last portion of the recording, playing a chorus of hot trumpet before the announcer tells the passengers that they have reached their destination of Chicago.

William "Chick" Webb (1905–1939) was just starting his musical career and wasn't anywhere near financially stable. By 1928, he had only one recording session to his credit.[31] Eventually, his band was able to take on all challengers, even beating heavyweights like Duke Ellington and Benny Goodman. Webb's future stints at Harlem's Savoy Ballroom had him crowned "The Savoy King."[32]

Although work was scarce, Webb did manage to book a three-week stint at the Savoy Ballroom in September.[33] During the engagement, the union delegate appeared at the Savoy and discovered Williams didn't have the proper card. He was a member of the Mobile musicians union, but he wasn't yet a member of the New York musician's union Local 802. Cootie was more interested in playing his trumpet than the business end of music, so it wasn't a priority. But since he didn't have membership in the New York union, Williams had to leave the gig. Webb was adamant in his defense of Williams, so much so that he got into an argument with the union representative. It was a bad miscalculation on Webb's part. The rep told Cootie, "I'll tell you what I'm going to do, boy, for you. I'm going to let you put in your transfer. Now, I give you privilege to work with anybody else in New York but Chick Webb."[34] Webb responded, "Well, I ain't going to let him work with anybody else. I'll just keep him out here." Recounting the episode years later, Williams said, "[I]f I had of had my transfer in, my card in, it would have been different. But I didn't have no card

"Fletcher Henderson, The Colored King of Jazz and His Orchestra" taken at the Roseland Ballroom, ca. January 1929. Front Row: Fletcher Henderson—piano; Buster Bailey, Benny Carter, Coleman Hawkins—reeds; Cootie Williams, Bobby Stark, Rex Stewart—trumpets. Back Row: Clarence Holiday—banjo; Kaiser Marshall—drums; Jimmy Harrison, Charlie "Big" Green—trombones. (Courtesy of Frank Driggs Collection)

in. I didn't think about nothing like that. So he wouldn't let me work with Chick Webb." Since Cootie wasn't able to work, Webb took care of him by giving him some money every now and then.[35]

Another opportunity presented itself when Fletcher Henderson's lead trumpet, Russell "Pop" Smith quit the band suddenly. Cootie was soon called to substitute. Lipscomb's insistence on discipline and reading paid off for Cootie— "I'll tell you. By him doing that, I got a break. I got one of the biggest breaks in my life. That's how I became known, by him making me do that. Someone told Fletcher about me. I was working with Chick Webb then, but Chick wasn't working. So he came by, and asked Chick could I go to work with him. And Chick said, "Yeah, I'll let you have him to go out on this trip." So I went with Fletcher. No rehearsal or nothing. Playing first trumpet."[36]

Henderson's arrangements were challenging and different. Cootie said "the arrangements was [sic] terrific. And he played in all hard keys, funny keys, everything. Sharps and flats. Five flats, five sharps, six sharps, everything."[37] "I wasn't nervous because of that right upbringing [from Charlie Lipscomb].... Fletcher was very conscious of sound, and he'd think about the brilliancy of certain things being geared to certain keys. He played no favorites. It seemed like ABC then, and I remember Coleman Hawkins saying [about me], 'Ain't that kid somethin'?"[38] Tenor saxophonist Ben Webster said of his time with Henderson, "They had some of the hardest music I've ever seen. In that band you'd play from B flat, B natural up the scale, every key on the keyboard. And all those guys were master readers. As we say, they could see round the corner."[39]

Pianist, arranger, and bandleader Fletcher Henderson (1897–1952) was the product of a middle-class Georgia family. He had a degree in chemistry from Atlanta University, an uncommon achievement for African Americans at this point in time. Despite his educational background, he decided to become a musician. He landed in New York in 1924 and organized what was originally a dance band (as opposed to a jazz band). But a young Louis Armstrong brought a strong jazz element to the band. Many major talents passed through the Henderson band—trumpeters like Henry "Red" Allen and Roy Eldridge, saxophonists including Russell Procope, Chu Berry, Lester Young, Benny Carter, Dexter Gordon, and Coleman Hawkins.

Tenor saxophone founding father Coleman Hawkins (1904–1967) was with the Henderson orchestra when Cootie joined in January 1929.[40] Cootie was surprised to discover that "Coleman [Hawkins] hated Louis [Armstrong]. It was when I was in the Fletcher Henderson band that I learned about this. I knew Hawk then and he just couldn't even stand the name Armstrong! I used to love Louis so much and when I'd speak about him Hawkins didn't like it at all. I don't know why, except that Hawkins seemed to think he ought to have had the recognition Louis had—a bit jealous, I think."[41]

With the lead trumpet chair filled, the Henderson band left New York to tour for a few weeks. When they returned home in mid-February, Cootie thought his term of employment was over. Cootie assumed "the arrangement was that I was only to go on the road with him until he come back [to New York]."[42] However, he was mistaken—he received frantic word that the Henderson band was in the midst of playing a Sunday matinee at the Roseland Ballroom without its lead trumpet! Cootie rushed down to the Roseland to take his chair. This mistake earned Cootie the wrath of one of the band's trombonists, Charlie "Big" Green (ca. 1893–1935). Cornetist Rex Stewart described Green as "a big bruiser" who was "6 foot plus" with a "rough and loud" personality. Plus, "he always appeared ready for a fight at the drop of a wrong word."[43] Of Green, Cootie said he "used to sit right behind me in the band, and he'd lean over and say, 'Boy, I'm going to kill you, kill you, kill you,' and Bobby Stark, the trumpeter, [who] sat next to me, and he'd say, 'Big, leave this boy alone. What's the matter with you?' Big Green scared me to death. . . . So, I'm shaking like a leaf."[44] Although Bobby Stark was a small man, his words to Green had their intended effect. "[After] Little Bobby done talked to him like that, I won't be afraid of [Big Green] no more. When [Green left] the bandstand, he don't said a word to me . . . I got the fear out of me, and I went on playing then. And I wasn't afraid on him no more." Rex Stewart wasn't as fortunate as Cootie. In his posthumously published autobiography *Boy Meets Horn*, Stewart describes the abuse and mental anguish he suffered under Green—"Big Green rode me out of Smack's [Henderson's] band."[45] Stewart also didn't fare well with Cootie:

> Coots started kidding Bobbie [Stark] about some girl and Bobbie retorted by kidding back, making fun of how green and country Cootie looked when he had first arrived in New York. I stay back, egging them both on, hoping that in the heat of their argument they wouldn't notice how often I was hitting our communal bottle. They didn't, and if I had left well enough alone there'd be no story. Anyway, they traded insults jokingly until it was just about time to return to the stand, when Bobbie told Coots, "Yeah, you're just a country boy lost in the big city." I remember I was coming up the stairs and I chimed in, saying, "Bobbie's right, Coots."
>
> The next thing I knew, I was desperately clinging to the stair railing, trying to keep my neck from being broken. Coots had knocked me down the stairs. After all that guff from Bobbie and I had hardly said a thing! I didn't even know he was angry.[46]

This was one of the earliest examples of Cootie's sometimes volatile temper. Heavyweight saxophone talents in the Henderson band like Benny Carter and Coleman Hawkins made no impression on young Williams. He wasn't interested in anyone that didn't play the trumpet. His ears were drawn to Bobby Stark. "Bobby Stark was the only one that moved me." And despite his treatment of Cootie, he added Big Green as a musician that grabbed his attention. But eventually he was seduced by the reed giants: "A little later on, I used to listen to Hawk and Benny Carter battle each other. Sometimes used to have jam sessions right on the bandstand."[47]

There is no recorded documentation of Cootie's time with Fletcher Henderson, save a 1929 formal photograph of the band. Cootie remembered making a single recording session while with Fletcher Henderson, but "[t]hey didn't let me do no solo."[48] *Hendersonia*, the authoritative Fletcher Henderson biography by Walter C. Allen, has no session that fits Williams's recollection. Although later in life Cootie estimated he was with Henderson almost a year, it was actually only three to four months.

PART II *Duke Ellington (1929)*

COTTON CLUB STOMP

Pianist, composer, and bandleader Edward Kennedy "Duke" Ellington was born in Washington, DC, on April 29, 1899, and had come to New York City in 1923. In 1927 he was offered the spot at Harlem's Cotton Club. (Ironically, the great King Oliver turned down the job.)[1] Williams had heard the Duke Ellington band on the radio but wasn't impressed: "They used to sound funny. I thought that was comedy music."[2] Williams had a friend in the Ellington band, saxophonist Johnny Hodges, who was someone that "was with Chick before me," Williams said.[3] Hodges and Williams met through their mutual friend Webb.[4] Williams didn't get to hear Hodges's playing for a while because Hodges "was up to the Cotton Club," and he wasn't allowed to enter. Like a lot of venues of the time, the club would employ Black musicians, entertainers, and staff (waiters, hostesses, and so on) but would not allow them as patrons.

Fletcher Henderson had no problem with Cootie leaving him for Duke Ellington. Cootie said, "[Fletcher] said, 'Okay, go right ahead.'"[5] Coleman Hawkins tried to get Henderson to retain Williams, but to no avail. In Hawkins's mind, "that was the worst thing Fletcher ever did." Hawkins preferred Cootie's huge lead sound over that of Russell Smith.[6] Hawkins said Cootie "would have been a great asset."[7]

According to Ellington, it was Chick Webb who told him about Williams—"Hey, man, I got a hell of a trumpet player for you. He was with me for a while, but he's too much for me. Fletcher [Henderson] heard him and hired him, but that style don't fit Fletcher's band. He's a hell of a player, man, and for you he'll be a bitch!"[8] In later years, "[Webb] used to tell Duke, 'I'm going to get my two men back from you one day.'"[9] Cootie Williams gave credit to Johnny Hodges for his job with the Ellington band. After Bubber Miley was fired, "'Why don't you get Cootie?' Johnny told him."[10] "And so I left and went up there with Duke. I used to laugh when Tricky would start to blowing, you know. It sounded funny to me. I never played no music like that."[11] The style of music that Ellington was playing at the time was labeled "jungle music." Mysterioso clarinets and plunger muted brass were some of the characteristics of this "exotic" music.

Cootie's predecessor James "Bubber" Miley (1903–1932) had joined Ellington in the fall of 1923. His musical stylings made a huge impact on Ellington: "Our band changed its character when Bubber came in. He used to growl all night long, playing gutbucket on his horn. That was when we decided to forget all about the sweet music."[12] While a great and original musician, Miley had an Achilles heel—alcohol. Cootie said, "The reason why [Duke] fired Bubber Miley was every time some big shot come up to listen to the band, there wasn't no Bubber Miley. And the whole band had been built around Bubber Miley."[13] He would die of tuberculosis aggravated by his alcoholism at the age of twenty-nine in 1932. The plunger stylings of Miley along with trombonist Joseph "Tricky Sam" Nanton (1904–1946) were foundational to the Ellington sound. Their contributions echoed throughout the entirety of the Ellington band.

At the time Williams joined the Ellington band, it was just a little over a year into their employment at the Cotton Club. The Cotton Club was one of the most prominent New York nightclubs at this time and its audience drew "the cream of New York society."[14] Still it its formative stage, the band at that time was only eleven pieces, not the fifteen to sixteen musicians that would become the standard big band in a few years.

Cootie was impressed with his new situation: "everything was still so new and exciting for me . . . The music, the whole show and especially the dancing girls with all their glamour, their furs, their jewels. What I would have given to have one of them as a friend! But they were just very cordial to us young musicians. It only dawned on me later that they [did so to protect] us from the gangsters. I was then around twenty or twenty-one years old then, a very inexperienced young man, and I couldn't take my eyes off the dancing girls, who responded with a movement to every nuance of our music. But they were only interested in visitors with money, they had to fend for themselves. I blew like crazy back then, just to impress them. They acknowledged that with a friendly smile or say 'Cootie, you play great!' But that's it."[15]

Valve trombonist Juan Tizol (1900–1984) joined Ellington just a few months after Cootie and Williams described him as "a quiet fellow; he was not a troublemaker." "[H]e was a very nice fellow and kept to himself; he didn't bother nobody. He played his part the best way he could, and that was all, [and] take his solos. Because one time Cootie was a terrific swing man, you know? When he first came in the band, oh, he could swing any tune. He was the real get-off man in the band, as far as the trumpet section was concerned."[16]

"Duke Ellington and His Famous Orchestra," 1929. Center: Duke Ellington—piano. Front row: Freddie Jenkins, Cootie Williams, Arthur Whetsel—trumpets; Harry Carney, Johnny Hodges, Barney Bigard—reeds. Back row: Joe "Tricky Sam" Nanton, Juan Tizol—trombones; Sonny Greer—drums; Fred Guy—banjo; Wellman Braud—bass. Sonny Greer inscribed the photo to Juan Tizol and his wife Rose. (Photo courtesy of the Steven Lasker collection)

Cootie's first vocal recording and record label credit.

Cootie Williams, at just seventeen years old, made his first recordings with "The Jungle Band" for Brunswick on March 1, 1929. "The Jungle Band" was one of the several pseudonyms used by Duke Ellington and his Cotton Club Orchestra to allow them to record for multiple record labels. Three titles were recorded at Cootie's inaugural session: "Rent Party Blues," "Harlem Flat Blues," and "Paducah." The last title was a blues by Don Redman and features Williams's first solo with the Duke Ellington orchestra,[17] a single twelve-bar chorus of the blues on open trumpet with the Armstrong influence front and center.

For their March 7 RCA Victor date, the band used the "Duke Ellington and his Cotton Club Orchestra" moniker. "Hot Feet" featured Williams's first recorded vocal and it resulted in his first mention on a record label—"Vocal refrain by Charlie Williams." (Charles or Charlie would be used instead of Cootie on occasion until about the mid-1930s.) "Hot Feet" is an up-tempo number, with Cootie's contribution consisting of gruff scat phrases traded with the trumpet of Freddie Jenkins.

When Williams joined the band, he had never played growl (plunger) trumpet. It was something he didn't take seriously, and as mentioned before, he would laugh at the sounds that master plunger trombonist Joseph "Tricky Sam" Nanton made as they played their gigs. Freddy Jenkins had taken the Bubber Miley role after his departure,[18] but eventually a revelation hit Williams: "I sat there for about six months, and it come to me that [Duke] had hired me to take this fella's [Bubber Miley's] place. I kept listening to Tricky Sam with the plunger. I used to take the plunger home and rehearse it and rehearse it. So one night Duke said, 'You got it.' So I went 'wah, wah, wah.' And he said, 'That's it! You got it!' And I've been playing plunger ever since."[19]

There are different stories about the origins of the art of plunger muted brass playing. Some of the earliest practitioners include Joe "King" Oliver (1885–1938) and Johnny Dunn (1897–1937). It's not as simple as waving the plunger in front of the instrument. Trombonist Al Grey (1925–2000), a star soloist with Count Basie, wrote the book *Plunger Techniques, A Plunger Method for Trombone & Trumpet*, an entire treatise on the proper way to use the plumber's helper. (One of Duke Ellington's tongue-in-cheek statements was that the plunger had been actually invented specifically for the trumpet "and they've found other uses for it now.")[20] Using the plunger can also cause intonation issues. Mercer Ellington said, "Musicians like Lawrence Brown and Quentin Jackson did very well, too, when they growled on trombone, but they moved their tuning slide, something that Tricky, Cootie, and Ray Nance never did."[21] When playing with the plunger, some brassmen use the pixie mute, a small mute that's almost entirely inside the instrument. This mute makes it easier to keep the horn in tune and also gives the sound a different timbre.[22]

Saxophonist Otto Hardwick described the plunger lineage: "Bubber taught Tricky his growling technique and was constantly besieged by valve men. The only answer they could get out of him as to 'how' he did it was: 'I don't know how I do it. I'm just crazy.' Bubber often said he wasn't going to teach anybody how to take his job from him. That's why there's a dearth of growl trumpet players today. Cootie Williams, who followed Bubber, got his schooling from Tricky and that's all, brother!"[23]

Six months after his first Ellington recording session, on Friday the 13th of September, Williams made his plunger debut on an Ellington composition titled "Jazz Convulsions." At the time, he probably didn't think that from this beginning it would become impossible to think of Cootie Williams without thoughts of the plunger mute being far behind.

CATHERINE

Another big change occurred for the young man in 1929. Not too long after his 1928 triumph at the Band Box, Charles Melvin Williams went dancing at the Savoy Ballroom. There, he met a strikingly beautiful young lady named Catherine Henrietta Smith. (How long they dated before they got married is unknown, but it could have been at most eighteen months.) Catherine was born in Chicago on June 24, 1913. They lived near each other before their marriage; the marriage certificate records that Catherine lived at 100 W. 139th Street, while Cootie's apartment was at 36 W. 138th Street, making their dwellings within a block of each other, just across Lenox Avenue, a five-minute walk.

The couple was young; Cootie was eighteen and Catherine was sixteen. They were married on October 28 at the residence of the wedding officiant, Rev. W. Abner Brown, at 22 W. 130th Street.[1] Rev. Brown was the assistant pastor at Metropolitan Baptist Church. The size of the ceremony and whether any of the band was present is unknown, but the Ellington band is known to have worked at the Cotton Club that night.[2]

Their wedding day was also the day dubbed "Black Monday." On this date, the US stock market experienced its largest drop in history up until that time. The following day, there was no rally, just an additional drop, cementing the start of the Great Depression. If there was a honeymoon for the newlyweds it must have been delayed, because Williams was in the Brunswick studio on October 29 recording with a subset of the Ellington band dubbed "The Six Jolly Jesters." (Despite the name, there were ten musicians in the group.)

October 29, the day following the Williams's nuptials, saw the release of a short film that featured Duke Ellington and his orchestra, "Black and Tan." Filmed the previous August, the film marked the film debut of both Duke and young Cootie.[3] Although in later years the song "Black and Tan Fantasy"

Catherine Williams in a Maurice of Chicago studio portrait from the early 1930s. It is personalized to Ellington drummer Sonny Greer and his wife Mildred. (Photo courtesy of the Steven Lasker collection)

Cootie and Catherine Williams in 1935. This photograph is part of actress/journalist Fredi Washington's photograph collection and may have been taken by her. (Connecticut Museum of Culture and History, Fredi Washington Collection)

would be a feature for Cootie, understandably, in the film, the song is given to the veteran trumpeter Arthur Whetsel (1905–1940). The brief story line features Duke Ellington as a struggling composer and musician on the verge of having his piano repossessed. Fredi Washington (1903–1994) plays Duke's girlfriend and a dancer at the nightclub where Ellington and his band perform. (Washington's best known role was in the 1934 drama *Imitation of Life*.)

The band was drawing rave reviews. A reviewer for the *Baltimore Afro-American* gave a bold yet accurate assessment of the band's future: "If these youngsters stay together, they will hold the diadem of supremacy indefinitely."[4] The following year, the band traveled to Los Angeles to film musical segments in a comedy starring two popular white comedians in blackface, Freeman Gosden and Charles Correll. They portrayed Amos 'n' Andy, owners of the Fresh Air Taxi company. The band makes a notable appearance playing "Old Man Blues," a chance to see the young band in action. Unlike some filmed appearances, the sound was not recorded separately and mimed on film. Juan Tizol and Barney Bigard, of Puerto Rican and Creole heritage respectively, are seen wearing dark makeup in order to make sure viewers don't think the band is racially mixed. Cootie is a visually animated presence on screen. Cootie has no solo in this segment; that task is handled by Freddie Jenkins (1906–1978). Williams thought highly of Jenkins. In a 1963 interview, he said, "I think someone should mention him now and then. He helped build the band. I never read an article on him—why?"[5]

Coinciding with the band's time in Hollywood, Cootie's hero Louis Armstrong was at Sebastian's Cotton Club in the Los Angeles suburb of Culver City. (This club had no affiliation with the Harlem Cotton Club.) Cootie said, "We played [Sebastian's Cotton Club] one night and when we came off the stand and Louis came on, it was an amazing thing just to sit and listen to that man play. He played thirty-two choruses on 'Ding Dong Daddy from Dumas' and I never will forget that. The longer Louis played the stronger he got, and all the choruses were different. The guy was the most crazy musician to do things that I ever heard in my life and there never was anyone I heard who could come up to compare with Louis Armstrong as a jazz artist. Most jazz musicians repeat themselves so many times in playing a song. If they play two or three choruses most jazz musicians start to repeat themselves but that is one thing that Louis Armstrong never did in his heyday. That's why I give him credit for being the greatest jazz musician that ever lived."[6]

During Williams's first tenure with the Ellington band, the orchestra made two more film appearances, *Murder at the Vanities* and *Belle of the Nineties*, both filmed and released in 1934. The latter film starred Mae West and introduced the song "My Old Flame." It would become a standard and Cootie recorded it several times during his career as a leader.

Through Ellington, Williams was enjoying the kind of career success and visibility that would not have been possible with Webb or Henderson. Neither of them appeared in a Hollywood film during their entire careers. Besides being one of the few Black bandleaders to make appearances in mainstream (white) movies, Ellington was also receiving major distribution and thus visibility with his recordings on RCA Victor. Cootie's first composition "Echoes of the Jungle" appeared on the label. Recorded on June 16, 1931, it was credited to Cootie Williams and Irving Mills. (Irving Mills added his name to many of his clients' compositions in order to claim 50% of the royalties. He made no musical contribution to any of the numerous pieces under his name. The current ASCAP database lists 364 pieces with Mills as coauthor. Besides Williams, Mills "co-authored" pieces by Duke Ellington, Hoagy Carmichael, Cab Calloway, and Fats Waller.) Eddie Lambert describes "Echoes of the Jungle" as "a sixteen bar blues with a beautiful singing, melancholy melody."[7] Perhaps because he is the composer, Cootie is the main soloist on this recording. In his open trumpet bars, Williams shows his deep Armstrong influence.

BUGLE CALL RAG

Because of the national exposure that came with being one of the major solo voices in a prominent band, Cootie had an influence on and was a role model for the playing of others. One such musician was a future star of the Count Basie band, trumpeter Wilbur "Buck" Clayton (1911–1991). Although they were born just a few months apart, Williams was able to get a big-league career going before Clayton. Clayton became aware of Williams before he knew about Louis Armstrong. "I was crazy about Cootie Williams with Duke Ellington. . . . I learned as many of Cootie's solos as I possibly could, playing the record over and over again until I got it almost perfect. . . . The only thing I couldn't do with Cootie's solos was to growl like he did. . . . But just the same, I was playing Cootie's solos, growl or not."[1] Not being able to growl turned out to be a liability—Clayton got fired from a job because he was unable to do so.[2] At Clayton's 1934 wedding, Cootie and Tricky Sam Nanton "growled the wedding march." Clayton said, "I never had any idea they could make the wedding march sound like something right out of Harlem, but they did."[3]

An example of Cootie's hot trumpet work can be heard on a 1932 recording of "Bugle Call Rag." Buck Clayton said, "Now 'Bugle Call Rag,' that's a special one for me because of Cootie Williams. The breaks, the solos, it's all Cootie. And I could never forget playing because I had to learn it. That second break, boy, that was hard for me but I finally got it. You know, I had to rehearse the damn thing six hours a day." Clayton said, "at the time I was trying to form a style I knew many of Cootie's solos note for note. We used to get the Ellington records as they came out, and I would put the needle down on Cootie's solo, write it down real quick, then put the needle back again and so on until I had the whole thing."[4] (The transcription process was a lot more arduous before computers and digital music files.) The third and fourth bars of the break

Cootie Williams's virtuoso second break on Duke Ellington's 1932 recording of "Bugle Call Rag."

are obviously the most technically challenging. Cootie tosses off the octave displacements with casual virtuosity. Williams was such a technically adroit trumpet player that many of his performances are deceptive in their difficulty.

Recorded at the same February 9, 1932, session that produced "Echoes of the Jungle," "Dinah" features Cootie's singing. Although Cootie sang periodically over the years, he didn't show the enthusiasm for it that his model Louis Armstrong did. "Sonny Greer did most of the singing for the band before Ivie Anderson joined. Duke used to try to get me to sing and though I did a bit I didn't like it."[5] He professed this reluctance throughout his career, although he sang to the end. He was most successful when he lent his vocal talents to blues and non-serious numbers; his attempts at more serious pieces and ballads don't come off well. Ivie Anderson joined the band as their regular vocalist in early February 1931. Her first recording session with the band, on February 2, was "It Don't Mean a Thing (If It Ain't Got That Swing)." While the song was composed by Ellington, Cootie claimed the expression was a catchphrase of his devising.[6] When Cootie was asked to define swing, he replied "Define it? I'd rather tackle Einstein's theory!"[7]

♪

The Ellington band would prove to be sui generis. This music of Duke Ellington wasn't based on classical conventions or even those rules that were being laid down in the jazz world. "We violate more laws of music than anyone else and then just go right along violating," Ellington said.[8] Ellington also didn't manage his personnel in an orthodox way either. (Leaders like Glenn Miller and Cab Calloway were known for their discipline.) Cootie appointed himself an enforcer of order: "If Johnny [Hodges] or Barney [Bigard] or any of them were in an argument, wasn't playing the music right, I'd holler at them. Because Duke would never say nothing to them. I'd be the one that had taken over that spot . . . [and] get them on the ball."⁹ The practical jokes the band played on one another didn't amuse Williams. He also found the antics and drinking of Sonny Greer irksome: "I couldn't do anything with Sonny . . . Even Duke couldn't do anything with Sonny."¹⁰

Bassist Major Holley, who played in the band for a short time in 1964, said "[Y]ou couldn't talk to Ellington about anything other than the extension on a G minor 9th chord. He didn't want to know about domestic or personal problems; he was impervious to all that. All he wanted to do was talk about music."¹¹ Louie Bellson (1924–2009), who joined the band in 1951, said "Duke's discipline was very much different to anybody else. Duke, his idea, he told me many times, he said: 'Look, if I had to worry about my band, I'd be six feet underground. All my guys are over twenty-one years old. If this guy acts up for two or three days, all I can do is go to him and say, "Are you OK, are you all right?" I can't worry about them, they're men. They should know how to handle themselves.' So as a result, sometimes the discipline would fall apart at times."¹²

9

THE FIRST EUROPEAN TOUR

Duke Ellington and His Orchestra in Dallas, Fall 1933. Standing—Cootie Williams, Lawrence Brown, Wellman Braud, Arthur Whetsel, Joe Nanton, Otto Hardwick, Fred Guy, Duke Ellington, Harry Carney, Juan Tizol, Louis Bacon, Sonny Greer, Earl "Snakehips" Tucker. Crouching—Johnny Hodges, Bill Bailey, Freddie Jenkins, Derby Wilson. (Connecticut Museum of Culture and History, Fredi Washington Collection)

On June 2, 1933, the Ellington band departed New York on the S.S. *Olympic* for their first European tour, arriving in Southampton, England, a week later.[1] It was probably only the second time Cootie had been on a ship. Cootie found was astounded by the reception accorded to the band: "I never will forget that. Because when we got off the boat, and when we got to the hotel and went out, everybody knew you. The same as in America. They knew you better than the people did in America. And they would invite you to their home, and they had all your records. Knew what to talk about. Knew when you were born, what was the first record you ever made."[2] "See, on jazz, the people in Europe, they're very well educated on jazz, which the American public are not. Any place you go in Europe, the general public are very much educated. On jazz music. That's something that we don't have here in America. . . . It's a pleasure to play for people that understand your music and understand what you're doing. Now, sometimes you play here in America, and the people don't understand your music and what you're doing. Because they don't know jazz. They don't know nothing about jazz, some people that come to concerts. And some of the universities and things we played, some of them have never heard of Duke Ellington. You know? And it's kind of hard to play to an audience, you know, that don't know nothing about jazz."[3]

After arriving in London on June 9, they performed concerts in the capital city for a little over two weeks before making a tour of UK cities that included Birmingham, Glasgow, and Liverpool. The Ellington band even got a chance to rub shoulders with a member British royalty. Cootie said, "[The Prince of Wales] was always around. We used to see him quite often."[4] The future King Edward VIII was nicknamed "The Wale" by Sonny Greer.[5]

After a concert in Holland, they arrived in Paris on July 27.[6] The French critic Hugues Panassie (1912–1974) was particularly intrigued and puzzled by Cootie Williams. First, he found Williams hard to identify, physically: "[W]henever there is a face hard to identify [in Ellington band photos], you can be sure that it is Cootie's. He changes so much from one photo to another that, even forewarned, one finds it hard to believe it is the same man."

Panassie also had a hard time comprehending the reserved nature of Williams's personality and the versatility in his playing: "I questioned Cootie eagerly, for I wanted to know which were the solos played by him on the [orchestra's] records, never having been able to be certain on this subject. At this time, it was supposed that only Cootie was responsible for the wa-wa growl solos and that he did not play many without mute. "Is it you or Freddy Jenkins," I asked him, "who is the trumpet in the second chorus of *Ducky Wucky*?" Cootie looked at me vacantly; there was nothing on his face to show that he had understood or even heard my question. After a few seconds of silence, however, he said to me in as neutral a tone as possible, "It's me." Curious person, I thought to myself. I asked again: "But it is Freddy Jenkins who plays the short trumpet passage in the last chorus?" And I looked at him intently to try to be quite sure that he clearly understood my question. His face remained as inexpressive as before, the same silence prevailed, and then Cootie said, "No, it's still me," as if he were pulling out the words with difficulty. I put several more questions to him about other trumpet solos on various records of Duke's. The reply was always the same: "It's me." And Cootie's expression—dull, vague, half-dazed—never changed as he rolled between his fingers a cigarette from which he occasionally took a nonchalant puff. "He is completely stupid," I said to myself, "and I have wasted my time with these questions; the fact that he has always replied 'it's me' is proof enough that he has not even paid attention to what I was asking." But I did not have long to wait to recognize my error: in the course of the concerts, I saw Cootie execute all the passages in question, even those I had always attributed to Freddy Jenkins. And still later I had the opportunity to verify that Cootie's sleepy manner did not prevent him from realizing very well what one way saying to him, and to reply with a precision one seldom encountered among the other musicians."[7]

Panassie was to become a huge fan and advocate for Williams. In his review of Ellington's Paris concert for *Jazz Tango Dancing* magazine he wrote, "the revelation of the [Ellington] orchestra for me was Charlie 'Cootie' Williams, who does most of the hot work on the trumpet and plays not only the muted Bubber Miley choruses, but most of the open ones." He raved that "inspiration never left him. I know few hot trumpets more moving" and that Williams "had flights worthy of Louis, infinitely surpassing his performance on the disc."[8]

In the December 1945 issue of *Hot-Revue*, Panassie wrote a seven-page, 4,200-word article extolling Williams's trumpet virtuosity, "The Case [for] Cootie":

I consider Cootie to be one of the greatest living jazz musicians. Alone among the trumpets, Louis Armstrong is above him.

Do you have to have heard Cootie in the flesh to measure the beauty of his sound? I dare not affirm it. However, I must note this: when I only knew Cootie from the record, I did not find his sound superior to that of other trumpets. Hearing it for the first time in the flesh in Paris in 1933, I was suddenly dazzled by its sound. Johnny Hodges, Barney Bigard, Tricky Sam didn't surprise me: they sounded just like on the records. Cootie, on the contrary, seemed to me another man incomparably more moving than in records.

In 1938 and 1939, I heard him again in New York and Paris. I realized that he was a hundred times better than I had thought. Once again, his sound overwhelmed me, his playing was a real revelation. Once again his records took on a new meaning for me. And since then, they have continued to look more and more beautiful to me. Such has been my experience. I do not claim for that that one cannot fully enjoy Cootie with the help of the records alone. I tend to believe the contrary. But it must be more difficult.

What is striking, when you hear it, is the power of its sound, a superior power higher than that of all jazz trumpets except Louis Armstrong and perhaps Tommy Ladnier. While being extraordinarily strong, its sound is round, fat, bright and mellow: it is a real delight for the ear. What further enhances the effect produced by this sound is the particular quality of Cootie's playing.[9]

The huge, majestic sound Cootie had on trumpet is something that is repeatedly remarked upon by musicians and fans throughout his career. Vince Prudente, who joined the Ellington trombone section in April 1972, sat in front of Cootie.[10] Prudente said Cootie "had the biggest trumpet sound I ever heard in my life. It was very powerful, really great. Not loud, powerful. You know what I mean? Some trumpet players play loud, and it hurts your ears. Being a trombone player, I've sat in front of a whole lot of trumpet players. Some of them have a sound that tears your ears up."[11]

Bassist John Lamb was with the Ellington band from 1964 to 1967 and said: "That growl thing that he did was always unique. It always fills up *everything*. I thought, my goodness this guy has a big sound. He'd turn his horn down towards the floor and you can feel the vibrations all through the entire room. I mean it was powerful, I mean you can really feel that. It wasn't just a note he was playing; I'm talking about the emotion behind it, the power, the energy that he put into that. I don't know if anybody else felt it or not. They might have taken it for granted, but I heard it and I felt it."[12] Trombonist Art Baron was hired by Ellington in 1973: "He would play a few notes and just floor the audience. He could get them, jumping up and down, smiling, laughing, [or] crying ... He got the essence of music, which is communication. Cootie spoke volumes in just a few notes."[13]

Most evaluations of Cootie's sound mention the power described by Panassie, Prudente, and Lamb. For those who were not fortunate enough to experience the sound of Cootie Williams in person, there is a way to put his recorded sound into perspective. There are numerous trumpet players who have recorded his transcribed solos, such as on "House of Joy" and "The Shepherd," to name just two. Play their recordings and compare them to Cootie's. No matter how great the trumpeter is, the sound suffers in comparison.

Panassie also goes on to say that Cootie didn't miss his notes:

There is one thing, however, that Cootie's beautiful technique does not explain. It's that he almost never misses a note, doesn't [fluff] like the musicians when all the trumpets fluff frequently.

We immediately notice a trumpet fluff, but we realize much less quickly a trumpet never fluffs. It took me almost ten years to realize that Cootie never misses. When I shared this remark with friends, I saw that they had never thought of it either. And I will always remember Louis Bacon's astonishment when I asked him why, in his opinion, some trumpets [did this] and others did not, citing the example of Cootie. He could give me no explanation and suddenly realized how strange this phenomenon was. He, too, had never thought of the fact that Cootie didn't fluff, and yet, as soon as I made my remark, he saw that it was true.

This is an anomaly that defies all explanation. Some trumpeters have a dizzying instrumental technique, like Louis Armstrong, Rex, Roy Eldridge, fluff quite often. Other trumpets, who possess their instrument less well, fluff much less. How is it possible? It should be noted that a trumpet like Louis Armstrong plays very difficult passages impeccably and fluffs on a note extremely easy to play. It is therefore not always the difficulty that provokes the fluff—at least among the great jazz trumpets. Could it be above all a question of nervousness and calm?

Panassie concluded his laudation with "He is one of the most dynamic musicians there is. And he's also one of the greatest jazz musicians. As long as Cootie lives and plays, real, beautiful jazz music will live with him."[14]

10

WILLIAMS, WHETSEL, AND STEWART

The hot trumpet wasn't Cootie's only strength. The year 1934 saw the debut of "Solitude," an Ellington composition that was to become a standard. A ballad, it featured Williams on an open trumpet solo. Of the recording session, Ellington said, "The sound engineer was half crying. It filled everybody up. To make people cry, that's music at its highest."[1] A large part of that mood is set by Cootie.

When writing an arrangement, the usual practice is to have parts for the first alto sax, second alto sax, first trumpet, and so on. Ellington would write for the person, not the instrument. Regarding Arthur Whetsel, Cootie said, "He played a lot of the first parts. Well, I'll tell you, Duke switched parts around. On one number, sometimes I'd be playing second, I'd be playing first, and like that, on the same tune."[2] In another interview, Williams said, "Even outside the lead, if he had a note he wanted dominant, he would give it to me. If it were tender, Whetsel would be the one."[3] "With Duke, we were a good team of friends. Arthur Whetsel was in charge of charming the ladies by playing softly and with feeling, Freddie Jenkins was the showman, he played with velocity to impress the gallery. This is why the Duke is an extraordinary leader. In his orchestra, everyone has a well-defined role. He chooses guys who have different styles but who get along well musically and humanly."[4] Of Jenkins, Cootie also said, "he had a peculiar style . . . but he could play."[5] He also felt that Jenkins didn't get enough credit for his contributions to the band.[6]

Cootie said during his entire time with the band, it was only that early trumpet section of himself, Whetsel, and Jenkins that truly blended. "It's a matter of staying under the lead, and blending in with the lead, and blending in with the second." What changed? His former section mate from the Fletcher Henderson orchestra, Rex Stewart joined the band on December 28, 1934, replacing an ailing Freddy Jenkins.[7]

Duke Ellington's 1936 trumpet section: Rex Stewart, Cootie Williams, and Arthur Whetsel. (Duke Ellington Collection, Archives Center, National Museum of American History, Smithsonian Institution)

Rex Stewart's style was unconventional. Garvin Bushell (1902–1991), a reed player who worked and recorded with the likes of Bessie Smith, Fletcher Henderson, Cab Calloway, and John Coltrane in his long and varied career, admired Rex but found him lacking in some aspects of his musicianship. He said, "In a way, Rex represented one of the great faults of Black musicians. In creativity they were tops, but since many of them didn't have basic training to begin with, they did a lot of things wrong, and it showed up in bands—like weaknesses in overall range and intonation problems. They became such great creators because jazz was their main object, not whether they could play in tune or not. . . . Anyway, Rex had a great ear, and could almost play whatever he heard. He could move fast and had the range. He just lipped and fingered his horn wrong."[8]

Cootie said personnel changes caused difficulties: "Well, as changes came along, different guys resent you telling them anything. And so that's the way it went. You'd let a guy set up there. You wouldn't open your mouth to him. Let him play what he wanted to play. There was always arguments when Cat [Anderson] was there. He was supposed to be in command, and they'd have fights and things, you know, and arguments. But they didn't have that in the days when I'm speaking of." But despite this, Cootie said the reed section were the bigger offenders.

Ellington would sometimes use his musicians' enmity to goad them into competition. For example, 1939's "Tootin' through the Roof," an up tempo swinger, featured the talents of Williams and Rex Stewart. After an Ellington introduction, Harry Carney states the main theme, with Cootie taking the bridge. Johnny Hodges and Lawrence Brown have short solos before Stewart and Williams trade four-bar phrases for a chorus like boxers exchanging blows. They then join up in a duet, climaxing in a high-note finale. One wonders if Cootie was irked by playing second to Stewart's lead.

Trumpeter Bill Berry played with the band in the early 1960s and described his approach to bandleading as being Ellington-influenced: "I feel everybody should be utilized as an individual. I don't like to think: here's the trumpet section; I like to think of four trumpet players, every one of whom plays differently. What I try to concern myself with, as far as possible, is what each does best. . . . If you have a Cat Anderson sitting there and you don't utilize his uniqueness, it's a shame."[9]

Author Claire P. Gordon (1919–2016) was a friend of Stewart's and said: "Cootie resented that [Rex] was in the band. He didn't think that Duke needed another major trumpet player." Gordon got to know Stewart well when he moved to Los Angeles in the early 1960s. He was asked to write an article for the *Los Angeles Times* by the Calendar section editor, Charles Champlin. As Gordon explained, there were some problems: "he did not have a typewriter, he did not know how to type, and he also didn't know how to spell the long words that were part of his vocabulary. He sounded like a college professor, but he dropped out of school at age thirteen. So I was his co-writer for years." She assembled Stewart's posthumously published autobiography *Boy Meets Horn* from his notes.

"He read all the time. He was a little fat guy, and he had these big pockets and would have these pocketbooks in his pocket. He was always reading a book. Well, a few of the other guys will talk about baseball games and prizefighters and Rex is talking about literature. And so this is another reason for the [band's] animosity; they thought he was stuck up. They thought he was trying to be grand and something he wasn't and so that that was another reason for the problem. I think that most of the guys did not like Rex at all. I mean he didn't fit in; he just was not one of the guys. So it wasn't just Cootie. The only other person he hung out with was Tricky. Tricky was another pretty bright guy, another reader. They were the only two [readers in the band]."[10]

Sonny Greer also remarked on the relationship between Williams and Stewart, saying "I don't think Cootie Williams ever forgave Duke for hiring Rex. I believe Cootie's jealousy of Rex is what caused him to leave the band."[11] It certainly didn't help that newcomer Stewart got solo space on all the selections for the first three sessions in 1935.[12] John Hammond wasn't happy about this and said that "[t]he only sad part about some of the sides is that they feature Duke's new "exhibitionistic high-note trumpet" instead of the peerless artist known as "Cootie" Williams, "just about the best trumpeter in the country."[13]

John Hammond (1910–1987) was an ardent jazz fan and promoter. He was one of those boosters who did a lot for music and social causes. Hammond could afford his passion; he was a Vanderbilt heir, the great-great-grandson railroad magnate Cornelius Vanderbilt. He rubbed a lot of people the wrong way because of his strongly held opinions—he wasn't shy about voicing them and didn't care if he stepped on a few toes in the process. He certainly thought Duke Ellington could have a better band, despite Ellington's own musical vision. In his autobiography, Hammond wrote, "It's impossible to like jazz without liking Duke Ellington. Yet I know I have puzzled or annoyed Duke's many admirers by my criticisms of his bands and his music."[14]

ECHOES OF HARLEM

The band made their first recording session of 1936 only three days into the new year. Two of the four selections recorded that day were showcases for two of the musicians, Cootie and Barney Bigard. "Barney's Concerto" was also known as "Clarinet Lament," while "Cootie's Concerto," not to be confused with the later "Concerto for Cootie," was widely known as "Echoes of Harlem."[1] *Metronome* listed "Echoes of Harlem" as one of the best recordings of 1936, saying "Cootie Williams's trumpet concerto that just swings like nobody's business, and in which Cootie's trumpeting should be everybody's ditto."[2] It also inspired *Down Beat* to list Cootie as one of the "Colored Musicians not always given credit to them" saying he was "one of the most natural artists in Duke Ellington's group."[3] Lionel Hampton said it "borders on the unreal realm of things, of what might have been."[4]

Although "Echoes of Harlem" was copyrighted by Ellington as sole composer,[5] Williams claimed he wrote the piece, saying:

> Most of Duke's compositions in the late 1920s and the 1930s were composed with the musicians assisting. If any member of the band wrote a tune it was thought of as an honor for the band to play it; we didn't think of the money value or nothing like that. Everybody contributed something on their own also—Tizol, Hodges, Bigard, Carney, and myself—but Duke used to get credit for them. Sometimes we would write a complete number and Duke would still get all the credit and all the money. I did "Echoes of Harlem" and "Concerto For Cootie" and they were entirely mine, but Duke got his name on the label. I didn't mind.[6]

A *Pittsburgh Courier* columnist wrote in 1936: "So it was Cootie Williams of Duke Ellington's band who wrote 'Echoes of Harlem' and not Duke? Never heard that [until it was] announce[d] via radio until last week."[7] But Cootie's assertion isn't entirely true. The bridge for "Echoes of Harlem" is the same as the main theme of "Blue Mood," a 1932 composition credited to Duke Ellington and Johnny Hodges.[8] Continuing the musical genealogy, "Blue Mood" was based on "Basin Street Blues"![9]

In the band's live performances, "Echoes of Harlem" stood out in the press reviews. "The thing that caught my fancy most of all about the Duke Ellington show was a cornet [sic] concerto played by 'Cootie' Williams. I think the tag of it was 'Echoes of Harlem,' and it sure was a pip."[10] *Tempo*, a short-lived Los Angeles–based publication, stated: "Cootie Williams stole the show when Ellington appeared at Loew's State [in NYC]. The success of the Cootie's Concerto has inspired the Duke to compose others for Rex Stewart and Lawrence Brown."[11] *Metronome* weighed in: "Cootie has a conception of savagery and force on the instrument that cannot be equaled. His work with the with the wa-wa mute is more expressive than speech."[12]

♪

Cootie said, "It was Irving Mills's idea [to form the small groups] to keep us main figures in the band happy and to make us extra money."[13] There were five nominal leaders, and they were to pick various combinations from the full band. The leaders chosen were from the main soloists in the band—Cootie Williams, Rex Stewart, Johnny Hodges, and Barney Bigard. Perhaps Lawrence Brown turned down a spot; he was only to record two albums (*Slide Trombone* for Verve in 1955 and *Inspired Abandon* for Impulse! in 1965) under his leadership during his entire professional career. The groups recorded on Mills's newly formed label, Master Records. Mills set himself an aggressive goal for recording his stable of artists for his new label with a goal of 200 recordings by April 1 and thereafter seventy-five per month![14]

The Williams sides were under the banner of "Cootie Williams and His Rug Cutters." (It's almost forgotten slang today, but to "cut a rug" meant to dance.) The group's first session was on March 8, 1937, and five titles were recorded. Eight of the band's fourteen members were used (Williams, Joe "Tricky Sam" Nanton on trombone, saxophonists Johnny Hodges, Otto Hardwick, Harry Carney; Duke Ellington on piano; Hayes Alvis on bass; Sonny Greer on drums). Cootie Williams used Johnny Hodges on all his Rug Cutter sessions and Hodges used Williams on all his small-group sessions, an indication of their friendship and mutual regard for one another.

A 1937 theater ad for a Duke Ellington stage show appearance. Note that the small groups are given billing. (*Wisconsin State Journal*, Courtesy of Newspapers.com)

The repertoire for this inaugural session was like the type of fare that would be typical for the rest of these sessions—original music, popular standards, and occasionally a vocal. Three of them were from outside composers; the ballad "I Can't Believe That You're In Love With Me," by Jimmy McHugh and Clarence Gaskill, dated from 1926. Most likely, this song was on Williams's mind from Louis Armstrong's swinging 1930 version. The other "outside" compositions, "Diga Diga Doo" and "Tiger Rag," had been previously recorded by the full Ellington band in 1928 and 1929, respectively. There were two originals, "Blue Reverie" by Carney and Ellington (According to *Variety*, "Blue Reverie" was composed in the studio by Ellington)[15] and "Downtown Uproar" by Williams and Ellington.

Helen Oakley Dance was under the impression that the bands' session creations were spontaneous, but that was far from the truth. Cootie said, "[M]ost of the small-group recordings were rehearsed beforehand and not made up in the studio. Barney [Bigard], if he had a date, would work hard getting his music together and we all did the same thing, along with Duke."[16] Critic Barry Ulanov summarized Cootie's small-group output as "reflect[ing] his own personality and that of his horn. The growl of good cheer, the grunt of ironic jeer, the musical sneer and leer and sorrowful inner stirrings."[17]

Cootie's extracurricular activity also included recording with combos led by Benny Goodman sidemen Lionel Hampton and Teddy Wilson. The Teddy Wilson session of March 31, 1937, included three Ellingtonians. Besides Williams, Johnny Hodges and Harry Carney were part of the backing for Billie Holiday for three numbers. (The fourth number recorded, "Fine and Dandy," was an instrumental.) Cootie's backing work on "Carelessly" is especially fine.

For Hampton, Williams made two sessions. On "Stompology" the band is swinging so hard that it's clear that it came to a grinding halt due to the three-minute recording time limit.

Later that month, Cootie recorded in a small group setting with the Gotham Stompers, a combo made up of musicians from the bands of Duke Ellington and Chick Webb. Notably, Chick Webb himself was at the drums, thus making the only time Cootie was able to record with his friend and former boss. (Two years later Webb would be dead at a young age from complications of the illnesses he had suffered since his youth.)

Lionel Hampton was also starting a small-group tradition. Hampton said, "In 1937, Eli Oberstein, who was recording director at RCA Victor, came and told me that any time I want to record, I had an open invitation." Hampton used these opportunities to assemble swinging combos from the best players in New York. A virtual who's who of jazz at that time recorded with him; a small listing includes Dizzy Gillespie, Charlie Christian, Chu Berry, Benny Carter, and Harry James.[18] For his April 14 session, he drew Cootie Williams, Lawrence Brown, Johnny Hodges, and bassist Billy Taylor from the Ellington band; from the Goodman organization, pianist Jess Stacy and guitarist Allan Reuss; and, from the Cab Calloway band, Cozy Cole playing drums.

Overall, Williams recorded on a staggering ninety-seven titles in small-group settings during the period from 1936 to 1940, which was nearly half of the nearly 200 songs made for the Ellington small groups. All the titles were gathered together in a 2006 reissue by Mosaic Records, *Duke Ellington: The Complete 1936–1940 Variety, Vocalion and OKeh Small Group Sessions*, which included thorough and knowledgeable liner notes by Steven Lasker. These liner notes would be a good substitute for a stand-alone book; they weigh in at approximately 20,000 words.[19] Unfortunately, the Mosaic set is out of print, so unless one is already in possession of one of the limited run of 10,000 seven-CD sets, they aren't publicly available.

♪

In their April 1937 issue, *Metronome* magazine had a short article titled "The Duke Ellingtons [sic]—Cotton Clubbers En Mass." It featured a group portrait of the band at their most elegant, wearing tie and tails. Beneath the portrait, thumbnail descriptions were given for each musician. For Cootie it read:

> Cootie Williams (trumpet)—a statuesque figure with great esprit de corps who just gives and gives in whoops . . . terrific over-eater and chronic gambler . . . but a smart one . . . good adviser on both music and commercialism . . . another bridge fiend[20] . . . always borrowing somebody's trombone to emit the best gut-bucket choruses in the band.[21]

Briefly, the trombone was Cootie's instrument of choice when he was very young. Fortunately, there's an extant example of Cootie's trombone playing. It was recorded after the February 24, 1938, recording in which the band recorded "Skrontch" and "If You Were In My Place," both featuring vocals by Ivie Anderson.[22] Leonard Feather (1914–1994) was an English-born jazz fan, composer, and journalist recently transplanted to America. Feather described how the recording came about:

> After the date was finished Duke was kidding around at the piano, singing a novelty song he'd written called "I Want to be a Rug Cutter." With the brazen bravado of youth, I asked him if he would make a special copy of it for me to take home to England. Duke agreed without hesitation, asked the engineer to set up an acetate, and proceeded to sing and play his way through the number. As an added bonus, Cootie Williams, who was still in the studio and for some reason was playing a trombone, did so for the other side of the record. As a result, on the back of "Rug Cutter" I had the only known example of Cootie on trombone, playing the blues, with Duke at the piano. The autographed copy of these two numbers is still the only one in existence and remains in my possession after a half-century.[23]

CARNEGIE HALL

One of the most historic nights in jazz history occurred on January 16, 1938. On that night Benny Goodman gave a concert of jazz music at New York City's fabled Carnegie Hall. Presenting jazz at a concert hall was a rare thing at that time. It was considered music for a nightclub or a dance hall, but not for a venue as distinguished as Carnegie Hall. Cootie Williams, along with fellow Ellingtonians Johnny Hodges on soprano and alto sax and Harry Carney on baritone sax, participated in the historic evening. Members of the Basie band were there, too, along with their leader.[1] Ellington decided against joining in, preferring to wait for the day when he, too, could play Carnegie Hall as a leader, which turned out to be five years later. But he was there as an audience member. Slyly, he did offer the services of clarinetist Barney Bigard.[2]

Cootie said of the event, "That was really the best. It was marvelous, thrilling . . ."[3] He only played on one song, however: "Blue Reverie," one of the pieces his Rug Cutters group had recorded ten months prior. Despite the brief time on stage, it was enough to catch the attention of reviewer George Simon, who wrote, "Cootie was cocky, grinning and grumbling into his mute."[4] The concert featured a jam session that used "Honeysuckle Rose" as the vehicle for solos by an ensemble that included Lester Young and other Basie band members, along with Carney and Hodges. Cootie would have been a natural in this setting, but perhaps he wasn't included because the trumpets of Buck Clayton and Harry James were already in the ensemble.[5]

THE SECOND EUROPEAN TOUR

The band left for their second trip to Europe on March 23, 1939, aboard the SS *Champlain*. World political tensions were high at the time. The front page of that day's issue of the *New York Times* was filled with stories about Hitler, Mussolini, Lithuania, and France. The *Pittsburgh Courier* reported that the "largest crowd of the season turned out to see Ellington and his crew off to Europe."[1] The tour lasted slightly over a month, but due to union regulations, there would be no concerts in Great Britain.

After arriving at the port of Le Havre a week later, the band departed over land to Paris.[2] While in Paris, "Ellington and his men had a night off ... Some of the men wanted to visit a bordello, but Ivie [Anderson] wouldn't allow Cootie to join them, instead entertaining him privately in a hotel room."[3] Rex Stewart said even the men "who had resolved to remain faithful" to their spouses, including himself, gave in to temptation during the tour.[4] How long the affair between Anderson and Williams lasted is unknown, but it definitely would have ended when Williams left the Ellington band. Juan Tizol said, "[Cootie] used to fool around with Ivie, but it didn't last long. Because they got in to a little trouble one time in the Pullman [train car], and he started to grab one of those hatchets out there in the Pullman—but nothing ever happened too strong."[5]

After Paris, the tour went on to make successful and memorable stops in Belgium, Sweden, Norway, Denmark and the Netherlands. With Europe on the verge of what would become World War II, the Ellington organization had a brush with the German government. While the band's valet (band boy) Richard Jones, known as "Jonesy," was transporting Sonny Greer's drums via automobile, Ellington reported in *Metronome* that Jonesy "was stopped at the

Page from a Swedish fan's autograph book with signatures of the Duke Ellington band collected during the 1939 European tour. Cootie Williams's signature is on the left and fourth one down. Duke Ellington and Ivie Anderson signed on separate pages. (Author's collection)

Dutch-German border and thrown into jail as a spy." Fortunately, he was only held for a few hours.[6]

The band returned to America on May 10. Shortly afterward, on June 16, drummer and bandleader Chick Webb died in his hometown of Baltimore. Cootie had fond memories of his time with Webb and recalled that Webb wanted Williams and Hodges to rejoin his band. (Webb would periodically kid Ellington, saying "One of these days, I'm going to take back my men.")[7] Williams thought "Chick was perhaps the greatest natural bandleader jazz has ever known. He found more talent and did more with it than anyone else. Any musician that worked with Chick became a great musician."[8]

In 1940, March 15 was just another Friday in the workaday world of Duke Ellington; the band was in the Chicago RCA Victor Studios for a recording session. They were in the midst of a Midwestern tour, just another round of their constant life on the road. At the beginning of the month, Ellington had just signed with RCA again, which, at the time, was one of the top record companies in the world. This was their second recording session for RCA, but one recording from this date turned it into a decisive moment for Duke Ellington, Cootie Williams, and the world of jazz.[9]

Three titles were recorded on this date: "Conga Brava," "Concerto for Cootie," and "Me and You," a vocal feature for singer Ivie Anderson. The band was enjoying a new burst of creativity and hitting an artistic peak. With the recent additions of bassist Jimmie Blanton, tenor saxophonist Ben Webster, and composer/arranger Billy Strayhorn, this edition of the band soon reached sonic and artistic heights previously unheard of in the world of jazz. This incarnation of the orchestra became known as the Blanton-Webster band, after the two influential short-term members who made a permanent impact on the Duke Ellington sound and on jazz in general. While the recordings of this date were eventually considered essential masterpieces for Duke Ellington and his Famous Orchestra, it was "Concerto for Cootie" that set events that would shake the world of popular music.

From a musical standpoint, it is innovative in many ways. Instead of the standard eight-bar phrases, there are several ten-bar sections. While not new, the idea of a single soloist on a song was also fairly unusual at the time.[10] But what was even more unusual was that it wasn't the bandleader getting all the solo space. In a little over three minutes, Williams showcases a wide variety of trumpet techniques and sonorities: lip trills, plunger-muted growling, pianissimo whispers, and a soaring full tone during his open-horn work. At no point does the work sound like a checklist of effects; it is a fully integrated virtuoso performance. (Eventually, "Concerto for Cootie" was outfitted with lyrics and became a popular hit for Ellington as "Do Nothin' till You Hear from Me.")

"It was quite different. Everyone in the band would pitch in and help write songs, everything that, almost, Duke did in those days. Someone in the band helped to do them. And in later years, I mean it got a little different, and people stopped doing things like that because they weren't paid for them properly. We only got $25.00 for a song if we gave it to him," Cootie said.[11] "And one of the biggest things that I did there was 'Concerto for Cootie.' I had to beg him to take that." [12] Cootie said he wrote the first part of the tune and Ellington wrote the second strain.[13] Williams said that some of the musicians had seller's remorse and sued Ellington for their share of royalties. He cited Barney Bigard for "Mood Indigo" and Rex Stewart for "Boy Meets Horn" as examples. For himself he said, "I believed in if I sold a person something and he paid for it, I didn't believe in going back, you know, and saying that I didn't mean it that way."[14]

Billy Strayhorn had an authoritative statement about the composition controversy. He felt that "only a few notes is hardly a composition. It may be the inspiration, but what do they say about 10 percent inspiration and 90 percent perspiration? Composing is work. So this guy says you and he wrote it, but he thinks he wrote it. He thinks you just put it down on paper. But what you did was put it down on paper, harmonized it, straightened out the bad phrases, and added things to it, so you could hear the finished product. Now, really, who wrote it? It was ever thus. But the proof is that these people don't go somewhere else and write beautiful music. You don't hear anything else from them. You do from Ellington."[15]

Down Beat raved over the coupling of "Concerto for Cootie" and "Me and You": "Haul out the superlatives and grab a new needle, 'cause these two 3-minute examples of Ellingtonia stack 'way high on the month's mass of releases. Cootie's side is, of course, all Cootie, mostly with mute and plunger, either of which is a guarantee of the finest brand of jazz. And note how the band (especially Jimmy [sic] Blanton's bass) cooperates in the background."[16]

In 1954, French jazz critic Andre Hodeir published a detailed analysis of "Concerto for Cootie," which was reprinted in his 1961 book *Jazz: Its Evolution and Essence*. The first point he makes is that the piece has aged favorably. Many times, in listening to something from the past, one wonders what they ever liked about it. Not so with this piece, as "there can be no doubt that the test of time has favored Ellington's 'Concerto for Cootie.'"[17] Hodeir has subsections of the chapter describing structure, harmony, and sonorities, among other points. In his summary, Hodeir lauds Williams's versatility, saying: "Cootie covers a [wide] range; he seems always to be discovering something. For all that, he doesn't lose his identity. This man of a thousand sonorities is still one whose particular sonority you would recognize in a thousand."[18] Cootie himself said that in the Ellington band "I played all types of trumpet—the Armstrong style, the Eldridge style, sweet, hot, growl, and legitimate first."[19]

Dr. Edward Green, an Ellington scholar and editor of *The Cambridge Companion to Duke Ellington*, enthused that "you never know in that wonderful piece what's coming next! Will Cootie give us a sweet tone on his trumpet? Or one that growls? Sounds that thrust aggressively at us, or are winningly shy? Dark, uncertain sounds? Or soaring, confident, bright tones? We just don't know; we're on the edge of our seats. So much happens in those three minutes of music! Yet—and this is the point—even as the concerto gives us a portrait, through sound, of a world which can never be summed up, which changes moment-by-moment and is amazingly various, it also gives us a continuous, coherent melody. From beginning to end, there's a melody that connects it all."[20]

Williams's solo contributions to the Ellington band could be ingeniously simple. For example, on "Rumpus in Richmond," there are only four phrases that are used in his sixteen-bar solo. The notes in bars 1 and 2 are merely transposed up a half step in measures 3 and 4. The same process is followed for measures 9 and 10. Measures 5 through 8 are repeated exactly in measures 13 through 16. Williams constructs a varied and interesting solo over sixteen bars with only three motifs.[21] Recorded on the same date as "Rumpus in Richmond," "Harlem Air Shaft" is another example of the heat, drive, and swing that Williams contributed to the band.

On September 5, 1940, two months before his departure from the Ellington orchestra, Williams recorded another memorably melodic solo on "In a

Mellotone." It starts quietly, with Williams using a pixie mute and a closed plunger. The first eight bars consist almost entirely of variations on the phrase played in the first bar. The second eight bars are a simple paraphrasing of the melody. At all times, Williams is aware of the sax figures going on behind him, never getting in their way. Author and saxophonist Loren Schoenberg called Cootie's ability "to work within a predetermined compositional context" the "most highly developed art of the big band idiom."[22]

PART III *Benny Goodman (1940)*

14

WHEN COOTIE LEFT THE DUKE

Benny Goodman had disbanded his orchestra in the summer of 1940 while he recovered from back surgery. By the fall, he was ready to rebuild.[1] One of his new trumpet players, twenty-three-year-old Jimmy Maxwell, played his copy of "Concerto for Cootie" on the Goodman orchestra's band bus not too long after it had been released. "I used to carry around this windup phonograph and a cardboard box full of Louis Armstrong and Duke Ellington records," said Maxwell. One of the records he played "all the time" was "Concerto for Cootie." "One day Benny came back and asked us, '[W]ho is that trumpet player?' and Irving [Goodman, Benny's brother] said, 'You've got to be kidding, Benny. That's Cootie Williams.' Benny just nodded and said, 'Yeah, that's a pretty good solo he plays there.'"[2] Perhaps Goodman could be forgiven for not remembering Cootie since they had only played one number together at the Carnegie Hall concert over two years prior.

Cootie mentioned trumpeter Irving Goodman as one of the people whom he considered as a friend during his time with the BG. But just a few months prior to helping facilitate the Ellington-Goodman deal, Irving and two other Goodman brothers, Harry and Gene, wanted Benny to drop the idea of a mixed band. Although there is no explanation given for the brothers' opposition, it's not unreasonable to suppose that at a minimum, they didn't want the social and economic pressure that would come with the change. But on the other side of the equation was John Hammond, who would soon become Goodman's brother-in-law when his sister Alice Hammond Duckworth married Goodman in 1942. In his autobiography, the wealthy Hammond said he wasn't motivated by financial gain but rather by a need to "change the world," something that was instilled in him by his mother.[3]

In October, Benny Goodman asked his brother Irving to see what it would take to get Williams in his band. "[T]he first time I was contacted by Goodman, I told [Duke] about it . . . And we used to go out and talk, talk about it, so he would tell me what to tell him the next time he called. And [Ellington] set up the deal for me," Cootie recalled. Ellington made sure to stipulate that Cootie was only to play in the Benny Goodman Sextet, not the Benny Goodman Orchestra. "You'll get lost, sitting back there in the band." As Cootie reminisced, "[W]e used to go out at night. And he [Ellington] said, 'Well, go ahead on. You've got a chance to make some money. And make a name for yourself.' And I left. And I said, 'Well, I'll be back in a year, after the contract is over with.'"[4]

In his public dealings, Cootie never intimated that he was unhappy to leave the Duke Ellington band. But in private, he was deeply hurt that Duke didn't make a counteroffer.[5] Stephen James, Ellington's nephew, wrote that the lack of a counteroffer "remained a lifelong offense to Cootie despite his deep admiration for Duke as a composer and musician."[6] Section mate Rex Stewart wrote in his autobiography that "no one wanted to see Cootie leave Ellington despite the certainty that he'd be bettering himself financially" and this was concerning "as we heard that the amount involved was only 25 dollars a week." The difference may have only been $25 per week (the equivalent of nearly $450 today), but there were other factors at work. Europe was at war and that translated to anxiety and a tightening of the economy in the United States. Stewart noted that in the time period prior to Williams's departure, bookings and attendance had been down for the band.[7] Additionally, Johnny Hodges asked for extra pay to double on soprano sax. Turned down by Ellington, 1940 was the last time his Sidney Bechet–inspired stylings were heard in an Ellington recording session.[8]

The lack of discipline in the Ellington band played a factor in Williams's decision to go with Goodman, saying, "That was one of the main reasons why I wanted to leave, too. Because they didn't care. [Sonny Greer would] get drunk and fall off the drums and things like that. And it wasn't no good for me."[9] Cootie had a musical vision and it required discipline. "I was serious about the music always and got mad at the rest [of the band] if they fooled around!"[10]

Cootie Williams leaving the Ellington band was akin to Babe Ruth leaving the Yankees. Unlike most big bands, the Ellington band was known for the stability of its personnel. In his eleven years with the orchestra, Williams had become a franchise-level musician. The event moved bandleader Raymond Scott to compose and record "When Cootie Left the Duke" to mark the occasion.[11] Jack Hall, the featured trumpet soloist, played a solo that mirrored the structure of "Concerto for Cootie" with sections for muted, plungered, and finally, open trumpet. *The Billboard*'s article on the hiring was titled "Ellington 'Fixture' Leaves Duke for BG," another reminder for those of us today who have no concept of the shocking nature of this move. They added that although Cootie would have a one-year contract with Goodman, "Ellington has never had contracts with his men."[12]

Ellington gave one of his trademark insouciant statements on the matter as quoted by the *Pittsburgh Courier*: "I feel like the fond parent who just reared a barefoot boy into young manhood, and, after finally getting shoes on him and, eventually, a collar, necktie and long pants, sees him desert the old homestead in a new-found spirit of independence. I'm sure it is not a question of salary, since there is so little difference between what I offered Cootie to stay and what he accepted from Goodman. I commend Mr. Goodman for his American viewpoint on musical appreciation, which has nothing to do with race or creed."[13] The short-lived publication *Jazz Information* (1939–1941) printed the last sentence of Ellington's press statement, which was omitted by the *Courier*: "I assume that the obvious distinction of working with a white band was the determining factor in his decision."[14] Ellington was sanguine about the future of Williams's chair in the orchestra. "If we can't find somebody who can growl well, we won't growl. . . . Anything is likely to happen to us. We just go on doing things."[15] Given that plunger-muted brass was a significant part of the Ellington sound pallet, "we won't growl" wasn't to be taken seriously.

Several trumpeters were mentioned to be in contention to take Cootie's empty chair, including Wilbur "Dud" Bascomb[16] (1916–1972), Sidney DeParis (1905–1967), Taft Jordan[17] (1915–1981), and Roy Eldridge. According to Eldridge, he was offered the job by Cootie himself, but he turned it down because he was happy with his current situation, which was leading a band at New York City's Kelly's Stables.[18]

But it was Ray Nance who joined the Ellington band as the replacement for Williams. Ellington didn't like the idea of "replacement," saying, "Cootie is not being replaced by Nance. We do not put in replacements in our orchestra. To the contrary we add new styles and new attractions to see how they fit into our organization. We are always looking for something different, you know."[19]

Apparently Goodman was eager to try out his new musician; he convened a rehearsal session with the new Benny Goodman Sextet on October 28 and fortunately it was recorded. This was even before Williams completed his duties with Ellington. November 2, 1940, marked Cootie's last date with the Duke Ellington organization as part of a small group led by Johnny Hodges in Chicago. (It produced the first recording of "Day Dream," a beautiful Billy Strayhorn ballad that Hodges would play for the rest of his life.)[20]

Ellington and his crew threw a farewell party for Cootie, an honor befitting a departing comrade, at a Chicago hotel where it was said there were "beverages and tears."[21] From Chicago, Cootie drove to New York with a stop in Cleveland to visit relatives. (His brother Isaac Jr. lived there.)[22]

14. WHEN COOTIE LEFT THE DUKE

Four members of the Benny Goodman Sextet. From left to right: George Auld, Benny Goodman, Cootie Williams, Charlie Christian. (Duke Ellington Collection, Archives Center, National Museum of American History, Smithsonian Institution)

Cootie wasted no time in transition. His official start date with Goodman was November 6. The next day, on November 7 in New York City, he made his first recording with Benny Goodman.[23] Guest pianist Count Basie, bassist Artie Bernstein, drummer Harry Jaeger, and tenor saxophonist Georgie Auld joined Goodman and Williams.[24] (It was rumored in the trade press of the time that Basie was considering disbanding his group and joining Goodman.)[25] Rounding out this small ensemble on electric guitar was Charlie Christian, the innovative genius of that new instrument. He had joined Goodman in August 1939.[26] Christian had jammed with Williams in Oklahoma City when the Ellington band passed through there sometime in the mid-1930s. He couldn't have known back then that he'd wind up in the same band with him.[27] Less than two years after this recording session, Christian would succumb to tuberculosis at the age of twenty-five.[28] (That same evening, Goodman's new big band debuted with Henry "Red" Allen temporarily in the trumpet section.)[29]

Today, most references merely state that the Williams's departure can be summed up as a longtime player leaving a band and having it commemorated in song. The contemporary ripples were more severe. The story was on the front page of the November 1940 issue of *Metronome*, under the large headline, "Cootie Williams Joins Benny!"[30] in a font that was almost in line with the declarations of war that were coming the next year. *Down Beat*'s front-page story, under a similarly large headline, was "BG Grabs Cootie for Hot Chair."[31]

Front page of the November 1940 issue of *Metronome*. Note the prominence given to Williams's move from Ellington to Goodman. (*Metronome*, Courtesy of RIPM Jazz Collection)

The same issue of *Metronome* also ran an editorial on the subject, "Cootie and the King." It started with: "Benny Goodman has taken Cootie Williams from Duke Ellington. He has taken one of the brightest stars from the great aggregation jazz has ever known. He will pay him well, and possibly bring him greater recognition. But what has he done to Duke?" They concluded with categorizing "the Ellingtonians among the untouchables. But then along came the King, and he not only touched, but he took. And we feel pretty badly about it all."[32] In response, a letter writer admitted that the magazine had accurately described fandom's feelings about the matter. However, he boldly and incorrectly predicted "Duke will go forward with unslackened pace and in time the name of Cootie Williams will be just another legend in Ellingtonia and no one will mark the spot where he stood."[33]

In late 1939, a *Down Beat* editorial had posed the question, "Should Negro Musicians Play in White Bands?" Bandleaders and sidemen were polled and asked to weigh in. None of those against the proposition wished to be quoted by name and even a few of those in favor chose to stay anonymous. White musicians feared losing their jobs and some also thought that the virtue of white women would be endangered in the presence of "colored" musicians, especially in "an atmosphere of drinking, where normal restraints are gone."[34] White musicians courageous enough to publicly endorse the concept of a mixed band included Jimmy Dorsey, Artie Shaw, and Shep Fields(!). Harpist Casper Reardon (1907–1941) said, "Good for Benny! I'm for him. His ideas are like mine. If a Negro is a better performer[,] use him. One cannot hope to draw a color line in music or any other art."[35]

Oddly, at that time, Woody Herman was lukewarm to the idea, saying, "[I]n spite of the tremendous debt we one Negro musicians and composers for our style we would not consider that the addition of one or more Negroes would enhance [our blues-based] style, any more than the addition of a white musician would improve Duke Ellington's orchestra. . . . We have too much respect for the vitality and imagination of Negro musicians to ask any one of them to sacrifice his integrity."[36] But in later years, Herman would have Black musicians like tenor saxophonist Gene Ammons and bassist Oscar Pettiford as members of his band.

It would be assumed that Black musicians would be in favor of the idea of a mixed group, if only for economic reasons. It may have been due to the limited number of people polled, but only Ella Fitzgerald ("Both races have a lot to offer each other") and Teddy Wilson ("an excellent idea") are quoted. The Black press predicted this type of move would mean the end of the Black bands. Goodman was accused of "tread[ding] on the toes of many jazz purists" in hiring Williams.[37] The Baltimore *Afro-American* said that "music fans felt that the Sphinx of Egypt would sooner move that that Cootie and the Duke would part."[38] Another newspaper wrote, "Benny Goodman tossed a depth charge in Duke Ellington's famous band."[39] One newspaper letter writer stated that "the gain to Goodman can never be as great as the loss to Duke."[40]

Although Goodman had employed other Black musicians prior to hiring Cootie (including Teddy Wilson, Lionel Hampton, and Charlie Christian), with the notable exception of Count Basie they didn't come from bands with the visibility of Ellington's, nor were they seen as integral to their orchestra's vision.

The short-lived jazz magazine *Tempo* had predicted in 1937 something like this happening: "Duke has some of the best men in the business. If the bar (public opinion) that prevents Negro and white musicians from working together is ever dropped there will be an immediate raid on the Duke's band by some white bandleaders."[41] There wasn't a wholesale dropping of the color bar. Rather, it was a chipping away at it by leaders like Benny Goodman, Charlie Barnet, Artie Shaw, and Gene Krupa. Like Goodman, Barnet didn't see himself as a social crusader. He said, "I never made a point of hiring Black musicians to change the social order. I hired them because of how well they played, not with any idea of starting a racial revolution."[42]

Without any basis, some letter writers speculated that perhaps Williams wanted to play with white musicians. And while they admitted to admiring Goodman's racial policies, they didn't see how Goodman's gain could outweigh Ellington's loss.[43] *Pittsburgh Courier* columnist Billy Rowe said, "Music circles are still wondering the whys and wherefores of the Duke Ellington-Cootie Williams break." After incorrectly stating that Ellington could have matched Goodman's salary offer, Rowe speculated that "it wasn't a change for betterment so, as those in the know have said, the change must have come about due to a personal feud between members of the band or the over-emphasis Ellington put on Rex Stewart, notwithstanding Cootie's 13 [sic] years with the crew. Whatever the cause, Cootie is gone, and with him a part of the heart of the master who created a new kind of American Negro music."[44]

The controversy was so large that Williams was given an interview in the form of an article that was allegedly written by him that appeared in the second issue of a new music magazine, *Music and Rhythm*. The magazine was the brainchild of John Hammond and Carl Cons, an owner of *Down Beat*. Due to an untenable relationship with his partner Glenn Burrs,[45] Cons found it necessary to sell his half of *Down Beat* and pitched in to the new venture. Unfortunately, *Music and Rhythm* folded after a little less than three years of operation, publishing fewer than thirty issues. The article was titled "Why I Quit Duke Ellington After 11 Years" and appears to be Cootie's first solo interview. Notably, the subject of salary was discussed with Williams saying, "I will be getting $200 a week." This salary made Williams by far the highest paid Black sideman in the country. The second highest was trombonist J. C. Higginbotham, who was making $150 per week with the orchestra of Louis Armstrong.[46] This was at a time when the country was still trying to recover from the Great Depression—unemployment was 18 percent and the average wage was $1,368 per year.[47] That equates to $26.31 per week; to make the comparison to Cootie's salary, the average American was making barely a tenth of what Williams was earning.

Cootie predicted that "with Benny, I expect to be able to stick more to my own individual style. I won't have to think so much about other styles. This will allow me to devote more time to some of the other things I want to do. Playing in all the various styles [with Ellington] has been a tough job . . . [with the Goodman small group], I probably won't have to use such a variety of styles. I am going to enjoy this because I think the smaller group will give me a chance to play more in the style which is closest to my heart. I think I will be able to explain to Benny's bunch exactly what I want. My type of playing is really a soft style which I think will fit in perfectly with a small group."[48] To illustrate where he wanted to go stylistically, Williams wrote, "Of all the records I have made, one of my favorites is *Chasin' Chippies*. That is the kind of playing I want to do more of, and I expect to do it easy [*sic*] in Benny's combination. My whole heart is in rhythm. I have to hear something rhythmic in order to give me inspiration. If a band is good, I'm good, and I have reason to believe Benny's will be plenty good."[49] ("Chasin' Chippies" was a Williams composition recorded by his Rug Cutters in August 1938.)

In the interview, Cootie confirmed he was going over to play in Benny's small group as was negotiated by Ellington.[50] Yet, less than two weeks into his official contract start date, on November 13, Williams is in the trumpet section (along with Alec Fila, Jimmy Maxwell, and Irving Goodman) for a Columbia recording session by the full Goodman orchestra. Despite the negotiated deal, Williams continued to play with the full orchestra throughout the yearlong contract. Interestingly, the pianist on this session is Cootie's band leader boss from his first days in New York, Fletcher Henderson. Cootie solos on "Benny Rides Again," wasting no time in making himself at home in his new place of employment.[51]

15

BENNY RIDES AGAIN

Williams was optimistic about the time to come: "My year with Benny will be something entirely new and different for me, and, as much as I hate to leave Duke and the boys and the music they stand for, I am sure I will get a lot of intense pleasure from my new job."[1]

The African American press avidly followed Williams's moves with Goodman. Even Cootie's first radio appearance with Goodman, on the December 10 edition of CBS radio show *We, The People*, was deemed pressworthy.[2] With the addition of Williams, the Goodman band had three Black musicians, Fletcher Henderson and Charlie Christian being the other two. An item from the Baltimore *Afro-American* eagerly mentioned that Goodman was going to make a short film at the start of 1941 and the three "will greet their fans from the screen."[3] Sadly, that film never happened.

The naysaying critics predicted "Benny Goodman won't do so well by Cootie Williams as the Duke did, because Benny's arrangements are not styled so personally as Duke's are for his bandsmen."[4] They neglected to say that Ellington was pretty much alone in customizing his music for his musicians. George Frazier, writing for *Down Beat*, said Cootie "was an enormously more moving musician when he was with Ellington" and speculated that perhaps he was added to the Goodman band because he "went as far as he could possible go with a big band and that the time [had] come for him to try something different."[5] But this ignores the fact that many jazz artists are wont to experiment, especially in the early years of their career.

In her autobiography *I Had the Craziest Dream*, Helen Forrest (1917–1999), the Benny Goodman band's female vocalist during most of Cootie's tenure, unabashedly declared that "Benny Goodman was by far the most unpleasant person I ever met in music. Almost anyone who ever worked with him will

> **COMING FRIDAY**
> IN PERSON
>
> # BENNY
> *"The Swing Master"*
>
> # GOODMAN
>
> HIS *New*
>
> HIS *Greatest*
>
> ## ORCHESTRA
> featuring
>
> **HELEN FORREST**
> Vocalist
>
> **"COOTIE" WILLIAMS**
> "Duke Ellington's Great Trumpet"
>
> **THE GOODMAN TRIO & SEXTETTE**

During Cootie's time with Goodman, he received special billing in most of the band's advertising. (*Bradford Evening Star*, Courtesy of Newspapers.com)

agree." Her harsh words were published while Goodman was still alive.[6] Benny Goodman was notorious for two things by those who knew him. The first was the withering stare he would affix to any musician whose playing (rehearsal or performance didn't matter) he didn't feel was up to snuff. This was known as "The Ray."[7] The second was his chronic absent-mindedness about everything except music and the clarinet. Unable (or unwilling) to remember names, he called everyone "Pops." Jimmy Maxwell became a beneficiary of that forgetfulness. When he told Goodman that his favorite band was Duke Ellington's, an offended Goodman fired him. Shortly after, Maxwell joined some of his former bandmates in a jam session. Goodman happened to catch some of the music and hired Maxwell based on what he heard since he needed a new lead trumpet, having forgotten that the musician he had fired and the newly hired guy were one and the same.[8] But Maxwell also found that Goodman could be quite generous on occasion, he just preferred that it didn't get publicized, telling Maxwell that, "[I]f they knew about [my generosity], everybody in the country would be coming to me with their hands out."[9] Pianist Jess Stacy had a simpler explanation for all of Goodman's quirks: "There's nothing wrong with him, he's just crazy."[10]

Crazy or not, Williams thought highly of Goodman. In later years, he said, "He is a great musician. He has talent, and I love him for it. Another thing, he's the same with everybody. He's just Goodman, not one way with this man and another way with someone else. That same with everyone. I think I was happier in music the first year I was with him than I ever was."[11] Part of the happiness had to stem from Williams being relieved of his self-appointed role as band discipline monitor. Williams disliked that some of the Ellington musicians would coast: "In Duke's band, even in the old days, there were some guys who didn't care. Sometimes for weeks they wouldn't play, just sit there not really blowing. And Duke wouldn't say anything. I'd be the one to scream and holler and do his work for him."[12] This statement becomes ironic considering Williams's later years when on many occasions he would only put his horn to his lips for his solos.

With Goodman's sextet, it was a different situation—"Each man could take care of himself. The thing would just move, that's what I enjoyed. There was never a let-down. Soon as one guy stopped playing, here came another, right in on top. With Benny no one could sit back and *he* couldn't sit back, either."[13] Cootie loved playing in the small group—"Everybody in the sextet was great. And each man that you had to follow to play behind, you had to play. And that sextet used to romp. And there wasn't no slack there."[14]

Goodman's new orchestra made its debut on November 9, playing a benefit at NYC's Manhattan Center. A reviewer said of the evening that although they "still can't hail the new Goodman Sextet as good as the old, no question that Cootie Williams sounds fine with Benny."[15]

The Benny Goodman groups performed at the Broadwood Hotel on November 28 for a Thanksgiving dance. *The Billboard*'s scribe, Maurie Orodenker, wrote an extremely enthusiastic and knowledgeable review that ran under the title, "New Goodman Band Potentially Greatest of BG's Whole Career." Although only a few weeks into his year contract, Cootie was dubbed a "show-stop," which he literally did—the audience "stopped dancing for his solo set," which included "Concerto for Cootie." Williams also played in the trumpet section for this date. His presence highlighted some weakness in the brass as "when Williams joined the section" and gave it "the force and body it lacked all evening."[16]

There were two notable big band features for Williams during his time with Goodman: "Superman" and "Fiesta in Blue." "Superman" is a jaunty piece composed and arranged by Eddie Sauter. It's a long piece, issued on a 12-inch 78 RPM record instead of the standard 10-inch format. Williams exchanges puckish phrases with the band on his plunger mute, before switching to open horn. Unfortunately, unlike an Ellington feature, he's not given the entire arrangement for himself. Tenor saxophonist George Auld has a solo midway before Williams growls over a coda and then takes it out at a slower tempo and eventually ending on a lipped-trilled high C. It's ironic that Cootie felt he would be able to play in fewer styles while with Goodman, since this piece is a showcase of versatility.

"Fiesta in Blue" was recorded on March 27, 1941, with the full Goodman orchestra for Columbia. Originally titled "Cootie Growls," it was a Benny Goodman composition arranged by Jimmy Mundy.[17] "Fiesta in Blue," like "Concerto for Cootie," features Williams as the only soloist. Its bluesy sensibility is a perfect vehicle for Williams to again explore the sonorities of his plunger-muted and open trumpet and gives him a chance to display his gift for melody as well as variations on melody. Like his musical idol Louis Armstrong, Cootie preferred to explore a melody over "running the changes." "Some people play on chord construction. I don't play on chord construction. I like to have a melody. I like to read the music down and see what the composer intended for it to be. In order for me to play it, to get a feeling out of it. Now, if you've got this chord construction there, you ain't got nothing but chords," Cootie explained in 1976.[18] But much earlier, in 1941, he said, "I think every hornblower should know something about the piano and about harmony. I didn't go in for harmony much myself, but I feel that I've learned a great deal by actually playing with bands."[19] "Fiesta in Blue" was also recorded in 1941 by Count Basie as a feature for Buck Clayton. It reached the market well before Goodman's, which wasn't released until the beginning of 1945.[20]

Economy and melodic logic are hallmarks of Cootie's style. In his March 13 solo on "Air Mail Special" he plays a four-bar phrase, which is answered in the next four. For the second eight bars, another phrase is introduced and reused with variations. The bridge is a sequence of diminished chords. Cootie navigates this progression with a simple chromatic scale making, quite a contrast to the approach used by Goodman, Christian, and Auld. The final eight bars uses just two notes, relying on the plunger to provide interest. The original title for the song was "Good Enough to Keep" and for Cootie this proved to be true, since he reused this solo when he recorded "Air Mail Special" on his 1958 *Cootie Williams in Hi-Fi* album and in live performances.

Cootie's melodic method of improvisation yielded phrases that led to other songs. For example, part of his solo on the 1931 version of "Rockin' in Rhythm" became a Harry James "composition," "Peckin'." James recorded it first with the Ben Pollock orchestra in 1936 and then with Benny Goodman the following year.[21] James said, "I stole the tune from the Duke, and the lyrics from Cootie Williams."[22] (Cootie's small group recorded it in 1937, with a comic vocal by the leader and bizarre backing vocal from the band.) His solos on "In a Mellow Tone" and "Tutti for Cootie" became vocalese subjects for Lambert, Hendricks, and Ross and Mark Murphy, respectively. Johnny Hodges credits the main phrase of "Stormy Weather" to Cootie Williams, saying it was something Cootie used to play that was adopted by one of the songwriters of Cotton Club's 1933 revue.[23]

♪

In 1939, *Metronome* started a poll of musicians to select an All Star Band, saying it was "comprised of the country's *leading* musicians as chosen by the country's *smartest* musicians." The winning musicians then met and recorded, with the proceeds going to charity, specifically, the New York Musicians' Union Unemployment Fund.[24] Cootie's star had risen to the point where he was selected as one of the trumpeters for the 1941 edition of the All Stars, the other two being Goodman alumni Ziggy Elman and Harry James. The prominence of Goodman musicians in the polls prompted the complaint that poll voters "feel that the only good musicians are of necessity the ones in [Goodman's] band" and "that being with Goodman is tantamount to being the best on whatever [instrument] you play."[25] The new year of 1941 saw him winning slots in the all-star bands of *Metronome* and *Down Beat*.

The group of heavyweights assembled, somewhat chaotically, on January 16, 1941, at RCA Victor's New York studio. Benny Goodman, Benny Carter, Count Basie, Coleman Hawkins, Buddy Rich, and Charlie Christian were just a few of those in the band.[26] Two songs were recorded, "Bugle Call Rag" and Count Basie's "One O'Clock Jump." The arrangement of "Bugle Call Rag" was from the Benny Goodman library. Due to the approximately three-minute time limit on a 78 RPM record, each soloist was only allotted a single sixteen-bar chorus. *Metronome* couldn't help patting themselves on the back, saying, "Few thrills equal the succession of Cootie, Ziggy and Harry. . . . Who could ask for more[?]"[27]

Down Beat's "All-American Swing Band" for 1940 was not a recording organization like *Metronome*'s. Williams and Elman were common to both groups, but Muggsy Spanier was the difference in the *Down Beat* group.[28] It was a point of pride for the Black press that "[f]ive of the 17 spots went to Negro swingsters, three of them—trumpeter Cootie Williams, guitarist Charlie Christian and arranger Fletcher Henderson—being members of Benney [sic] Goodman's otherwise 'ofay' [white] unit."[29] The following month, Goodman presented the awards to Williams, Christian, and Henderson on his Fitch Bandwagon radio show.[30] It was only the third time Black performers had been featured on this show, which had been running since 1938. The integration of the show wasn't caused by an awakening of the broadcasters but rather the threat of a national boycott.[31]

Two days prior to the all-star date, the Goodman band recorded a novelty number called "Let the Door Knob Hitcha" which featured Williams as a vocalist. The first few words tell you everything you need to know about the song: "Cut out, be gone, step back and let the door knob hitcha. Cut out, be gone, step back and let the door knob hitcha in the back." (The arrangement is by Margie Gibson [1916–1990], one of the few women arrangers of that era. Unfortunately, not much is known about her except that she also worked for Harry James and Artie Shaw in addition to Goodman.)[32] But the song had fans, even at the highest levels of the government. The Goodman band performed at Washington, DC's Mayflower Hotel for President Franklin D. Roosevelt's Birthday Ball on January 30, 1941.[33] Once again, Cootie gathered special mention: *Down Beat* reported that First Lady Eleanor Roosevelt said she "particularly enjoyed Cootie Williams's vocal on *Don't Let the Doorknob Hitcha*."[34]

Taking a cue from his Ellington days, Cootie assembled a small group under his leadership, largely from the Goodman band's personnel. Two of the four songs recorded on the May 7 date were by Williams, "G-Men" and "Blues In My Condition." "G-Men" is an "I Got Rhythm"–derived piece based on a riff Cootie recycled from his own solo on Ellington's 1937 recording "Harmony In Harlem." "Blues In My Condition" is a direct throwback to Ellington's small-group sound. It's very easy to mistake this as something from the Ducal catalog.

Fats Waller's "Ain't Misbehavin'" is given a bouncy reading. The last side of the session is Cootie's take on Louis Armstrong's 1928 classic, "West End Blues." It was an audacious move to take on a performance indelibly associated with Armstrong and especially one so technically challenging. *Down Beat* said "it's only honest to report that Williams does more than mere justice to the classic. In fact, it's a better performance than Louie's [1939] Decca and the equal of the Armstrong original. . . . If you know anyone around at this late date who needs convincing as to Williams's genius, this is the disc."[35] The *Baltimore Sun* declared, "His hair-raising, breath-taking note holding, and his hot phrasing remind us of the good old ad libbing days when nobody knew who was going to do what when."[36]

By midyear, Cootie was playing in the trumpet section of the big band on a more regular basis. Irving Goodman had to leave for military service and Jimmy Maxwell was out with a mouth infection, leaving temporary vacancies for Williams to fill.[37] Williams appreciated the discipline of the Goodman organization—"[W]hen the band hit, they hit." In Ellington's band, a set might start with half of its members absent. But Williams was proud of the fact that during his 1929–1940 stint with Ellington, he was never late. "I always disciplined myself," he said. The Goodman punctuality was nothing strange to him, and it was a very welcome departure.[38] In 1962, Jimmy Maxwell finally got a chance to play in the band of his hero, Duke Ellington, as a short-term substitute for Cat Anderson. It was a study in contrasts. He observed, "I realized I couldn't have lasted a month with that band. It would have driven me crazy the way everyone showed up three hours late for rehearsal and all that casual anarchy.... Cootie had no tolerance for that, so he liked being with Benny's band."[39]

♪

Texas-born pianist Teddy Wilson became the Jackie Robinson of jazz when he joined Benny Goodman as part of a trio with Gene Krupa in 1935. With the addition of vibraphonist Lionel Hampton the next year, who was also African American, the trio became a quartet. Wilson and Hampton, however, didn't play with the big band like Williams. However, on occasion, Hampton would man the drums in the big band if the regular drummer wasn't available. In his autobiography, Hampton praised Goodman for providing security for the Black members of the entourage when the band toured the South.[40] But Goodman didn't see himself as a social crusader; he simply wanted the best musicians for his band.[41] Regardless of the motivation, Hampton had nothing but praise for Goodman's racial stance, saying that when he and Teddy Wilson were with the band they "had it better than Black musicians in the all-Black bands. Benny was courageous and always insisted that we all—Black and white—stay in the same white hotel."[42]

Staying at the same white hotel was not without complications. Jimmy Maxwell had joined Goodman in 1939 and was just starting out on a career that would make him one of the most sought-after lead trumpet players in the business. Maxwell was Cootie's roommate on the road. He reminisced about his experience as a roommate with Cootie:

> I generally like to room alone, but we would get into a place like Ohio or someplace and they wouldn't have any place for Cootie to stay. So I would check-in in both names and then Cootie would come in the room. And it broke my heart the first time he said, "You check in and I'll carry the bags in and act like I'm the bandboy." I said, "Bullshit. I'll check in and you walk in, and I'll carry my own bags. That much I'll do." Then he didn't want to go down to the dining room and he said, "We'll have room service." I didn't want to go out and eat and leave him alone, so it cost me a lot of money. But when I said, "Look, we'll go down to the dining room. You don't have to do anything. If they say anything at all, I'll pop them." And he said, "No, I don't want to embarrass the band. Leave it alone. It's all right."[43]

But there was the occasional silver lining—"When there were black waiters, though, if you ordered a steak, they would bring you three of them."[44]

Roy Eldridge, who joined the Gene Krupa orchestra in April 1941, said "you never know how colored you can be until you make the rounds with the ruling classes and you don't have to go south of the Mason-Dixon Line to find head-breaking prejudice if you forget the lines of demarcation."[45] While Roy was vocal in the press about his mistreatment in white America, there are no similar statements to be found by Williams. Eldridge grew up in Pittsburgh and perhaps growing up with northern racism hadn't prepared him for the unfiltered racism of the South. He carried a gun with him for protection "because you never know."[46] Eldridge stayed with Krupa until May 1943, when the band broke up due to Krupa's incarceration on a marijuana charge. He was with Artie Shaw from the end of 1944 until the fall of 1945.

Like Eldridge, Oran "Hot Lips" Page (1908–1954) was employed as a trumpeter with Artie Shaw. Page joined Shaw in August 1941 and stayed until Shaw disbanded to join the Navy in early 1942. For the band's Southern tour, the promoters wanted Shaw to drop Page in order to perform there. Shaw said no, so instead they proposed Page could play, but he had to be no closer than fifteen feet from anyone in the band. Again, Shaw said no and cancelled the tour altogether. Like Goodman, Shaw didn't appease the racists.[47] (It's interesting that most of the star African American musicians in white bands, such as Page, Williams, Eldridge, Charlie Shavers, and Jonah Jones, were trumpeters.)

In a bit of candor rare for the time, in 1944 Ellington saxophonist Otto Hardwick gave his opinion of the racial situation in America, saying "I find an undercurrent of evil feeling among white people wherever we travel. Of course, they do not always show their discriminatory practices to us [Duke Ellington and his Orchestra], but to others outside of the organization, there have been several occasions where people I know have been discriminated against. Race relations are supposed to be getting better, but I feel they are getting worse in spite of all the civil rights organizations, race relations meeting[s], labor unions, etc."[48]

Racism was codified in law and openly practiced at the time. Laws and signage in the South dictated the separation, while in the North, it was done by custom, as Jimmy Maxwell's Ohio example illustrates. Life on the road for musicians is hard enough, but for many years in this country, the Black musician had to deal with the added burden of Jim Crow. For a time, the Ellington band traveled and slept in their own Pullman cars and were able to avoid worrying about finding lodging, but other Black bands of the era had to obtain their food and lodging with local private citizens. Some musicians shrugged it off as part of a necessary condition of life in the United States. But others, like trumpeter Roy Eldridge as part of the Artie Shaw and Gene Krupa bands, found it galling to the point that they became extremely bitter. "I hated that the people that wanted my autograph were the very same people who would deny me a drink in a bar or a room in a hotel," said Eldridge. In pleading for a hotel room, he did slyly promise the hotel clerks that he "wouldn't rub any black off on the sheets."[49]

Even the younger generation wasn't always forward thinking. The college newspaper of Catholic University of America, located in Washington, DC, opined that Cootie Williams was holding the Benny Goodman band back: "We like colored musicians as musicians but when it comes to mixing the bands, we do not approve."[50] Teddy Wilson said that "[p]rejudice against mixed bands will disappear whenever prejudice against Negro bands themselves disappears. As soon as a colored band can get the pick of the good hotel jobs, plenty of airtime and all the rest of the consideration given white bands, then there won't be any more prejudice against colored and white musicians playing together."[51]

But apparently, the racial aspect didn't color Cootie's view of his Goodman tenure. Looking back years later, Cootie observed: "[T]ell you the truth, that was the most relaxed thing that I ever had in my life in music. Any job or anything I ever had in my life in music. That year."[52] Goodman thought highly of Williams. When you consider he had great musicians like Bunny Berigan, Harry James, and Ziggy Elman playing trumpet for him at various times, it's even more impressive that Goodman said that "Cootie Williams was by far the most versatile man that ever played in the section. He was a fast reader, had the biggest tone and unlimited power. Nobody can play lead like Cootie, and his solos are great."[53]

♪

At the end of May 1941, the Goodman organization took a break. Goodman was successful enough to have the luxury of being able to pick and choose his workload.[54] Cootie and Catherine Williams used the opportunity to take a vacation in Chicago.[55] Midway through his year's contract with Goodman, the press asked Cootie for a progress report. "I hated to leave Duke and the boys and the music they stand for, but I get a lot of pleasure from my new job." He also expressed that the "change would let him rest up a bit and work on his individual style." As in his 1940 interview with *Music and Rhythm*, he repeated that the kind of music he wanted to play more of could be exemplified by his 1938 small-group record, "Chasin' Chippies."[56]

The great drummer Sidney "Big Sid" Catlett joined Goodman in June and the story was headlined in *Variety* as "Benny Goodman Employs Third Negro Musician."[57] (Of course, Williams and Christian were the other two. Fletcher Henderson was gone by this time.) When bassist John Simmons joined the Goodman band at the end of July, the press reported that Goodman now had four "sepia" musicians. (Incidentally, Simmons was paid $125 a week.)[58] With Jonah Jones in Charlie Barnet's band and Roy Eldridge with Gene Krupa, it almost seemed like progress.[59] The move earned Goodman well deserved respect in the Black community with the *Detroit Tribune* saying, "Goodman's actions make him a topnotcher so far as the Negro is concerned. He is doing what was once thought impossible."[60]

While the presence of "colored" musicians still disturbed the social norm, Goodman had commercial clout on his side and wasn't afraid to exercise it. Jimmy Maxwell said, "I've heard him stand up, even in the New Yorker [a luxury hotel], the first time we went in there. We had Sid Catlett, John Simmons, Charlie Christian, Cootie Williams . . . and I remember the manager saying, 'I don't want these black guys coming in through the lobby and through the restaurant. In fact, I don't even want them here.' And Benny said, 'Well, I'm sorry. This is my band. If you don't want them in the band then screw yourself. We're walking out.' So then [the manager] said, 'Well, they'll have to go through the kitchen.' Benny said, 'They do not go through the kitchen.' Then [the manager] said, 'All of the musicians go through the kitchen.' And Benny said, 'None of the musicians go through the kitchen.' 'Well, then, they can't wear their uniforms when they come.' 'All right, they won't wear their uniforms.' But he stuck up for them. It wasn't just [that] he put black guys in the band and then said, 'Good luck.'"[61]

The *New York Age* was certainly optimistic, running an editorial "Democracy In Entertainment." It said:

> That overworked word, "democracy," may have a new meaning for colored entertainers if the present tendency in the theatrical and music world of integrating Negroes into white organizations continues. . . . The practicing of picking colored musicians for outstanding white bands was started by Benny Goodman, who now has John Simmons, Cootie Williams, Sidney Catlett and Charlie Christian in his band. His example has been followed by Charlie Barnett [sic], who in addition to having Helena [sic] Horne as vocalist has recently added Jonah Jones, trumpeter; and Gene Krupa, another popular band leader, has recently added Roy Eldridge to his trumpet section.

The *New York Age* also wrote: "If the practice continues, the day may not be far distant when the Metropolitan Opera Company will see the advisability of employing Negro soloists instead of so many foreign stars. . . ."[62]

Goodman continued to break racial barriers with his African American sidemen. The *Chicago Defender* presented virtual orchids to BG and called it a "precedent-setting act" to take a mixed band into the Panther Room at the city's Sherman Hotel. They noted that it "hasn't been done before and perhaps

The seven-member Benny Goodman Sextet in a print advertisement for Adam Hats. Although it is hard to fathom today, an integrated group advertisement was controversial at the time. Front row: Cootie Williams, Benny Goodman, George Auld; back row: Art Bernstein, Dave Tough, Bernie Leighton, Charlie Christian. (Solo Flight—The Charlie Christian Legacy website)

Cootie Williams featured in front of the Goodman orchestra at Ohio University's 1941 Junior Prom. "The solid Jive of Goodman's ace trumpet man pleased enthralled Prom-goers." (Ohio University Archives)

won't again soon, until someone comes along who is just as big as Benny Goodman ... [Williams, Simmons, and Catlett] don't play in the sextettes only as did Teddy Wilson and Lionel Hampton. No sir, they are full-fledged member of the ork."63 The praise from Chicago's *Daily Times* hasn't aged well: "as for the band itself, you will appreciate three colored boys who have their race's rare gift for rhythm."[64] Optimistically and prematurely, the Baltimore *Afro-American* thought that "mixed bands may be [the] rule." They wrote, "The use of black arrangers for white bands and white arrangers for Black bands was seen to be a not unusual practice."[65]

During Cootie's time with Goodman, the orchestra would occasionally play concerts that featured classical music in the first half and a swing concluding half. The first was held July 31 at Philadelphia's Robin Hood Dell. Goodman's large audience was second only to Paul Robeson's during that concert season. After being introduced by Goodman as "the outstanding trumpeter of our day," Cootie played "Superman" and "Dear Old Southland." Charlie Christian was not on the stand due to illness, but with Catlett and Williams present, "it would appear that Mr. Goodman is determined to use colored musicians in his band, whenever and wherever possible."[66] Goodman saw jazz as something American: "Swing is just one outgrowth of the freedom permitted in this country." And "I pick members of my band on their ability and not on their looks, race or religion. Many colored men are superior when it comes to playing a tune the way I want to play it."[67]

For an August 11 concert in Chicago's Grant Park 100,000 fans turned out on a Monday night. As part of the classical portion of the night, Goodman played Mozart's "Clarinet Concerto." Catlett and Williams inspired the "hep cats . . . to stir": "While Mr. H. Sidney Catlett, the Negro drummer, beat out 'Don't Be That Way,' the hep cats, from children of 8 to blossoming college freshman, beat their beat. And as Mr. 'Cootie' Williams, the Negro cornetist, put in some hot licks, a crescendo of joyous screams warned that the voodoo was drawing near, in other words, things started rolling." Cootie "brought the addicts to their feet" with his renditions of "Concerto for Cootie" and "Deep River." Of the latter, the newspaper went a bit overboard trying to describe it: "'Deep River,' as Mr. Williams sold it to them, sounded like a swarm of huge tropical birds, all trying to get into one nest. The birds fit. A lion says good morning to his wife. The river spreads its tentacles like an electric sign over Michigan avenue. You jive."[68]

A similar program played at New York's Lewisohn Stadium for an audience of 15,000 fans elicited another enthusiastic reception. Cootie was featured on his two showcases, "Concerto for Cootie" and "Superman." "The audience was electrified" and the "jitterbugs" took to the field to dance.[69]

The end of Williams's time with Goodman was marked by two extended engagements. The band played a four-week booking at New Jersey's Meadowbrook Club. The venue broadcast a Saturday afternoon program (at 5:00 p.m.), "Matinee At Meadowbrook." Fortunately, several of these broadcasts are preserved as aircheck recordings. The newspaper noted that "[a]t least one period of musical madness is promised WCAX listeners when Cottie [sic] Williams,

15. BENNY RIDES AGAIN

Cootie Williams solos as a member of the full Goodman orchestra. This photo was taken at the band's Meadowbrook booking, which started on September 9, 1941, and lasted for four weeks. (*Metronome*, Courtesy of RIPM Jazz Periodicals)

Goodman's famed Negro trumpeter, goes to town on the new tune, 'Superman.'"[70] After the lengthy Meadowbrook stand, there was another long-term booking at the New Yorker Hotel starting on October 9 and lasting until January 2. Here, it was said that the band was deemed to be "better for listening than for dancing," and "Cootie Williams's fine trumpet gets a lot of solo spots."[71]

Cootie's contracted employment with the Benny Goodman organization ended in November 1941, in the middle of the New Yorker job. Cootie had expectations to rejoin Duke Ellington at this time. He said, "After the contract was up, I contacted [Ellington] and I said, 'I'm ready for my job. The year's up.' He said, 'Oh, no, you're too big now. You can make a whole lot of money.' He said, 'Go ahead on.' He said, 'I don't need you right now. Time I need you, I'll let you know.'"[72] Since Ellington was never one to show his cards, it would be pure speculation to guess why Williams wasn't taken back into the fold. One reason Ellington may have pushed Williams aside is that Ray Nance, his replacement, was working out very well. Not only was he a fine trumpet player, but he also doubled on violin and sang and danced as well. Earlier in 1941, Nance had waxed a splendid solo on Billy Strayhorn's "Take the 'A' Train" that was so perfect that it was included, or at least referred to, in nearly every performance of the song, like Illinois Jacquet's tenor sax solo on Lionel Hampton's "Flying Home." Another reason for Ellington's demurral may have been financial; perhaps Ellington didn't want to start a salary war, particularly since his alto saxophone ace, Johnny Hodges, had made noises about moving on.[73] When faced with the prospect of his band being raided, Ellington said that "They'll have to talk real money to get my men. Small change won't do."[74] But a decade later, in 1951, Hodges finally did strike out, not with another band, but on his own, taking trombonist Lawrence Brown and drummer Sonny Greer with him.

Cootie's story makes for a nice, neat narrative, but the truth was the press was reporting rumors that Williams was leaving Goodman to start his own band as early as September.[75] As late as October 25, *The Billboard* was reporting that Cootie "denies reports he is leaving the Goodman band."[76] Interestingly, John Simmons had a different account for Cootie's departure. Simmons said Goodman told Williams, "'I'm going into the New Yorker [Hotel]. You stay with me, and I'll help you form your own group.'" While Simmons and Catlett were enjoying drinks at a Harlem bar, Simmons said "Cootie comes walking in the door, crying big crocodile tears [and] he called [Goodman] every name in the book. 'He fired me, after promising me everything.'"[77]

The *Pittsburgh Courier*, an African American newspaper, lamented that Cootie's departure from the Goodman organization would leave the King of Swing with no Black musicians: "Benny Goodman will be without the service of any sepia musical satellites for the first time since his rise to fame in the swing world."[78] Just a few months prior to this, it was noteworthy that the band boasted four "colored" musicians: Cootie, guitarist Charlie Christian, bassist John Simmons, and drummer Big Sid Catlett. Catlett and Simmons were "let out," and Charlie Christian left due to illness in mid-1941.[79] *The Afro-American* even accused the orchestra of "going through a 'bleaching' process"![80] *The People's Voice* dubbed it "the here-today-gone-tomorrow tactics of Benny Goodman." This was ironic considering the Black press just a year earlier had predicted that the hiring of Black musicians by white bands would destroy the Black bands. Additionally, it didn't acknowledge the huge risk Goodman faced head-on in taking his bold and pioneering moves.[81] Like Cootie's hiring, his departure was also news in the mainstream press. *Variety* wrote "Benny Goodman's band is without a colored musician in its ranks for the first time in years." They also noted that Williams's last night with the band was November 13, during the band's long New Yorker Hotel stint and noting that "Williams apparently is not going back to Ellington. He has expressed a desire to front a band of his own."[82] Jimmy Maxwell, who indirectly was responsible for Cootie's joining the Goodman band, suggested Roy Eldridge as a replacement. Goodman didn't like the idea, saying, "I do all the fast high note playing in this band."[83]

16

BUILDING A BAND

Starting a band is a daunting task that requires an investment in capital. There were musicians to be hired, uniforms to purchase, building a library of music, obtaining bookings, and so on. Cootie used some of his own money to start the new enterprise.[1] This caused friction in the Williams household. Cootie said of Catherine, "She doesn't care about nothing but money." Apparently realizing how harsh that sounded, he quickly added, "I mean in the line of business." Catherine believed the money could be more practically spent—"With all that money you've spent we could have bought a home!" Cootie's retort—"Money? You've got to invest money before you can make it."[2]

At the beginning of Williams's contract with Goodman, the *New York Amsterdam News* saw that Cootie's move to go out on his own was inevitable, writing "The only possible benefit to Cootie Williams, and the other who may join the Goodman band is that when they come out they are automatically band leaders. They'd be too big to go into another colored orchestra."[3] Teddy Wilson and, more successfully, Lionel Hampton became bandleaders after their time with Goodman.

Williams had approached Benny Goodman for financial help with his band, and Goodman offered money but advised Williams against taking it,[4] saying, "Cootie, I think you should come up the hard way. If I should do something for you, you'll never know what life is, and what having your own band is."[5] That was how Goodman got started, so he felt others should follow the same path.[6] Williams took Goodman's advice to heart and didn't accept any funding from him. Despite getting no monetary help, Williams, in a mild bit of deception, used the Goodman name to lure some reticent musicians: "Some of the boys weren't too anxious to go in with me, but I told them, 'Benny is behind me!'"[7] However, Cootie said Goodman "helped me immeasurably to get started with my own outfit" by offering Williams "the use of his entire musical library which consisted of more than five thousand numbers."[8] Williams was grateful because "in the end I owned my own orchestra and today I'm glad."[9] Williams also asked Duke Ellington to invest. While Ellington was enthusiastic, he couldn't help.[10] Ellington had huge financial responsibilities of his own and appeared almost indifferent to money matters, preferring to focus his attentions on music.[11] But talent scout, music critic, and Vanderbilt heir John Hammond (1910–1987) did pitch in some money and advice for Cootie's enterprise. Hammond was a man of firm convictions and tastes who wasn't at all shy about expressing his opinions. In a column for *The People's Voice*, he applauded Goodman's pioneering integration efforts and singled out Artie Shaw and Charlie Barnet for having the courage to take the same move in the 1930s.[12]

Williams went to Kansas City looking for talent assuming "Count Basie, Andy Kirk and the rest of the Southwesterners left any good musicians."[13] On the advice of Hammond, Williams travelled to Houston, Texas, to recruit tenor saxophonist Arnett Cobb for his orchestra. Cobb (1918–1989) was one of those big-toned musicians from the state known as the "Texas Tenors." (Others of that school included Herschel Evans, Buddy Tate, and Illinois Jacquet.) Cobb had been a high school classmate of Cootie's younger brother, Leroy Barney Williams. (Ike Williams, with a new wife and his youngest son, moved to Houston after Ike had lost everything in 1928.) Cobb said that the younger Williams obtained the nickname "Barney Google," after a popular comic strip of the time. Leroy played trumpet, too, but not at well as his famous brother. Cobb recalled that he "he couldn't play. He played in the school band, [and] he played out the side of his mouth."[14] Apparently, there was no equivalent to Charlie Lipscomb available to Leroy Williams in Houston to set him on the correct path.

At this time, Cobb was a member of the Milton Larkin band. Williams went to one of their gigs and liked what he heard and offered Cobb the tenor saxophone chair. Unfortunately, Cobb couldn't accept the job. Cobb's wife didn't want him to give up his day job as an insurance agent for a full-time music career.[15] Disappointed, Williams went to the kitchen during the band's break, thinking about the money he had wasted traveling so far for nothing. Some of the band members stayed on during the break to do their own thing. The alto saxophonist, a young Houston native, was singing the blues, something he didn't normally do with the band. Cootie heard him from the kitchen and decided to move back to the front of the house and said to himself, "This is what I want."[16]

His discovery was named Eddie Lee Vinson Jr. (1917–1988), nicknamed "Cleanhead" because of his bald pate. He lost his hair in a botched attempt at straightening his hair with the lye products of the time. Williams hired Vinson and arranged for him to come to New York for rehearsals. Besides Vinson, Williams recruited trombonist William "Billy" Luper from the Larkin band.

Unfortunately, Luper contracted meningitis en route to Chicago from Houston and died in St. Louis at the tender age of twenty.[17]

When Williams went down to the New York City train station to meet Vinson and escort him to a rehearsal of the new band, he was shocked to see the musician carrying his alto sax without a case. Cootie knew that showed a lack of sophistication and professionalism that would be mocked by the band members. The first order of business was to obtain a new instrument with a proper case.

The band was rehearsing in Harlem's Renaissance Ballroom. Because many of the musicians were from out of town, they needed salary advances to pay their rent and other expenses. Unfortunately, this had to come from Cootie's pocket, to the consternation of Mrs. Williams.[18] Bassist John Simmons had left Benny Goodman a few months prior, but although he had no intentions of joining Cootie's new band, he played the rehearsals just for the money. He didn't want to enlist because Catherine Williams "ran things . . . She'd make out the checks and pay the fellows off and everything. Cootie didn't have a word to say. So I knew I wouldn't like that."[19] The *Pittsburgh Courier* didn't see that as a negative; she was given credit for her guidance of her husband's career. But in the same breath, it added she was "one of the best looking [bandleader's] better halves."[20]

Tenor saxophonist Franz Jackson wasn't with the Williams band very long, but provided a great assessment of his work methods:

[When Cootie] decided to go out on his own, he showed an uncanny ability to organize and rehearse a band in a relatively short period of time and make them sound like something. He would do it overnight. I remember many things that I found unique about Cootie. Sometimes he would stand in front a band and would be counting off for a tempo, and to the audience, it must have seemed as though he was taking forever, but we understood what he was doing. You could actually hear him humming and when he finally got the tempo that he thought he wanted that song to rock on, he would give the downbeat, and you can bet your bottom dollar, when he gave the downbeat, the tempo was right. He had a sense for setting tempo unlike any musician I ever worked with. Cootie had a peculiar kind of personality, somewhat like Hawk [Coleman Hawkins]. Maybe that's the badge of genius. He did not communicate after rehearsals. There was nothing other than music that Cootie would talk about. We would get on the bus and ride for 300 miles, and he wouldn't open his mouth, even if he was spoken to, unless he thought it was something important. We initially thought it was because he had worked with the great Duke for so many years, but it is my understanding that that was his attitude with the members of the Ellington band all the years he was there. He did his job, but never had anything to say.[21]

Alto saxophonist Charlie Holmes (1910–1985)[22] was a childhood friend of Ellington saxophonists Johnny Hodges and Harry Carney.[23] He considered Cootie a friend and knew it would be no problem gaining a slot. But Holmes had a condition—"Well, look, I don't want any solos." And he was content to play second alto sax instead of first (lead) alto. (The hard work he had put in during his time with the Louis Armstrong orchestra made him desire an easier gig.) Williams had no issue with the request, responding that he already had Vinson to play lead and do the solo work.[24] Charlie Holmes said of Vinson's first day: "Naturally, he's scared to death. Anybody just comin' right out of Texas and set in a band up here in New York with a bunch of New Yorkers, you've got to be scared to death, or else you [are] crazy."[25] Cootie recalled that after the rehearsal, Vinson was intimidated and unhappy with his new situation and told Williams, "Oh, I want to go back home! I can't make it, and I done spent my money. . . ."[26]

Holmes goes on to say that Vinson was "good," but the problem lay in his sight reading: "[H]e was a very slow reader. He didn't read good at all. He could read, but very slow." Because Holmes didn't want to play lead, he went to great lengths to help out Vinson. Holmes said Vinson "was working like mad." Vinson had a heavy load to carry in the band; besides his lead work, he also soloed and sang.

Williams continues:

I had to bring him up to my house and talk to him. I said, "You'll be okay, man, don't worry about anything. Don't worry about a thing. Oh, you're going to make it. You're going to make it." [Vinson was intimidated by these musicians, saying] "I can't compete with these boys. I can't do this." [Cootie] said, "Yeah. You're going to make it. You're better than these boys." So the next day, in rehearsal, I took him to the piano player. I said, "What was them blues you was singing down there? You should sing those blues so they can get an arrangement on them." So he said it was in the key of F or something. So I said, "Start the blues in the key of F." Said, "Come on, sing the blues." He got up and sang them blues, and everybody was all over him."[27]

Holmes said, "Everybody was trying out and Cootie was very generous. He had plenty of whiskey there. And it was just like they was having a party or something. So we would rehearse a number, and then we'd stop and take a break, have a little taste and so forth. Well, they would take up the afternoon, you know, take up the time, and come back the next day."[28]

George "Butch" Ballard (1918–2011) auditioned for the drum chair. Ballard recalled that "Big Sidney Catlett told me that Cootie Williams was forming a band like Duke Ellington's, so I went down to the rehearsal hall, and I saw 99 sax players, 99 trombone players—all auditioning to get the job. This drummer sat in, that drummer sat in, and then I got my shot. As luck would have it, the number he called out was 'Airmail Special,' and I knew it because the [band he was formerly in] used to play it. So I felt right at home. Then we went on to play some blues, and I was nervous, but after I got past the first chorus, I was okay. About two weeks later, I got a call from his office saying that I'd been hired for the job. I almost fainted."[29] Williams had high praise for Ballard, saying he was "the most promising young guy I've run across in my search for sidemen." [30] Unfortunately, he didn't last long as Williams's drummer—the Navy called him up in 1943. The *Pittsburgh Press* quipped that "[a]side from ability to play or sing[,] an important essential to get work with a band these days is a draft deferment."[31] Ballard would go on to play with the Duke Ellington orchestra for most of 1953 and have a long career in music.[32]

While the work of recruiting for the new band continued, Williams still worked around town. He was the lone horn player, "playing straight trumpet"[33] in an unusually instrumented band accompanying Jack Leonard, a singer from Tommy Dorsey's band. The backing consisted of Cootie's trumpet, four string players, and a rhythm section.[34] Cootie solos on only one song from the session, "Madeleine," and it's a straight, but moving, reading of the melody.[35] Sitting in here and there also helped him keep in playing shape. At the end of November, he was the guest star of the Providence [Rhode Island] Swing Club's jam session.[36] He also found time to sit in with Charlie Barnet (1913–1991), a white bandleader who greatly admired Duke Ellington and Count Basie. (Like Goodman, he also had integrated bands. Over the years, he employed Black musicians like Frankie Newton, Al Killian, John Kirby, Clark Terry, Bunny Briggs, Oscar Pettiford, and Howard McGhee.) Of the December 1 Barnet radio broadcast, the review noted that Cootie's "fine playing never did fit in as well with Goodman's crew . . . his appearance with Barnet, frequently called the white Ellington[,] worked out perfectly."[37]

But apparently Cootie's career moves weren't public enough or proceeding quickly enough. The *Chicago Defender* wrote "'Cootie's silence worries his fans' since he's made no public mention of his plans since leaving the Goodman troupe and his fans are wondering why."[38] As always, whenever there is a lack of available information, rumors rush in to fill the void, like Cootie would ditch his plans to form his own orchestra and join Barnet's instead.[39] Or if he did form an orchestra of his own, the piano chair would be manned by Billy Strayhorn![40]

Late in the year, Cootie filled the information vacuum and publicly announced that he had begun his planning with the help of Willard Alexander of the William Morris Agency. At the time, Morris represented Count Basie, Earl "Fatha" Hines, and Vaughn Monroe, to name a few. As reported by

Metronome in December, Cootie said, "I'm just starting to get men, so I won't be ready for a while. So far I have Sandy Williams [trombone], Charlie Holmes [alto sax], Louis Bacon [trumpet and vocal] and Joe Guy [trumpet]. I think I'll go to Chicago soon. I know some boys there I'd like to get." Bacon had been a member of Duke Ellington's trumpet section for a few months starting in 1933. He was incorrectly reported to be Ivie Anderson's husband, but they were romantic partners, not man and wife.[41]

Williams wanted a generationally mixed band. The older, experienced musicians included Charlie Holmes, Greely Walton (1904–1993),[42] Louis Bacon (1904–1967), and of course, the leader. The youth contingent consisted of Canadian pianist Ken Kersey (1916–1983), George "Butch" Ballard, tenor saxophonist Bob Dorsey (1915–1965), and trumpeter Joe Guy (1920–1962). Cootie explained that the "older men are steady and experienced and the youngsters have fire and enthusiasm. Each group passes some of its qualities on to the other."[43] Holmes had trouble understanding the younger musicians: "[A]ll the young ones, they were nuts. Believe me. They didn't care about anything. But they could play."[44] Cootie decided the band's style would be "built around me. Before I would let [arrangers] write for the band, they had to come hear the band in person. . . . I haven't patterned [my] band after any other band. Good music always sounds good, no matter in what particular style it is played, and that's our goal: to play good music."[45]

Cootie closed out 1941 by recording in another edition of the *Metronome* All Star Band. Harry James joined him in the trumpet section again, but this time the third man was Roy Eldridge. Williams won again in the *Down Beat* poll, too. Eldridge and Elman were his cowinners.[46]

While building his new band, Williams continued to work sporadically with Goodman on a freelance basis. Goodman did two more of his combination classical and swing concerts in the first week of January 1942. The first, on January 4, was in Cleveland with Artur Rodzinski conducting the Cleveland Orchestra. The critic sent to review the program admitted he didn't know much about swing music, and it shows: "I cannot pretend to appreciate all of [swing's] fine points, though I heard most of its rough ones. I was particularly interested in one Cootie Williams, who made the trumpet sound like a sneeze and whose contortions suggested the colic or some violent form of hysteria." At least Cootie got mentioned by name. Peggy Lee was described as "a young lady who sit[s] in front of the band and smile[s] knowingly when anything of special merit takes place." She "uttered sounds which did not resemble singing and were unrecognizable as English, but they undoubtedly have special meaning for those accustomed to this sort of thing."[47]

Two days later, on January 6, 1942, Benny Goodman played a similar dual-themed concert with the Pittsburgh Symphony Orchestra under the direction of Vladimir Bakaleinikoff at the Syria Mosque concert hall. Since the songs to be performed were subject to whatever Goodman decided to call, they weren't listed for the last portion of the program. Instead, it read "Program by Benny Goodman and His Orchestra, Peggy Lee, Vocalist and Cootie Williams, Trumpet."[48] The popular music critic at the *Pittsburgh Post Gazette* gushed over the performance of the Goodman band and Peggy Lee and Cootie Williams fared much better in the review. Lee was mentioned by name and "the charming young lady" knew "the business end of the microphone when she sees it." Cootie gave out "irrepressible sendings" and described "as sweet a trumpeter as has held the stage of the Mosque."[49] *The Billboard* said, "Cootie Williams' scorching interpretation of Duke Ellington's *Concerto for Cootie*, abetted by his showmanly front-stage parading that suggested a cross between a bounce and a hop, proved show-stop. When he finished soloing on the *Deep River* encore, Benny had to wave the audience to quiet in order to proceed with the program."[50]

However, the classical music critic at the city's *Sun-Telegraph* panned both segments of the concert saying, "As a classic [sic] musician Goodman appears completely without distinction. His reading of the Mozart [Concerto for Clarinet] was casual, without virtuosity, albeit smooth and without mishap. Later a few tones from our own clarinetist demonstrated what a symphony soloist could do with the same instrument." He was not impressed with Williams's offerings, either: "Cootie Williams, cornetist [sic], might play well if he ever stopped shrieking through his horn."[51]

Another Williams-Goodman pairing took place in the studio on January 16, when they were included in the band "Metronome All Star Leaders." After a short introduction, Cootie states the melody of "I Got Rhythm." Given the amount of soloists[52] that needed to be heard within the limits of a 78 RPM recording, that's all the time Cootie is afforded.

In 1939, the Daughters of the American Revolution (DAR) infamously refused to let African American contralto Marian Anderson perform at their Washington, DC, venue Constitution Hall. It created a huge furor and resulted in First Lady Eleanor Roosevelt resigning her membership in the group. Eventually, Anderson gave a concert in front of the Lincoln Memorial instead. On January 25, 1942, Benny Goodman and his Orchestra played yet another joint swing/classical concert at Constitution Hall. With this concert, Cootie Williams was hailed as the first African American to play Constitution Hall. "When Cootie Williams stood with Benny Goodman on the stage of Constitution hall last week, where Marian Anderson couldn't stand, and blasted out on Duke Ellington's 'Concerto to [sic] Cootie,' D.A.R. ghosts fell shuddering from the eves [sic] at the thunderous applause...."[53] The Washington, DC, *Evening Star* made no mention of the racial import of the event but stated that Cootie

Charlie Christian and Cootie Williams in the studio during a Benny Goodman Sextet recording session. (Duke Ellington Collection, Archives Center, National Museum of American History, Smithsonian Institution)

"took to the middle of the stage to quiver his soul out."[54] Recalling the event in 1980, Williams said, "I was the first black to play in Constitution Hall. The manager of the hall tried to put pressure on Goodman to get rid of me during the booking, but Goodman wouldn't have any of that. He told them the band wouldn't play if I didn't play. So we played and we were a smash."[55] Lost in all of this is that African American tenor Roland Hayes sang at Constitution Hall in 1931, meaning Williams was not really the first Black person to perform there. The anti-Black prohibition was put into place in the mid-1930s.[56] Regardless, it was said that not everyone in the crowd was pleased. Diplomats, senators, and other VIPs were there and "they say that some of the Senators turned a nice shade of pink at the guest spot that Benny gave Cooty [sic] Williams; jazz had never been heard in the hall before, let alone Cooty's growls."[57] Perhaps the shock was even more intense since it wasn't announced in advance that Cootie would be present.[58] This probably wasn't sabotage or subterfuge; Cootie was just days away from making his debut as a leader in Chicago and his availability may have been in doubt up until the last moment.

In its January 31 issue, the *New York Age* breathlessly announced that the lineup for Cootie's band was set. "Cootie, Louis Bacon and Joe Guy are on trumpets, with Cootie and Bacon sharing the vocals. Trombones are R. H. Horton, Jonas Walker and Sandy Williams; saxes, Eddie Vincent [sic], Charlie Holmes [who was on Cootie's first recording session in 1928], Bob Dorsey, Don Stovall and Greely Walton. Rhythm includes pianist Kenneth Kersey, from Red

Allen's band; guitarist-arranger, Roscoe Fritz, and drummer George Ballard. The bassist and a fourth trumpet were still to be set at press time."

Fritz (1914–1965) wasn't supposed to be the guitarist in the new band. That spot had been promised to Charlie Christian. But he never returned to playing after taking a leave of absence due to illness from Benny Goodman's groups in the spring of 1941. He succumbed to tuberculosis on March 2, 1942, at the tragically young age of twenty-five.[59] Given the size of Christian's talent, the band probably would have been molded around him in addition to Williams. Roscoe Fritz only played with the orchestra for a few months and wasn't present at the time of the band's April 1, 1942, recording debut. By the summer he was working in a group backing vocalist George Tunnell, better known to the public as "Bon Bon."[60] According to *Down Beat*, Fritz was doing most of the arrangements for Cootie's band.[61] Unfortunately, this can't be verified, but may have been true in the early days of the band's existence. But Don Redman, Mary Lou Williams, Bill Doggett, Don Kirkpatrick, and Franz Jackson[62] among others are known to have contributed to the band's book during its five years of existence.

The rehearsals in Harlem were said to be going well, with *Down Beat* saying that "it appears that Cootie Williams will be the first bandleader to step out in 1942 with a really outstanding new organization." At the time the story ran, the location and date for the band to go public hadn't been determined.[63] Although he was working hard to build his band, Cootie was in the social columns, too. He and Count Basie were reported as guests at a party given in Joe Louis's honor in early January.[64]

PART IV
Cootie Williams, Big Band Leader (1942)

17

FLY RIGHT

The place and date for the debut of Cootie Williams and His Orchestra turned out to be Chicago's Grand Terrace Café on Friday, February 6, 1942. World War II was almost two months old for the United States and it was hardly the best time to start a new band. The newspaper headlines of that day were all war related—the Japanese movements in Rangoon and Luzon in particular.

The Grand Terrace Café was the longtime home of pianist and orchestra leader Earl "Fatha" Hines. The club, started by Ed Fox in 1928, didn't do great business at the beginning and the Great Depression the following year didn't help matters. But the club was doing well enough in the early 1930s to have mob boss Al Capone extort a 25 percent ownership share of the club in exchange for "protection." The mob would occasionally conduct business meetings at the club and of course the musicians knew to deny any knowledge of the clientele or any packages that might be exchanged among these gentlemen.[1] Cootie and Catherine arrived in Chicago on February 1 and stayed at the Southway Hotel on Chicago's South Side.[2] (Ellington stayed at the Southway Hotel when he was in Chicago, too. Known for his love of food and big appetite, the Duke rated the hotel's "cinnamon rolls and filet mignon the best in the world and [gave] high grades to the shrimp creole and barbecue ribs.")[3]

The *Chicago Defender* printed a picture of fellow bandleader Andy Kirk, who had the previous booking at the Grand Terrace, passing a baton to Cootie Williams on his opening night, with the heading "Welcome, Cootie." In addition to the band, the show also had comedy from "The Three Loose Nuts" ("[t]hey do a satire on Hitler that is terrific and another about a Spanish queen that is the tops")[4] and a "Fast Florid Floorshow" with Billy Nightingale, Lovey Lane, the Basie Brothers, Mitzi Mitchell, Muriel Jones, and Lucille Wilkins. Sadly, all of these performers are obscure today. The floorshow also touted

Handbill for Cootie Williams's 1942 orchestra debut at the Grand Terrace Café. The initial four-week booking was extended twice. (Author's collection)

"The Grand Terrace Ensemble of 10 SEPIA BEAUTIES." Trumpeter/vocalist Louis Bacon was the only band member featured in the handbill for the job. That would soon change as Bacon would prove to be neither an audience nor critical favorite. The standout in the band, aside from Williams, would be young Eddie "Cleanhead" Vinson.

Cleanhead could almost be considered a costar in the Williams band. "Saxer Vinson is the clan's chief vocalist and clown, even overshadowing Cootie's own horn virtuosity. His voice is good for blues, which the band features frequently, his sax sorcery blows up enough steam to excite, and while his idea of comedy is on the corny side, on him it looks good and meets with the desired response."[5]

Several fellow bandleaders sent congratulatory telegrams and flower arrangements to the thirty-year-old newly minted bandleader. Duke Ellington and his band sent an arrangement of roses that "stretch[ed] a third of the stage's width." But Benny Goodman didn't send flowers. Instead, he sent a telegram with $100 (which is almost $2,000 in today's dollars) and a prophetic message that read, "This will serve as a better bridge than will flowers when you need to be helped over your first 'rough and tough' sledding."[6] Benny Goodman was in New York at the time the Williams band made its debut but was able to catch the radio broadcasts. Through a press release, he gave his stamp of approval and said, "the band has come a long way in a short time and with a few more rehearsals will take its place among the fine colored bands in the country." Goodman had hated to lose Cootie, but they parted on good terms.[7]

An early review in the *Chicago Defender* said: "To classify 'Cootie's' band one would call it strictly commercial with plenty to offer in that line. Cootie himself is the star of course but there are others like Louis Bacon who also serves as vocalist and the sax playing of Eddie Vincent [*sic*] who doubles at chirping blues that set the place on fire. This boy is the most natural blues singer to hit the main stem in many, many moons."[8] One of Cootie's strengths as a bandleader was talent scouting; this was just the beginning.

Charlie Holmes said "the type of music that Cootie was playing, it wasn't for no high-class people. I mean, he was playing the rugcutters' music . . . He had a dance band, a dance-hall band. And boy, we was wailin'! And this is a high-class night club, [and the music] did fit in the place . . . We were there practically all winter. It's cold in Chicago, too."[9] Holmes said that "at that place, you did not have to blow loud to be heard . . . And we hit down there like a ton of bricks. Boy, people were holding their ears, and he was playing his favorite number, "Rollin'" [*sic*, "Roll 'Em"] and boy, it was loud. I don't know if the people liked it or not. It was really too loud, you know."[10] Besides calling them loud, Holmes also offered a colorful characterization the band's musical abilities: "I've never in all my life played with such a bad band that sounded so good. There were more people in there who couldn't read a note as big as a house, and they had no more conception of music than the man in the moon, but they could play, and they could swing, and it sounded good."[11] Despite problems with the band's musicianship during these early days, Cootie Williams had public goodwill behind him—"The band isn't terrific but Cootie works mighty hard and the patrons will string along with him until he arrives."[12]

Holmes noted that the band was heavily promoted during their Chicago stand, saying that they were "billed like a circus."[13] A regular radio remote broadcast also helped publicize the band.[14] The shows, carried on Chicago's WBBM, were late-night affairs, usually at 12:30 or 1:30 a.m.[15] The band was worked hard during their Grand Terrace gig. Trombonist Sandy Williams (1906–1991) (no relation) said, "We had to play four shows a night there and I'd been on to Cootie for a raise. When it didn't come, I got mad, because I couldn't send enough money home. I went to the hotel that night and let my bags and golf clubs out the window at the back. I just had enough money to take the bus home, and when I got to New York I had one nickel in my pocket—subway fare uptown."[16]

During the engagement, Cootie was presented with his trophy for his win in *Down Beat*'s 1941 "All-American Swing Band," his second consecutive win. The *Chicago Defender* ran a photo of the ceremony participants, which included Count Basie, Al Monroe from the *Defender*, and Bob Lock, *Down Beat* editor. In a bit of intra-city rivalry, the *Defender* refused to identify the publication, only referring to *Down Beat* as a "well known magazine."[17]

The young band continued to improve. In March, it was announced that the Grand Terrace engagement had been extended from its original four weeks for yet another four weeks.[18] But musical improvement wasn't the only thing the band needed. There was a problem with Cootie Williams himself. The next gig, at Detroit's Paradise Theater, was almost lost because management was unhappy with Cootie's stage presence—"he can't talk like an emcee."[19] Since the engagement went forward, apparently Williams was able to improve his hosting skills enough to assuage theater management. Later, there were some who felt that his stage demeanor went too far, with him "hopping around and rolling his eyes and conforming to the stage caricature of a Negro jazz musician." In rebuttal, Cootie replied, "That is showmanship. I'll have to do that as long as I front a band. I can go out and hit a note that nobody else can, but who's going know it? When I started the band I didn't use any showmanship at all. We had a very tough time. And, Mister, I was playing a lot of horn!"[20]

The new band entered the recording studio for the first time on April 1 at the Chicago studio of OKeh (Columbia) records. "Sleepy Valley"[21] and "Marcheta"[22] were arranged by Don Kirkpatrick and "Fly Right" was arranged by Bob McCrae. Cleanhead made his recorded singing debut on "When My Baby Left Me," an original blues credited to Cootie and Cleanhead.[23]

"Fly Right" was used as the band's theme song.[24] The composition on this first recording was credited to Thelonious Monk, Kenny Clarke, and Cootie Williams. It wouldn't be the only time a Thelonious Monk melody would be used as a theme by Cootie Williams.[25] *Metronome* said that these recordings, "when and if issued, will introduce a great, new, little known band to the world, outside the northeastern United States."[26] "Fly Right" would sometimes later be used as a set closing theme by Monk under the title "Epistrophy," which was only credited to Monk and Clarke. (Williams's name would not appear on future recordings.) Looking back, Eddie "Lockjaw" Davis remarked that "Epistrophy" was "considered avant-garde in those days," and especially so to use it as a theme at the Savoy Ballroom.[27] The chromatic chord movements and tritone intervals in the melody certainly set it apart from standard swing era big band music. Williams played the melody at the beginning and concluding choruses of the recording, playing the first chorus open and the last chorus tightly muted for variety. He left the improvised solos to pianist Kenny Kersey and trumpeter Joe Guy. Perhaps Williams didn't find the chord structure conducive to his style.

Shortly after the recording session, Cootie may a quick trip to New York City and appeared as a guest at Eddie Condon's jam session. Guitarist Condon (1905–1973) hosted a series of jam session–type concerts at New York's Town Hall over several years, starting in 1942. Cootie, along with "blues singer" Billie Holiday, James P. Johnson, Dave Tough, and others were featured at the fourth concert in the ongoing event, held on April 11. (Unfortunately, the recording of the concerts from radio broadcasts, didn't start until 1944.)[28] Condon had his own issues with the DAR. In 1946, Condon tried to rent Constitution Hall for his monthly concerts but was rebuffed by the organization. Essentially they feared that jazz rowdies might "damage the building." In response, Condon, well known for his wit, promised to ban all DAR members from his concerts.[29]

Cootie was happy with the results of his Grand Terrace gig, saying "it's been very encouraging. The house has been full, the trade papers and dailies have given us encouraging reviews and we've gotten good reports about the band from listeners over our CBS wire. We've already recorded for the OKeh label—something very unusual for a band as young as ours."[30] Cootie enjoyed his new role, too: "I like being a leader. I get a kick out of fronting a band and seeing something that you've worked hard on for a long time take shape. I was fortunate of course, in having worked with two of the greatest leaders in the business—Duke Ellington and Benny Goodman—and during those years I picked up a lot of tips on how a leader handles problems quickly and efficiently."[31]

By the end of the Grand Terrace residency, *Down Beat* said the band was "still rough but not as rough" and was much improved from opening night. Williams's time with Goodman continued to be a critic's punching bag, with the reviewer saying Cootie's playing reminded them of his Ellington days and he was "playing much better than he ever did during his stay with Benny Goodman."[32]

BACK TO NEW YORK

After over two months at the Grand Terrace Café, the band left Chicago, playing a few gigs in the Midwest on their way east to New York. For their May 11 date at Detroit's Greystone Ballroom, the band got paid $400. "The driver of our chartered bus said I owed him $1,000." Cootie told the driver, "You insult me! You don't want to carry me any further? Then we are through!"[1] This forced a change in transportation. "I put the fellows on a Greyhound bus so that we could come to New York and open at the Apollo Theater, in Harlem. I told the fellow that the bus company didn't want to carry a big musician like me, and I had them so fussed that they wanted to kill that driver."[2]

Williams had to stretch the truth to keep his band's morale up. "I would tell the fellows, 'Don't worry about a thing. Benny is behind me. He's going to take care of us. Next month we are going to follow him into the Hotel New Yorker.'" This was a complete fabrication on Williams's part. "We had as much chance of playing the New Yorker as [the interviewer]. They don't ever book a Negro band. Other times I would tell the fellows we were going to California. This went on for two years. The fellows would believe me because they knew that I was a big musician. That's how I kept the fellows together, by lying to them."[3] Black bands would continue to fight for hotel bookings for many years. For their part, the big hotels feared booking "Negro talent" because it would attract "Negro patronage."[4]

The new Williams band faced the demanding crowd of the Apollo Theater for the first time when they were booked for a week's engagement starting on May 15.[5] Sharing the package with the Mills Brothers, Cootie wound up with second billing, a sign of his band's untested box office drawing power.[6] In their review of the show, *Variety* noted "the absence of big marquee names with the exception of the Mills Bros." But the review said that the "band goes over

Cootie Williams's band made their debut at the Apollo Theater on May 15, 1942. He would appear there twenty-one more times over the next sixteen years. But the first time here, the veteran Mills Brothers got top billing over the novice band. (*The People's Voice*, courtesy of NewsBank/Readex)

big."[7] "Cootie Williams looks like a click. He's not quite ripe for top picture house bookings but could easily make the grade by switching a couple of his orchestrations so as to avoid the sameness of his jam sessions. After the third they all begin to sound alike." Presciently, they added he should "retain 'Cherry Red Blues' . . . an unusual novelty which Eddie Vincent [*sic*], sax, vocalled for fine returns. Vincent should climb fast. He is a rasping, high-pitched, but nonetheless effective voice, with a double entendre and frankly blue interpolations of 'Cherry Red' heightening the effect." Apparently, Cootie continued work on his hosting skills were paying off: "Williams handles m.c. assignment satisfactorily."[8] "Cherry Red Blues" aka "Red Blues" would become a major hit for Williams and Vinson, but the AFM strike would prevent them from recording it for a year and a half.

Metronome was more enthusiastic, saying the band's New York debut at the Apollo was "an exciting and an auspicious one. Few bands, colored or white, make inaugural appearances this fine in every way." Vinson was singled out, given a whole paragraph in the six paragraph column: "Visually,

Eddie Vinson was the high spot of the show. A thrilling altoist in the Hodges tradition, Eddie is also a fine blues singer, with a cracked voice, a powerful beat and a very happy ability to put the meaning of his songs and his singing on his face, in his gestures and in his general stance. He killed this audience with *Cherry Red* and *Outskirts of Town* and could have remained on for at least another four numbers."[9] The reviewer, Barry Ulanov, also liked Pearl Bailey, saying she sold her songs "with some of the best use of hands and body and smile and all around showmanship this reviewer has ever seen." And not least, Bailey "also, fortunately, showed a find jazz voice and manner and a beat that was really solid."[10]

While *Variety* was sold on Williams as an emcee, Ulanov was not: "[Cootie] needs to learn one important lesson for theater appearances—the necessity for good diction. His mumbled announcements made it impossible to make out the names of performers or tunes." Part of the problem may have been Williams's southern accent. But overall, Ulanov was highly pleased with Williams's musicianship and his "abundant talents. His trumpet, open, plungered, buzz-muted or hand-muted, paraded through everything the band did. . . . [H]e led a band that showed forthright and unmistakable musicianship in everything it played."[11]

Cootie's talent-spotting skills were certainly accurate when it came to Vinson and Bailey, and he would go on to make many other stellar discoveries. In early reviews of the band, they may not have cited him by name or misreported his surname as "Vincent," but they uniformly reported that his blues singing was a crowd favorite—"that guy in the band who sings the blues like nobody else can, really broke it up."[12] Another report said, "You just wait, you're going to hear plenty about Eddie Vincent [sic], the sending blues singer, with "Cootie" Williams's band . . ."[13]

Music and Rhythm ran a monthly column called "Let's Buy a Band." The premise of the column was stated below the title banner: "Are you looking for a band? Whether you are a hotel man, ballroom operator, night club promoter or just a member of the Prom committee, *Music & Rhythm*'s band directory will help you select the kind of entertainment you want." Cootie Williams was one of the bands listed in the April 1942 issue:

> There aren't a lot of outstanding negro bands in the field, but Williams, former Ellington and Goodman trumpeter, has a good chance to break into the top bracket quickly. His trumpet playing is marvelous, his stage personality excellent. The band, made up of outstanding colored soloists is still a little rough, but has plenty of fire and attack. Red hot for ballrooms (Williams already has a name). The band will be due shortly for location.

Cootie's band was selected as *Music and Rhythm* magazine's "Band of the Month" in its May 1942 issue. (*Music and Rhythm*, Courtesy of RIPM Jazz Periodicals)

Quite a range of styles were included for the "buying"—other bands featured in this same column included Erskine Hawkins, Jack Teagarden, Paul Whiteman, Blue Barron, and Xavier Cugat, just to name a few.[14]

In the next issue of the magazine, Cootie Williams and his orchestra was named *Music and Rhythm*'s May "Band of the Month." In giving them the honor, they stated, "Williams has produced in a few short months one of the outstanding Negro orchestras of the day. A capable musician and a capable leader, Williams and his orchestra have forged another link in the great tradition of swing music."[15] (Previous honorees included John Kirby, Teddy Wilson, Gene Krupa, and Bud Freeman.) The two-page story included paragraph length biographies of each musician in the band and a half-page interview with Cootie. A paragraph rating the band stated: "The newest of the Negro bands, Cootie William's [sic] orchestra seems unquestionably destined for success. Leader, long a name in the music world, is an ace performer on the trumpet, a capable showman as well. Band, though still rough in spots, has dynamic rhythm section, exciting soloists, excellent spirit. Two band members [Eddie Vinson and Louis Bacon] handle vocals."[16] The publicity that the magazine gave Williams may not have been entirely altruistic since John Hammond, cofounder of the magazine, was an investor in Williams's band.[17]

In June 1942, Cootie Williams hired Mercer Ellington, Duke's twenty-three-year-old son, as his road manager.[18] The road manager handles a group's logistics, such as herding the musicians, obtaining lodging, interfacing with the venue, and so on. As a boy, Mercer was taught the trumpet by Cootie and would wind up playing the instrument in his father's band in the 1960s. "Cootie Williams said I had chops that were good for the trumpet, so he bought me a trumpet."[19] Mercer Ellington said, "Cootie knew that, in preparation for my once-dreamed-of engineering career, I had studied math. Seemingly he felt that bookkeeping and math were one, for he insisted that I become his temporary manager. I left the [East] coast and went with Cootie." This temporary assignment lasted only seven months,[20] but Mercer would return as Cootie's road manager in 1954.[21]

19

THE IMPACT OF WAR

Following the successful week at the Apollo, the band performed dates along the East Coast, with stops including New Brighton, Pennsylvania, Buffalo, and Annapolis. Apparently, Benny Goodman found himself down a trumpet player, for on June 17, Cootie joined the Goodman trumpet section once again for a recording date. Four titles were recorded, all featuring vocals by Dick Haymes, but Cootie didn't solo on any of them.[1]

♪

The United States was experiencing changes on a large scale due to the now six-month-old war. (Of course, these hardships were not as significant compared to having war being fought on your home turf, as Europe had experienced for nearly two years.) There was virtually no aspect of life that was untouched. Gasoline, tires, coffee, tea, sugar, meat, and other staples that people took for granted in their daily life were now subject to rationing. For example, the government was mandating tea and coffee consumption reduced by 50 percent and 25 percent respectively.[2] The Office of Defense Transportation (ODT), per its official government description, "coordinated and directed the utilization of domestic transportation facilities during World War II."[3] Because of the need for gasoline and tires for the war effort, on June 22 the ODT prohibited bus non-essential bus travel. This edict included travel by the bands.

As a workaround, the ODT suggested that the train be substituted for the buses. It turned out the bus ban was not only expensive, but inconvenient and impractical. There were two problems with using trains. First, most train stations weren't near the hotels and theaters that the orchestras needed to travel to, thus there was still a need for ground transportation from the train depots.

Second, the Black bands faced an additional problem with the trains—Jim Crow. In the South, they were forbidden to travel on the trains in many cases. All the itineraries originally expected to be traveled by roads now had to be rerouted. It created a "superhuman job" for the agencies that specialized in booking "colored outfits" like those of Joe Glaser and Moe Gale.[4] (In the 1930s, the bands of Cab Calloway and Duke Ellington had private Pullman cars that could be used for travel and once they arrived at the station, the cars could be detached and used as lodging.)

To add insult to injury, there were exceptions to the bus policy. For example, *Music and Rhythm* printed a picture of buses being used to ferry customers from the Mt. Vernon train station to the Empire race track under the caption "Uncle Sam Nabbed Leaders' Buses . . . But Not These."[5] Like most aspects of American life, your political lobby determines your outcomes.

During the summer of 1942, New York's *The People's Voice* newspaper announced it was starting a series of guest columns to be "written by the most prominent bandleaders, both Negro and white."[6] Benny Goodman, Count Basie, Tommy Dorsey, and others were listed for future contributions. Cootie Williams was given the honor of providing the inaugural article (which was most likely ghostwritten) and was published in the June 20, 1942, edition of the publication. The headline reflected Williams's dark view of the music business—"Future Looks Gloomy Says Cootie Williams."

> It is reasonable to assume, providing the present law governing the utilization of buses and other motor vehicles is upheld that the end of Negro bands is in sight. To begin with, there are now only three major spots in the country where Negro bands can really display their wares in top form; the Hotel Sherman in Chicago, the Trianon in Los Angeles and the Savoy Ballroom here in New York.
>
> Because the majority of bands travel mostly by bus and there are but comparatively few Negro bands who get the real breaks, each Negro musical organization above the combination size will be seriously curtailed in its activities between New York and Los Angeles should this business of commandeering buses continue over any great length of time.
>
> [T]here are approximately 150 spot jobs within the New York area alone, but only one, the Savoy, offers a permanent location for Negro bands. It seems obvious that with such a limited field for our bands, this bus trouble is certainly going to sound the death knell for Negro bands.
>
> . . . [O]ne-nighters are really the life blood of the Negro band schedule. Without them our bands face virtual starvation. Perhaps you have already heard about the 73 per cent cut in the recording business. Both Negro and white bands depend upon the record business to make up the

deficit of spot jobs. Now that the record business has diminished, what is there left for Negro bands[?] There will always be enough work for white bands because there are so many hotels, night clubs, restaurants, and radio commercials, so the outlook for them isn't so bad, but frankly, what is to become of our bands now? As the situation now stands, I can see very little hope for them.[7]

Syndicated excerpts of this gloomy article appeared in other Black newspapers. The August 8 edition of the *Philadelphia Tribune* published a story headlined "Future 'Looks Bad' For Race Bands, Says Cootie Williams In Interview." Williams predicted that only "three colored bands" would survive the war and beyond—Duke Ellington, Count Basie, and Cab Calloway.[8] The high price of wartime travel made Williams think that eventually the government would ban non-war-related travel altogether. Fortunately, that prediction didn't come true.[9]

With the prohibition on bus travel, Cootie's band was only able to make a few jobs in vicinity of New York; Worcester, Massachusetts, on June 27[10] and a three-day stint at the American Legion Fair in Trenton, New Jersey. from July 7 through 10.[11] Williams was supposed to play the Dartmouth Green Key summer prom on August 8 but had to cancel due to their bus transportation woes.[12]

In the midst of dealing with all the turmoil needed to keep his band going, Cootie did stumble into a lucrative situation. The band was booked to play at Colgate University, located in the central part of New York state, on July 12. For only ninety minutes of work, the band was paid $450, the equivalent of nearly $9,000 today.[13] From there, they spent a week in Boston at the Tic Toc Club before returning to New York City. A young George Frazier saw the band in Boston and proclaimed that Cootie's band "impressed me as the best colored band to come up since Basie came out of Kansas City a few years ago."[14]

By mid-July, *The Billboard* declared in a banner headline that "ORKS DROP LIKE FLIES." The military draft and transportation issues created a list of bands "teetering on the brink" that was "depressingly long." They also reported that "Cootie Williams, who has been doing fairly well with his new band, will probably call it a day to join the new Raymond Scott outfit on CBS."[15] Like so many opportunities, studio work was denied to African Americans, so this would be a new frontier for Black musicians. But taking the job would mean going back to the position of sideman in a band.

Just a few months into the war, the government realized they had a problem with African American support for the effort. It wasn't that "Negroes" were pacificists and it certainly wasn't that there was any sympathy with Nazi ideology; rather, it was that the African American population felt "that they don't belong" and didn't feel that "Uncle Sam is for them." In order to try to counter these sentiments, the Office of Facts and Figures (OFF) sent out a memo to the radio stations to suggesting that they can help "by remembering Negroes whenever a program is being worked out on which they or their contributions can be included—and included unostentatiously."[16] One result of the memo was CBS tasked Raymond Scott with organizing "medium-sized house band" which was "to contain sepia tooters" (slang for Black musicians). While the formation of the band was set, the number of Black musicians was not.[17] Raymond Scott (1908–1994), born Harry Warnow, was the very definition of a polymath. Besides being a composer, pianist, and bandleader, Scott was also an inventor. In the spring of 1942, he had a successful limited run radio show on the CBS network with a program named *Powerhouse*,[18] titled in honor of one his most memorable compositions.[19] Scott was lured back to CBS during the summer and given carte blanche in the formation of his new group, and Louis Shoobe, the director of orchestra personnel at CBS, was "under orders to get anyone Scott wants."[20]

With a heavy heart, Cootie put his band on notice. Andy Kirk was able to lure away two of Cootie's stars, Eddie "Cleanhead" Vinson and pianist Kenny Kersey. Duke Ellington made a play for Vinson, offering a chance to record with the band in Chicago. In a comedy of errors, Vinson arrived in Chicago and "wandered around vaguely for three days" with Duke and his organization hunting for him. Eventually, Vinson was able to phone Ellington at the recording session.[21] But there was another complication—Vinson had no idea where the studio was located and didn't have cab fare to travel there anyway. After a while, he finally arrived but by then the session was over. (Vinson eventually decided to return to New York and rejoin Cootie Williams.[22] He may not have had the option to rejoin Kirk since Kirk had no idea where Vinson was and considered him "AWOL.")[23]

It wasn't easy for Raymond Scott to recruit the mixed group he was tasked to form. After a month, he only had former Goodman pianist Mel Powell and former Ellington bassist Billy Taylor.[24] Although Cootie Williams had committed to joining the new Scott band, he changed his mind when he found out the job paid scale, about $150 a week, far less than what he was making with Goodman and less than what he hoped to make as a bandleader. The title of the article in *The Billboard* summarized Cootie's position perfectly— "Cootie Williams Won't Go For CBS Offer of Peanuts." Instead, Williams decided to give his booking agency, William Morris, another chance. Williams decided to keep his options open—if the big band didn't work out, he'd take the Scott gig.[25]

Cootie encountered yet another headwind during that summer, but he was not alone in facing it. For several years, American Federation of Musicians argued that royalties should be paid when a recording is played for broadcast. They couldn't get the record companies to agree, so at midnight on the night of July 31 the AFM went on strike. Union members were forbidden to record after that date. The strike wouldn't be fully settled until 1944, resulting in a twenty-month gap in recording opportunities for the new big band.[26]

♪

With intense lobbying from John Hammond, Cab Calloway, and the NAACP's Walter White, a solution was reached for the prohibition on buses. In exchange for buses, the bands would agree to perform at least twice a week at United Service Organizations (USO) camps.[27] It was only a temporary plan, lasting three months. At the end of that time period, it would be reviewed, and another ruling would be made. This solution was more palatable to Southerners than extending rights to African Americans by dropping the Jim Crow train restrictions. Calloway received high praise for his role in obtaining the buses. It was noted that there really wasn't anything in it for him since his band seldom used buses.[28]

Cootie Williams and his orchestra played one of their obligatory camp dates at New York's Camp Edison in September, just a few weeks after the settlement.[29] He quickly became a favorite among the military. At Camp Shanks (near Orangeburg, New York), they voted him "King of Swing."[30] Charles Melvin Williams had registered for the draft on October 16, 1940, just a few days before starting his new job with Benny Goodman.[31] He was called before the draft board three years later, on October 27, 1943. He was "rejected for military service. An ear ailment resulting from a mastoid operation which was performed before he went to Europe with Duke Ellington several years ago accounted for the board's action."[32] (It's not known if the operation was before the 1933 or 1939 European tour.) He was classified as 4-F by the War Department's Draft Board. He was fortunate that he didn't suffer the same fate as Chuck Peterson, a trumpet player in Woody Herman's band. Peterson was also classified 4-F, but when the draft board found out he was a musician, he was told, "we'll put you in 1-A, you can be a musician in the Army as well as you can in civvies."[33] At the beginning of 1943, it was estimated that 10,000 to 15,000 musicians were taken by the draft.[34]

He could take some comfort from the support he received from the troops he entertained. One letter he received said, "You are doing a swell job on the outside for the men in the service, so stay out there and carry on. You don't have to be a soldier to do your part. A little fun now and then means a lot to us."[35]

Cootie's band is the headliner of the show at their second Apollo Theater appearance in mid-October 1942. (*People's Voice*, courtesy of NewsBank/Readex)

The band played at the Apollo Theater for the second time in October. This time, the band had enough of a following to not need an insurance act like the Mills Brothers. Although Louis Bacon was still one of the vocalists with the band, he was no longer billed—Vinson and, although less prominently, Bailey were featured in the newspaper ad.[36]

MOE GALE AND THE SAVOY BALLROOM

> If you loved music and you loved dancing, the Savoy was the place to go....
> Nobody but the great dancers went, or at least those who thought they were.
> —FRANKIE MANNING[1]

Cootie was rumored to be in line for yet another studio job in October, just two months after turning down Raymond Scott and CBS, this time with Irving Miller's NBC orchestra. It didn't come to fruition because the need was urgent and would require Williams to drop everything immediately.[2] Williams was not going to give up his band easily.

Instead, Cootie decided to change management. He dropped William Morris and instead signed with Moe Gale and his agency. (For a short period of time in the interim, Cootie, unsuccessfully, tried to manage the band himself.)[3] By signing with Gale, Williams was able to get gigs at the Savoy Ballroom, because Gale gave preference to artists managed by him into that venue. As Cootie had said in his *People's Voice* column, "only one [venue], the Savoy, offers a permanent location for Negro bands" in New York City. "That public at the Savoy, they know! If they really like a band, you know it's going places."[4] Gale's agency specialized in Black talent, and at the time Williams signed with them, they had a roster that included Ella Fitzgerald, Erskine Hawkins, the Ink Spots, and Lucky Millinder. Moe Gale (born Moses Galewski, 1898–1964), besides owning the agency, was part of the team that owned the Savoy Ballroom, which consisted of his father, Charles Gale, and Charlie Buchanan. Buchanan (1898–1984), of African descent, immigrated to the United States at the age of six from Barbados. He owned a 35 percent share in the Savoy Ballroom, with the Gales owning the balance.[5] As manager, Buchanan was the face of the venue.

There was a problem in signing with Gale; he wanted 50 percent of the band in exchange for his management services. As Cootie said, "[D]uring that period of time, you had to give up some part of your band in order to be a success."[6] Bill Kenny of the Ink Spots described the deal they signed in 1939: "Gale took 20 per cent of our income for his cut. The New York State law allows only 10 per cent agent's fee, but Gale got away with it by promising other services. Aside from the 20 per cent[,] he also took 50 per cent of the balance to pay for advertising."[7] Doing the math, Gale's total cut worked out to 60 percent of the group's income! Kenny lamented that "Colored performers are the most exploited in the world. It's time we stopped letting other people take our money from us."[8] Bandleader and pianist Earl "Fatha" Hines weighed in on the matter, saying, "This is just a good illustration of how Negro artists have been bilked by booking agents and it offers conclusive evidence that something is wrong in the field of entertainment."[9] Moe Gale had also managed Chick Webb. There was no known contact between them and according to Gale's son, their agreement was a "handshake" deal.[10] It's hard to imagine that Gale didn't exact half of Webb's earnings, too.

Harlem's Savoy Ballroom was located at 596 Lenox Avenue, between 140th and 141st Streets.[11] It opened its doors on March 12, 1926. The grand opening featured "Fletcher Henderson And His Roseland Orchestra, The Charleston Bearcats, Direction Duncan, Fess Williams's Royal Flush Orchestra and A Brilliant Vaudeville Show."[12] At the opening, the *New York Age* reported:

> There is no amusement place uptown to compare with the new Savoy. When one enters the building he finds himself in a spacious lobby set off by a marble staircase and cut glass chandelier. The hall itself is decorated in a color scheme of orange and blue. One half of the floor is heavily carpeted. There are tables, settees, etc., where guests may rest between the dances or watch those on the floor. . . . The dance floor is about 200 feet long and about 50 feet wide. It is made of the best quality maple flooring, polished to [the] highest degree. Two band stands and a disappearing stage are in the rear. Above are spot lights which create a beautiful effect as they play their vari-collored [sic] lights on the dancers.[13]

Over time, the Savoy's dance floor would be nicknamed "The Track."[14]

The Savoy Ballroom was home turf for Cootie's early bandleader boss, drummer Chick Webb. Webb was fiercely competitive and loved the musical battles the Savoy regularly featured. The ballroom's two adjacent bandstands made these head-to-head competitions easy and also allowed two bands to alternate in order to provide continuous music. Pre-Gale, Cootie was booked at the Savoy for a single engagement on the night of August 30, where his band "battled" the Earl Hines band. In the newspaper ad for the event, the veteran Hines gets a larger photo and much more prominent billing. The large audience of 4,258 resulted in a "fine" gross of $3,085.[15]

These "Battles of the Bands" was something that Cootie took very seriously. On December 26, 1938, Duke Ellington's band met the Jimmie Lunceford Orchestra at Philadelphia's Penn Athletic Club.[16] In his autobiography, Barney Bigard recalled it as a battle that Ellington could have lost if not for Cootie's competitiveness:

> The first time Ellington met the Lunceford band in a battle of music, Lunceford led off with a string of Ellington compositions, plus their score of "Rose Room," a feature for Willie Smith on clarinet which was clearly based on the recorded Ellington arrangement. When the Ellington band's turn to play came the leader persisted in calling slow, quiet numbers which made little impact on the audience. The band became increasingly angry at this policy and its effect until Cootie Williams shouted, "For crying out loud, play something!" whereupon Duke turned his musicians loose—their blood well up—on "St. Louis Blues" and "Tiger Rag." That was the end of the Lunceford challenge for that night.[17]

After the "battle" with the Hines band, Cootie Williams played the first week of September at the Savoy Ballroom for the first time as a leader. As Williams noted in his August article for *The People's Voice*, the Savoy Ballroom was the only venue in the New York area that offered a "permanent location for Negro bands." But Moe Gale, owner of the Savoy, only booked acts that were managed by the Gale Agency, a firm run by Gale and his brother Tim. It's probable that this booking was an audition for the Gale Agency since it was shortly afterward that the press announced that Gale was negotiating to procure Williams from William Morris.[18]

Metronome sent Barry Ulanov to review Cootie's band in performance at the Savoy; he had reviewed them a few months prior at their New York debut at the Apollo Theater. The article was titled "Cootie's Crew Worthy Of Its Leader" with a subtitle "Trumpet Star's Band Kicks Like Mad, Offers Listeners Musicianship, Showmanship and Cootie Williams." Cootie had taken the criticism of his lack of showmanship to heart and in Ulanov's opinion, he had corrected that deficiency: "Cootie, who was just a great trumpeter, but no murder as a showman, with Duke and with Benny has turned into one of the most ingratiating and most showmanly leaders in the business. . . . His singing, his grimacing as he trumpets, his affable handling of the crowd, both by smile and by word—these things are big time."[19] (Another reviewer knew Cootie's true nature was the cause of his hosting difficulties—Cootie's true nature was to be "quiet and shy offstage.")[20] But not everyone thought the hosting was good; one *Down Beat* reviewer thought "his showmanship would make Ted Lewis cringe."[21]

The Billboard said that due to Cootie's "dynamic personality and torrid trumpeting," he made the right decision to nix the Raymond Scott offer. Cootie "seems to be at the peak of his playing skill. Working with open horn or mutes or plunger, the man doesn't play a note that isn't thrilling, exciting or merely wonderful. And watching him blow that horn is a pleasure." But they wondered if the band was a good enough for him. The reviewer notes that the band seemed to be made up of 3-As and 4-Fs[22] and as a result it may be why the band "sounds as tho [sic] it has been places, rather than as if it were going places." In summary, they predicted that once the band was tightened up, reaching "the top is a cinch."

Overall, in only eight months, the critics were declaring the band a polished unit. Ulanov praised their musicianship, saying "Much attention has been paid [to] the ensemble and the sections that go to make it up. Result is lots of smoothness, on the whole good intonation, and an impressive evenness of attack." The overall rating was A minus, a very good rating for a new band.[23] "On the asset side is the band's boffo opener, 'Rollem' [sic, "Roll 'Em"], and a mid-bill group of tunes including 'Western Blues' [sic, "West End Blues"] and 'St. Louis Blues' is the standout, with Vinson a close second. His impromptu dancing and personality singing of 'Cherry Red Blues' get guffaws and palm thumping from the mob. Vocalist, Pearl Bailey, a looker, shows oomph but poor taste in trying to swing a ballad, 'At Last.' She improves on 'Hip, Hip Hooray' and 'Git It.'..."[24]

Pearl Bailey (1918–1990) was born in Newport News, Virginia, which was also the birthplace of Ella Fitzgerald. (Bailey was just eleven months younger than Fitzgerald.) They had something else in common—they both won the Apollo Theater's Amateur Night in 1934.[25] Cootie and Pearl clashed; the two of them had different visions for her style. Cootie said, "I had a very hard time with Pearl." Williams believed that she had something within that wasn't being presented. "She'd say, 'Well, I can't do this this way.' And I'd say, 'Well, you're going to do it this way.' And I made her do it that way."[26] As the boss, Cootie prevailed; ultimately it came down to "she was going to do it my way. And I made her do it my way. And that's the reason why she became a success." Although there was resistance, Cootie was able to say, "she thanks me today."[27] In her autobiography, Bailey did indeed credit Cootie for his advice saying, "Cootie had a great influence on my getting together a basic act."[28]

Bailey recalled it wasn't easy being the band's singer: "He never called me for one song; I sat on that cotton-picking bandstand till I wanted to cry, waiting my turn. Then he would call me to do about six numbers at once (no dancing).

Everyone else wanted me to throw in that fast buck dance, but then I thought of myself as strictly a vocalist."[29]

The band's popularity was increasing. They packed in the crowds at a November stand at Baltimore's Royal Theater. ("SRO for all four shows").[30] Working at the Savoy gave Williams a level of stability and visibility. And from the Savoy, he was able to broadcast late night (12:30 AM) over the Mutual Broadcasting System (MBS). His show was broadcast by most of the network "coast-to-coast," giving him an audience that still was not able to hear him on records.[31]

TRUMPET STUDENT

John Hammond, a fervent fan and booster of Cootie Williams, told *Down Beat* a story about Cootie's trumpet virtuosity:

> Adolph Busch, the conductor of chamber orchestras, was preparing for a series of Town Hall concerts presenting Bach's six Brandenburg Concertos. The 2nd Brandenburg has the most difficult trumpet part ever written, and Busch had been unable to find a symphonic player able to play it properly. In desperation he came to me, asking whether there was anybody in the jazz world capable of doing it, and I suggested Cootie, who was breaking in his new band at the Savoy Ballroom.
>
> It was necessary to find either a small F trumpet [piccolo trumpet], or an even tinier archaic instrument, of which Benny Baker was the only possessor in New York. This was immediately borrowed, and Cootie came down to the apartment of Rudolph Serkin, the great pianist who is married to Busch's daughter, and read the part practically without a mistake. The two classical musicians were astonished and delighted, but they were unable to use Cootie for the concerts. It seemed that the difference in embouchures was so great that it might affect the solos on his nightly broadcasts from the Savoy! Bitterly disappointed, Busch had to substitute a clarinet for the trumpet, and Cootie was robbed of perhaps the greatest publicity break and musical experience of his career.[1]

Robert Lawrence, a music critic at the *New York Herald*, said of Williams: "He can produce a high 'F' that would shame any symphony man who parades the difficulties of Bach's brass parts. He can give out a hot trill that sounds like a death rattle; his entire tone is gaudy and beautiful."[2] If Cootie Williams had

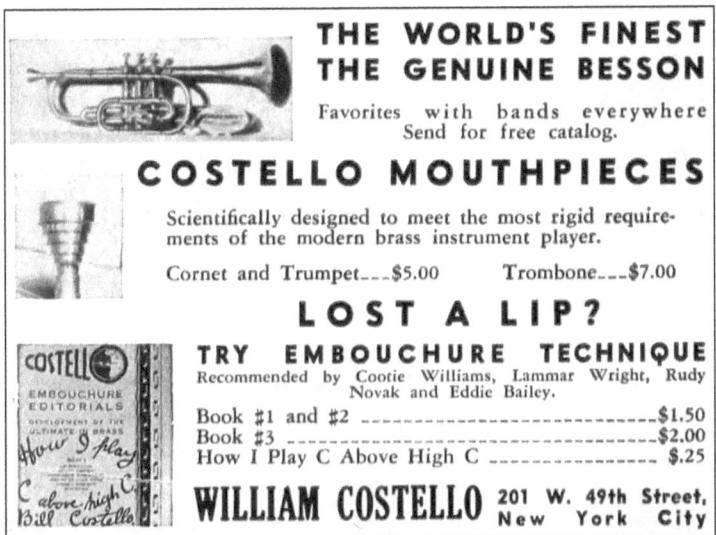

Advertisement in the January 1941 issue of *Metronome* for the William Costello School of Music featuring Cootie's endorsement. (*Metronome*, Courtesy of RIPM Jazz Periodicals)

been born later, perhaps he could have pursued a career in both the classical and jazz fields, like Wynton Marsalis did many years later.

Cootie was a serious student of the trumpet. Long after Charlie Lipscomb's lessons back in his Mobile youth, Williams continued to study the instrument. When he left Ellington in 1940, Cootie said, "Sure, I'll miss him, but I'll have more time to study and rest my lip."[3] He took lessons from William Costello in New York after he joined Ellington and said in 1972, "[i]f I didn't have to travel on the road all the time, I'd still be studying."[4] Costello was a respected "legit" trumpet player and played for the Philadelphia Symphony Orchestra and New York's Paramount Theatre. He was famous for his no-pressure embouchure system and his focus on a proper high-note embouchure. One of his students recalled (in an undated anecdote): "I do remember the day when I was in the studio and in walked Cootie Williams. He was there for music reading lessons with Bill Costello, however what transpired in the studio was interesting. We could hear Bill Costello challenging Cootie by his climb up the scale to a double high C. That did not stop Cootie. He climbed up to the stratosphere and matched the double high C. Soon after that they got down to work on Arban exercise from the scale section on. I don't think that Cootie had much trouble. Bill was an excellent teacher."[5] When Costello died in 1956, he bequeathed his trumpet to Cootie.[6]

William Costello had a semi-regular brass advice column for *Metronome*. In his December 1937 installment, he used Cootie as an example to encourage a student who thought his lips were too big for the trumpet: "You mention

For a few years, Cootie Williams deviated from his devotion to Conn trumpets to endorse Rudy Mück's trumpets. (*Metronome*, Courtesy of RIPM Jazz Periodicals)

colored boys having no embouchure trouble. I happen to be the teacher of Cootie Williams and [Lammar] Wright, the first-named with Duke Ellington and the latter with Cab Calloway. These men are tops without doubt."[7] (Wright would later be a member of Cootie's big band's trumpet section.) Costello was kind compared to *Down Beat*'s advice columnist who told someone doubtful about success on trumpet due to lip size: "If they would look about them they would see such men as Louis Armstrong, Roy Eldridge, Cootie Williams; these boys have Ubangi lips in comparison to the [prospective trumpet student], and it don't stop them from playing a mess of trumpet."[8]

♪

Cootie endorsed and played Conn trumpets throughout most of his professional life. It's not known exactly when he started with them, but in 1932 an advertisement appeared in *Metronome* for the "New Connqueror Trumpet with {New Principle} Vocabell."[9] In the ad "Charlie Williams, 1st Trumpet Duke Ellington's Orchestra" is quoted, saying "Have just ordered one of the new 40B Trumpets in burnished gold. After trying it I knew I could never be happy until I owned one. What a horn!" At the bottom of the advertisement, there's a statement to inform readers that the enthusiastic reviews are sincere: "All Conn testimonials are guaranteed to be voluntary and genuine expressions of opinion for which no payment of any kind has been or will be paid."[10]

It may have been the influence of Costello that caused Williams to switch from his Conn trumpet to an eponymous Rudy Mück brand trumpet around 1937.[11] Mück made the mouthpieces Costello was famous for. But at some point, Cootie switched back to Conn and played that make until the end of his career.[12]

Cootie told *Music and Rhythm* about the importance of proper training in 1941: "I've studied a lot with teachers during the 15 years that I've been playing. You can learn a lot about legitimate trumpeting, breathing, attack, etc. by keeping on your toes and keeping an eye on the legit stuff—which can be turned into a very valuable asset in jazz playing."[13]

Additionally, Williams was always open to listening to other trumpeters and learning from them. "In the 1920s and 1930s I would sit at home and play records and listen to Bix Beiderbecke, Red Nichols, Louis Armstrong, Bunny Berigan, and others. I would listen and compare them to see what made them tick and what they were doing. Later on I would listen to records by Roy Eldridge and others." Later listening material included Dizzy Gillespie and Miles Davis. "It gives you ideas if you listen to others and keeps you alive in music."[14] On another occasion he said, "Many jazz players of today listen to just one person, and after a while, they become that person. They never find themselves."[15]

CLOSING AT THE SAVOY

Usually Cootie appeared on radio with his band, but he made an appearance without his trumpet or orchestra for a show hosted by critic Leonard Feather on a music-based quiz show on New York radio station WMAC called *Platterbrains*. The format consisted of a panel of musicians, journalists, and critics being invited to answer musical questions submitted by listeners, usually involving a short musical segment played by the host. If the listener's questions stumps the panel, they are rewarded with a subscription to *Metronome*.[1] Cootie participated in the November 14, 1942, show along with pianist Joe Sullivan and writers/critics George Simon, Bob Bach, and Barry Ulanov. Fortunately, a recording of this episode exists, housed in the Leonard Feather Collection at the University of Idaho. Cootie's participation is minimal; he seems to be the shy young man described in earlier press accounts.

♪

Being based out of the Savoy gave Williams the opportunity to live out of his own home instead of a hotel room on the road. He was able spend Christmas at home in 1942 and he and Catherine hosted a "bang-up" party at their 555 Edgecombe Avenue apartment.[2] The Ellington band was in Detroit at time,[3] so the wives of Otto Hardwicke and Harry Carney were in attendance, along with actress Fredi Washington, who was married to trombonist Lawrence Brown.[4]

This Savoy stint ended on January 3, 1943, but he had already built up a fan base. They were said to "eagerly await his theme 'FLY RIGHT' over the ether waves!"[5] *The People's Voice* said, "Cootie Williams and his growling trumpet came up with one of those good old good ones Sunday afternoon on the broadcast from the Savoy. 'Solid' is a thoroughly overworked Harlemese

Ring in 1943 with Cootie Williams and more at the Savoy Ballroom. (*The People's Voice*, courtesy of NewsBank/Readex)

adjective, but that's the only word that could adequately describe the rhythmic riot that they pitched."[6]

The ODT bus exemption was not renewed upon its January 1943 expiration due to the shortage of gas and tires being even worse. (Tires became a valuable and rare commodity. *Music and Rhythm* published a photo of a smiling Count Basie sitting on a set of tires gifted to him by a fan.)[7]

According to the band's tenor saxophonist, Eddie Davis (who had yet to gain the nickname "Lockjaw"), Cootie was eager to engage his old boss Duke Ellington in a battle of the bands at the Savoy Ballroom. That happened on March 9, 1943, when Ellington was booked for a one-night engagement in honor of the Ballroom's seventeenth birthday along with Cootie's band. As Davis described it, it was "excellent. Duke gave more a concert and we're swinging. And Duke [played in a] sophisticated, concert style. Ellington didn't emphasize swing. He emphasized soul [and] . . . more depth musically." Cootie's "attitude was coming from a different dimension [with a] swinging orchestra, with good soloists."[8]

Alto saxophonist Charlie Holmes remembered it differently. The Ellington band started off slowly and was thrown off a bit because Duke wasn't present at the start of their set. So the Ellington band played with a lack of focus and "they didn't sound good. So anyway, Cootie got on the stand and played his numbers, to get that first whack in. So man, the house was comin' down, boy. They applauded and applauded. And next time we went up there he put Eddie Vinson on, sing[ing] his best numbers and so forth. While you got 'em down you keep 'em down, you know. So man, he was carryin' on."

Holmes continued: "[E]ven the wives of the Ellington members were saying, 'Yes that's right. Duke got cut tonight.' Well, they was as much for Cootie as anybody else, because all the wives knew Cootie from Duke's band. And they were saying, 'Yes, Duke got cut tonight.' Well, Duke wasn't in form that night, and the band wasn't in form—believe me . . . We had a loud band. Of course, all the notes wasn't always right, but they could play loud."[9]

Metronome reviewed the Cootie Williams band performance on April 11 at a 4:00 p.m. Sunday matinee. The reviewer had high hopes: "Cootie is the number one threat in the field of new bands today. With every conceivable obstacle in his way, Cootie has persisted through unbelievably discouraging experiences and finally emerged with the combination of his heart's desire." Taking from his time with Duke and Benny, and his own requirements, he "has developed a band that jumps, plays in tune, has amazingly unexpected sustaining beauty and power."[10] At the end of that review, the reader was advised to "go and catch the band, and hear and thrill for yourself."

Due to popular demand, Cootie Williams was in the midst of his second holdover at the Savoy.[11] But soon that opportunity would evaporate. Cootie Williams and His Orchestra was still the featured attraction, along with the Savoy Sultans, when on April 17, just a few days after the date of the performance that generated that glowing review, the Savoy Ballroom was shut down by the US Army and the New York Police Vice Squad. The publicly given reason was that the Savoy was a place known to facilitate prostitution and that numerous soldiers contracted venereal diseases from these encounters.[12] The real reason: the Savoy was an integrated club, one of the few in the country. Popular opinion held that it was closed "to put Harlem out of bounds for white civilians and soldiers."[13] While no one denied that women could be obtained at the Savoy, it wasn't something that couldn't be found at numerous other clubs around the country—it was a bare fig leaf of an excuse. The Savoy Ballroom was one of the few integrated venues in the country. And as an integrated place, it continually drew attention from those who didn't like "race mixing." It was closed because "there is no color line at the Savoy [and] whites mingle freely with colored. . . . management frequently had been warned of this co-mingling."[14] Pressure to change or close the Savoy had been building for several years. In order to appease the authorities, over a several year period, the venue stopped booking white bands, ceased advertisement in white newspapers, and stopped selling liquor. But none of this was enough to stop April's closure.[15]

The bands of Erskine Hawkins and Taft Jordan and the Sunset Royals Orchestra were scheduled to follow but were suddenly left in a lurch. The closure also put a staff of sixty-five people out of work.[16] Cootie wasn't immediately affected by the Savoy Ballroom shutdown; in May he had weeklong stints in New York City at the Apollo and the Hurricane.

23

FILM VODVIL

Screenshot of Cootie Williams and His Orchestra from Columbia's *Film Vodvil*.

In the first part of June 1943, the Cootie Williams Orchestra started work on what would become their only appearance on film. Columbia Studios, over a two-day period, filmed the group at their Movietone Studios for a movie short subject as part of the *Film Vodvil* series.[1] It was part of a Columbia series of films dedicated to generating musical content to screen in theaters. Others in the series included the orchestras of Saxie Dowell, Art Mooney, and Bobby Byrne. The finished product was only ten minutes long, and it played in theaters around the country, part of the fare that filled out a movie package, along with newsreels, cartoons, and so on. Jazz film historian Mark Cantor calls it "one of the most important band shorts of the decade." Why? There are several reasons—it's the only documentation of this band, it's not bogged down by a ridiculous story line, it's just a straight music presentation. Also, it's the only footage of Cootie Williams leading his band. Equally rare are the film appearances of musicians like Eddie "Cleanhead" Vinson and Sam "The Man" Taylor at this early point in their careers.[2]

After the credits, an attractive young lady, who seems to be uncomfortable on camera, is shown holding a title card that reads "COOTIE WILLIAMS/ His Hot Trumpet/and Orchestra." Then the band, seated on a three-tier riser, appears playing "Get Hep" with vigorous conducting by Cootie Williams. (This song is sometimes misidentified as "Wild Fire.") The song is a brisk blues, and the first chorus of solos is split into four-bar segments for the rhythm section of pianist Fletcher Smith, bassist Norman Keenan, and drummer Butch Ballard. Next, a whole chorus each for trombonist Ed Burke and tenor saxophonist Sam "The Man" Taylor. Cootie takes three choruses, and his solo is nearly identical to one heard on the May 1944 Jubilee session recording of "Roll 'Em." While Fletcher Smith (1913–1993) isn't well known, Dizzy Gillespie was impressed with him, saying "[he could] play some piano."[3] Charlie Holmes said that Cootie "had a lot of good piano players come in that band. In fact, all the piano [players] he ever had was [sic] outstanding. . . . But they were comin' in and goin' out, changing the piano. And Cootie was just as nice as he could be to them."[4]

Next, after changing from his band uniform to street clothes, Eddie "Cleanhead" Vinson is featured on "Things Ain't What They Used to Be." Vinson sings, or rather lip synchs, the song in a deadpan mode with both hands in his pockets. As the song ends, he's shown leaving the scene's frame with a shuffle step.

After Vinson, the title card announces the "Douglas Brothers, Acrobatic Dancers." From Chicago,[5] Albert Lee Roy Douglas (1913–2004) and Maurice Frederick Douglas (1915–2000), known as Al and Freddie, dance to an unknown number. In the first part of the 1940s, they performed in theater bills with Jimmy Dorsey, Andy Kirk, Fletcher Henderson, and Erskine Hawkins. Despite this exposure, they never broke into the big leagues, with this being their only filmed appearance. Fayard Nicholas of the more famous Nicholas Brothers dance team "remembered them and commented that they were skillful, professional dancers who 'had their own thing going. Of course, they weren't the Nicholas Brothers!'"[6]

The next segment is "Laurel Watson, Harlem's Heat Wave Singing 'Giddup Mule.'" The song features the band singing background and supplying hand clapping. Watson (1911–2001) was another talent that didn't get the recognition she deserved. Except for a late-in-life comeback, she was sadly under the radar through most of her singing career. Before this appearance, she sang with the bands of Don Redman and Roy Eldridge.[7] Pearl Bailey had left the band in May and "Giddup Mule" was one of her vocal features.[8]

The last full segment features two pairs (Russell Williams and Connie Hill, Leon James and Dottie Mae Johnson) of "Lindy Hoppers"[9] engaged in an exuberant dance routine while the band plays "Let's Keep on Jumping."[10] As was the custom of the time, the soundtrack was prerecorded, and the visuals were mimed. Thus, during this song, Cootie can be heard playing a short trumpet solo while he's busy conducting the band with the horn nowhere near his lips. As always, Cootie's trumpet work was notable. The press noted that "Cootie's trumpeting won the raves of the sound technicians, who are very hard customers to please."[11]

Cootie was quite exuberant in the film. How much that might have been juiced up for the filming is not known, but one suspects it wasn't too far from his usual stage demeanor of the time. Based on this film, one critic said Williams was "leaping about like a demented Cab Calloway."[12] In an interview around that same time, he was asked if "he liked hopping around and rolling his eyes and conforming to the stage caricature of a Negro jazz musician." For those who criticized his stage demeanor, he replied, "That is showmanship. I'll have to do that as long as I front a band." The interviewer told him he was good enough of a musician to get by on his playing. Williams disagreed. "I can go out and hit a note that nobody else can, but who's going to know it? When I started the band I didn't use any showmanship at all. We had a very tough time. And Mister, I was playing a lot of horn!"[13]

The finished product was released into theaters on October 8 with the movie trade publications designating it for "colored patronage"[14] being "a natural for Negro [movie] houses"[15] while providing "entertaining fare for the jive addicts."[16] The film was even used to entertain the Negro troops in North Africa. A soldier writing from the war zone wrote, "I was pleasantly surprised yesterday while sitting in a show, when an up-and-coming bandleader in a short subject was flashed upon the screen. It was good all the way through, only much too short. First, he played wild swing, then mellow ballads with a girl vocalist, then featured himself in a couple of numbers, which had a touch of Ellington." He can be forgiven for getting a few of the details of the movie wrong.[17]

The band was booked into another successful week at the Apollo Theater starting July 30. This would be the third of five appearances for 1943, a solid indication of the Cootie's popularity. *Variety* gave the appearance a rave review, stating that the show was "tiptop start to finale with every act registering." Acknowledging the popularity of the Williams band, they called it "the draw," but had to take a swipe at Cootie's stage presence saying, "the rotund leader hopp[ed] vigorously about while giving out [well known songs]." Cleanhead

This newspaper advertisement for a Chattanooga, Tennessee "dance and concert for colored" is typical of those run during Cootie's 1943 southern tour. (*Chattanooga Times*)

was "his usual droll self, galloping off with most of the evening's laughs as a result of his singing and impromptu dancing."[18]

Press hype said that Cootie was solidly booked on the East Coast, preventing him from taking care of the audience demand in other parts of the country.[19] But it wasn't true; the band undertook its first southern tour in mid-August, starting in Norfolk, Virginia. For two months, the band played in North Carolina, South Carolina, Alabama, Tennessee, Georgia, and Florida. For their September 24 gig in Chattanooga, the arrangement was for Cootie to play an 8:00 p.m. "concert for white spectators" to be followed with "dancing for Negroes to begin at 9."[20] There was talk that the band would use the tour to work their way to the West Coast for appearances at either the Hollywood Casino or Culver City's Casa Manana,[21] but after playing Macon, Georgia, the band returned to Philadelphia for a week's engagement with Billy Eckstine on October 15.[22] During the years he was away from Ellington and Goodman, Williams's visits to the West Coast were rare.

Sometime during this same year, Benny Goodman unsuccessfully offered Cootie $350 a week to return to his organization.[23] The following year, Cootie said Goodman "sent me a wire offering me four fifty a week. My wife opened it. She grabbed me and brought me down here. She said she can't wait five years and that this is the end of the band now. I half wanted to go back to Benny, but I decided to stick it out. My wife wouldn't speak to me for three days. I would have dinner and she would sit there and not eat with me."[24] (This implies Catherine Williams gave Cootie five years to try his luck as an orchestra leader.)

While the critics and audiences were raving about his band, Cootie still was not as successful as he could have been. "It's high time some[one] started a Society For The Prevention of Obscurity For Cootie Williams. When this magnificent musician paid a visit to Harlem's Apollo Theatre a few weeks ago, his own performance, as well as that of his band, made one reflect what a musical tragedy it is that the Williams aggregation is being restricted to colored one nighters and theaters, and has never yet crashed the lucrative white theatre dates and locations with airtime."[25] *Variety* noted that Cootie didn't have a strong white following—"Among the ofay trade [his reputation] may not be as strong as in Harlem."[26] This lack of crossover would limit his touring and earnings potential. Cootie said, "In the music business, if you were made by a white person, you were a standard name in both fields of black and white, but, if you were made by a black person, then you were only in the black field—for a certain time and then you died out."[27]

As a result of several months of legal maneuvers and editorial acrimony, the Savoy Ballroom reopened on October 22 after being dark for six months. In an act of continuity, the bands that were playing there when it was shuttered (Williams and the Savoy Sultans) were booked for the opening. In a concession to the authorities, the Savoy management had made some changes—personnel were added to the ballroom's staff to make sure there wasn't any more of the type of illicit activities that were the putative cause of the closure. And the scale for the sidemen playing there was raised from "$38.50 per week to about $50," a raise of 30 percent.[28] This applied only to the second bands, like the Sultans, since Williams and other name bands were already paid more.[29]

The Friday night reopening was a hugely successful affair. The fire marshal limited the capacity to 1,500 patrons, frustrating an estimated 10,000 people standing outside hoping for a chance to get in. *The People's Voice* reported that "Those fortunate enough to gain admittance were treat to an evening of high jovality [sic] with the bands of Cootie Williams and Al Cooper outdoing themselves as they virtually played their hearts out."[30] A surprise awaited those who managed to get in—the hugely popular Ink Spots, who were not on the bill, did a spontaneous set and sang a few songs for the crowd.[31]

Like *Metronome*, *The Billboard* raved about the band: "The band has almost everything necessary to boost it into the commercially successful class of Count Basie and Lionel Hampton. First there is Williams himself; his playing is a byword in music circles and his fronting is fun to watch. Second, there is Eddie Vinson who has built up a tremendous following with his robust alto sax work and blues singing, sold with tremendous showmanship." They named the small band within the band as the third element and added that the full band "kick[ed] like a mule."[32]

After the triumph at the Savoy, the band moved just a little over a mile away to the Apollo Theatre for a week's booking. By the end of the year, reviewers were noting the small band as a standout attraction, even though the names were badly mangled—"Eddie Binson on alto sax, Ves Paine on drums, Buddy Powell on piano . . ."[33]

A RETURN TO THE STUDIO

At the end of December, *Esquire* magazine announced the results of their expert-derived "All-American Jazz Band." (The results were published in the February 1944 issue.) Louis Armstrong won first place (Gold) for trumpet, with Cootie taking second place (Silver). Armstrong also placed first as male vocalist. In his analysis of the results, Belgian jazz author Robert Goffin expressed happiness with the high ranking given to Cootie Williams, especially because it meant lower rankings for someone like Harry James, "whose playing has become commercial and correspondingly bland."[1] This was *Esquire*'s first real jazz poll. In 1943, Goffin alone had selected their "All-American Band"[2] and perhaps *Esquire* realized there was something odd about a foreigner generating an "All-American" list.

When Williams went into the Commodore studio with a group of Esquire All-Stars to record under the supervision of Leonard Feather, it had been over a year and a half since he had put music on wax. (Commodore was one of the first small independent labels that settled with Petrillo's musicians union.) Besides Cootie Williams (Silver winner), Edmond Hall was on clarinet, Cootie's bandmate from his teen years. Hall was the only non-winner to appear, but he certainly deserved to be in this company. The gold and silver winners for clarinet, Benny Goodman and Barney Bigard, respectively, weren't available. Fellow Henderson band alumnus Coleman Hawkins was also a member of the group.

Given the limitations of recording time during that era, giving everyone a chance to solo on these star-laden session resulted in short statements from everyone. On "Esquire Bounce," Cootie's only solo is heard on the bridge of the opening theme statement. The great piano virtuoso Art Tatum gets a whole

The Esquire All Stars in the recording studio, December 4, 1943. Cootie and his trumpet are the center of attention for most of those assembled. From left to right: Art Tatum, Al Casey, Coleman Hawkins, Big Sid Catlett, Cootie Williams, Edmond Hall, Oscar Pettiford, Leonard Feather (Pictorial Press Ltd/Alamy Stock Photo)

Full page ad for "The Big Three" tour from the January 5, 1944, issue of *Variety*. (*Variety*)

chorus, and Al Casey, Edmond Hall, and Coleman Hawkins split choruses. "Boff Boff" is taken at a tempo brisk enough to allow full chorus solos from Tatum and Hawkins and a hot Williams closing the recording out with a chorus and a half. "My Ideal" is a ballad feature for Tatum and Hawkins at their best. Hall's only solo on the session is heard on "Esquire Blues" but at least he gets two choruses, compared to Cootie's single chorus.

During the first week of December 1943, the band was booked at the Savoy Ballroom. The run was very successful, with Cootie breaking all previous attendance records.[3] Additionally, the band continued to draw rave reviews. *Down Beat* reviewed the band at the Savoy Ballroom during this booking:

> "Holy Moley, what a band!" Gents, this is *it* and if anybody in the audience thinks that Cootie Williams made a mistake when he left the Duke to build his own band, anybody can hop over to the N.Y. Paramount theater in a few days and change his mind. The first obvious item of interest in this full-blooded band in the leader's amazing trumpet work. I don't want to malign either Harry James or Charlie Spivak, but the bald truth is that Cootie can play their kind of pop tune and out-puretone them with several yards of sweet notes to spare. But the sweet stuff, of course, is just a by-product; Cootie's real music coming in with the jazz beat. As far as I'm concerned, Cootie represents on trumpet what Benny Goodman stands for on clarinet: the unbeatable king of them all, whether you're talking about tone, phrasing, ideas or you name it. And when you add Cootie's unique growl style to his list of accomplishments, the contest becomes a walk-away.[4]

December saw the announcement that Cootie Williams and His Orchestra would begin a thirty-three-week cross-country tour. This promised to be an exceptional undertaking. As *The People's Voice* said, "[t]he general rule with bands is to have one or two acts that are moderately known in their show, but this will be a triple-starred affair with The Ink Spots and Ella Fitzgerald sharing honors. It's fast company, which means all concerned will stay on their toes, with the result that it should be a bang-up show."[5] To round out the show, there was dancing from Ralph Brown plus a comedy dance team, Moke and Poke. The price attached to this package was $9,500 (which would be over $160,000 in today's dollars) per week, plus a percentage based on business.[6] The stage show would be paired with a movie and there were usually four to five performances per day. (According to the Ink Spots' leader singer Bill Kenny, the idea for the tour came from him "lock, stock and barrel.")[7] But Ella Fitzgerald and the Ink Spots had done a similar Gale tour in mid-1940. The backing band was Ella Fitzgerald and Her Orchestra, an organization that existed briefly when Ella took over Chick Webb's band upon his death.[8] The 1940 tour logged 18,000 miles and hit thirty-six of the forty-eight states.[9] This touring group was sometimes billed as "The Big Three," a reference to the "Big Three" leading World War II's Allies—the United States, the United Kingdom, and Russia.

The outlook for the band certainly seemed bright. It may have been a factor in Cootie gifting wife Catherine with "a fine mink coat" that Christmas.[10] Given the long tour ahead, it was fortunate that Cootie and the band were able to stay home for the holidays, with gigs at the Savoy Ballroom, the Golden Gate, and the Renaissance Ballroom filling the calendar for the month of December.

♪

January 1944 found the Cootie Williams orchestra finally making their sophomore recordings, after nearly two years in existence, for the Hit Record label. The recording ban would still be in effect for a few months thereafter until Decca, one of the big three labels, agreed to the union's terms in September. A number of the smaller independent labels had reached a settlement with the musicians' union.[11] Hit Records, run by Eli Oberstein (1901–1960), gained the right to record union musicians in November 1943.[12] Hit, along with Decca, the record label for the Ink Spots and Ella Fitzgerald, came to an agreement before the bigger firms, RCA Victor and Columbia.[13] *Variety* reported that Cootie's deal was not long-term, but on a single date basis.[14] But by mid-year, Oberstein was offering multiple date recording contracts.[15] Oberstein had continue to release new music during the recording ban, but they were legal because they were recorded in Mexico, where the AFM (American Federation of Musicians) had no authority. The problem was that Oberstein's story wasn't true. But he was able to feign ignorance about the provenance of his recording stock, saying that he bought them in good faith.[16]

On January 4, the band's "sextette" recorded four songs. Two days later, the sextette was in the studio to record an additional set of four songs. Later that same day, the full orchestra convened to record four more songs. Recording twelve songs in a two-day period was probably because the upcoming tour meant it would be several months before the band would be available to record again. Oddly, the full band was only used as backing for the vocals of Vinson and Bailey and didn't record any instrumental selections.

These recordings are the first made by pianist Earl "Bud" Powell, already a monster player at age nineteen. This was also the first time in the studio for tenor saxophonist Eddie "Lockjaw" Davis (1922–1986). Davis described Williams as "easy to work with. But very demanding. He didn't tolerate any

Cootie's Hit label album, *Echoes of Harlem*, featuring darkie artwork that was offensive and outdated even in 1944.

nonsense [like] being late or not playing your part properly. [He was a] very conscientious music man."[17]

The eight sextette sides were released individually, but they were also issued in album form under the title *Echoes of Harlem*. *Metronome* was enthusiastic in their praise: "This album presents all his trumpet moods and styles—the famous growl technique, the less famous but just as thrilling open tone; riff numbers and exquisitely played melodies; every aspect of this man's unbounded talent is represented here."[18]

One of the "sextette" numbers was Fats Waller's "Honeysuckle Rose," but the melody that everyone is familiar with was not played. Instead, a contrafact was used, one "which was so fascinating that we're willing to bet every small band in the country will be using it on 'Honeysuckle' within three months." This prediction didn't come to pass. Williams could have claimed this contrafact as an original and kept the royalties for himself. But Fats Waller had died the previous month, so one suspects it was decided that the disk would be more saleable as "Honeysuckle Rose."

Unfortunately, the album featured a horrible "darkie" style cover, which *Metronome* castigated them for: "Hit Records should be ashamed of the insulting, minstrel-style pictures of Negroes on their album cover, which will hurt the sales in colored districts."[19]

The full band was on hand that same day, recording for only the second time in their almost two years of existence. All four tracks included vocals, two each by Eddie "Cleanhead" Vinson and Pearl Bailey. Although Bailey had left the band in May 1943, apparently she was coaxed backed temporarily to record.[20] It may have been thought that she was needed to counterbalance Vinson's vocals.

Bailey's two numbers, "Tess's Torch Song" and "Now I Know," were arranged by the great Don Redman.[21] Both songs were from the Danny Kaye/Dinah Shore movie musical *Up in Arms*, which was released that same year.[22] Bailey's version made a one-week appearance on the *Billboard* music chart at #19.[23] These would become the only documentation of her work with the Cootie Williams Orchestra. The day after this session, the band would begin touring with Ella Fitzgerald as the featured vocalist, so Bailey was no longer needed.

"Red Blues" also known as "Cherry Red Blues," was a big hit for Williams and Vinson. It was part of Vinson's repertoire until the end of his life.[24] The song was written by Pete Johnson and Big Joe Turner and recorded by them in 1939 under the group name Pete Johnson and His Boogie Woogie Boys, with Turner taking the vocal honors on the disk.[25] Vinson and the song even figured in the memoir of one the shoe shiners at the Savoy, one Malcolm Little—"My friends now included musicians like . . . Cootie Williams, and Eddie 'Cleanhead' Vinson, who'd kid me about his conk—he had nothing up there but skin. He was hitting the height then with his song, 'Hey, Pretty Mama, Chunk Me In Your Big Brass Bed' [*sic*]."[26] (Little would later convert to Islam and become Malcolm X.) The tune starts with a short fanfare played by Vinson's alto, with the introduction completed with a short growling statement by Williams. After two choruses of Vinson making a strong instrumental statement, he sings five choruses with plunger muted answers from Cootie. Delivered with his trademark voice breaks, squeals, yelps and good humor, it became a calling card for Vinson. The ending lyrics were both humorous and (for the time period) risqué, closing with "Take me, pretty mama, chunk me in your big brass bed / Rock me, mama, 'til my face turns cherry red, cherry red."

The song was banned by New York radio station WOV—"no discs with off-color lyrics are ever played on WOV record shows." The station abided by a "clean jive" policy and "believes [the] smut element in certain recordings, of which 'Red Blues' is characterized as prime example, will hurt all jive." The station emphasized that they play other recordings by Cootie Williams that have passed a "purity test."[27]

"Red Blues" only managed to land on the *Billboard* Music Popularity Chart once (in August)[28]—"It wasn't very popular with the white people," said Cootie.[29] But it was a fixture on the "Harlem Hit Parade" (*Billboard*'s segregated charting of the Negro music trade) for thirty-nine weeks.[30] Its popularity was such that one columnist said it was a requirement for accompanying a good meal: "I enjoy my food most when I can hear Cootie Williams's band making with *Cherry Red Blues* and the like."[31]

The *Billboard* music popularity charts were segregated. The chart without any qualifying adjectives was the popular, mainstream or white records. "The Harlem Hit Parade" was the Black records and "folk" or "hillbilly" was what is now called country and western. "Red Blues" was able to make all three charts. On August 26, 1944, it made the white charts once in position #23.[32] During the same year, it also made the folk charts several times.

Perhaps as a small contribution to the war effort, Williams composed "Got to do some war work, baby." While the lyrics don't rival Cole Porter, the sentiments seem sincere. The overall theme of the song relies heavily on the sentiments of "Giddup Mule," featured in the previous year's short, *Film Vodvil*, which among other thoughts said, "we'll have to farm to win this fight." Recorded by a sextet of Cootie Williams, saxophonists Eddie "Cleanhead" Vinson, and Eddie "Lockjaw" Davis and a rhythm section of Bud Powell, Norman Keenan, and Vess Payne on January 4, 1944, after an ensemble statement of the thirty-two-bar theme, Cootie takes the vocal. After three short eight-bar solos by Williams, Davis, and Powell, the last eight bars of theme with a two-bar tag with a last vocal exclamation of "I'll guess I have to take the farm." (In Cootie's Alabama inflection, "farm" comes out as "fom.")

Radio and records were important financial and promotional tools for any band. While Cootie had a radio outlet, his first orchestra recordings from the April 1, 1942, session for OKeh weren't immediately released due to the wartime shellac shortage.[33] In early 1942, the WPB limited shellac usage to 30 percent of the amount used in 1941 and later in the year slashed it to 5 percent of the 1941 total![34] To add insult to injury, Cootie's 1941 recordings had been taken off the market by 1942.[35] "Fly Right" wasn't released until 1962 when it was included as part of a three-LP Columbia anthology *Jazz Odyssey, The Sound of Harlem*. These Hit recordings would be the first commercially available disks from Cootie Williams and His Orchestra.

After a full day of recording on January 6 by Cootie's band, Moe Gale's "Big Three" package of the Ink Spots, Ella Fitzgerald, and Cootie Williams and His Orchestra started their national theatre tour on January 7, 1944, with a three-day stint at Rochester, New York's RKO Temple Theatre. The audience was "overflowing." The reviewer from the local newspaper referred to the troupe as "masters and mistress of their material." Of the band, he said, "The orchestra was a first-rate outfit; every player knew his job, and Cootie Williams had all under control and blending into a variety of rhythms." For Cootie himself, he "displayed his marked skill on the trumpet. He played it straight, and he made an amusingly whimsical instrument. The audience showed unmistakable pleasure."[36]

Virginia-born Ella Fitzgerald (1917–1996) was one of the greatest vocalists of all time. Her diction, intonation, and swing were without peer. She got her start with the orchestra of Cootie's late friend Chick Webb.[37] When Webb died in June 1939, she was named as leader in his stead and kept that position until the spring of 1942.[38] The Ink Spots were a popular vocal quartet with a formula that was almost invariable for their songs, with the main features being the falsetto voice of the lead singer and the lyrics being recited (not sung) by the bass vocal over a hummed background. Fitzgerald and the Ink Spots were both best-selling artists on the Decca record label. Gale had a reciprocal agreement with Dave Kapp of Decca Records whereby Gale artists were signed there.[39] Why wasn't Cootie a Decca artist too? At the time Cootie signed with Gale, he may have still been under an agreement with OKeh.

With Rochester, the touring package was off to a successful start, critically and more importantly, a financial success. On this first stop, they were only fifteen dollars away from breaking the house record.[40] There was one blight on this first date—Moke (Fletcher Rivers) and Poke (Leon James) were arrested on marijuana charges at their hotel.[41] Fortunately for the show, the comedy team wasn't detained for long, rejoining the retinue at their Cleveland stop at the end of January.

The troupe broke ground by being the first Black attraction to ever play Cincinnati's Albee Theater.[42] Perhaps that's why the reviewer from Cincinnati approached the show as study in anthropology: "The Williams outfit plays its music in the Harlem manner, with plenty of primitive rhythmic drive and nerve-tingling stimulation to be derived therefrom." But at least they recognized that the band could swing: "Only a man with sawdust in his veins can withstand the temptation to toe tap or clap hands when Cootie rides high on the trumpet and the band works out on 'Good Enough to Keep' [aka "Air Mail Special"]."[43]

Cleveland's Palace Theater may have seen Cootie reunited with his oldest brother Ike Jr. A local columnist reported that Ike worked at Alma Lue's Confectionary at Cedar and 71st and that his younger brother is "leader of one of the best bands in the land and possibly the best trumpeter."[44] Alma Lue Frost, the owner of the store, was Ike's (and Cootie's) aunt via her marriage to their mother's younger brother, Baalam Frost Jr.[45]

Chicago's *Down Beat* magazine reviewed the touring group when it rolled onto their home turf. It had been exactly two years since the band had launched during a two-month stint at the city's Grand Terrace Café. *Down Beat* considered the bill "over embellished" with the Ink Spots and Ella Fitzgerald. The magazine remembered that Cootie was "quiet and reserved with Ellington and BG" and had "become zestful in front of his own orchestra. Cootie plays, walks and manually batons in rhythm, with vocal accents when hot breaks pop up." The reviewer singled out the drummer Sylvester Payne (a "lighter and more relaxed" style "than is usual today") and pianist Earl Powell ("sparkling pianistics") for praise.[46]

Madison, Wisconsin's self-described "hard-to-please audiences" were "literally rocked" and "wore out No. 18 coupon shoe leather" (a reference to the fact that even shoes were being rationed for the war effort) taking in the music of "Cootie Williams and his 14 jivesters."[47] During their week in Minneapolis, even the -11 degree temperature didn't deter audiences; the gross was over $25,000 despite the pairing with a now-forgotten mediocre film (*Around the World*).[48]

But in Omaha, the cold weather kept the show from drawing the crowds they had become accustomed to. Charlie Holmes said there were times when "you could throw a baseball out there and it wouldn't hit nobody."[49] The extreme cold weather delayed the start of the show on a few of the days.[50] Despite this, they managed to gross a very respectable $18,000 for the week.[51] Omaha's *Central High Register* enthused, "The Orpheum [T]heater really hit the jack-pot last week with its all-sepia stage review." While they grew bored with the Ink Spots ("each [song] was like the one before it"), they loved Ella (she "deserves every bit of praise she gets and then some"). But the highest praise was reserved for Cootie and his band, "a marvelous organization" where "the brass bite everything, and the rhythm trio is one hundred per cent fine." The review ended with "Cootie was wise to form his own band. He is much too fine a trumpeter and leads his orchestra far too well to be stuck in the back row of any man's band, even the Duke's or the King's! This band has great things in store for it. All it needs is an opportunity to display merit. Then keep an eye peeled and an ear pinned on **Cootie Williams and his band!**" (The bolding of the font was in the original review.)[52]

While there were many positive and enthusiastic reviews, not every critic was a fan of "le jazz hot." "Of course one doesn't expect anything sweet from an orchestra such as Cootie Williams', and one doesn't get any. The elect seem to recognize the various band numbers, but to the ear of this old fogie all of them sound just alike. The band might just as well have stuck to one number and played it over and over."[53]

Traveling from home in New York, Catherine Williams joined her husband in San Francisco, where the package played the RKO Theatre from April 12 through 18.[54] They moved across the bay to Oakland for a date on April 19 and 21. The tour rolled into the small central California town of Fresno and surprised everyone with their drawing power as "Friday night is supposed to be an off night for entertainment." Four thousand fans, evenly split between Black and white, turned out to hear the groups. The reviewer was impressed with the band, predicting that, given publicity from records and radio, it could "surpass Count Basie among the Negro jive bands."[55]

"Strange As It Seems" was a syndicated cartoon in the mold of "Ripley's Believe It or Not." No other documentation of this alleged feat has been found. (*Lock Haven [Pennsylvania] Express*, Courtesy of Newspapers.com)

The touring group started a seven-day stand at downtown Los Angeles's Orpheum Theater on April 25. The show was described as "solid from start to finish." The Los Angeles crowds packed the house, filled the lobby and had a long line that went down the street.[56] The initial schedule called for five shows a day, but with 2,000 people in line after the last show of the evening, a sixth show was added for the duration of the week's booking. But everyone got paid for the overtime, including theater employees, with the band receiving about $1,000 additional compensation. The show set an Orpheum box office record with a whopping haul of $43,007, shattering the record previously held by Amos 'n' Andy, Xavier Cugat, and Cab Calloway.[57]

Metronome wasn't impressed with the headlining Ink Spots, saying they were "just a blotch." But they had high praise for the band. Cootie Williams "went into West End Blues on a dark stage. The effect was stupendous, and Williams, with his masterful control and sureness of melodic line, provided the finest part of the show with this two-minute solo exhibition."[58] The *Los Angeles Examiner* was enthusiastic for everyone in the show and picking a favorite is a "tough proposition" but gave the win to the Ink Spots "by a photo finish."[59]

The first of May was their last day in Los Angeles and, on a day where they still had to perform six shows, the group recorded selections from their act for *Jubilee*, an entertainment program created by Armed Forces Radio Service for Black troops. Running from 1942 to 1953, it featured the top Black entertainers of the time like Duke Ellington, Lena Horne, and Jimmie Lunceford. White musicians like Charlie Barnet, Harry James, and Stan Kenton also contributed programs. The shows were not broadcast domestically.[60]

The program by the Big Three for *Jubilee* broadcast #78 gives the best surviving example of what the touring package was presenting during their epic 1944 tour. While presented as if it were a live show, in reality, the songs were recorded in a studio and stitched together with announcement by host Ernie "Bubbles" Whitman and dubbed applause. Basie's "One O'Clock Jump" was used as the theme music and is played by the featured band for each show. The Williams band then demonstrates the swing and power they were capable of with their rendition of Mary Lou Williams's "Roll 'Em." The band backs Fitzgerald on the song that was her earliest hit, "A-Tisket, A-Tasket," followed by the "Concerto for Cootie" derivative, "Do Nothing 'Til You Hear from Me." ("Concerto for Cootie" was back in the news during the summer of 1944 courtesy of Walter Winchell's syndicated column. He wrote that "Do Nothing Till You Hear from Me," a popular favorite of the radio program *Your Hit Parade*, was written by Cootie Williams. "Its real name is "Concerto for Cootie." Cootie peddled it to Ellington for $25."[61] Ellington had started performing the song in 1943, but because of the recording ban, he didn't get to make a commercial recording of it until November 1947 for Columbia.)

The Cootie Williams Sextette makes an appearance, playing "You Talk a Little Trash," erroneously titled on most releases as "Let's Toot" due to the announcer's exhortation at the beginning of the song. It's taken at a brisker tempo than the recording four months prior, and Bud Powell is almost in a boogie woogie mood in backing Cootie's solo. The Ink Spots have the next three songs, with sporadic organ-like chording from the orchestra, before the last song, a torrid "Air Mail Special," by the full orchestra.

In addition to the Los Angeles *Jubilee* recording session, it was reported that the troupe would appear in a film.[62] Unfortunately, that did not come to pass.

Catherine Williams had joined Cootie in San Francisco and stayed with the tour to Los Angeles. From the City of Angels, she attempted to return home but ran afoul of the war's travel restrictions. *The People's Voice* reported in mid-June, five weeks after the touring group had left, that Catherine was "frantically trying to get reservations out of Hollywood to New York. Each time she thinks she's all set, along comes a priority and she's shoved back for another two weeks. The morale [sic] of this little story is, if you don't have to travel on important business, you'd better stay home."[63] At least there were some diversions—*The People's Voice* reported that "she met more stars . . . than you can

Newspaper advertisement for the Atlanta, Georgia, appearance of "The Big 3 Unit." In the upper right—"For White Patrons Only." (*Atlanta Constitution*)

shake a stick at" during a party hosted by actress Rosalind Russell.[64] It would take until June 26, a nearly two-month delay, for Catherine to finally return home to New York.[65] By this time, the touring package was in Pennsylvania on their last stop of their long tour.

Big crowds and big theatre grosses followed the Big Three wherever they went. But something else followed them in their travels—Jim Crow. In some places (including Chattanooga, Tennessee, and Birmingham, Alabama) the show played to an audience of one race, with the other placed in the balcony as spectators. In some cities (Oklahoma City, Atlanta), there were race-specific performances held on separate dates. Fredi Washington by this time was a theater columnist for *The People's Voice*, a Black newspaper based in New York City. The Atlanta ad specifying "White Patrons Only" was sent to her by a soldier stationed in Georgia who wrote: "I think it the most outrageous thing I've ever seen. Are those appearing so broke they must take such bookings—and humiliation? It's really a disgrace—even in Georgia." The column goes on the say that since the artists are from New York, they hadn't had to live with the type of entrenched racism found the Deep South. This ignores the fact that Cootie Williams and Ella Fitzgerald grew up in the South. Washington wrote that the artists should place a clause in their contracts that disallow "whites only" patronage, following the lead of artists such as Paul Robeson, Hazel Scott, and Marian Anderson.[66]

Norman Granz took over Ella Fitzgerald's management from Moe Gale at the end of 1953.[67] He had an ironclad rule against segregated audiences. Unfortunately, Cootie Williams didn't have that type of management and continued to be booked in segregated venues well into the 1950s.[68] It's interesting to speculate what Granz could have done for Williams's career. Charlie Parker's recordings for Dial and Savoy largely feature his working groups. But when Granz recorded Parker for his various labels, he featured him in diverse settings such as a big band, a Latin jazz group, a vocal choir, and, perhaps most famously, "Bird with Strings." Granz prolifically recorded pianist Art Tatum in solo and group settings. The Gale Agency wasn't a firm that was interested in artistic development or fighting for their artists; they only cared about bookings.[69] Trombonist Sandy Williams complained that Moe Gale was "the cheapest man going." He may have been cheap, but he had a reputation as being "well liked."[70] Gale had an excellent press agent in Art Franklin, who was able to wrangle positive PR such as a *Saturday Evening Post* article that portrayed him as a "Great White Father" to the people of Harlem.[71]

Despite their treatment as second-class citizens, the touring group did their part to lift wartime morale for the soldiers. The group performed at the dedication for the opening at a new amphitheater at the Tuskegee Army Air Field on May 31. The Tuskegee base had opened three years earlier as the home of the training program for Black pilots. Under dark skies that unsuccessfully threatened rain, the Big Three performed for "a capacity crowd who filled every available square foot of space."[72] The *New Journal and Guide* printed a photo montage of the show in their June 17 edition. They show the troupe in high spirits and some of the "record breaking crowd."[73] The amphitheater stills exists and is part of a complex honoring the legacy of the Tuskegee Airmen. Today, the literature describing the amphitheater says, "Ella Fitzgerald and the Ink Spots were the first performers who played the venue," with no mention of Cootie Williams.[74]

During a three-day stop at Charleston, South Carolina, at the beginning of June, the touring group played several shows at the Folly's Pier venue. As part of the war effort, the Ink Spots, Ella Fitzgerald, and the Cootie Williams Sextet played an hourlong program for the patients at Stark Hospital's Red Cross Auditorium.[75] Cootie's music proved to be so infectious that it caused a man who had been shot in both legs to dance on his crutches.[76]

The tour that started on January 7 finally came to an end on June 29 at Philadelphia's Earle Theatre. Cootie Williams made a solid impression: "Maestro is a wizard on the trumpet and has a first-rate band back of him."[77] "The heat's really on here. Put together a band of crack colored performers and you really have a show. From the insistent blare of Mr. Cootie Williams's educated trumpet to the dulcet balladeering of the Ink Spots, the Stanley's stage hour is not so much one of charm as of sizzle.... Mr. Williams has a band guaranteed to sky the temperature and pin the ears back on a brassy beachhead."[78] Always on the search for new talent, in Philadelphia Cootie tried to get an impressive young bass player named Ray Brown to join his band, but his parents wanted him to finish high school first.[79] Brown (1926–2002) would go on to a stellar career as one of the greatest bass players in jazz and for a few years was married to Ella Fitzgerald.

Bill Doggett, who was on the tour as pianist for the Ink Spots said, "it was more like a family tour."[80] Charlie Holmes said, "everybody in the band was just as happy as they could be" and "the money was floatin' around."[81] Although the money "floated," it wasn't easy money; Vinson said "we [were] making $100 [per week]. But there again, you had to work hard for it, man, about four or five shows a day."[82] The marathon tour of 1944 was a national highlight of the year, with Black performers "reaching almost giddy heights in all branches of the entertainment world." Cootie, along with musicians like Eddie Heywood and Billy Eckstine, were singled out as "new faces destined to stay up there a long time."[83]

The Billboard proclaimed the box office haul was "the best in history" for "Negro names." The reason given is that "Negroes are earning plenty of dough now, and they're the first ones to spend it on having a good time," engaging in the stereotype of the Black spendthrift. The magazine said Cab Calloway grossed $750,000, Ellington $600,000 and the Williams-Fitzgerald-Ink Spots "over $500,000." The Big Three "averaged $11,000 in theaters on guarantees, getting more than that in many spots." The success of Gale's touring package inspired Joe Glaser to mount a touring package that featured Billie Holiday, accompanied by her orchestra led by husband (and former Cootie Williams trumpeter) Joe Guy, and combos led by "Big Sid" Catlett and Al Casey.[84] It was also credited as the inspiration for a combination featuring the Nat "King" Cole Trio, Benny Carter and his orchestra, and vocalist June Richmond.[85]

25

'ROUND MIDNIGHT

As part of his conditions for taking the job, Charlie Holmes had negotiated that he wasn't going to play any solos and didn't want to play the lead (first) alto parts, leaving all of that on Vinson's shoulders. But one night he needed to impress a young woman who was disappointed that she wasn't hearing him taking any solos with the band. Holmes approached Williams during one of the breaks and asked for "something to play." Holmes relates "Cootie said, 'Nobody wants to hear you play. My name is in the lights downstairs, not your name. Nobody wants to hear you. The people come in here to hear me.' So when he said that, I looked at him and said 'Okay.'" Holmes packed up his sax and said "You stay here and blow all you know. I'm gone. Goodbye."[1] Eddie "Lockjaw" Davis also left the band around this time, "[B]y the time we got back to New York I'd had enough of that band. We changed bands in those days the way you'd change shirts."[2]

With hardly any break from the long tour, Cootie Williams started a run at the Savoy Ballroom on July 2. But Cootie was able to take a much-deserved vacation at the beginning of August.[3] Coincidentally, the Ellington band was given a rare twelve-day break[4] and Cootie and Catherine were able to relax with Harry and Dorothy Carney in Old Orchard Beach, Maine.[5] More than likely, they stayed at the Cummings' Guest House, a boarding house catering to Blacks since the local hotels were off limits. Duke Ellington was known to stay there when he was in town. (The Cummings' Guest House was placed on the National Register of Historic Places in 2004.)[6] Old Orchard Beach wasn't just a tourist destination; its Pier Casino ballroom was a stopping point for the major talent of the day. In 1940 alone, it hosted Louis Armstrong, Harry James, Andy Kirk, Guy Lombardo, and Erskine Hawkins, to name a few.[7]

This cartoon biography of Cootie Williams appeared in several African American newspapers starting in the spring of 1944. (*Ohio State News*)

♪

In August, Cootie's band made their third date for Hit Records. The August 22, 1944, recording session is historic in that it marked the first time the jazz standard "'Round Midnight" was commercially recorded. It was to become the band's theme song, replacing "Fly Right" (aka "Epistrophy"), giving Thelonious Monk authorship of two consecutive theme songs for the band. It was one of a pair of instrumentals recorded at the session. "Blue Garden Blues," a variation of the old standard "Royal Garden Blues," was the other one.

Each instrumental was paired with songs featuring the singing of Eddie "Cleanhead" Vinson. "Somebody's Gotta Go" and "Is You Is or Is You Ain't" were paired on disk with "'Round Midnight" and "Blue Garden Blues," respectively. "Is You Is" was a cover of a 1943 Louis Jordan hit and it proved to be so durable that it was almost always part of Jordan's set list.[8]

One of Bud Powell's close friends was pianist and composer Thelonious Sphere Monk (1917–1983). According to Williams, Monk liked to hang around the band as it rehearsed at the Savoy Ballroom.[9] At the urging of Powell, Monk

25. 'ROUND MIDNIGHT

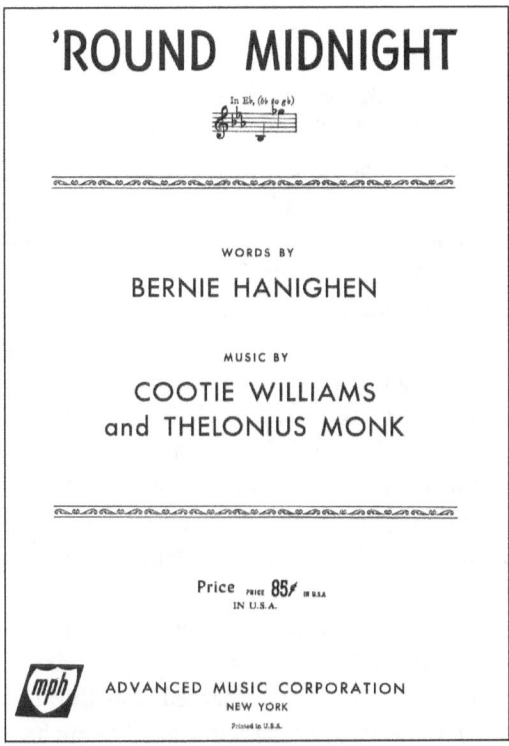

Original 1944 sheet music for "'Round Midnight." Not only did Monk get third billing, his first name was misspelled too. (Author's collection)

demonstrated his song "'Round Midnight" for Williams—"He wanted me to listen to it. And I listened to it. And I says, 'Okay, give it here. I'll put the verse to it." And it turned out to be okay." Cootie said of his contribution, "[N]obody never did play the verse, or interlude, or whatever they call it. Nobody but me." Cootie's contribution to the piece is not included the 1944 sheet music, further adding to its obscurity. Although Cootie wasn't aware of anyone using his part of the composition, there was at least one person who incorporated it into his performances. Pianist Barry Harris used Cootie's contribution as an introduction to his version of "'Round Midnight" in his performances of the piece. An example can be found on Harris's 1976 album *Live in Tokyo*.[10] There are some who see Williams's name on "'Round Midnight" and see it as another case of a musician being exploited by another. But as Williams explains, that wasn't the case—there was an actual contribution by him. If Williams's name had been appended to another, less popular Monk ballad like "Reflections" or "Ask Me Now," it would be a small footnote in the history of jazz.

Song authorship can be a messy subject. The popular jazz standard "Stompin' at the Savoy" provides an example. According to Rex Stewart, it came out of some spontaneous riffs that his band would throw around in rehearsal. Stewart said, "I am particularly sorry that I was not given credit for the bridge of "Stompin' at the Savoy." How I regret not having that standard included in my ASCAP catalog!"[11] At its first recording on May 18, 1934, by Chick Webb and His Orchestra, it was solely credited to Edgar Sampson. (Sampson had been the arranger for Stewart's band.) When Benny Goodman recorded the tune on January 24, 1936, the names of Goodman and Webb had been added to the "composer" credits!

By 1944, Cootie Williams already had an impressive musical career—featured on many recordings as a star soloist with two major jazz orchestras and now a bandleader in his own right. Thelonious Monk was only six years younger than Williams but would only see a recording studio for the first time in October 1944 as a sideman for Coleman Hawkins. In 1947, he was recorded as the leader of his own group for the first time. He finally was able to make his first recording of "'Round Midnight" at his third leader session on November 21, 1947. Ironically, with nearly a quarter of the twenty-first century passed, the reputations of Williams and Monk are vastly different. Monk is rightly revered as an original and creative voice in music both as a performer and composer. The Thelonious Monk Institute of Jazz (which was renamed for Herbie Hancock in 2019) was founded in 1986; there is no institution named after Cootie Williams. Monk was awarded a posthumous Pulitzer Prize in 2006.[12] Monk has been the subject of several biographies, with the best and most notable being *Thelonious Monk: The Life and Times of an American Original* by Dr. Robin D. G. Kelley. He's the subject of a graphic novel, *Monk! Thelonious, Pannonica, and the Friendship Behind a Musical Revolution*. He's also been the focus of a few documentaries, 1988's *Straight, No Chaser*, and a PBS American Masters series documentary. Also, several folios of his compositions and solo transcriptions have been published. Projects consisting of the complete compositions of Thelonious Monk were recorded in a quartet setting by pianist Frank Kimbrough and solo guitar by Miles Okazaki. The readers of *Down Beat* elected Monk to the magazine's Hall of Fame in 1963 while he was around to receive the honor. By contrast, Cootie Williams is not in the Hall of Fame and is largely remembered only in the context of Duke Ellington and his Famous Orchestra.

Billboard's review for the coupling of "Somebody's Gotta Go" / "'Round Midnight" was centered on the former, with barely any attention paid to "Midnight": "For the lowdown back-biting race blues chants with its characteristic two-timing wimmin [sic], Cootie Williams picked a dandy in the familiar *Somebody's Gotta Go*. With Eddie Vinson's excellent blues shouting in who-ee style, this slow blues drag is dynamite. The band packs plenty of power behind the voice, with Cootie scraping the ceiling on his horn. The maestro's trumpet is showcased for *'Round Midnight*, a mucky and moody blues ballad for which

Hit Record advertisement from December 16, 1944, issue of *The Billboard*.
(*Billboard*)

his horn gives fine expression in spite of a minimum of melodic appeal to the tune."[13] This composition, with its "minimum of melodic appeal," has gone on to become the most recorded jazz standard written by a jazz musician.[14]

Unlike the theme songs of Duke Ellington ("Take the 'A' Train") or Benny Goodman, ("Let's Dance"), in choosing "'Round Midnight" Cootie went the dark and somber route like Artie Shaw's "Nightmare." The somber arrangement was written by Bill Doggett.[15] It starts with three ominous chords, reminiscent of Rachmaninoff's "Prelude in C# Minor." Cootie, on open trumpet, is the only soloist. After a single chorus of the melody, Cootie's eight-bar contribution is played (approximately two minutes into the recording), followed by a reprise of the last eight bars of the form and a two-bar ending.

Earl Rudolph "Bud" Powell was born in New York City on September 27, 1924.[16] Cootie described him as "young and wild" but "he could play."[17] That was the case by the time he was with Williams. Before he joined Cootie's band, "he drove everybody crazy. He couldn't count bars."[18] Williams said he first heard Powell when the latter showed up at a band rehearsal and played, possibly on the invitation of trumpeter George Treadwell.[19] "Oh, he was something else. He was something else in his young age. And I think he was around 16 or 17."[20]

Band Leader magazine singled him out for praise writing, "The piano player is really something special. He's Earl Powell, a 19 year old New York boy, and some say, 'he's as crazy as he plays.'" Cootie added that Powell was a true devotee of his craft: " He plays all the time. I can't stop him."[21]

Williams's tenor saxophonist, Eddie Davis, who was later to be better known as Eddie "Lockjaw" Davis, remembers it differently. "One night Cootie Williams came into the club. He had a listen and then hired me, Bud Powell, who was on piano, and a guy called Sylvester Payne, who played the drums, for the big band."[22] Although some books and articles have reported that Cootie Williams acted as Powell's legal guardian, according to Powell biographer Peter Pullman, that wasn't the case. Williams was just his boss and merely got his mother's permission to take the young man on the road.[23] Dizzy Gillespie had offered Powell a job in his band, but Bud's mother thought that with Williams being better known than Gillespie at that time, playing with Cootie was the better gig.[24]

Cootie had a high regard for Powell—"[h]e was a terrific pianist" and "[h]e was what you call a real genius."[25] But Bud Powell was headstrong and had his own ideas about music. Charlie Holmes gave an example:

> So we would start off, and pretty soon Cootie would stop the band and said, "Wait a minute." He said, "Bud, don't improvise on this number. Just play what's on the music, just like it is." Okay, Cootie starts again. Here we go. [SINGS THEME] And Cootie stops the band again. "Bud, I asked you not to improvise. Just play what's on the music." "Okay, all right." So we go off again. Here we go. [SINGS] Cootie stopped the band. He said, "Bud, how many times do I have to tell you, don't improvise. Play what's on the music." Bud looked at Cootie and said, "If you think I'm gonna play that sad stuff, you're crazy." He said, "I ain't playin' nothin' that sad." I couldn't believe it! I had to look around. I said, "Well, who is this kid talkin' to the leader like that?" Bud ain't but about 17 years old, and he's up there talkin' to the leader [like that] . . . He's lucky to be in a band. And he told him, "I'm not gonna play that sad stuff." Well, I come to find out Bud was right![26]

For the night of January 19, 1945, Cootie had a one-night-stand gig at Philadelphia's Mercantile Hall.[27] Bud Powell came in late and "full of something." Cootie said, "He jumped up on the bandstand, and jumped up on the piano while the band was playing. And after the date, he didn't go back with us on the bus. And they called me the next morning and told me—I think the police called me here in New York and told me they had one of my men locked up over there in jail. They didn't know what was wrong with him, so they had beat him on his head, with this blackjack or something. And I told them to call his mother [in New York]. And I gave them his mother's phone number and everything, and they got in touch with his mother. So his mother goes over to pick him up. So his mother couldn't pick him up, because he was just a raving maniac . . . [S]he had to hire a special car to bring him back to New York. And to put him in Bellevue Hospital. And that started his trouble. Right then, from then on." The rough treatment by the police was hardly necessary, "[w]ith a little guy like him, the police, all they had to do was pick him up with one hand and shake him . . . They had no business hitting him with no blackjack."[28]

Powell never returned to the Williams band. Later, he was to become one of the leading voices in the new music dubbed "be-bop" in his short and troubled life. He suffered health consequences from his police beating for the rest of his days and died at the young age of forty-one in 1967. Part of his life story was used as the basis for the 1986 movie 'Round Midnight.

Blending swing players and boppers was fairly radical at that time, although Cootie said, "[I]t made sense to me." While this was a deliberate strategy by Williams, it may have been born out of necessity—the raging war made available musicians a scarce commodity. The younger musicians were sometimes hampered by substance abuse problems, but Cootie said, "but when they were right, [they] played so wonderful."[29]

♪

Cootie didn't actively seek out acting opportunities, but he was rumored to be a prospect for the lead for a Black version of the Broadway play *Little Orpheus*. The play was written by Howard Baker, husband of Dorothy Baker, author of *Young Man with a Horn*.[30] It was reported that he turned down parts in the movies.[31] This may not have been a wise move—the saying goes that "any publicity is good publicity." His bandleading peers Louis Jordan, Cab Calloway, Louis Armstrong, and Fats Waller made non–plot essential appearances in several movies during this same time period. They were also able to appear in full length, all-Black movies like *Stormy Weather* (Waller), *Cabin in the Sky* (Armstrong and Ellington), and *Beware* (Jordan). If the fear was that movie work would detract from the music business, these examples say quite the contrary.

After his short vacation, the "Big Three Unit" did a few dates in New York. And for a few dates in September, Lena Horne toured with the backing of Cootie Williams and His Orchestra. Their Boston opening date "opened very big indeed."[32] The pre-show estimate was $45,000 for the week,[33] but the actual take was nearly 50 percent better, a significantly higher $65,000, breaking records at Boston's RKO Theatre.[34]

Next on the agenda was a grueling two months of one-nighters in the South and Midwest for the Cootie Williams orchestra, without their touring partners Ella Fitzgerald and the Ink Spots. Starting in the second week of October, the band played Newark, Baltimore, Roanoke, Indianapolis, and many more cities before winding back up in New York in mid-December.[35] While the grind was tiring, it was financially rewarding. Williams was able to get a $700 to $750 a night guarantee. Typically, he could have expected about $400 a night, but the new postwar economy and demand for entertainment down South raised the stakes.[36]

Reviews continued to consistently characterize the band's volume: "Band obviously out to draw blood, and gets it with as loud and wild a scramble as they come, Williams putting them through the wringer for an added decibel."[37] "In commenting about their work anyone will have to agree that the boys have the loudest—if not the best—band heard here in some time. There's never a quiet moment when they get the down beat. Cootie is an exponent of trumpet blasts and toots, which, I presume, are big stuff among the swing-wise set."[38]

PERSONNEL CHANGES

For the band's December 1944 stay at the Savoy, the *Chicago Defender* reported they would be without Cleanhead since he "quit the band following a row."[1] But one of their columnists stated it was the other way around—Williams "took a sock" at Vinson after he said he was quitting the band and starting his own band.[2] This is the earliest known press reporting on Cootie's volatile temper. But plans for a new band were superseded by Uncle Sam—Eddie "Cleanhead" Vinson was inducted into the Army on January 31, 1945.[3] Vinson's replacement was the great Charlie Parker (1920–1955). (According to record producer Teddy Reig, Charlie Parker first substituted for Vinson on January 3, 1945.)[4] How Cootie and Bird came together is not clear. Maybe Cleanhead introduced Parker to Cootie—Vinson's playing displayed a Charlie Parker influence; they were briefly section mates in the Jay McShann band in 1941.[5] Cootie and Bird were at the same jam session and perhaps this is where they first met.[6] Or he could have been brought to Cootie's attention by Bud, Monk, or any other of the young modernists in the band. Charlie Parker wasn't in the band for very long. Williams could tolerate bad behavior from a good or great musician like Parker and Powell, but he couldn't tolerate bad musicianship. "[M]usic is a very serious thing with me. More than the money part to it. I love music. And I don't like to see anyone mess music up."[7]

Parker's work with the Cootie Williams orchestra only survives in an aircheck from the Savoy Ballroom on February 12 recorded as part of the *One Night Stand* series, a radio show that ran from the World War II years all the way up to the Viet Nam era. The broadcast is the only known recorded documentation of the collaboration of Bird and Cootie, and unfortunately, Parker only solos on the sole sextet number, "Floogie Boo." The band took part in another episode of the show the previous week, February 5, but it's not known if Parker was there. If he was present, he didn't solo. But a clue can be found on "You Talk a Little

The Cootie Williams Sextette. From left to right: Fletcher Smith, Norman Keenan, Sam "The Man" Taylor, Cootie Williams, Eddie "Cleanhead" Vinson, George "Butch" Ballard. (Duke Ellington Collection, Archives Center, National Museum of American History, Smithsonian Institution)

Trash," a number normally played by the sextet. On this broadcast, it is played by a quintet, sans alto. According to Williams, he only used Parker as a soloist. "The only thing that he [Bird] didn't like, I wouldn't let him play parts. I had him just as a soloist . . . [b]ecause he didn't blend in with my [sax] section."[8] This seems like an odd usage for a musician, especially since Charlie Holmes had made it clear to Williams that he didn't want to play lead alto sax, which was Vinson's role.[9] Besides the significance of documenting Parker's short time with the band, these two live broadcasts from the Savoy Ballroom are two of only four known airchecks of Cootie Williams and His Orchestra.

Cootie was proud of having had both Charlie Parker and Bud Powell in his band—"they were musicians. Oh, they could play!" Of Parker, he said, "There never was a musician before that influenced all the instruments—saxophones, drums, trumpets, piano." But that great influence also proved to have a negative side. Before Parker, "[e]verybody had his own style in those days. Now everybody's Charlie Parker." Parker was the avant garde of the 1940s, but the new developments of 1960s jazz left Cootie cold: "My nerves are not good enough to go along with the crowd of musicians that are coming up. I went in Smalls', in Harlem, a while back. A young tenor man—you'd know his name if you heard it—happened to be playing there. I listened. I thought, "This can't be true." I left, and I came back and listened again, and it *was* true. I thought, He sound[s] like a *beginner* to me."[10]

♪

Esquire announced their second "All-American Jazz Band" in their February 1945 issue. Cootie displaced Louis Armstrong as the first place (Gold) winner, with Roy Eldridge taking second (Silver). The "New Stars" trumpet category (for up-and-coming musicians) was won by the musical director of the Billy Eckstine band, Dizzy Gillespie, "creator of a highly esoteric trumpet style" and "the most copied instrumentalist to emerge in recent years."[11] Besides a gold statuette, nicknamed "The Esky," Cootie, like the other first place finishers, received a $500 War Bond.[12]

Later that month the band recorded what would turn out to be their last session for Eli Oberstein and Hit Records. Although Williams didn't mention Oberstein in any known interview, his fellow bandleader, clarinetist Artie Shaw, didn't have kind words for him: "Musicians who want to do things of lasting value simply don't belong in companies that are run by men like Oberstein. And a lot of them are finding it out—this isn't just my fight by any means! Oberstein told me what I should record, and how, despite that my contract clearly stated I was to have full authority. Why should I, or any bandleader who want to do things that are worthy of respect from musicians and people who know good music, take orders from someone like Oberstein?"[13]

The records Williams made for Hit Records didn't serve him well. The first eight selections, gathered in the album *Echoes of Harlem*, are all performed by the sextet, which, although featured in his regular shows, was a side attraction to the full orchestra. The big band sides all feature vocals, with only two exceptions, "'Round Midnight" and "Blue Garden Blues." Thus, "Blue Garden Blues" was the only commercially available example on the market of the band in hot mode, with pieces like "Roll 'Em," "Air Mail Special," and "St. Louis Blues" unrecorded to the general public. Given Shaw's comments, it seems like Oberstein is to blame for this imbalance.

With Vinson out of the band, it seems that Williams was pivoting away from blues vocals to a crooner in the mold of Billy Eckstine. His last session for Hit seemed designed to appeal to the pop music market. Only two songs were recorded, Duke Ellington's "I'm Beginning to See the Light" and "Saturday Night (Is the Loneliest Night of the Week)." Both were features for baritone singer Warren Evans (1931–1959), who was sometimes billed as Tony Warren, as he was on this release. Besides Williams, Warren sang with Sammy Price, Buddy Johnson, and Count Basie. Despite being billed as a "Sepia Swoon Star"[14] and "The Chocolate Sinatra,"[15] Evans's career never caught fire.

On Monday, February 26, in order to conserve energy resources, a midnight curfew was implemented by order of the War Mobilization Department.[16] It was the first (and so far) only time a curfew had been imposed in the United States.[17] The day after its implementation, the headline on the front page of New York's *Daily News* blared "Business Is Lousy And Town Is Blue As Curfew Rings." They reported the business was off anywhere from 10 to 60 percent.[18] Against this backdrop, the Big Three Unit of the Inks Spots, Ella Fitzgerald, and Cootie Williams and His Orchestra were reassembled for another tour, starting with a four-week stay at New York City's Paramount Theatre on February 28.[19]

The tour got off to an inauspicious start when there came a report of friction between Cootie Williams and Bill Kenny, the lead singer of the Ink Spots: "There was quite a display of fireworks backstage at the Paramount" with "Bill Kenny . . . feuding with Cootie Williams, the trumpet genius." It's noteworthy that this item was reported in the white (aka mainstream) press.[20]

While counting down the tempo for a number on the second night at the Paramount, Cootie stomped so hard that he dislocated his knee. "I leaned over and pushed it back in place and finished the show. Then I fainted in the wings."[21] The audience was none the wiser to Cootie's ordeal, thinking it was part of the show. Despite the pain, Williams didn't miss a single show during the Paramount booking.[22] Despite the curfew, the theater managed to squeeze in five shows per day, making a "socko" $80,000 during their first week. (To the relief of a war-weary population, the curfew was lifted in April.)[23]

Fortunately, this iteration of the tour wasn't a long thirty-three-week ordeal like the 1944 version. But it did extend until the end of September. The *Variety* review called the band "the surprising component in the overall impact" of the show. "Williams is an animated personality who does a convincing job of stirring enthusiasm in his band and consequently in the audience. Musically, the band is okay; it's main point, however, is the way it entertains. Leader is one of the best trumpeters in the business and proves it at various times."[24]

The group was in Pittsburgh on May 8, when victory was declared in World War II's European Theater and in Philadelphia on Mothers' Day, May 13.[25] Both days resulted in big drops in theatre grosses, but not for the touring group. They were apparently impervious to outside forces and broke the attendance record at Pittsburgh's Stanley Theatre.[26] Oddly (and to almost comic effect), the *Pittsburgh Press* sent a critic who was a self-professed square to review the show: "Despite years of listening to the swing tunes, I never have become an enthusiastic booster for this hodge podge of off-beat stuff." Of Williams he said: "Cootie is of the 'hot' trumpet school and pushes all sorts of queer noises through the curleycues [sic] of his trumpet. Not to be outdone, his bandsmen go berserk on the various instruments, to the delight of the hep cats. I just felt old, rather than critical, when the rhythms failed to 'send' me."[27]

From Pittsburgh, the package moved to the Earle Theatre in Philadelphia. Fortunately, *Variety* sent a savvier critic to review the show. They wrote: "Cootie Williams's hot trumpet is in rare form and that means solid." The band "keeps customers bouncing in their seats." It was also noted that attendance was at capacity, with those waiting for seats standing "five deep" in the lobby.[28]

After the Philadelphia stand, the group moved on to DC's Howard Theater. Unfortunately, Ella Fitzgerald missed the opening due to transportation problems and angry management canceled her from the rest of the engagement.[29] Even with Savannah Churchill replacing Fitzgerald, the show still garnered long lines around the theater.[30] Ella rejoined the tour at their next stop at the State Theater in Hartford, Connecticut. The Friday through Sunday stand also included a show to entertain the patients at Bradley Field Station Hospital.[31]

CAPITOL RECORDS

Cootie Williams and Ella Fitzgerald on stage on cover of the July 15, 1945, issue of *Down Beat*.

The only time Williams ever appeared on the cover of *Down Beat* magazine occurred with the July 15, 1945, issue. Featured with his touring partner Ella Fitzgerald, they are captured on stage. "Cootie Williams and Ella Fitzgerald have been knocking out the customers on their current road and theater tour.

Cootie Williams and His Orchestra recording for Capitol Records in their New York studio on May 29, 1945. (LaBudde Special Collections, UMKC University Libraries)

On the cover pic they seem to be knocking themselves out as well. Cootie's fine band now records for Capitol records, first releases are due soon."[1]

Williams was able to terminate his contract with Hit Records due to "pressing and distribution problems."[2] *The Billboard* wrote, "Williams had no trouble in canceling the Majestic [Hit had become Majestic by this time] pact as he proved that platters cut by his combo were only being distribed [sic] in next to nothing amounts which brought in very small royalty checks."[3] Cootie Williams and his Orchestra were then able to sign with Capitol Records, a big career boost.

It was big news for Capitol Records, too. The story was on the front page of their May 1945 newsletter. "Cap Wax Pact for Cootie's Combo."[4] (Billy Rowe, columnist for the *Pittsburgh Courier*, complimented Capitol's promotion of their artists, but wondered why they didn't see the "value in advertising in the Negro press.")[5] Capitol Records was relatively new at the time, having been founded in April 1942 by the team of Glenn Wallichs, Buddy DeSilva, and songwriter Johnny Mercer.[6] Initially based out of Los Angeles, by 1945 they were able to lease recording studios in other parts of the country so that their artists could record locally if need be.

Cootie's first Capitol session was on May 29. Although Capitol was a Los Angeles–based record label, they leased studios in New York and other locations in various parts of the country. Cootie's sessions were recorded at radio station WMCA.[7] Cootie never recorded for Capitol in Los Angeles. Unlike

A half-page Capitol Records ad for Cootie Williams in the September 1, 1945, issue of The Billboard. (Billboard)

Oberstein's methodology, the four songs recorded seem to have been chosen to represent different aspects of the band's repertoire: a ballad ("Mood for Coot," composed by Cootie Williams), a blues feature for Cleanhead ("Juice Head Baby"),[8] a jump number ("Salt Lake City Bounce"), and a novelty song ("Jitterbug Serenade"). "Juice Head Baby" was written by Cootie Williams and Holmes Daylie.[9] Cleanhead was newly returned to the band. He was a smoker and had been given a medical discharge from the Army due to asthma.[10]

The band was back at WMCA for their second Capitol session, which was just a little over three weeks after their initial waxing for the label. Again, four titles were recorded and like the first Capitol session they show the band's variety—a blues ("When My Baby Left Me"), a foxtrot ("Everything But You"), a ballad ("Mood for Coot"), and barn-burning swing ("House of Joy").

The Cootie Williams band had recorded "When My Baby Left Me" at their very first recording session on April 1, 1942, for the OKeh label. But OKeh hadn't released the side. Unbeknownst to Williams at the time, it would be over twenty years before that side would see the light of day, long after the big band had dissolved. "When My Baby Left Me," is a blues in B♭ and, except for a four-bar instrumental introduction, is all a vocal feature for Eddie "Cleanhead" Vinson. Like "Red Blues," it would be a part of Cleanhead's repertoire for the rest of his career.

Hype is a necessity in show business since everyone else does it. Cootie's composition "Mood for Coot" was the subject of such publicity. The news stories claimed it was written in thirty minutes at a party when Cootie lied to his new bosses at Capitol about having an unrecorded song that was "slow, pretty and moody."[11] The result "has caused such a sensation in music circles and with his recording firm, Capitol Records, in particular, that President Johnny Mercer and Vice President Glenn E. Wallichs, of Capitol made a special plane trip from the West Coast last week to personally supervise a recording of the tune." It was also reported that John Hammond (now in the Army), who was on a military leave, attended the session.[12] The stories go on to say that Duke Ellington and Harry James wanted to be the first to introduce the song on the radio, but Cootie wanted to hold on to the song until his own recording was released.[13] The first recording on May 29 was rejected for unknown reasons. Unfortunately, this second record wasn't released in Williams's lifetime, seeing its first airing in Mosaic Records' 1997 box set *Classic Capitol Jazz Sessions*. But the song was performed publicly. The reviewers came away with different views of the piece, ranging from "disappointing . . . drew only scattered [applause]"[14] to "one of Williams's best efforts to date."[15] It had an Ellingtonian quality, with its front line of muted trumpet and trombone and clarinet very reminiscent of "Mood Indigo."

"House of Joy" is a Cootie Williams composition. The composer credits also cite lyrics by Bernard Hanighen, although no vocal was recorded or reported in any performance review and no sheet music is known to exist. The song derived its name from Cootie's fan club.[16] The song had been in the band's repertoire since at least the previous December, with great audience reaction.[17] Perhaps Cootie withheld recording it for Oberstein's Hit Records or maybe Oberstein himself didn't want to record it. It's a simple riff piece on the "I Got Rhythm" chord changes in the key of B♭. There are no introductions, interludes, or modulations, just five choruses of hard swing. Robert Horton takes the first chorus' bridge with a growl trombone solo. Interestingly, Cleanhead, now back in the band, gets the most solo space on this recording with two choruses as opposed to only one by the leader. But Cootie makes the most of his chorus, showcasing his abilities to play hot and high on open trumpet.

In live performances, the song was opened up to feature most of the band. One story reported the band played "House of Joy" for forty-seven minutes![18] On many occasions, it worked the fans into a dancing and stomping frenzy. Cootie's home base, the Savoy Ballroom, "advised Cootie to play the song less frequently because the sudden impact of 2,000 heavy pairs of feet on the floor might cause a cave-in."[19] At New York City's Renaissance Ballroom the number caused the "frenzied lindy hoppers" to dance "with such vehemence that Manager Bob Douglas" feared "for the safety of the building and dancers." Douglas requested that Williams exclude the number from the rest of the 1946 engagement as it was too much for the club to handle. Williams complied

Publicity photo for bandleader Eddie "Cleanhead" Vinson ca. 1947. (Author's collection)

Gale Agency publicity photo of Bob Merrill, ca. 1945. (Author's collection)

and took it all in stride, saying "I've had a lot of compliments paid me for my trumpeting but that's the first time I was ever told that I played TOO GOOD!"[20] The fans at the Savoy were so taken with the song that they asked the ballroom's management to change the venue's slogan from "the Home of Happy Feet" to "The House of Joy." Unfortunately, the request was denied.[21]

Cootie apparently still kept up with Ellington's pursuits. The reverse side of "House of Joy" was a new Ellington composition, "Everything But You." It was so new that Ellington had only recorded it for RCA Victor just two and a half months prior. Duke's version was a ballad, sung by Joya Sherrill and concluded with a majestic baritone saxophone solo by Harry Carney. Cootie treated the song as an instrumental bounce, with solos by himself and tenor saxophonist Sam "The Man" Taylor.

Although Hit Records invested in trade ad publicity for Cootie Williams, Capitol wound up doing more. Capitol Records had their own monthly magazine *Capitol News* and used that in addition to the trade press to publicize their new releases and the activities of their artist roster.

After this recording session, the Big Three resumed touring, spending July 1945 in the Midwest, with dates in Chicago, Omaha, Minneapolis, Milwaukee, Madison, and Detroit. Cootie took four days off at home[22] afterward before heading to Baltimore's Royal Theater for another week of shows in September. *The Billboard* proclaimed, "Cootie has come a long way as a showman since he started his band four years ago. He makes a neat front both musically and visually." They also singled out the band for their "excellent . . . backing of acts."[23] The press declared that "his band is no longer a little big band on the make. It is strictly bigtime[,] able to take its place among the best in the business."[24]

Eddie "Cleanhead" Vinson, as always, was an audience favorite and his "Red Blues" was a best-selling record on the "race charts." Given his success with the Cootie Williams orchestra, Cleanhead finally made good on his previously aborted attempt to strike out on his own to lead a big band. He was doing what numerous other musicians did during this time. Certainly, he had to look no further than what Cootie himself had done as an example. But there was a big problem with Cleanhead becoming an orchestra leader—he wasn't suited for the task. His former section mate Charlie Holmes said: "People think all you got to do is put your name up there and that's it—well, somebody sold him a bill of goods with this band, you know. And it didn't work out. Because he knew nothing about handling a band or anything, [it's] no easy job handlin' a band." There was another complication, too—Vinson's drinking. Holmes said, "Eddie's a nice guy—just a dual complex. He's one way when he's sober and another way when he's drinkin'. . . ."[25] But at least Vinson, like Cootie, had an eye for talent. His 1949 band had pianist Red Garland, trumpeter Johnny Coles, and saxophonist John Coltrane, who at that time were all under twenty-four years of age.[26]

Supposedly, Vinson's departure was under amicable terms, at least as far as the public was led to believe. The Black press published a picture of Cootie and Cleanhead examining a contract together, saying as much.[27] Years later, Cootie said of Cleanhead, "How could I ever forget him—he made me a lot of money! We sold well over a million copies of him singing 'Cherry Red Blues.' He's a very fine jazz musician, too, an all-round jazz personality."[28]

Trumpeter Bob Merrill joined the band to replace the role created by Eddie "Cleanhead" Vinson of instrumentalist and blues vocalist. Cootie was able to use Merrill as a front-stage trumpet foil on several numbers that went over well with audiences.[29] He was born Robert Alphonso Merrell (not Merrill) on November 12, 1918, in Claremore, Oklahoma.[30] Merrill made his last recordings in 1961, but it's not known exactly when Merrill passed away. His son, Robert Merrill Jr., who died in 2009, didn't discuss his father with his children, so he is a figure of mystery even to his own family.[31]

At the end of 1945, it was reported that a group consisting of Cootie Williams, along with Lucky Millinder, Erskine Hawkins, Nat King Cole, and boxer "Sugar" Ray Robinson were teaming up to give Harlem a radio station. The musicians saw that others were getting rich from their production and besides keeping money in Black pockets, they hoped to uplift the Black community. While the press goes on to say that there would be regular meetings to accomplish the goal of the group, there is no evidence that the project went any further than the talk/idea phase.[32] But the group was far ahead of their time—WERD in Atlanta became the first Black-owned radio station *in the country* at the end of 1949.[33] New York City would not get a Black-owned station, WLIB, until 1972![34]

Cootie's interest in radio also extended to shortwave radio. He applied to the FCC for a license to obtain a shortwave radio telephone for usage in his new automobile. With the ubiquity of the cell phone in today's life, it's hard to conceive how exotic, rare, and expensive the car telephone was in the 1940s. Cootie's "application makes him one of the first non-newspaper personalities who have asked for this new invention."[35] Cootie said, "Music isn't the only media in which a forward looking bandleader must watch for new developments. Anything new that helps make the work run smoother is of extreme value. This gives me the chance to drive into the city, conduct any and all business, and listen to my band rehearsing, all at the same time."[36] The distance from Cootie's St. Albans home to the Savoy Ballroom was only sixteen miles. Perhaps traffic would allow Williams the time necessary to accomplish his list of tasks.

Cootie's name was also tied to the possible reopening of clubs that played a big part in his history—New York's Cotton Club and Chicago's Grand Terrace Café. Of the latter, it was said that he was "quietly investigating the possibilities" of restarting the club where he launched his career as a bandleader.[37] Just a few months later, at the start of 1947, Williams was approached by a group of investors that were interested in restarting the Cotton Club. Williams would be the opening attraction and also an investor. Supposedly, he had "long contended that a properly run major club in Harlem would be a money maker."[38] But neither proposition came to pass.

28

MAINSTREAM PRESS ATTENTION

Cootie received mainstream press coverage with a short feature in the May 15, 1945, issue of *Look*, a photo-journal magazine. The subtitle of the article, "He is to a trumpet what Goodman is to a clarinet," was indicative of his level of musicianship. Describing him as "good-humored" and "hard-working," with the "ambition to lead the greatest band in the country, but some critics say he's achieved that already."[1]

The following year, Cootie was again featured in *Look*. The August 6, 1946, issue ran a photo essay titled "Hot Trumpeters," who have "piped the blues, the boogie and the be-bop which have crystallized into an original American art." Of course, the lead trumpet was the great Louis Armstrong, whose portrait was almost a full page. The remaining eight trumpeters (Bunk Johnson, Cootie Williams, Harry James, Rex Stewart, Roy Eldridge, Bobby Hackett, Dizzy Gillespie, and Pete Condoli) were each given a quarter page. *Look* was a large-format magazine, so the portrait space was generous. Each artist was also given the briefest of biographies.[2]

Shortly after this, Cootie was featured in a full-page interview published in a Sunday edition of the newspaper *PM*. In it, Cootie's early life was detailed in brief, but the main focus of the article was the formation of his orchestra. Baltimore's *Afro-American* newspaper lamented that "the only time colored entertainers can break through is when they hit the top . . . otherwise they don't exist."[3]

Esquire named Cootie the Gold winner for the second time in their 1946 edition of their All-American Jazz Band. Charlie Shavers won silver while the previous year's winner, Roy Eldridge, was penalized because he was "less than adequately heard during his long term in the Artie Shaw band, away from New York."[4] The available winners were assembled in concert on January 16, but

Recording session with the 1941 Metronome All-Stars. Gene Krupa—drums, Lou McGarity and J.C. Higginbotham—trombones, Roy Eldridge, Harry James, Cootie Williams—trumpets. The reeds and the rest of the rhythm section are not shown. (*Metronome*, Courtesy of RIPM Jazz Periodicals)

once again Cootie couldn't make the date. His long-term booking at the Club Zanzibar conflicted with the concert. This was to be Cootie's last major poll win. The following year saw Armstrong return to the top of the *Esquire* poll, which also happened to be the last year it was held. Dizzy Gillespie and Miles Davis would top the polls in *Down Beat*, *Metronome*, and others signaling a changing of the guard and awareness of a new musical style that was dubbed "be-bop."

Jazz "wars" between the varying schools of music are nothing new and they persist to this day. The factions change and so does the fervor with which they are argued. The music of Dizzy Gillespie and Charlie Parker, known as be-bop, created a rift with swing and the more traditional (sometimes known as "Dixieland"). Cootie thought bop was a "passing fad" since "few people can understand and appreciate it." Williams said:

> I personally like be-bop and get kicks both out of playing and hearing it. Still, you can't overlook the fact that the mass of people don't like or understand it. Any art form that appeals to a limited audience must be short-lived. That is the inevitable fate of be-bop. I feel sure that 10 or 20 years from now you won't hear be-bop recordings classified as popular classics such as is the case with Louis Armstrong, Bunny Berigan, Bix Beiderbecke, Sidney Bechet and their like. Of course, their styles aren't necessarily in the pattern of today, but they all had a basic quality that will live forever because it is sound music form. The best you

Cootie Williams was not only popular with music polls, he was also popular enough to endorse shoes. (*Pittsburgh Courier*, Courtesy of Newspapers.com)

can possibly say for it is that it is a passing fad and will last no longer than any other fad. [5]

Throughout his life, Cootie mainly listened to other trumpeters when he played recordings. He started off with Louis Armstrong and Joe "King" Oliver, but as the years went on, he also listened to Dizzy Gillespie and Miles Davis. He saw a danger in listening too closely to only one person. . . ."[6]

Esquire poured gasoline on the fire by favoring the older style of jazz and almost completely ignoring its newer developments in its 1947 *Jazz Book*. It favored traditional jazz so much that some dubbed it an "Eddie Condon press manual" as only two of its ninety-one pages listed the poll winners. The issue was edited by Ernest Anderson, Condon's manager, which *Down Beat* snarkily said was "strictly by accident."[7] Nineteen of the twenty-three jazz experts that made up the magazine's advisory board, including John Hammond, Leonard Feather, Norman Granz, and Barry Ulanov, resigned in protest.[8] Additionally, a bevy of heavyweight musicians wrote a protest letter. Thirty-four musicians signed the letter. Besides Cootie, the signatories included Duke Ellington, Louis Armstrong, Billie Holiday, Miles Davis, and Ella Fitzgerald.[9] The original copy of the letter became a prized possession of Leonard Feather.[10] The *Esquire* poll was mortally wounded after the controversy and became the last one in the short series.[11]

Cootie had been the winner of the *Esquire* Gold Award for trumpet for the years 1945 and 1946. It turned out that 1946 would be the last year Cootie would win a music magazine's national or international jazz poll. Louis Armstrong won the *Esquire* Gold Award in both the trumpet and vocal categories.

Armstrong's wins in the *Esquire* poll was an anomaly amid prevailing winds of jazz trends. The Silver Award trumpet went to Dizzy Gillespie and the New Star winner was Miles Davis. *Metronome* had given Cootie their top award in 1941, 1942, and 1945. By the late 1940s, the torch had been passed to Dizzy Gillespie and his disciples.

A CHANGE IN MANAGEMENT

According to those who knew him, despite outward appearances, Cootie had a good sense of humor. On occasion, he would even prank the press. During a run at St. Louis's Club Riviera, a young journalist noted that Williams didn't say much during their conversation:

> In desperation, I asked him about his band, his "book" and his men. I remember that on a previous visit his drummer, a noisy four-beater, was named Alvin York, and a quick look behind me verified that he still held that spot in the band. His spikes of pomaded black hair and the angular face were easily enough remembered. "You still have the same drummer you came through with last time," I ventured. When Cootie countered with "Drummer" I said, "You know, 'Drummer York.'" ('Drummer York' had the nickname drawn in black on his white pearl drumheads.) Cootie still looked surprised, and we explained that his drummer's name was York. "You don't say," Cootie mumbled in dead seriousness. He turned and looked behind him at York, "Hey, you!," Cootie shouted up at him. "Is your name York?" York said it was so. "Yeah, that's his name," Cootie certified.[1]

Toward the end of the Club Riviera engagement, Jack Teagarden and Lionel Hampton sat in with the band and provided a set that "was the wildest here in modern times." They played "House of Joy" for forty minutes and at the end Hampton's vibes "crumpled to the floor under a smashing blow."[2]

After St. Louis, Cootie and Ella traveled to Oklahoma. Their October 21 date in Tulsa met with opposition from a local minister. Three days prior to the date, Rev. William P. Mitchell came forward and demanded that the dance be cancelled because it fell on a Sunday. He not only had a problem with Sunday dancing, but with *any* kind of dancing, saying that "dances of any kind are contrary to the Christian religion, especially those held on Sunday."[3] A police detective found a city ordinance that prohibited dancing on Sunday and a triumphant Mitchell said, "once you let the bars down the sheep get out and you can't get them back in again." The dejected promoter, "Kid" Redick, would have to refund all the tickets at a loss to himself.[4]

But on Saturday, with just hours to spare, a solution was found. Since the dance was scheduled to start at 11:00 PM on Sunday, Redick decided to move the time to 12:01 AM, Monday morning. Thus, no Sunday dancing. Rev. Mitchell wasn't happy and said the move was "in a spirit of violation."[5]

From there, Cootie and Ella played dances at the Army's Camp Gruber (Oklahoma) with October 23 for "colored personnel" and "a repeat performance for white personnel" on the 24th. Ella and Cootie also visited the camp's hospital patients before the second performance.[6]

The Fitzgerald/Williams team moved to the Deep South in November 1945. They played a dance for Blacks in Columbia, South Carolina, on November 16. The price of admission was $1.65 ($1.40 in advance), with white spectators charged $1.30. (The next day, Benny Goodman played a dance at the same venue for white patrons, with the ticket price of $2.25 and colored spectators admitted for $1.50.) Cootie Williams and Ella Fitzgerald sans Ink Spots continued through the south, returning to New York City for a long-term booking for a revue at the Café Zanzibar. Capitol Records thought that Cootie's gig at the Café Zanzibar was notable enough to be featured on the front page of their October 1945 newsletter with the headline-making note that Williams was following his former boss Duke Ellington into the venue.[7] "The fortunes of the band looked bright. After their engagement at New York's Café Zanzibar, management was so pleased they signed Cootie to a contract to appear annually for a period of ten years.[8] Unfortunately, the Café Zanzibar closed in 1947.[9] When it was rumored that the nightclub might reopen shortly after the closure, it was hoped that Cootie Williams would be the first headliner, given his drawing power at the time.[10]

Cootie was one of the big stars at Moe Gale's agency. In advertisements for the 1945 holiday season, the Gale Agency proclaimed the collective relief of the time—"Season's Greetings To A World At Peace." Cootie was one of a quartet featured with large photographs in a full-page layout, the other three being Erskine Hawkins, Ella Fitzgerald, and Lucky Millinder. The Ink Spots, despite their popularity, are only mentioned in the accompanying list of eleven other artists. Perhaps their lawsuits against the agency had bumped down their status.[11]

Program from Café Zanzibar's December 1945 to January 1946 show. (Author's collection)

Cootie caught the flu during this long engagement. He was able to play through that, but an onstage mishap was something he couldn't just shake off. During dancer Ralph Brown's segment of the show, Brown's foot hit Cootie's horn while he was playing, resulting in a split lip, sidelining him for a few days.[12] But the almost two-month-long residency, spanning December 1945 to January 1946, was an artistic and financial success. The *Chicago Defender*'s Joe Bostic thought so highly of the show that he thought the show, "The International Laugh-Lease Revue," should be christened "The Unbelievable." Ella Fitzgerald gave "the best singing performance of her ten-year career," while the Ink Spots "completely justify the honored position" of being the headline act.[13] Interestingly, Cootie Williams and his Orchestra didn't appear onstage at all. They were confined to the pit, with Williams acting as conductor and musical director for all the acts. The band was singled out for dance music that was "soothing and hot in turn." It was so effective that "the dance floor resemble[d] a tightly packed sardine can."[14] Despite the acclaim, the band members were reminded that being popular didn't cancel out being Black because they couldn't get a taxi to stop and pick them up outside the Zanzibar.[15]

A residency of almost two months was becoming a rare thing. The economics of the entertainment business had changed a great deal by the time 1946 started. Previously, theaters could put bands in for one- to two-week bookings and make them profitable because they could run four to six shows

Cootie making a point at a Capitol Records studio session ca. 1945. (LaBudde Special Collections, UMKC University Libraries)

a day. One week was a hard and fast rule for the Apollo Theater; beyond that there was a falloff in business. Charlie Buchanan said that sometimes even a whole week was too long to be profitable at the Savoy. While the white bands were seeing some gains in the movie, radio, and nascent television sectors, the Black bands were seeing a continuation of the color line there too, reducing their opportunities.[16]

The Cootie Williams and Ella Fitzgerald show also broadcast from the Zanzibar. A review of the January 13 show deemed the band "impressive." The reviewer was very taken with the bass playing of eighteen-year-old Jimmy Glover, another Cootie Williams discovery. The January 21 show survives as an aircheck, the show an episode of NBC's *Let's Go Night Clubbing*. "Jumpin' at the Zanzibar," a Cootie Williams blues in B♭, was recorded at the next day's recording session as "Jumping to Conclusions." Overall, the band sounds a bit tired.

The next day, January 22, 1946, the band went into Capitol's New York recording studio and recorded four titles—"Jumping to Conclusions" (recorded in two parts), "Someone I Knew," and a vocal feature for Bob Merrill, "You're the One for Me Sweetheart." None of the recordings from this session were issued at the time and sat in Capitol's vault until the 1990s.[17]

The band was in the studio a week later to record another four sides. This time, they fared better; three of the four titles ("Stingy Blues," "Echoes of

Harlem," and "That's the Lick") were released, but it would take two and a half years for "Stingy Blues" to see the light of day, press stories notwithstanding.

The unissued song, "He Should'a Flip'd When He Flop'd" was composed by young Mercer Ellington and sung by Johnny Mercer. Although the arranger is uncredited, it's not a stretch to believe the younger Ellington could be the author. Interestingly, the Capitol Records chief sat in with the band delivering a lyric about a guy who suffered the effects of gravity. After a bright statement on the melody by the band, there's a bit of banter between Mercer and Williams before Mercer sings a chorus. But Cootie's concluding trumpet solo steals the show as a stellar example of his open trumpet work. He confidently soars over the ensemble in his best Armstrong-inspired manner, complete with a forceful conclusion on a high E♭. With solid, swinging backing from the band, novelty lyrics and a stellar solo from Cootie Williams, this song had no chance to prove itself in the commercial market since it remained unissued until 1997.[18] It's especially ironic when the record was given advance hype in the *Cleveland Call and Post* ("Mercer Joins Cootie in Recording Date"),[19] Los Angeles's *California Eagle* ("Johnny Mercer Paired on New Record with Cootie Williams"),[20] and other Black newspapers. And on top of it all, it was a song by one of Capitol's honchos!

"Stingy Blues" was another slow blues that was popular with the band's fan base. Bob Merrill sings the lyrics, another tale of a man done wrong by a woman. In this case, she's "got all my money and won't give none to me." During the brief instrumental interlude, Williams, playing open, climbs up to the trumpet's high G before descending to the middle range to deliver a strong solo. There was a human-interest story behind "Stingy Blues." It was composed by Elaine Blackman (1924–1986), who was described as a "pretty crippled girl"[21] in the condescending manner of the times. But her disability was not the issue; she was serious about composing. The previous year, she provided Eddie "Cleanhead" Vinson with "Kidney Stew Blues," a song that became one of his signature tunes. Lorenzo Pack and Bob Merrill manage to get composition credits on the label. Most probably, it was for their promotional efforts, which was a common practice in those days.

Beginning the week of June 25, the orchestra started a week's stand at Philadelphia's Earle Theater. The headliner was the great dancer Bill Robinson (1878–1949), better known as "Bojangles." The run broke attendance records and Robinson was well pleased with the band's backing. At the end of the final show, he requested that the band remain in their seats. No one knew the reason for this unusual command, so all in attendance were surprised when Robinson pulled out envelopes with a "substantial cash bonus" for each member of the band. It may be hyperbole, but the press proclaimed that "this was the first time in the history of Negro show business that the principal on a

```
╔══════════════════════════════════╗
║      THE NAME OF FAME            ║
║    **Cootie Williams**           ║
║    The KING of The TRUMPET       ║
║    AND HIS SENSATIONAL ORCHESTRA ║
║  AT THE **RENAISSANCE BALLROOM** ║
║  7TH AVENUE AT 138TH STREET,     ║
║         NEW YORK CITY            ║
║    **SUNDAY, JUNE 23rd**         ║
║    Dancing From 9:00 p. m. Until!║
║  General Admission—$1.25 (plus tax)║
║      NYLONS        PRIZES        ║
╚══════════════════════════════════╝
```

1946 advertisement from *The People's Voice*. As a sign of the times, note that nylons were used as an incentive for attendance. (*The People's Voice*, courtesy of NewsBank/Readex)

vaudeville bill has made such a gesture to the members of the entire orchestra."[22] Robinson's generosity was legendary. Unfortunately, his generosity and gambling losses combined to make a precarious financial situation. By the time of his death two years later, Robinson was broke.[23]

Cootie's penultimate session for Capitol produced five titles, with three of them being released into the contemporary market. "Wrong Neighborhood" was another vocal blues feature for Bob Merrill. Perhaps to fake out the audiences, the arrangement starts with the now famous introduction used in "Red Blues." Merrill also takes the vocal duties on "I May Be Easy, But I'm No Fool," a song cowritten by Cootie. Cootie is cocomposer and vocalist on "Let's Do the Whole Thing or Nothing At All."

Cootie Williams and Erskine Hawkins made a joint appearance at Carnegie Hall on August 24, 1946, as part of a concert to crown the winners of *Look* magazine's "All-American Amateur Swing Band" contest. A series of preliminary regional bouts led to the culmination show at Carnegie Hall. The concert also featured a jam session between Hawkins and Williams that "will never be forgotten in the annals of jazz." Sadly, there is no known recording of this event.

Six trumpeters sponsored trophies in their name for the winners. In addition to Williams and Hawkins, they were Harry James, Louis Armstrong, Randy Brooks, and Pete Condoli. Wally Holmes won the Cootie Williams trophy, which was presented to him by Catherine Williams, with Jimmy Flanagan being presented the Erskine Hawkins trophy by Florence Hawkins.[24] (The wives of bandleaders had public visibility, too. The *Chicago Defender* said the "best dressed band wife in the business is Mrs. Erskine Hawkins; prettiest is Mrs. Cootie Williams; cutest is Mrs. Lucky Millinder; best business head belongs to Mrs. Cab Calloway; best 'carriage' belongs to Mrs. Jimmie Lunceford; most eligible for pin-up election is Mrs. Noble Sissle.")[25]

For Waldo Thomas "Wally" Holmes (1928–2021), winning the Cootie Williams trophy was a significant event, "For the first time I thought I had a shot as a professional musician." His career, besides playing the trumpet, included song writing and artist management. He managed the Hues Corporation and wrote "Rock the Boat" for them.[26] The song was a huge hit in 1974 and is considered to be the first disco hit.[27] (Please don't blame Cootie for disco . . .)

Cootie recorded for Capitol for what would be the last time on September 11, 1946. Three titles were recorded, all of them written or cowritten by Williams— "Bring 'em Down Front," "Ain't Got No Blues Today," and "Rhapsody In Bass."

For a short period in 1946, Cootie used two double bassists in his band, Jimmy Glover and Norman Keenan. It was something Duke Ellington did periodically throughout his career. An artistic rivalry existed between them onstage, and Cootie wrote "Rhapsody in Bass" to feature them. *Down Beat* described it as a "battle for basses."[28] By the time it was recorded in the studio, only Keenan was left. To cover, the second bass line was covered by pianist's Arnold Jarvis's left hand.[29]

"Bring 'em Down Front" was another occasion for Williams to sing, and for "Ain't Got No Blues Today," the vocals were handled by Bob Merrill. Merrill's vocal would see the market within a month of its recording, but Cootie's wouldn't be out until July 1948, quite a few months after Capitol released him from his contract.

Two days after the September 11 recording session, Cootie played a week at the Apollo Theater, once again with Ella Fitzgerald along with The Vagabonds, a male singing quartet, the dance duo of Honi & Brown, and comedian Spider Bruce. *Variety* gave the show a good review: "Orch[estra], fronted by Williams who blows a vigorous trumpet, is off to a noisy opening with 'Lets [sic] Do the Whole Thing.' Stick-swisher serves up swing at its best in 'House of Joy,' a cacophony of din which sends sidemen and Williams into a virtual frenzy. [The latter], on a trumpet solo, really gets hep and gets plenty of palm whacks. 'Mood for Coot,' an original by Williams, features muted clarinet, trumpet and trombone in a pale blue spot. Though a welcome change of pace, this instrumental number was disappointing and drew only salvos." Apparently "applause" can only be used in an entertainment magazine so many times, hence synonyms like "palm whacks" and "salvos."[30]

After a week at home in New York, it was time for the band to hit the road again. The last part of September was spent in Pennsylvania and Ohio. Then it was on to Michigan and Illinois in October. November and December took the band through the South again, consisting of twenty-five one-nighters and more than 28,000 miles on the road.[31] The tour marked Cootie's first appearance Jackson, Mississippi, which rated above-the-fold coverage on the front page of the *Mississippi Enterprise*. In Louisiana, the students of Southern University voted Williams's band as tops during their November poll. They also selected "House of Joy" as "most exciting arrangement of the year."[32]

The band also broke another racial barrier when they became the first Black group to play at the Brooks Field (now Brooks Air Force Base) Officers' Club in San Antonio, Texas, on November 23. One of the base's officers proclaimed: "Not only have we just finished winning a war for the democratic ideal but the Army has shown us the way in honoring the memory of a Negro hero; for us to cling to anti-democratic practices would be to ignore the principle for which Brooks died." Oddly, some thought the pilot for whom the base was named for, Sidney Johnstone Brooks Jr., was Black, but that wasn't the case. His father's full name was Albert Sidney Johnston Brooks, having been named after Confederate general Albert Sidney Johnston, who was most famous for the Battle of Shiloh. The confederate-sympathizing family would be less than amused to be confused for African American. (It wasn't until 2023 that a base would be named for an African American when Fort Polk in Louisiana was renamed for WWI hero Henry Johnson.)[33] Treatment that should have been mundane becomes noteworthy when it's extended to "Negroes": "The Williams band was not only warmly received by all the guests at the dance but had a number of special courtesies extended to them by the hosts. Among these latter was a buffet supper just before the dance."[34]

After the San Antonio date, the band continued east with gigs in Galveston, Prairie View, Port Arthur, and New Orleans before playing Mobile on December 9. Cootie's return to his hometown was a triumphant affair. Since he had left in the mid-1920s, he had made numerous recordings and appearances with the orchestras of Duke Ellington and Benny Goodman, but those groups hadn't played in Mobile. Now, the prodigal son was not only returning home, but he was also an award-winning trumpeter leading his own renowned orchestra. The local auditorium was filled to its 2,500-person capacity. The patrons were treated to a show that "brought down the roof." At the intermission, Cootie was presented with a loving cup and the key to the city.[35]

The return home also brought a reunion with Cootie's first trumpet teacher, Charlie Lipscomb. Now sixty-four years of age, the old tutor had to be proud of his star pupil. The press staged a photo of Lipscomb standing in front of a seated Williams playing his trumpet. (As a side note, Williams is wearing sandals in the photo. This footwear was apparently novel enough in the 1940s to attract press attention: "Ralph Cooper and Cootie Williams are just two Harlemites who wear those toeless, heel less slippers in summer weather.")[36]

Charles Lipscomb passed away on January 14, 1949, at the age of sixty-six,[37] just over two years after this reunion. He had taught many other students over the years: "Many old Mobilians credited Lipscomb for teaching them the instruments in which they are teaching someone else right now."[38] He willed his trumpet to Cootie, who one would imagine was his favorite pupil. There's no doubt he was the most successful student.[39]

Perhaps inspired by "Black, Brown, and Beige," Duke Ellington's "tone parallel to the history of the American Negro," around this time period Cootie was reportedly working on a large-scale project to be titled "A Cavalcade of Jazz." Unlike Ellington's work, which was a long suite, Williams's opus was to be a show with actors and musicians that would "trace the influence of Negroes on the American musical idiom from the spirituals through the jazz evolution up to the present day, emphasizing the instrumentalist whose styles have affected popular music." Williams's collaborators were to be Shirley Graham (1896–1977) and Shepard Edmonds (1876–1957).[40] Graham would become the second wife of famed Black scholar Dr. W. E. B. Du Bois. Shepard Edmonds was a man of many talents; he was a vaudevillian, composer, and private detective over the course of his life. But no record of this ambitious work has been found beyond the discussion phase.

Another alleged large-scale work was publicized under the headline "Cootie Goes Longhair!!" Williams had allegedly written a six-minute trumpet concerto after two years in the works. Said to be a serious piece, "A Trumpet Concerto" was to be premiered at the Paradise Theater in Detroit in October 1946. Unfortunately, there is no piece of music copyrighted by Williams under that name and there are no recordings or further press on it.[41]

At the DAR's 1946 Atlantic City convention, the organization refused to strike the "for white artists only" clause from their Constitution Hall operating contract.[42] Perhaps the memory of his treatment five years ago prompted Williams to send a strongly worded letter to Mrs. Julius Talmadge, head of the DAR. He wrote:

> I note with considerable concern the recent action of your organization endorsing the infamous Rankin Committee. This action following your completely un-American stand with reference to the artistic performances in Constitution Hall gives me and every other artist in America cause for real alarm.
>
> It would seem to me that both of these positions taken by you in these vital matters are in direct opposition to every concept and precept that motivated Crispus Attucks, George Washington, Paul Revere and other heroic Americans in their fight for freedom. These actions are indeed a desecration of the noble purpose for which the revolution was fought.

There remains but one further act to round out an infamous trilogy of anti-American positions, to wit: your blessing of the Ku Klux Klan. I am watching with apprehension and bated breath for the announcement of such an endorsement.

I, in all sincerity make this very positive suggestion to you, that you either discontinue the desecration of the ideals of the glorious revolution and the embracing of undemocratic ideologies or change the name of your organization to one more appropriately in line with your thinking as indicated by recent actions.[43]

Since the language of the letter doesn't match that displayed by Cootie in his interviews, more than likely the letter was dictated and polished by a publicist or lawyer. But the larger point is that Williams allowed these sentiments to be published under his name. Cootie's letter was a small part of the fight against the DAR but at least he decided to speak out. The DAR didn't rescind Constitution Hall's exclusionary provision until 1952. The following year, Marian Anderson finally performed there for the first time.

In order to strike at the discrimination prevalent in government jobs and the defense industry, President Franklin D. Roosevelt signed an executive order creating the Fair Employment Practices Committee (FEPC) in 1941. It prohibited "discrimination in the employment of workers in defense industries or government because of race, creed, color, or national origin." It wasn't a panacea, but it resulted in some small gains. Unfortunately, the FEPC was not a permanent organization and was subject to renewal by Congress.[44] In the campaign to make the FEPC permanent, Cootie was one of those lending his voice to the struggle. He wrote a letter that was sent to Congressional leadership that was published in several newspapers:

> Men of all creeds and all races have just concluded a victorious fight to preserve the dignity of individuals no matter what their station. Our whole national history has been predicated on the premise that every citizen has the right to support himself by the fullest exploitation of his skill. To deny any man that privilege because of race, creed or color is to violate the ideals on which this nation was founded and prospered. Hundreds of thousands of men are returning from heroic battlefields to take their place in our society as productive citizens. It is criminal to deny them their rights to work. The citizens of this nation look to you our elected representatives to intelligently legislate in the veterans' behalf. To do any less is to violate the trust of those who elected you and to desecrate your oath of office. You owe it to yourself and your constituents to Make A Permanent FEPC A LAW.[45]

Again, more than likely, this statement was written by a ghost writer. But in allowing the words to be published under his name, Williams clearly endorsed the sentiments that were expressed. Surprisingly, Williams apparently didn't come under FBI scrutiny like peers like Duke Ellington and Lena Horne[46]— there was no file for him under a search conducted of the FBI archives as allowed by the Freedom of Information Act (FOIA).[47] Ultimately, the FEPC effort failed and it took more than two decades for a successor organization, the Equal Employment Opportunity Commission, to come along.[48]

Cootie was able to show his support for labor in another situation just six months after his FEPC advocacy. In September 1946, the Seafarers International Union went on strike for higher wages in an event now known as the Maritime Strike of 1946. To support the struggle for labor, union members and sympathizers were requested to not board ships or cross picket lines. Williams received a letter "to walk off his ship."[49] "Williams was at first amazed but then recalled that for a period of two years prior to his breaking into the music field in New York he had been a member of the merchant marine as an able seaman."[50] He complied with the request. (This would have placed his time of service in the period of 1926 to 1928, when Cootie was living in Jacksonville, Florida. Unfortunately, neither the Seafarers International Union nor the Merchant Marines could find any record of his service.)[51]

Touring the South was always fraught with challenges for Black musicians. The constant presence of Jim Crow made the experience challenging. Food and lodging were hit or miss on the road. Despite providing entertainment for both Blacks and whites, once off the stage, the musicians weren't treated any better than any other Black person. A notable exception occurred when the Cootie Williams orchestra played at the Ocean Forest Hotel in Myrtle Beach, South Carolina. The waterfront Ocean Forest Hotel was considered one of the finest resorts in the South, if not the country. It catered to "the wealthiest families of the South."[52] One of the regulars was the state's governor, Strom Thurmond, an arch segregationist. Oddly, Cootie's band was booked at the Ocean Forest, becoming the first "colored" band to play in the sixteen years the hotel had been open.

Cootie and his band made quite an impression—"The management of the ultra-swank hotel was so pleased with the music and behavior of the Cootie Williams band that they accorded every member complete privilege of the resort. The bandsmen were treated as paying guests and were given rooms and meals in the hotel. They were also invited to swim on the beach and mingle with the guests."[53] It's a sad commentary that fair treatment for African Americans, enjoying their rights as full citizens in 1946, was newsworthy. [54]

African American celebrities faced conflicting pressures regarding the fight against Jim Crow. How does one fight and not get blackballed or come to physical harm? Passivity (or the appearance of it) gets one labelled as an Uncle Tom. Cootie Williams's involvement in the fight for civil rights can be illustrated in several events. In the parlance of the time, Williams was a "race man"[55] who "takes great pride in the achievements of his people."[56]

Cab Calloway had been invited to see Lionel Hampton perform by Hampton himself at the Pla-Mor club in Kansas City, Missouri, on December 22, 1945. Calloway and a friend were refused admission despite purchasing tickets at the door. When they wouldn't comply with the order to leave, the officer on duty hit Calloway on the head several times with his gun. When Hampton heard about the assault on Calloway during the intermission, he and the band walked off the job, forcing club management to issue refunds to 1,500 patrons.[57] Cootie, along with fellow bandleaders Lucky Millinder and Erskine Hawkins lent the "full weight of their prestige and popularity" and endorsed Hampton's walk-out. The three bandleaders sent telegrams of protest to the mayor and police chief of Kansas City.[58]

Cootie answered the call for talent to perform at a benefit concert for Isaac Woodard held at Lewishon Stadium on August 16, 1946. Woodard was a returning WWII veteran who was beaten and blinded by a southern sheriff for daring to request the use of a bathroom during a bus trip. The event was cochaired by Joe Louis and Carol Brice, and featured a "million dollars in talents." The list included Cootie Williams, Cab Calloway, W. C. Handy, Milton Berle, Orson Welles, Nat King Cole, Billie Holiday, and Louis Jordan.[59] The sold-out event raised $22,000 for Woodard.[60] (This would be the equivalent of $330,000 today.)

Cootie believed in the power of voting. His voting civic-mindedness wound up costing him a fair amount of money on one occasion. While at the Savoy, he was reminded that it was the last day to register to vote for the upcoming November 1948 election. Speeding home to St. Albans cost him $50 for a speeding ticket. He damaged his fender in the course of the trip, which cost $24 to repair. He sprained his ankle rushing down the stairs, incurring a $20 doctor bill. The roughly $100 incurred would be a stiff $1,200 today.[61]

A YEAR OF CHANGE

1947 would be one of the most eventful and consequential years in the life of Cootie Williams. It started off with a grand and historic occasion. On January 6, the orchestra performed at the New York Newspaper Guild's prestigious annual Front Page Ball. The Ball was an annual event that might be considering the press's equivalent to the movie industry's Academy Awards. Writers, publishers, and photographers were presented with awards celebrating their achievements of the previous year. In supplying the entertainment for the gala, Williams became only the second Black band to do so. (The first was Duke Ellington.) Williams's choice was "significant because of the consistent exclusion policy in the matter of using Negro bands practiced by practically all of the hotels in the Broadway sector."[1] They shared musical duties with a group led by Eddie Condon.[2]

During the early months of 1947, New York City experienced vaccination frenzy due to the discovery of nine cases of smallpox in a population of millions.[3] Cootie Williams decided it would be a good idea for the whole band to be vaccinated. Unfortunately, the band didn't agree and balked. In order to get the ball rolling, Williams led by example and agreed to be the first for the inoculation. Two days later, Williams came down with a mild form of the disease, developing a fever of 104 degrees. Despite his illness, he played his next gig before taking time to quarantine himself. (An unnamed band member joked "when the growler gets warm on that horn, it's a fever pitch anyway.")[4] Although no copyright information has been found for it, supposedly Williams composed a song with the title "Cowpox Boogie" to commemorate his ordeal.[5]

Besides leading by example, being a leader entails keeping order, but the degree of order and the level of discipline needed to achieve it was up to the individual leader. Cootie's brand of leadership meant implementing a fine system for lateness and "other infractions of discipline." They could take some comfort in the fact that their funds were going to charity "to aid the starving people of Europe."[6] Cootie's rationale was, "Most of the sufferers are members of minority groups, who suffered under the heel of the fascist marauders. I, as a member of [a] minority group, must necessarily feel a keen sympathy for their plight. But for the grace of God my people might very well be in their shoes."[7] Later the fines were designated to "organizations aiding displaced persons." Cootie said, "This painless extraction should help eliminate tardiness among the fellows. While I think all of them will try hard to avoid the fines, they certainly won't feel bad about it if they know that I am not keeping the money but using it to help in one of the greatest tragedies of all time."[8]

The Moe Gale touring package of the Ink Spots, Ella Fitzgerald, and Cootie Williams continued into 1947 and was still a huge draw in its fourth year of existence. At Washington, DC's new Music Hall, they "drew a banner opening crowd of 5,000, with the S.O. [Sold Out] sign going up as early as 10:30 p.m."[9] New York's Paramount saw "Williams's band scored solidly with its hard-driving tempo and then registered nicely with a mellow tune and as the background for Bob Merrill's provocative blues [singing]. The clear, true toning of the growl man's trumpet made it easy to understand why he won the Esquire magazine poll so handily."[10]

For years, Catherine Williams had longed to escape apartment living and own a home.[11] Part of the motivation was certainly driven by the lack of maintenance of their building at 555 Edgecombe Avenue in Harlem. It was described as the "swankiest of the swank apartment houses on New York's famed Sugar Hill." Besides the Williamses, it was home to celebrities like fellow bandleader Andy Kirk, boxing champion Joe Louis, actor Canada Lee, and the manager of the Savoy Ballroom, Charlie Buchanan. Despite the swank factor, the tenants weren't happy—the building wasn't being properly maintained. The complaints included "falling plaster, lack of water at intervals, heatless days, no hot water, and poor elevator service."[12] The Williamses had lived in the building since 1940.[13]

After years of patient waiting, Catherine was finally able to convince her husband that it was time to no longer live the tenant life and become homeowners. Their house hunting even made the gossip columns of the Black press. The *Chicago Defender* wrote, "Cootie Williams may add a palatial home in Long Island to the new high-priced car his wife's sporting along the boulevards."[14] On January 24, 1947, Catherine Williams signed the paperwork for the sale of 175–19 Linden Boulevard from Dr. Walter J. Lynch and his wife Dorothy. Cootie wasn't present since he was on the road on the day before (Monoa, Pennsylvania), the day of (Harrisburg, Pennsylvania), and the day after (Newark, New

Jersey). The house was in the St. Albans portion of Queens in a neighborhood known as Addisleigh Park. By the time the Williamses arrived, it was home to Count Basie and Lena Horne. Fats Waller was residing in Addisleigh Park at the time of his death in 1943. He was an early African American resident to the area—the neighborhood had restrictive covenants in place forbidding home sales to Blacks. At the time the neighborhood was being developed in 1926, its creator could boast that he had "land and house restrictions of the highest type."[15] The Williams's covenant did have a clause that allowed "that if a Negro lived in the home or the neighborhood for four months[,] a signatory to the covenant would void it."[16]

Ella Fitzgerald, Jackie Robinson, Roy Campanella, Mercer Ellington, Illinois Jacquet, and John Coltrane are among those who would call Addisleigh Park home over the years. The Addisleigh Park area was designated an Historic District by the NYC Landmarks Preservation Commission in 2011. In a neighborhood that didn't want African Americans, there is now a stretch of 113th Avenue renamed "Milt Hinton Place."[17]

The Williams home was built in 1931 in the medieval revival style. The two-story home had "approximately eight rooms, depending on whether the breakfast nook and sun-porch are counted,"[18] and a large basement. The basement was used for entertaining and it was said the Williams's "basement recreation room was constructed to set the fashion for all recreation rooms."[19] When Cootie was on the road, Catherine would take in Mercer Ellington's children to keep her company. She was godmother to Gay Ellington and Edward Ellington II, named after his famous grandfather.[20] Mercer considered the band as family when he was growing up, so it made sense that he would entrust his own children to the Williamses. He said, "They were like parents to me. Harry Carney would take me out to the beach with my big [stuffed] alligator. Cootie Williams would take me to the movies. Sonny Greer would give me a big barrel of pennies. . . . It was like one big family. I didn't really get to the stage where I could think in terms of these people being the big giants that they were musically."[21] Sometimes Dorothy Carney, Harry Carney's wife, would stay over too. Cootie turned into a carpenter for jobs around the new house, with his wife saying he was "doing a good job at it."[22]

♪

Williams was a teetotaler when he was with Ellington and Goodman. "I didn't drink at all until I got my band." When asked why he started drinking, he mused that "maybe handling men and seeing their reaction and going out on parties, with people inviting you out, and the thing that I never did drink. So I started to drinking."[23] In the midst of all the mayhem of bandleading, he's

30. A YEAR OF CHANGE

Cootie and Catherine Williams lived at 175–19 Linden Blvd from 1947 to 1962. This photo dates from 1940, nine years after the house was built. (Courtesy Municipal Archives, City of New York)

quoted as saying "Boy, if I had good sense, this would drive me crazy."[24] But he practiced a strange sort of moderation—"I never did drink steady. If I would drink two or three months, [then] I would lay off two or three months and check myself out. If I would drink this year, the next year I wouldn't drink. I found out that it makes you nervous. It works on the nervous system. I don't think you have the horn, the instrument under control, when—when you're not drinking, I used to always have my instrument under control. And I found that wasn't no good."[25] He was also aware of the effect it had on his playing: "Well, besides that, there's the fact that if you're drinking, and if you're being entertained, and you're the star or whatever, and you're drinking, even if you don't know it at the time, you know it the next day, that maybe everything wasn't just exactly the way you wanted it to be, because as you say, you're not really in control. If you're drinking, you don't know exactly just, you know, you're maybe not acting just the way you would be doing if you weren't drinking. I've been around many persons that drank and drank and drank, and it half killed a lot of good musicians. Famous musicians, alcohol has. And I see this thing has happened to them. And maybe, yes, when I look at them, and I see them, that's the reason I don't drink today [1976], again. It's been about 18 years since I had a drink of alcohol."[26] He also said that alcohol limited his technique and reflexes, "Things you want to do, by the time you'd be ready, they'd have gone right past. I wasn't in control."[27] He continued, "Remember, a lot of musicians sound bad when they're drinking. They are at their best when they're sober. I've heard fine big musicians sound like amateurs when they're high. Because drinking affects coordination—a drummer can't play up-tempos at all, and horns get sloppy all over. No, I've never seen anyone under the influence who could really play. They may *think* they're playing. . . ."[28]

Williams would tolerate errant behavior if the musician was talented, but a mediocre performance received no such grace, saying "if a musician doesn't have talent, I'm his bitter enemy while we're working. After I get off the stand, if we meet on other terms, we're all right. But when we go to work—I don't like him."[29]

The St. Albans neighborhood was a hotbed of activity for Black high society. One of the Williams's neighbors was Rose Morgan (1912–2008), who made a considerable fortune in Black beauty supplies. Her 1955 marriage to Joe Louis was a big event in the Black press and was even reported in the *New York Times*. The *Times* said that "among the wedding guests were Roy Campanella . . . Mrs. Campanella, Count Basie and Mrs. Basie, and Cootie Williams and his wife."[30] All those listed were St. Albans neighbors. (Unfortunately, the marriage only lasted three years.)

Her parties were covered in the society section of the Black press:

> Most novel soiree of the New York season was a combined house-closing and Christmas party hosted by Rose (Meta) Morgan in her St. Albans home. Christmas lights, strung on spruce shrubs, decorated the approach to the Georgian mansion; holly and Christmas ribbons festooned the four floors; and a maid greeted the 150 guests with a gift bottle of Bianca, Rose's latest perfume. Boasted the hostess: "This was the most inexpensive party I have given. With the help of Catherine (Mrs. Cootie Williams) and Elsie Mitchell I prepared all the food for the buffet supper, and people drank only $150 worth of liquor." But the combined wealth of the guests ran into about $10 million. Heading the list were two multi-millionaire French textile manufacturers, Robert Wassing and Max Berglas; Horace Titus, the writer-painter son and heir of cosmetic queen Helena Rubinstein; Maria (Mrs. Nat) Cole; Edgar Stern, owner of Hartz Mountain products for pets; and many other six figure socialites.[31]

Joe Louis and Cootie Williams had a long history together. Louis was a big fan of swing music. At one point in time, he wanted his own jazz band and he sought out Cootie for trumpet lessons. When the band idea didn't pan out, there was talk of him fronting Cootie's band as an MC, but that didn't come to fruition either. Knowing of Louis's love of music, Cootie offered to have his band play after Louis's 1948 training sessions for his upcoming fight with "Jersey Joe" Walcott.[32] It's not known if Louis took Cootie's offer for these post-workout sessions.

Sometime shortly after 1950,[33] the new home in St. Albans received a visitor—Cootie's father, Ike Williams. At that point, the senior Williams, then in his early sixties, decided to move in with his famous son. The former gambler and dockworker had a new profession—minister.[34]

It had been nearly twenty-five years since Cootie had left Mobile. In 1926, nine years after the death of Cootie's mother, Ike married Trudy Clabon, a divorcée five years older than himself.[35] Shortly afterward, he decided to expand his gambling activities to include horse race betting in New Orleans, about ninety miles from Mobile. He wasn't successful at the track and wound up broke. (It's ironic that Cootie even had a passion for horse racing considering it cost his father everything, but for him the hobby paid off.)

By 1930, Ike and Trudy had moved to Houston, Texas. Isaac Jr. and Elbert were no longer living with Ike, leaving only Leroy in the household. The 1930 federal census said Ike was employed as a foreman in the shipyards.[36] Cootie added an important detail to that description, saying "he was a sort of a strike breaker. When the men would go on strike, he would bring in other men to work." It was a dangerous job. During a strike in the fall of 1931, Ike refused to walk off the job with his fellow dock workers. This resulted in an argument with one of the strikers which escalated to a boiling point. A gun was drawn, and Ike got shot in the neck.[37] Cootie, with Ellington at the time, left New York and went to visit him at Houston's Jefferson Davis Hospital. Fortunately, Ike was able to pull through his injuries.[38] Despite the shooting, Ike returned to the docks after his recovery.[39]

In 1942, Ike and Trudy Williams moved to Alameda, California, which is on the eastern side of the San Francisco Bay adjoining Oakland. Perhaps the move was prompted by job opportunities created by the war. But the following year, Trudy died of colon cancer, leaving Ike a widower once more.[40] By the time of the 1950 census, Ike was living in Bakersfield, California.

Ike Williams had been many things by this point in his life—junk dealer, fur trader, gambling hall manager, longshoreman, and finally minister. Perhaps his near-fatal shooting in Houston caused the change, but Cootie knew his father well enough to be skeptical. He saw his father as "a good time man. [T]his was a new person coming to me and I couldn't understand it."[41] Cootie said, "My father was the type of man—his [way] was to get a dollar, you know. He was going to get that dollar from some kind of way. And maybe if he couldn't come through me he was coming through somebody. He was going to get that dollar."[42]

Unfortunately, Ike made the mistake of telling his adult son and wife how to run their household. Cootie said, "he came to live with me, and I provided a place for him. When I bought my home on Long Island, out there. So this time, when he came to me with all of this, different things, he shocked me. In my early days, of course, I used to like to drink and used to have parties and entertain. But he didn't want me to drink, didn't want me to have no company. I had a big bar in the basement of my home. He didn't want me to have no company that drank alcohol ... And I told him no. I said, 'No, Dad, that wouldn't work.' Not with my friends and my wife's friends. So he went and stayed with my younger brother [Leroy Barney Williams].

"So he stayed with [Barney] for a pretty good while. I told him that I would give him the money to stay any place else he wanted to stay. So he got mad with me. Because I wouldn't give up the [entertaining], you know. So he stayed in New York [with Leroy] for a pretty good while." Cootie said "[Leroy] was working at some club downtown. Just working as a layman."[43] What Cootie meant by "layman" is unclear, but at the time of his death in 1990, Leroy Barney Williams was working as a bartender.[44]

After "a pretty good while" in New York, Ike decided he wanted to go back to California. But he needed money to make the move. Ike and Cootie weren't on speaking terms. Cootie said, "He didn't want to see me, so he sent my younger brother out to the house to tell me that he wanted to go to California, he needed some money." Despite their estrangement, Cootie gave Ike money. Cootie said, "If there was anything I wanted while I was coming up, when he had money he gave it to me. So I wouldn't deny him of anything, you know. I gave him $300 (In 2024, that's the equivalent of almost $4,000.) [T]hat's about the last I heard of him, until he passed away." Williams said of his father, "My father didn't put enough money aside; now he envies me. But I have never forgotten that it was he who allowed me to learn to blow my trumpet. He lives in California; California is good when you're old! The sun warms your bones. Better to be poor in California than rich in New York. But I never go there."[45]

In the fall of 1959, Leroy Williams received word that Isaac Williams was seriously ill. In his 1976 Jazz Oral History Project interview, Cootie mentioned that the last he ever heard from his father was when he gave him money to leave New York. Cootie's estrangement from his father was such that he thought his father lived in California. Actually, he moved to Texas instead and spent the last six years of his life there.[46] After he got word, Leroy Williams flew to Laredo, Texas, to see his dying father.[47] Ike Williams had been admitted to Mercy Hospital on October 18 and succumbed from an ulcer of the duodenum eleven days later, on October 29.[48]

♪

In the thumbnail personality sketches of the Ellington band members in *Metronome*, one of Cootie's noted traits was that he was a "chronic gambler ... but a smart one." He had a lifelong love of horse racing, but his betting took on many forms. For Joe Louis's 1946 fight with Billy Conn, Williams bet against seven other bandleaders (Count Basie, Erskine Hawkins, Tiny Bradshaw, Lucky Millinder, Rex Stewart, Dizzy Gillespie, and Willie Bryant) to predict the Louis's winning round. Williams won, with the prize being six new suits, custom made for "his massive frame." Count Basie was dejected about losing, saying "Never did I feel a loss so keenly. A loss of money would have been quickly forgotten. But how I would have loved those six new outfits."[49]

On another wager, Cootie wound up betting against himself and lost, but he was "set up." He decided to take his new smaller band to Toledo to test its box office appeal. He bet the band if the crowd was more than a certain modest number, he would treat them to ringside seats at the upcoming Joe Louis/Jersey Joe Walcott fight. However, the pianist, Arnold Jarvis, had found out that the advance sale of tickets was so large that Cootie was just two hundred tickets shy of setting the record for the venue. Williams would have been none the wiser about the deception until he happened to overhear his men discussing the whole thing the following week. His loss cost him eight ringside seats.[50] Jarvis (1918–1975) occupied the piano chair for a long time, playing with Cootie off and on from 1945 to 1959. In June 1973, he was a wounded bystander when a patron shot up a Harlem bar. He never fully recovered from his wounds, dying some eighteen months later.[51]

Prize fights were a common item for Cootie's bets. But in addition to fights, Cootie would bet on the weather. During a torrential downpour just before a gig in Harrisburg, Pennsylvania, the promoter, fearing a loss from a lack of turnout, asked Williams to cancel the job and take the deposit and call it even. Williams decided to make his own offer—he wouldn't take the deposit, but instead would take 70 percent of the gate, no matter how small it was and absolve the promoter of any obligation. The promoter agreed, thinking that he would cut his losses. "Despite the torrential rains, Cootie drew more than 1800 patrons and made one of his tidiest 'hauls' of the year."[52]

He didn't win every bet, however. During a two-week Florida booking, Cootie made a comment about the rainy weather and how the weather was better in California. A friend disagreed and offered to pay one hundred dollars per night for any night where there was rain during Cootie's engagement. If it didn't rain, Cootie and his band had to provide the venue with an hour of extra music at no additional charge. Cootie wound up not collecting at all on this one.[53]

END OF AN ERA

The sound volume generated by the band and specifically that of the leader resulted in at least two lawsuits. In 1947, James Washington, described as a "vegetable and fruit peddler," was travelling in Harlem on his horse-drawn wagon. While stopped at "a traffic light on Lenox Avenue in front of the Savoy Ballroom, through whose windows was coming the pulsating rhythms of a hot jazz orchestra. And then above the throb of the other music there suddenly came the strident blare of a torrid trumpet solo." The trumpet solo allegedly startled Washington's horse, causing it to run up the street in a "mad dash" that only ended "when the wagon upset as the racing steed turned sharply into a side street." The judge ruled against Washington in that "it would be virtually impossible to prove that the noise from the instrument rather than any of many other normal sounds indigenous to life on Lenox Avenue was the causes of the horse's fright."[1] Cootie may have been lucky in this judgment since trumpeter Joe Newman recalled that "Cootie Williams was a very strong trumpeter player. I remember times when you could hear him two blocks away from the Savoy Ballroom."[2] It brings to mind that the legendary New Orleans trumpeter Charles "Buddy" Bolden (1877–1931) had a sound that was allegedly audible across the Mississippi River.

The following year, a Mrs. Elvira Singleton sued Cootie Williams for a broken eardrum "because she got too close to 'that powerful horn blower'" at a Shreveport, Louisiana, dance. Fortunately, Williams's lawyer was able to discover that Mrs. Singleton had received medical treatment for her ear condition several days prior to the event and as a result the case was thrown out. Afterward, Williams remarked, "Now I've seen everything. I've always taken pride in the power I've been able to inject into my horn blowing but this is the first time I ever heard of anyone trying to penalize you for giving your best to satisfy the customers. Well, thank heavens, the most of the customers like our entertainment."[3]

Cootie Williams returned to the Savoy Ballroom on January 16, 1947, not having appeared there since the previous June. The opening night was tumultuous. When the band attempted to leave for their break after their first set, they found their exit was "blocked by a frenzied mob of admirers who demanded encore after encore." The attendance was 1,697, a record for a weekday opening.[4]

At the end of January, he undertook his last tour as a leader with Ella Fitzgerald. They started out at Washington, DC's New Music Hall. In February, they were joined by the Ink Spots, thus reconstituting the Big Three tour that proved to be so popular and lucrative in 1944. The Big Three was booked into New York's Paramount Theater for the first three weeks of February and did record business. The third week only saw a drop in business because of a blizzard that was the worst seen in six years.[5]

The catchphrase "Open the Door, Richard" became nearly ubiquitous in 1947. Cootie's band "was the first musical organization to convulse Broadway with a personal presentation" of "Open the Door, Richard."[6] Cootie's blues shouter Bob Merrill performed the comedy routine. In the early part of 1947, several groups, including Count Basie, Louis Jordan, and Jack McVea had big selling records of the novelty item.[7] Why didn't Cootie capitalize on this song with his own recording? He was without a place to record it. At the beginning of the year, Capitol Records said they wouldn't be renewing his contract when it expired in June. But *The Billboard* reported if Cootie were to "come up with [a] hit record before that time, [Capitol] might change its mind. However, present attitude has maestro out of Capitol picture."[8] This seems to have been a preemptive move— big bands had been falling by the wayside over the last few months. But Capitol was merely reading the market and made 1947 a good year for them—they would gross "$14.5 million on 230 singles and 24 albums."[9] Although Cootie recorded twenty-four titles with Capitol, only thirteen, barely over 50 percent, were released during his time with the label. (Majestic, the next label that Cootie was to sign with, already had a version of the song in release by the Merry Macs and perhaps didn't want to cannibalize their own sales.)[10] Ironically, in March 1947, Capitol proclaimed that Cootie Williams's band was the top seller for the label for the year 1945. He was also the first trumpet-playing leader to hold this position. Previously, saxophonists had held this distinction.[11]

Fortunately, there was an option in Williams's Capitol contract that allowed him to obtain an early release. He signed with Majestic Records for a three-year term. In a bit of PR puffery, Majestic was said to have pulled off a coup when it "grabbed off one of the choicest jazz packages on the market today."[12] Majestic Records launched in 1945 when the Majestic Radio company bought the Hit Record label. The president was the former mayor of New York (1926–1932),

Jimmy Walker, and the general manager was Eli Oberstein, who was only with them for a short time. Walker was an odd choice to run a record company. His prior job was working as a garment industry executive and he confessed he wasn't a fan of what he called "the jive" (as the music was sometimes called during those days).[13] Majestic bought the Hit and Classic labels' catalog that was owned by Eli Oberstein.[14] So Williams was essentially returning to the label he had left for Capitol. But perhaps he was convinced that things would be different since Eli Oberstein was no longer part of the operation, having left for RCA Victor in August 1945.[15]

Majestic Records was a slipshod operation, so the two sessions Williams made for them have no precise dates attached to them. On a session only dated as "1947," Cootie Williams and his Orchestra recorded four titles: "Sound Track," "I Want To Be Loved (But Only By You)," "Inflation Blues," and "I Can't Get Started." But based on newspaper articles, the first Majestic session would have occurred in late March/early April 1947.[16] The *Baltimore Afro-American* reported that the band was to "begin recording chores under the Majestic banner on April 1," but that can't be confirmed by any recording logs. Cootie's first session for his new/old label consisted of four titles; two are mentioned by the *Afro-American*—"Inflation Blues" and "Cootie's Beauty."[17] Perhaps the latter title was the original for the song released as "Sound Track," an instrumental written by Cootie Williams and tenor saxophonist Eddie Johnson.

"I Want To Be Loved (But Only By You)," a ballad, was sung by Billy Mathews. His deep baritone voice belied his youth—he was only seventeen. He was introduced to Williams backstage at his March stint at the Apollo Theater by a mutual friend who had heard Mathews sing at a school party. Williams gave him an audition on the spot, and he joined the band almost immediately.[18] The song was written by Savannah Churchill and her recording was a big hit in early 1947. *Billboard* said Mathews "pipes it slowly and expressively but without its sultry nuances."[19]

Recording "I Can't Get Started" was somewhat controversial. The song became associated with trumpeter and vocalist Bernard "Bunny" Berigan when he recorded it in 1936 (for Vocalion) and in 1937 (for RCA Victor). His early death from the effects of alcoholism in 1942, just five years in the past, made the song even more sacrosanct. Cootie's version didn't include a vocal but it was a bravura display of his open trumpet work. In assessing Berigan's legacy as a jazz trumpeter, *Down Beat* rated him one of the "four most popular trumpeters of all time" along with Louis Armstrong, Bix Beiderbecke, and Cootie Williams himself.[20] Armstrong himself refused to play or record the song himself out of deference to Berigan.[21]

In 1947, the postwar economy posted an inflation rate of 20 percent.[22] "Inflation Blues" commiserated with the public's pain with another vocal feature for

Bob Merrill, lamenting "it's getting so lately, I can't even afford to buy a glass of beer." Williams was being squeezed by it on his business side; inflation caused the musicians' union to raise the pay scales, putting a bind on Williams's bottom line. Williams saw incorporation as a way to solve the problem.[23] It is not known if Williams actually followed through with this idea.

Majestic had access to the Hit Records catalog because Eli Oberstein had been involved with both companies. As such, Majestic rereleased old Hit label disks under its banner, a practice that caused some confusion for fans and critics. Majestic's 1947 release of "Echoes of Harlem" was thought to be a new recording, but it was from 1944. The *Hollywood Reporter* was fooled: "Cootie Williams's new version of 'Echoes of Harlem' is the best side he's made for Majestic. He should record more such tunes and steer clear of novelties."[24]

April saw the band make a short tour through Virginia, West Virginia, Indiana, and Illinois before their stop in Cleveland, Ohio. Although Williams had played Cleveland many times, this visit drew one of his largest crowds. Afterwards, Williams gave the band a two-day vacation, calling it a "spring fever" holiday. Cootie said that "when the first warm days come musicians, like anybody else, suffer the pangs of spring fever. I find that if you give the men a day or so to just relax and loll about they come back to work with more bounce than ever."[25]

The band was playing a dance at the Evansville, Indiana, Coliseum on April 27 when during the pre-dawn hours of Sunday morning, a fire broke out backstage. It burned the theater's electrical wiring and plunged the theater into darkness. Fortunately, Cootie kept the band playing and they were credited with averting a panic. Until the fire department showed up and ordered an evacuation, the patrons had no idea they were in danger.[26]

Perhaps the calm in the face of sudden darkness is something that Cootie and the band remembered as a lesson learned when they were ringing in 1947, four months prior to the Evansville fire, at North Carolina's Camp LeJeune. The base had arranged for the lights to go off and start a fireworks barrage at the stroke of midnight. Unfortunately, no one had thought to tell the band about the plan. When midnight struck there was darkness and explosions, so the band stopped playing and ran to the shelters in a panic. It took "several ranking officers" to convince the band that the base was not under attack and was safe to resume the dance.[27]

For May, the Gale Agency decided to create a new package tour. Cootie Williams, Ella Fitzgerald, and, in place of the Ink Spots, Illinois Jacquet and his small band would open in Chicago's Regal Theater on May 2.[28] This package also proved to be popular, once again setting attendance records.[29]

On May 11, Cootie Williams was booked as the inaugural band for the opening of the W. C. Handy Theatre in Memphis. Handy was someone Williams admired greatly. To show his gratitude, he started a college scholarship fund for trumpeters in Handy's name.[30] In addition to Williams and his band, the opening bill featured popular comedian Mantan Moreland and his stage partner Heywood Jones, and the Congaroos (a dance group). Cootie showed himself quite the fashion plate, "nattily dressed in a pearl grey double-breasted suit with white shoes and cravat to match." The band was "terrific" and "Williams's trumpet is one of the most amazing extant."[31] The package proved so popular that they performed a special late night "Ramble for Whites" at the neighboring whites-only Airway Theater. The show drew what was the largest audience to ever attend a performance in Memphis up until that time.[32] (The Handy Theater was in the Black part of town and was designated as a "colored" venue. In later years, the Handy Theater would host "Midnight Rambles," late night shows for a whites-only audience.[33] It closed in 1955 and by 1960s it was an unused eyesore. It was demolished in 2012.)[34]

The Handy Theatre opening was the beginning of what would be the big band's last swing through the South. Dates in Mississippi, Louisiana, and Arkansas completed the month of May. It was reported that Williams had to keep the peace during one of the stops: "Cootie Williams[,] who holds a deputy sheriff badge[,] was pressed into service while playing Alexandria, La., last week when a gang war started that the local cops couldn't handle."[35] It's unknown if it was Cootie's celebrity or his fists that quelled the violence.

♪

There are a lot of advantages to being a regular attraction at a club. No road weariness, getting to sleep in your own bed every night, and you don't have to lug equipment anywhere. Unfortunately, in Williams's case, the latter turned out to be a disadvantage when someone stole his trumpet from his dressing room at the Savoy Ballroom. It was even more of an inconvenience because he had a Majestic recording session the next day. But when word went out about his plight, no less than eight trumpeters loaned Cootie an instrument. The generous donors were heavyweights—Louis Armstrong, Erskine Hawkins, Harry James, Dizzy Gillespie, "Hot Lips" Page, Charlie Spivak, Cat Anderson, and the now obscure Randy Brooks. Considering his future relationship with Williams, Anderson's generosity is ironic. In keeping with Majestic's sketchy record keeping, Williams's second session for them has only been dated as occurring in July 1947 in discographies. But based on the newspaper reports of the incident, the date was probably July 24.[36] (Cootie had his horn stolen from the stage of the Paramount a couple of years prior to this. The "fan" who took it said he only wanted it as a souvenir and Cootie declined to press charges.)[37]

This would turn out to be the last time that Cootie's big band would be inside a recording studio. This version of the orchestra had a six-man(!) trumpet section. As a sign of changing tastes, all four of the songs recorded at this session had vocals. Three were of the novelty type and there was one ballad.

"If It's True" was aimed at the crooner market. It was another feature for Billy Mathews, but unfortunately it failed to chart. "Ooh-La-La" was promoted as Cootie's contribution for "the war on long skirts." He was able to generate further publicity for it by hosting an "Ooh-la-la leg contest" at his September booking at the Apollo Theater. "The object of the contest will be to find the prettiest pair of legs in the theater audiences at each performance of the all-star vaudeville show headed by the old growl trumpeter and his band during the week."[38]

"Save the Bones for Henry Jones" starts with a short bit of banter between Williams and Merrill before Merrill sings this novelty number. Cootie's solo is a clinic on the number of tonal inflections that can be obtained with the plunger mute. "I Should o' Been Thinkin' Instead of Drinkin'," another novelty with vocal by Merrill, also features a rare Merrill trumpet solo. Cowritten by Cootie Williams, it may have been a humorously regretful reflection on the amount of alcohol he was consuming.

These last two numbers were paired on a Majestic release and received mixed reviews. The *Hollywood Reporter* thought the band sounded good but "the Bob Merrill vocals are wasted effort. His intonation is poor and you can barely understand more than half of the words."[39] *The Billboard* said "it's a pairing of excellent race doggerels with Bob Merrell's [sic] rhythmic and lusty race blues shouting carrying the cuttings. The band setting down a solid base, Merell [sic] brings out the race humor flavor for both novelty pieces."[40] But *Metronome* was the harshest, offering that Majestic could help Cootie out "by forcing some good material on him." They called the Merrill songs "objectionable" and finished their review with "Cootie sounds like a combination of Dizzy Gillespie and Erskine Hawkins in trying for these many tasteless effects."[41]

An August 6, 1947, aircheck recorded for the *Midnight Jamboree* radio show series at Washington DC's Howard Theatre, is the last known recording of Cootie's big band. In what survives of the broadcast, the band can be heard playing two of the songs recorded the previous month and providing backing for Ella Fitzgerald on "Across the Alley From the Alamo."

With the touring package still drawing well, it puzzled Williams when the Gale Agency demanded that he shrink the size of his band. There were rumors that this move was coming. *Pittsburgh Courier* columnist Billy Rowe wrote, "Don't be surprised if Cootie Williams cuts his big band down to seven pieces. . . . The success of Louis Armstrong on the small combo tip has got all the guys thinking in terms of smaller aggregations. Eddie (Cleanhead) Vinson jumped

Publicity photo of Cootie Williams under the banner of Universal Attractions. (Author's collection)

into the field and is having unbelievable success."[42] Louis Jordan had been showing the viability (and profitability) for small-group music for some time.

But the era of the big band was coming to a close, leaving big name bands facing downsizing or disbanding altogether. Moe Gale told Williams it was too difficult to find places that were willing to pay for a full-sized big band and he would need to downsize in order to be marketable. Williams refused. Instead, in November he requested a release from his contract with the Gale Agency, which had three years left to run.

In order to settle the books with the Gale Agency, Williams had to write a check for money owed. Perhaps the sum was significant, because a week later, Williams asked for the check back and agreed to shrink his band and dropped his request to leave the Gale Agency. But Gale refused. Maybe Gale had tired of arguing with Williams and perhaps his vacillation had become too much—he agreed to let Cootie sign with Universal Attractions management agency and waived the exclusion period.[43] Universal Attractions, had been founded by Ben Bart (1906–1968), a former Gale Agency agent, in 1945. Some Gale clients, like the Ink Spots, went over to Bart's new firm. By 1947, in order to prevent Universal from poaching clients, the firms had an agreement in which they could not sign a Gale artist for three years.[44] In assessing the move, Cootie said, "I went with [Universal]. And they were strictly colored, you know. Dinah Washington, I think they had. And it didn't do no good. In fact, things started to dropping. And eventually, I got the house band at the Savoy. I had the house band in the Savoy until they closed it down."[45] As Williams said, Universal Attractions specialized in Black talent like the Gale Agency. Besides Williams and the Ink Spots, their talent roster included saxophonist Earl Bostic, Eddie "Cleanhead" Vinson, Dinah Washington, and blues singer Gatemouth Moore.[46]

Even though he disbanded his full-sized orchestra before other big name bandleaders like Cab Calloway and Count Basie, it cost Williams dearly. "I lost 50,000 dollars by insisting on keeping this big band. 50,000 dollars! But the sound was so beautiful. Wonderful! $50,000 messed up for the pleasure of being accompanied by a big band! I was crazy! My wife said to me, 'Buy yourself a good phonograph and play in front of *that*.' But I couldn't bring myself to dissolve it."[47]

Reflecting upon these times, Cootie said, "I organized a big band, and for a while, things were bad. But in 1943 I made two hundred and fifty thousand dollars. Half of that went to my backers. Everybody had backers in those days, or they would have sunk. Then I quit my backers and I sunk, and in 1948 [*sic*] I gave up the big band and took on a small one."[48] In his 1976 Jazz Oral History Project interview, Cootie summed up the times thusly: "Well, now, let me tell you. So I wasn't doing nothing [in 1942]. So the next year, I think I made $250,000." "I had 'Cherry Red Blues,' yeah. And 'Things Ain't What They Used to Be.' And they didn't squeeze me out. I got in all the major theaters cross country. And I played everything. [Gale] was in on fifty percent of that. So after I'd made all this money, I go to Moe Gale and tell him, I said, 'Man I can't give you fifty percent of my earnings.' There's no contract you can make with a man to get fifty percent of your earnings. So I knew that. And so now, I'm mighty well established see, and I'm rolling on. The next year [1945] I make $150,000.00. So I started to going down. And sure as shooting, it's a control on that business. Soon as I started giving up that fifty percent, I could see the difference in the bookings."[49]

Interestingly, in a 1945 interview, Cootie had mused about getting out of the music business entirely: "I want to get out of the music business while I'm still young. I'm going to get me a couple of apartment houses and live off that. All musicians—colored and white—live today and damn tomorrow. They live their money and when they die people have to take up a collection for their widow."[50] What would his legacy have been if he had done that? It's unknown, of course, but many musicians of his generation didn't continue in music through their life. Saxophonist Otto Hardwick left the Ellington band in 1946 and shortly thereafter quit music altogether.[51] Cootie wound up storing his orchestra's arrangements in his house, along with some unfinished arrangements that he hoped to complete in the future.[52] The current whereabouts of his band's archives is unknown at this time.

In his massive, nearly nine-hundred-page book *The Swing Era*, Gunther Schuller wrote that "Cootie and his orchestra fell prey to the risks and flaws inherent in being caught between two styles. Not fully committed to the incoming bop, and at the same time not quite able to relinquish the safe ground of swing, Cootie, both in his choice of personnel and in the performances of his players, seemed to waver, unable to assume a clear direction."[53] Schuller's assessment shows that he was unaware that Cootie's strategy of combining the old and the new was deliberate. During the 1942 to 1947 period in which Williams's big band existed, music was in transition, so it's unfair to say that Williams was "unable to assume a clear direction." (Of course, music is dynamic and always in transition.) Cootie said he was unconcerned with musical categories: "I get mixed up and confused with all that stuff. I don't know WHAT you'd call my band. I call it a band that plays good music . . . that's all. We just play good music the best way we know how."[54] Gunther Schuller doesn't attach much importance to Cootie's big band and gives it scant coverage. Cootie's band and that of Erskine Hawkins share a ten-page chapter and are the only subjects given that treatment. Out of the ten pages, Williams is only the subject of two and a half pages. Schuller gets a lot of dates and facts wrong in those few pages. As for Cootie's last years, Schuller dismissed Cootie's return to Ellington as "re-creating himself and Bubber Miley in endless one-night stand on the road with Duke." He also incorrectly stated that Cootie stayed "with Mercer Ellington's band until his death in 1985."[55]

Cootie Williams and His Orchestra existed for only about five and a half years. Cootie's legacy as an orchestra leader is not what it should be for several reasons. First of all, the recording ban of 1942–44 robbed him of visibility and sales just when he was getting his band off the ground. Secondly, except for his short stint at Capitol Records, he wasn't able to enjoy the distribution, advertising, and exposure that a major label could provide. Third, unlike Ellington, Basie, Calloway, Hampton and Armstrong, Cootie was not able to cross over to the white market.

PART V
Cootie Williams, Combo Leader (1947)

32

THINGS AIN'T WHAT THEY USED TO BE

In the fall of 1947, Cootie Williams scaled down from an orchestra of seventeen musicians to an octet. The postwar period had not been kind to the big bands. Changing tastes, an aging fan base, and the recording ban made it difficult to support large aggregations. Cootie wasn't alone in scaling down; his hero Louis Armstrong ditched his big band and began fronting a combo that would be his touring format until the end of his career.

Cootie's new combo was still able to provide solid musical entertainment. *Variety* wrote: "Cootie Williams band provides more sizzling syncopation in closing slot [of the show]. Fronted by Williams on trumpet, combo consists of three rhythm, trumpet and sax, with some of the lads doubling on instruments. They're plenty torrid and really cook on 'Typhoon,' 'Echoes of Harlem' and 'House of Joy' for plenty salvos."[1] Even in a small-group incarnation, the Williams group continued to be an "audience favorite." "Cootie Williams and his big little band . . . really set off the pyrotechnics with their jump and race tunes. Williams carries the burden of the [session] with his scat singing and trumpeting. Although most of the numbers are unidentifiable, they're plenty loud and seem just what the doctor ordered for this audience."[2]

An indication of lean times, Cab Calloway and Duke Ellington took on tours of the South during 1947, something they had avoided as much as possible in the past due to the dangers of Jim Crow.[3] Shortly afterward, Cab Calloway would disband his big band, despite being one of the three Black bands that Cootie had predicted would survive. Although he faced economic difficulties, Ellington never broke up his big band during the entirety of his career.

Cootie's current record label, Majestic Records, was struggling during the last year of the big band's existence. Drummer Ray McKinley terminated his deal with Majestic due to "dissatisfaction with the label's production and distribution of his disks."[4] The label was struggling financially; they would stop recording in December 1947 and filed for Chapter 11 bankruptcy the following February.[5] Like his other label associations, Cootie's tenure with Majestic was short, which like his past and future associations, was the rule, not the exception. He was able to quickly jump to Mercury Records, and in the period from 1947 to 1949, he logged only three sessions under his own name. (Cleanhead had started recording with Mercury in October.) Mercury Records was just a six-year-old concern at the time Williams signed with them. Williams's first records for Mercury were billed as "Cootie Williams and His Orchestra," but the "orchestra" was now an octet—two trumpets (Williams and Merrill), two saxes, and a four-piece rhythm section.

Of the four songs Williams recorded, three were originals either written or cowritten by Williams. "You Talk a Little Trash" was another visit to a Williams composition that he had first recorded for Hit Records at the beginning of 1944. "I Love You, Yes I Do" was a vocal feature for Billy Mathews and a backing group, The Balladeers. It had been recorded earlier by saxophonist "Bull Moose" Jackson, who scored a big it with it. "Typhoon" is aptly named; it's an exciting ride based on the standard "I Got Rhythm" changes. Taken at about 280 bpm, it was mostly a showcase for tenor saxophonist Bill "Weasel" Parker, but Cootie's chorus is an exciting dialogue with the ensemble.

Eddie Condon didn't recognize Cootie in the recording when it was played for him in a Leonard Feather blindfold test for the August 1949 issue of *Metronome*. He asked "Is most bop played at that bright a tempo? . . . This sounds like an aviary, too many birds flying around. What do I think is wrong with it? That's easy—the music is bad. This is just exhibitionism and nothing else. Well, give 'em one star just for being there that day."[6]

At the end of November 1947, Williams shared the bill with singer Dinah Washington at St. Louis's Club Riviera, an upscale venue catering to the Black trade. Dinah Washington (née Ruth Jones, 1924–1963) was a Lionel Hampton discovery. Like Cootie, she was from Alabama, born and raised in Tuscaloosa. She had hit records with "Salty Papa Blues" and "Evil Gal Blues" in 1944.[7] She left Hampton in 1946 and was at the beginning of a career that would make her one of the most successful singers of the 1950s.

Club Riviera's owner, Jordan Chambers, and singer Frankie Laine sponsored a Teenage Jamboree show for Saturday, December 13. The lineup was Cab Calloway, Frankie Laine, and Dinah Washington, an odd group for teenage tastes. The goal of the event was to give these underage people a taste of what they couldn't see in a nightspot.

The crowd of over 5,000 started to gather at 12:30 p.m. for the 3:00 p.m. show and the street was completely blocked a half hour before start time. Laine, Calloway, and Washington did their portion of the show to an enthusiastic audience. However, when Cootie's band performed "House of Joy," pandemonium ensued and the place had to be cleared, with the plate glass doors of the club destroyed in the process.[8]

Cootie's second Mercury session was as the backing band for Dinah Washington on December 30, 1947. Four tracks were made and released with the billing "Dinah Washington and Cootie Williams Orchestra." The "orchestra" was the same octet that Williams recorded for the first time just three days previous. These studio dates were necessary to stockpile materials, for on January 1, 1948, the musician's union second recording ban went into effect, just two days after the Williams/Washington studio date. The ban would last until November 13, an eleven-month interruption.[9] Dinah's "Record Ban Blues" from that date contained a dig against the AFM president near the conclusion that went, "Now you've heard my story, and that's the way it goes. So don't ask me when I'll record again, because only Petrillo knows."

At the end of April 1948, Cootie's band had just closed a successful run at Washington, DC's Club Bengasi. On April 26, at Washington, DC's Dunbar Hotel, the police were summoned to quelle drunken rowdiness involving Dusty Fletcher and Williams. Clinton "Dusty" Fletcher (1900–1954) was credited as one of the originators of "Open the Door, Richard," and according to the press, he was a friend of Cootie's. Williams and Fletcher had "engaged in a bit of imbibing" in Williams's room, which resulted in a bit of loud arguing. Hotel management was summoned at the behest of the patrons and the two quarrelers were separated back to their respective rooms. All was well until Fletcher returned to Williams's room to apologize. A woman in Cootie's room feared a reprise of the mayhem and called the police. (The newspaper didn't name the woman.) At some point this general disturbance, Williams "fell and cut [his] right thumb and [the] palm of [his] right hand."[10] In a case of life imitating art, one witness to the incident reported that Fletcher "ran from door to door in the hotel, shouting "Open the Door, Richard!'"[11] Williams and Fletcher were carted away to DC Precinct 13 but they weren't arrested since neither would swear out a complaint against one another. The police report said Williams "was taken to Freedmen's Hospital and refused treatment." Unfortunately, the injury was to his playing hand and playing the trumpet aggravated the wound which wouldn't allow it to heal. According to the press at the time, there was a possibility that the untreated wound could be career ending. Over four months later, he had surgery to graft skin from his arm to the injured area. The procedure was performed by Dr. Arthur Logan, who had been Duke Ellington's personal physician since 1937.[12]

For Cootie's May run at the Savoy Ballroom, someone (however, not Cootie) came up with a gimmick to have Williams take on any willing trumpeter in a cutting contest. Ostensibly, it was an answer to press talk about who was supreme on trumpet in the wake of battles pitting bop versus the older styles.[13] It's unknown how many (if any) responded to the challenge.

On May 29, Cootie Williams wound up in prison after the two-week May Savoy stand—not for any crime, but to play for the inmates at Elmira State Reformatory. It seems a friend who was recently a "guest" there told Williams that the inmates "seldom get to hear any major Negro bands, although many of the men are ardent admirers of race orchestras."[14]

The next southern tour by Williams and his band started on June 11 in Lynchburg, Virginia. While on their New Orleans stop, Cootie was honored by the New Jazz Foundation and presented with a certificate for his "meritorious contribution to American jazz."[15]

In mid-August, Cootie announced he planned to take four weeks off and vacation in Mexico for the last two weeks of it.[16] The vacation had been delayed due to his hand surgery.[17] He had another purpose in mind, too—scouting out musical ideas from the Mexican culture.[18] It was rumored that a pending movie short deal might cut short the vacation,[19] but that's not what interrupted his rest plans. The vacation didn't even get started. Just as they were getting ready to leave the country, Arnett Cobb was hospitalized for what was characterized as major surgery. Cootie stepped in and took dates that had been booked for Cobb at the Apollo, starting on September 10. He also filled in for Cobb at DC's Howard Theater the following week.[20]

At the Apollo, Cootie shared the musical chores with Ray Anthony's eleven-piece band. Cootie had seven men, with an instrumentation of trumpet, trombone, two saxophones, and a three-piece rhythm section. *Variety* gave an enthusiastic review: "Cootie Williams and his big little band close [the show] and really set off the pyrotechnics with their jump and race tunes. Williams carries the burden of the [session] with his scat singing and trumpeting. However, he gets splendid support from the [band] that background him. Although most of the numbers are unidentifiable, they're plenty loud and seem just what the doctor ordered for this audience."[21]

In September, most likely due to the scare caused by the hand injury, Cootie sought to insure his playing hand for $50,000, which is roughly equivalent to $615,000 in today's dollars. Unfortunately, his application was denied due to a hobby that was deemed to be too dangerous—playing bocce ball. But the insurance would be granted if Williams were to give up his pursuit of the game.[22] This may have been just a public relations story since three years prior, it was reported that Williams's right hand was insured for $30,000.[23] In the same story, Williams was said to be a big believer in insurance, with many policies—his twelve trumpets were insured against fire and theft for $1,500 and he carried approximately $50,000 worth of life insurance. He also carried policies on his home, furniture, cars, bus and even his dog![24]

Shortly after the southern tour, Cootie was in Chicago, and gave the interview published by *Down Beat* in their August 11, 1948, issue. In a July 1945 interview for *PM*, Williams had mused about getting out of the music business and did it again in this article. He planned to get out of the rut sometime in 1949, saying "I want to go into some other business maybe a hotel or bar. I have a house in St. Albans (Long Island), and I'd like to stay home with my wife. We've been married 19 years, you know." But he added, "I'll always play music. Probably in the bar and around." In evaluating Williams's current band, *Down Beat* didn't think much of tenor saxophonist Weasel Parker, saying he "played it loud, with blatant honks and screeches" and "there still wasn't much to the exhibition except a lot of released energy."[25] John Hammond, who always had the highest admiration for Cootie, went to see the band and "my ears were assaulted by innumerable choruses from a wild, screaming, and thoroughly unmusical tenor sax man [Parker], and the bleatings of a so-called blues shouter [Bob Merrill]. America's most naturally gifted trumpet player has been reduced to a minor attraction in a side-show, one of the real tragedies of the music business."[26]

It was understandable that Williams and the band didn't travel internationally during their early years due to the war. Three years after WWII ended, the notion of a tour to Australia was floated. Frank Johnson, publisher of the Australian music magazine, *Tempo*,[27] proposed a series of December 1948 dates starring Cootie. However, the planned concerts failed to materialize. There was also talk of touring the West Indies during the same time period. Supposedly, the Williams band would be "the first modern jazz band to visit the islands." But this was another touring opportunity that failed to come to fruition.[28]

After another week at the Savoy Ballroom in the middle of December, Williams and his band embarked on yet another southern tour. Christmas Eve was spent in Greenwood, Mississippi, and Christmas in Vicksburg. They welcomed 1949 at Laurel Air Base, also in Mississippi. Williams wouldn't be back in New York until the first week of February.

The increased reliance on the South reflected the fact that the business base was shrinking and ignoring that region was no longer the option it was in years past. The end of 1948 found Lionel Hampton undertaking his first southern tour in seven years. But because the big names were a rarity in the South, the promoters could charge triple the ticket price while only having half the audience size.[29]

For the rest of January 1949, the group made stops in Louisiana, Texas, and Oklahoma, before encountering bad weather in Kansas City, Missouri. That show, and a few subsequent dates, were disrupted by snow.

GATOR

Williams continued to scout for musicians, both at jam sessions and club gigs. One such jam session find was a young tenor saxophonist named Willis Jackson (1932–1987).[1] Jackson was from Florida, hence the nickname "Gator." He was a college man, a graduate of Florida A&M. He had only started playing the saxophone at age eighteen, which is rather late when compared to his peers.

Articles in the press were generated for the new addition's "athletic" style of play—"When he really gets into stride, he runs, jumps, twists, turns and practically turns somersaults—all while blowing his saxophone to the delight of the assembled crowds who flock to hear and watch him in action."[2] (Fortunately, there is surviving video of Jackson's 1955 appearance on the Ed Sullivan show. Jackson plays "Gator Tail," and we get to see a demonstration of his frantic, physical showmanship.)

Another publicity story backfired, to the embarrassment of Williams and Jackson. It was later attributed to press agent Joe Bostic and carried the headline "Jacquet Defeated in Tenor Battle." The article starts: "Youthful Willis Jackson, tenor sax sensation of the Cootie Williams band, has emerged as the unofficial king of the tenor sax following a two day running, 'battle of the blowers' at the Savoy Ballroom. . . ." It concluded by stating that "[v]eterans of the Harlem jazz scene agreed that this was the most exciting music event to stir the uptown community" since the days Chick Webb and Benny Goodman dueled.[3]

There was a huge problem with this tale; it didn't happen. Cootie Williams and Illinois Jacquet were at the Savoy on the dates in question, but there was no battle—just two bands in rotating, non-overlapping sets. Jacquet's press agent, Jim McCarthy, said that only in Bostic's "warped imagination" could Jacquet be "'carved' by a rank 15 dollar a night sideman"! Jacquet took it all in stride:

"I don't blame Cootie or Jackson for this story—it's just a case of a press agent shooting his big mouth off."[4]

Cootie was finally able to return to the recording studios after yet another long absence. March 2, 1949, marked the recording debut for Willis Jackson and it had been fourteen months since Williams had been in the studio. The band recorded three songs—"Let the Good Times Roll," a feature for the blues shouting of Bob Merrill, "Sliding and Gliding," and what could be considered a primer on R&B saxophonics, "Gator Tail." "Gator Tail" was released in two parts on a single disc. It was also unusual in being strictly a feature for the sideman Jackson; Cootie doesn't solo at all. Across twenty-nine choruses of a B♭ blues, Jackson honks and squeals his way across two sides of a 78 RPM record.

The record made an impact on author Jack Kerouac, meriting a mention in "On the Road": "[Dean] leaped out of the chair and put on a Willie [sic] Jackson record, 'Gator Tail.' He stood before it, socking his palms and rocking and pumping his knees to the beat. 'Whoo! That sonumbitch! First time I heard him I thought he'd die the next night, but he's still alive.'"[5] It wasn't a bad assumption to credit the disk to Jackson since he's the only soloist, but it made it hard to find the recording unless you knew it was under Cootie's name. Not many leaders (with the notable exception of Duke Ellington) put out records where they don't solo for a few bars. Perhaps the record should have been titled "Concerto for Gator."

Cootie's French champion Hugues Panassie caught the Williams combo at the Savoy in early 1949 and remarked that "Cootie is still a great trumpet player." But he didn't like the fact that Cootie greatly reduced his solo time in order to feature Jackson, who was a commercial draw. Not only did he find it boring to hear "a single note for three or four choruses . . . streaked with screams" he thought it was appalling to think that you could cross the street to another club and "hear another tenor sax player doing exactly the same thing."[6]

Universal Attractions, like the Gale Agency, liked to send its acts out in packaged units. At the beginning of March 1949, Universal sent out Dinah Washington, Cootie Williams, and the Ravens. The Ravens were a male vocal quartet and at the time, had several "race record" hits under their belt—"Write Me A Letter," "Old Man River," and "Bye Bye Baby Blues."[7] The tour started at the Philadelphia Theater on March 4 and was to last a month. The newspaper advertisements of the time give top billing to the Ravens.

While Cootie preferred a big band over a small group, at least a combo can travel with fewer seats and therefore smaller vehicles. In 1948, it was reported that Williams's band traveled in a customized "busette," which was described as "a cross between a bus and a station wagon."[8] The life of a traveling musician is full of travails—bad or scarce food, unobtainable lodging. On top of it all, there is the hazard of road travel. Musicians such as Bessie Smith, Chu Berry, Clifford Brown, and Scott LaFaro, just to name a few, were victims of their time on the road. On Friday morning, April 8, 1949, at approximately 8:30 a.m., the limousine carrying Cootie and a portion of the band suffered a broken axle while traveling through Franklin, Virginia, on their way to the next gig. As a result, one of the rear tires flew off the vehicle, causing the car to flip over four times. (As a reminder, this was in the time before seat belts and shoulder harnesses.) Williams "suffered severe bruises of the chest and shock" and wound up spending a little less than three days in the hospital in Norfolk under observation. The others injured were pianist Lester Fauntleroy, with a "broken back, broken spine and fractured wrist," alto saxophonist Rupert Cole, "broken ribs and serious cuts," road manager Howard "Bud" Shorter, "fractured ribs, spine and pelvis," and driver Marcus Coleman, "broken collar bone and contusions."[9] The injuries to Bob Merrill and Willis Jackson weren't severe.[10] Fortunately, the cars carrying Dinah Washington and the Ravens were behind the Williams vehicle and stopped to render assistance and drive the injured to nearby hospitals.

Cootie took only a little time off for recovery. When released from the hospital in Norfolk, Williams flew back to New York, hired replacement musicians, and rejoined his band at a Huntington, West Virginia, job on April 11, just three days after the accident. Bud Shorter sued Williams for $50,000 for injuries and damages from the accident. It took five years for Williams to win the suit.[11] (On the morning of May 18, 1954, Cootie's bus was involved in another road incident when it was sideswiped in Missouri enroute to a Ft. Knox, Kentucky, booking. Fortunately, no one was reported as injured during this accident.)[12]

Returning to New York in mid-April, the touring package split up. Cootie took a stand at the Savoy Ballroom. Washington and the Ravens, with George Hudson's orchestra providing the musical backing, moved into the Apollo Theater.

Williams was proud of his "the show must go on" reputation. In 1946, the band's vehicle broke down five miles outside of an engagement in Wilmington, North Carolina. The men weren't able to secure cabs. (It is unknown if it was due to lack of availability or Jim Crow.) But they were able to rent a horse-drawn cart from a local farmer to tote the instruments to the gig.[13]

Now in his late thirties, life on the road was becoming a bit tiresome and less appealing to Cootie. Domestic life, when available, suited him. At this point in his life, he preferred to stay home instead of jamming at clubs. When he had the chance to do so, he enjoyed playing pinochle or fishing. He said, "After traveling on the road with bands for the past 20 years, I like to sit down and relax . . . I sometimes wish I wasn't a musician. I could enjoy my home more then. I wouldn't have to worry about leaving only about coming back."[14]

Cootie Williams playing cards at the home of Fredi Washington, who is on the far left. Catherine Williams is on the far right. Date unknown. The *New York Amsterdam News* wrote "[w]hen he isn't playing, Cootie likes to fish and play pinochle with friends." (Fredi Washington Collection—Connecticut Museum of Culture and History)

Sunset Terrace Ballroom

ONE NITE ONLY **SUN., APRIL 30, 1950** HOURS 10 P. M. TO 2

ADV. $1.50 Tax Incl. **DOOR $1.75**

MAKE TABLE RESERVATIONS NOW AT SUNSET CAFE—RI. 0876

UNIVERSAL ATTRACTIONS, INC., PRESENTS

THE GREAT BIG 4 ATTRACTION
Mr. "Growl" Trumpet — In Person

★ **Cootie Williams**
and his Famous Orchestra

COOTIE WILLIAMS   FEATURING

★ **Willis Jackson**
WORLD'S GREATEST
TENOR SAX STAR
And Recording Artist

Plus

★ **HERB LANCE**
JUKE BOX KING
"CLOSE YOUR EYES"   "BECAUSE"
And Over 25 Other Hits

★ **EDDIE MACK**

BLUES SHOUTING SENSATION
He Needs No Loud Speaker

Cootie Williams in Indianapolis in 1950. (*Indianapolis Recorder*)

At the time, Cootie and Catherine, whom he called "Toots,"[15] had been married for nineteen years. They never had children, but they both loved dogs. In the 1950s, *Jet* magazine would report that "Socialite dog lover Catherine Williams (Mrs. Cootie) shops for her mutt, Poochie, at Gregg Juarez's salon for canines on Manhattan's East 55th St. where a pair of dog pajamas cost $65.50, hats by Mr. John are tagged at $35, and a specialty of the house is a perfume called Kennel No. 9 . . ."[16]

Another example of Cootie's domestic life could be found in the picture *Jet* magazine published of him and Catherine enjoying one of his favorite midnight snacks, the Italian hero sandwich. Cootie promised it was something that "will separate the men from the boys." Perhaps the sandwich wasn't well known to the audience of *Jet* at the time since they felt it necessary to list the ingredients (ham, Italian sausage, liverwurst, Swiss cheese, lettuce, tomatoes, pickles, and onions).[17]

Cootie Williams loved driving and fast cars. He gifted his wife Catherine with a brand-new LaSalle for her birthday in 1939.[18] Neither one of them knew how to drive at the time! (But she learned first.)[19] In May 1946, he applied for entry in that year's Indianapolis 500 race. As stated in the newspapers stated, "Should his entry be accepted, Williams will be the first Negro in history to have an auto officially starting" in the race.[20] It was bold of Williams to even consider the move, but perhaps he thought his celebrity could make a difference in the outcome. However, Williams was turned down. It took a long time before an African American was even a driver in a NASCAR event.[21]

In the fall of 1949, Williams acquired another blues singer in the Vinson tradition, Eddie Mack. Mack was born Matthews Mack Edmonson (originally, his surname didn't have a second 'd') in Beaumont, Texas, on March 15, 1914.[22] He was yet another Williams talent discovery, who called him "one of the best blues artists in the country today."[23] Mack possessed a loud voice and added to the continued Williams reputation for volume: "Small but loud, the Williams band all but blasted the audience's eardrums with several unidentified numbers, two featuring Willis Jackson, whose tenor sax playing finally blew him right out of his coat, one in which Cootie himself, took torridly to the trumpet. Using the microphone although he hardly seemed to need it, band vocalist Eddie Mack, roared his way through 'Big Fat Mama' and 'Evil Woman Blues.'"[24]

The size of the band Cootie led in the early 1950s fluctuated. The band that appeared at the Apollo Theatre in February 1950 was almost a return to a full-sized big band. It had eleven musicians, consisting of "four reeds, four brass and three rhythm."[25] When they appeared at the same venue in May 1951, they were down one sax and totaled ten. (*Variety* described the "four brass, three reed and three rhythm" as a "loud brassy crew that pleases the hepsters with its swingy rhythms.")[26] But by 1952, the band was back to a dozen members.[27]

After disbanding his big band in 1947, Williams had vowed his days with a big band were over. He gave two reasons for preferring smaller groups—economics and flexibility: "You can say without fear of contradiction, it'll be a long time before I re-enter the large band field. It is just too tough a proposition at this time."[28] But these gigs showed he wasn't completely done with larger groups after his 1947 disbanding.

In the old tradition of the band business, Willis Jackson left to form his own band.[29] (Initially, it was reported that Jackson would be joining Lionel Hampton.)[30] When Jackson left Cootie Williams in May 1950 to form his own band, it was with financial backing provided by Lionel Hampton.[31] In later years, Jackson said of his time with Williams: "Cootie Williams was a very smart bandleader and I was a blowin' motherfucker."[32] He was replaced by his predecessor in the tenor chair, William "Weasel" Parker (1921–1992). While Parker's R&B stylings weren't popular with the critics, he was an audience favorite at the Savoy, sometimes causing the dancers to stop and listen.[33] Allegedly, Cootie had to engage in a bidding war to retain his services again.[34]

A few years earlier, Cootie had predicted that be-bop was just a passing fad. Despite that prediction not coming true, Cootie turned his forecasting skills onto another musical phase. The line services reported that Williams saw a return to the glory days of the blues singers, "in the mold of Bessie Smith, Clara Smith, Ma Rainey, and the others." He said, "Blues music is hard time music. Whenever there is troubled times, you'll find people singing the blues."[35]

34

SAVOY BALLROOM CHAMPION

Cootie Williams and tenor saxophonist Buddy Tate share billing on the Savoy Ballroom's marquee in 1956, just two years before the venue was permanently shuttered and demolished. (Duke Ellington Collection, Archives Center, National Museum of American History, Smithsonian Institution)

At the end of September 1950, Williams completed a three-week stand at the Savoy Ballroom. This engagement happened to mark his forty-second engagement at the "Home of Happy Feet," breaking the record of forty-one, held in a tie by Chick Webb and Erskine Hawkins. Unfortunately, the event was not celebrated at the time of its occurrence because manager Charlie Buchanan hadn't checked his records until after the completion of the gig.[1] Ironically, despite his importance in the history of the Savoy, books like Norma Miller's *Swingin' at the Savoy* and *Frankie Manning, Ambassador of Lindy Hop* mention Cootie only once, just in passing. Arranger Van Alexander spent many evenings at the Savoy, yet he doesn't talk about Cootie in his autobiography *From Harlem to Hollywood—My Life in Music*.

```
DERBY RECORDS
Proudly Announces
The Signing of

COOTIE
WILLIAMS
and his Orchestra
─────
Watch For Initial Release
Soon To Be Announced
─────
DERBY RECORDS, INC.
520 W. 50th St., N. Y.
```

Derby Records announcing the signing of Cootie Williams.
(*Cash Box* magazine)

At the end of 1950, Williams signed a two-year recording contract with Derby Records,[2] a small label that didn't survive for very long. Cootie recorded only four songs for them and only two were released at the time. The two selections represented a real diversion from Cootie's normal repertoire—they fell into the "Hillbilly" category. ("Hillbilly" was the term that was being phased out at that time in favor of "Country and Western.") Sadly for Cootie, he gets second billing. The label on the single reads "Mack Edmondson with Cootie Williams and his Orchestra." "Shotgun Boogie" was written by Tennessee Ernie Ford and was Ford's most successful record. It stayed on the Country and Western charts for twenty-five weeks, with fourteen of those at the #1 position.[3] It was covered by a stylistically varied group of artists like Cab Calloway, Rosemary Clooney, and Cecil Gant.[4] Unfortunately, Cootie's version didn't chart nearly as well as Ford's did. The only reference to any chart performance is showing at #2 on the *Cash Box* charts for Richmond, Virginia,[5] and at #7 in Little Rock[6] in March 1951. "Divorce Me, C.O.D.," was on the reverse side. Written by Merle Travis, it too became a #1 ranked recording for him.[7] Cootie doesn't take this one very seriously. His solo is pure corn and more like a Clyde McCoy plunger solo.

"Beauty Parlor Gossip" and "Steam Roller Blues" stayed in the can until 2001.[8] It wasn't a loss that they weren't issued at the time of their waxing; they were additional Mack vocal features that were light on trumpet contributions from Cootie. This 1950 session turned out to be the last time that Cootie Williams would be in a recording studio as a leader for almost seven years. Eddie Mack last recorded in 1952 and faded from the music world in the intervening years. It's unknown how long Mack was out of the music business, but at the time of his death in 1984, just five days short of turning sixty-nine, he was a laborer at the Greyhound Bus Station in his native Beaumont, Texas.[9]

Cootie was matched with another bird-named singing group, the Orioles, for his summer touring in 1950. The Orioles, five strong, also had two of its members backing them on guitar and bass. *Down Beat* didn't seem too impressed with them, saying that "[o]ther than the peculiar jolt [lead singer Sonny] Til seems to give little Negro bobby-soxers, we can find absolutely no reason for [their popularity]. They just don't sing."[10] In December, Cootie was reunited with the Ravens. The previous month, the Orioles had suffered the loss of one of their group in a car accident that also left another singer seriously injured. By 1951, the "package" touring deals that had been Cootie's bread and butter were being seen as making it hard for the few remaining orchestras to work. It used to be that a big band could sell a show by itself, and the package tours were the exception. Amongst the Black trade, according to the *Baltimore Afro-American*, the biggest drawing orchestras were led by Lionel Hampton, Erskine Hawkins, and Buddy Johnson.[11] Except for certain cases, audiences liked the idea of seeing more than one act for their money, and of course promoters liked the idea of anything that sold tickets.[12]

Cootie's music was heard behind the Iron Curtain on the April 1, 1951, episode of Leonard Feather's *Jazz Club U.S.A.* A brainchild of Feather's, the show was sponsored by the Voice of America and intended as a propaganda tool for the US government, beaming jazz into countries that weren't friendly to the American way of life.[13] The program on April 1 was titled "Savoy Ballroom." Cootie didn't get the whole show, but shared with another band recorded at the Savoy, Buddy Johnson and his Orchestra. Although a specific date for the pre-recording is not specified, more than likely it was during Cootie's Savoy booking during the first week of February.

Cootie started his segment with "Echoes of Harlem," which was his theme song by this time. The program got under way with Weasel Parker taking his predecessor Willis Jackson's showcase, "Gator Tail." In his introduction, Feather expresses skepticism about the viability of this style of playing, saying "whether this is a legitimate jazz style is open to debate" and that Parker "claims he can play notes so high that only a dog can hear them." But he had to admit it went over well with the audiences.

Variety announced that Williams would start his by-now traditional tour through the South starting on June 12 in Suffall, Virginia, and ending the first week of July in North Carolina. In between, there would be dates in West Virginia, Alabama, and South Carolina.[14]

Segregated venues were the rule, not the exception at this time, not just in the South. In 1950, the Celebrity Club, a newly opened integrated venue in Providence, Rhode Island, decided to implement a "name band" policy. (They initially booked local talent.) Cootie Williams was chosen to be the first, opening on September 18. One of the factors for the selection of Williams was his box office performance for the previous year.[15] The club would go on to present artists like Louis Jordan, Louis Armstrong, Duke Ellington, and Erroll Garner. The Celebrity Club was the first integrated club in the New England area and because some weren't happy with the interracial policy, it was subject to frequent police raids as retaliation.[16]

Cootie was matched with R&B groups like the Dominoes and the Ravens again for his next package tour. The Ravens were not new partners for Williams, having toured with him in 1949. The Dominoes, another male singing group, were led by pianist and arranger Billy Ward. They were a hot commodity in 1951, taking the #1 position in the R&B charts for fourteen weeks with "Sixty Minute Man."[17]

Cootie brought in a twelve-piece band during the Apollo show that featured Dinah Washington during the summer of 1952. By this time, show reviews for Cootie were becoming less frequent and he was less prominent in them. In reviewing the show, *Variety* devotes a scant paragraph out of the five paragraphs reviewing the band. The focus of the single paragraph was the band's volume and the long tenor saxophone wailings.[18] But Cootie was catering to audience demands; R&B was becoming the music of the day. However, the critics' ears didn't seem attuned to the "new" music. And the critics certainly did not expect to hear it from Cootie Williams. The band would feature a succession of tenor saxophonists, playing in the honking, wailing, and screaming style of the day. Wilburt "Red" Prysock (1926–1993) was another R&B tenor saxophonist in the mold of Willis Jackson who was featured by Williams. (His brother was singer Arthur Prysock.) During an engagement at Montreal's Latin Quarter, Williams's music was branded as being for "devotees of the loud, brassy brand of jazz." It was noted that Cootie didn't play much, but instead left "the greater part of the solo work to a honking tenor saxophonist." Prysock worked all the R&B tricks—walking the bar, marching through the audience to the exit, and contortions and gymnastics. (The bassist for this gig was Richard Fulbright, a fellow member of the Alonzo Ross Deluxe Syncopators that brought Cootie to New York in 1928.)[19]

In order to enlarge the musical palette a small group presented; Williams mused to the press that he'd like to work on a "two-in-one" band concept. Given that certain musicians are proficient in their own styles, Williams proposed that having a roster of a few key players, rotated into the band as necessary, could alter the band's style to suit the gig at hand. Cootie said, "If the customers want be-bop as well as our usual swing style of music, we'll just have to give them what they want."[20] One of the ways Cootie changed the palette of his combination was the addition of an organ. In the small-group setting, Williams said, "You got a big sound with the organ. So it'd make it sound like a big band."[21] Count Basie, who occasionally played organ himself, was impressed with the sound of the group when he heard them at the Savoy Ballroom: "I went over to the Savoy to hear Cootie a few times. He's got a band and he's blowing. He's got that organ with him, makes it sound like 19 pieces. I don't remember the guy's name [Preston Brown], but he's real down. Yes, Cootie really had them. The big band opposite was in trouble the way Cootie had them."[22]

♪

The touring package of Dinah Washington and Cootie Williams was hugely popular at the Chicago's Regal Theater, described as "one of the hottest to hit the Southside in moons." Capacity audiences and long lines were the rule and "Cootie's tooting and Dinah's blues chirping had the house jumping from curtain to curtain."[23] Cootie Williams and Dinah Washington's next tour started in Phoenix, Arizona, on January 11. It was a rare visit to the western part of the country for Williams. It was the only time he had been out West since his fondly remembered swing through in 1944; the *Arizona Sun* wrote, "This is the first appearance of Cootie Williams since the war when he presented the very popular personalities, The Ink Spots and Ella Fitzgerald."[24] After this tour, Williams didn't appear again in the western part of the United States until he rejoined Ellington.

The Bay Area provided mixed results. The group had full attendance in San Francisco's Trianon, but they "bombed" attendance-wise across the bay in the Oakland Auditorium.[25]

Cootie was reunited with the Ink Spots for a fifteen-week tour that started in September 1952. This wasn't the same group that Cootie started out with in 1944. Various squabbles had created more than one group using the name and their biographer refers to this edition as "Charlie Fuqua's Ink Spots."[26]

The Orioles and Cootie Williams on tour again in 1952. (Author's collection)

♪

Cootie Williams and his orchestra was chosen as one of the thirteen groups to welcome 1954 over the radio. To be included in the Mutual Broadcasting System's "Welcome New Year" program was considered a "plum" gig. Cootie would be remotely broadcast from the American Legion auditorium in Roanoke, Virginia. Williams said, "I am very happy to have been so honored. You know, every leader likes to hit the airwaves and to be placed on such a program that has such large coverage is even more pleasing."[27] But radio was rapidly fading due to the rise of television. The Williamses were early adopters of the new medium; Catherine Williams bought their first television in 1948.[28] That year, only 1 percent of American households owned a television set.[29]

At the end of January, Cootie played New York City's Birdland Club, sharing the bill with someone from his early past, the great tenor saxophonist Lester Young. Cootie's future singer Wini Brown was also on the bill. From the *Variety* review, it doesn't appear Williams and Young sat in together with one another's bands. Cootie had a sextet at the time and was "still one of the best trumpeters around." In keeping with Cootie's goal of versatility, *Variety* said "this crew dishes up sounds that are [a] blend of traditional and modern jazz."[30]

Cootie reunited with Eddie "Cleanhead" Vinson for a series of jobs starting at Chicago's Regal Theater in 1954. After leaving Williams in 1945 to form his own big band, Cleanhead had a few hit records. He had rerecorded several of his popular songs with the Williams band—"Cherry Red Blues," "Somebody's Gotta Go," and "Juice Head Baby." He had a double-sided hit in 1947 with "Kidney Stew Blues" and "Old Maid Boogie."[31] But like Williams and so many others, he had to abandon the no longer viable big band format and downscale to a combo.

Cootie and Cleanhead reunited on records under Vinson's name in a session for Mercury sometime in February 1954. Two of the four songs were recorded and except for one blues chorus on "You Can't Have My Love No More," Cootie is only heard in an ensemble role.

In June, Williams and Vinson played the Apollo Theater. Frank Schiffman, the owner of the venue, kept neatly typed index cards on most of the acts that played there. For June 25, 1954, Schiffman noted that Vinson "[a]ppeared as vocalist with Cootie Williams Band. Gave a good performance. Did not draw any business." (During a 1951 gig, Schiffman said Vinson was "sober and cooperative." Vinson was a different person when he was under the influence.[32] It took a mid-1970s DWI for Vinson to finally join Alcoholics Anonymous and dry out.)[33] In addition to reuniting with Vinson, 1954 saw Cootie functioning as backup band for R&B singers and singing groups, not the headliner. In addition to Dinah Washington, Cootie was teamed with LaVern Baker, singer, and guitarist Danny Overbea, the Drifters, and the Checkers.

35

THE HOUSE BAND

Starting in 1953, Cootie was given the role of house band for the Savoy Ballroom. "... And eventually, I got the house band at the Savoy. I had the house band in the Savoy until they closed it down [in 1958]. They had to have a band that could draw and that could mean something." Cootie was proud of his musical versatility and adaptability. He felt it was the main reason he was able to maintain his long tenure at the Savoy Ballroom—"But the main reason why they kept me there [was] not because I was Cootie Williams, a jazz player. It was because I produced. They used to have certain nights for certain types of music. And I learned to play that type of music. They used to have on Wednesday nights, club nights, where they would have the older people there. And I learned how to play the waltzes and the slow music. On Monday nights and Thursday nights, that was jitterbug night. I had to learn to play their type of music. So they wanted me, the jitterbugs. And the older crowd that come there, they wanted me. And on Sunday afternoon, they would have matinees, club dances, and I used to learn how to play club music for that type of thing. So I was well rounded, with all types of music to play for the types of people that came to the Savoy Ballroom."[1] Charlie Buchanan, the manager of the Savoy, seemed to be describing Cootie's musical strategy when he said, "Give me the good, old-fashioned band that play an occasional waltz, foxtrot or a mambo or cha-cha."[2] Trombonist Dickie Wells also thought that less complicated arrangements and "very good rhythm" was why bands like Cootie's, Lucky Millinder's, and the Savoy Sultans were able thrive at the Savoy.[3] Williams also was sensitive to the needs of the crowd. Drummer Lester Jenkins observed that "Williams would slowly survey an audience to get a feel for them, next counting off the rhythm and performing a tune that would get them moving in their groove" and he was constantly aware of "the meter, keeping time, and the swing."[4]

Although some derided Cootie's late 1950s music as rock and roll, it was actually rhythm and blues. Buchanan wouldn't have rock and roll in his venue. "When rock and roll first came out we experimented with these new sounds and got a hundred complaints from life-long patrons who said it sent each feet [sic] in a different direction. That I couldn't take and out the window went rock and roll."[5]

While it offered steady employment, the house band job also carried a downside. Cootie wasn't on the road as often, which led to a lack of visibility to the general public and perhaps more critically, the press. And since he wasn't signed to a recording deal, he didn't have anything current on the market for sales or radio play.[6] Cootie's public visibility had fallen considerably since his heyday in the 40s; there are not very many mentions of Cootie Williams in the press for the years 1955 and 1956. In a review of a reissue of a Lionel Hampton record that included Cootie, the reviewer asked, "where is he now?"[7] John Hammond blamed "inept management and innumerable blunders [that] made his name all but unknown to the music fans of today."[8] His profile had gone so low that the syndicated newspapers printed this (perhaps apocryphal) anecdote about Cootie and his press agent Artie Franklin:

[Franklin] was busy typing one day when the phone rang and Cootie, who was play a long string of one-nighters, was calling long distance.

"What's cooking, Artie?" asked Cootie dejectedly, "I haven't seen any mentions in the paper for a few weeks now."

"Don't worry about a thing," Artie said, "everybody in New York is talking about you!"

Cootie brightened on the phone. "They are?" he exclaimed, "What are they saying?"

"They're saying," Artie answered, "whatever happened to Cootie Williams?"[9]

Leonard Feather analyzed *Down Beat*'s 1955 Readers' Poll and noted that the winners from ten years prior were nowhere to be found. Feather wrote, "What struck me most forcibly . . . was the fact that some of the real titans of the '30s and '40s couldn't even make [the minimum vote required for listing]. Coleman Hawkins for instance, and Earl Hines, Cootie Williams and Rex Stewart. How can musicians like this . . . be so completely forgotten?" But there were a handful of the 1945 winners that still ranked high—Harry Carney, Lester Young, Johnny Hodges, and the perennial Duke Ellington.[10]

Leonard Feather published *The Encyclopedia Yearbook of Jazz* in 1956, a 190-page survey of what was currently happening in the jazz world. It was intended to be the first in an annual series, but there was only one additional volume published in 1958. One of the components of the *Yearbook* was a poll of jazz greats—the "'Musicians' Musicians' Poll." One hundred and one jazz greats (Miles Davis, Dizzy Gillespie, Duke Ellington, and Teddy Wilson, just to name a handful) were asked to name the greatest ever on each instrument. Cootie's choice for trumpet was Louis Armstrong, the obvious choice for him. He picked Duke Ellington for big band and arranger, but Earl Hines got his vote for the piano. His other former boss, Benny Goodman was his choice for clarinet and combo. Ellingtonians Johnny Hodges, Harry Carney, and Jimmie Blanton were on his ballot, along with Coleman Hawkins, Ella Fitzgerald, and Charlie Christian.[11] Overall, the trumpet category was won by Dizzy Gillespie with forty-five of the 101 votes cast and Armstrong was a very close second at thirty-nine. Sadly, Cootie didn't receive any votes, a far cry from his polling ten years previous.[12]

♪

As an entertainer, endorsing political candidates can be risky career move. But the 1956 presidential election saw Cootie doing Harlem campaign appearance support for the Democratic challenger to President Dwight D. Eisenhower, Adlai Stevenson, as part of the effort to boost the Black vote. At the Savoy Ballroom, "Cootie Williams blew rock 'n roll from the bandstand and the crowds voted it the most man, the most." Stevenson gave a speech that was noteworthy for its strong support for civil rights, undoubtably one of the planks that drew Williams to support him.[13] Along with Cootie's friend Joe Louis, the rally featured former First Lady Eleanor Roosevelt, New York Mayor Robert Wagner, Tallulah Bankhead, and Shelly Winters.[14] Not to be outdone, Eisenhower's jazz supporters included Canadian Maynard Ferguson, Terry Gibbs, and Henry "Red" Allen.[15]

36

BACK TO THE STUDIOS

In a 1957 issue of *Down Beat*, Nat Hentoff wondered why it had been so long since Cootie had been recorded, but he added "don't [record] him with his present band."[1] Cootie Williams had made his last studio recordings in 1950 as a leader, seven years prior. John Hammond wanted to record a live Savoy Ballroom album, but that didn't happen. Given Hammond's tastes, he also probably suggested Williams make the record with another band.[2] *Melody Maker* also hinted that Williams's drinking may have been hindering his career, noting that "Cootie has been on the water wagon for about two years now."[3] Williams could be touchy on the subject of his drinking. When Henry "Red" Allen encountered Williams at a festival they were both playing, he offered to buy Cootie a drink. Williams "blew up, saying, 'Don't you know I'm not drinking?' I said, 'Okay, sorry I bothered you,' but my mind went back to the time when he and Ella Fitzgerald were having a scene together and Cootie used to get so drunk that Ella regularly had to carry him home."[4]

Fortunately for Williams, 1957 found the record industry frantically trying to sign talent. Steve Sholes had been the head of the County and Western division for RCA for about a dozen years at this time and it was announced that he had personally signed a group of country artists plus Cootie Williams. Sholes had struck gold when he contracted a young singer named Elvis Presley to the label in 1955. Sholes offering a contract to Williams is not as odd as it seems on first glance. In his youth, he played clarinet and saxophone in territory jazz bands.[5] Before moving over to the country division, he had recorded jazz artists like Jelly Roll Morton, Sidney Bechet, Coleman Hawkins, and Mezz Mezzrow for RCA.[6]

The *New York Amsterdam News* reported that Williams signed a contract with RCA Victor for "at least $100,000 per year over a period of ten years."[7] In today's dollars, that would be slightly over a million dollars. Cootie Williams had not been in a recording studio for seven years and his popularity had faded. Given his situation at the time, that figure is not realistic and the story can be discounted.

Cootie's first RCA session took place in their New York studios on March 29, 1957. Cootie's regular band at that time consisted of two saxes, Rupert Cole on alto and George Clarke on tenor. On organ there was Preston Brown, who was known professionally as "The Fabulous Preston Brown." Cootie said of Brown, "he could swing."[8] Larry Dale handled guitar and vocals in the group. "Larry Dale" was the stage name of Ennis Lowery (1923–2010), who worked as a blues session musician before he joined Cootie. He would return to the blues world after his time with Williams. His guitar work was heavily influenced by "T Bone" Walker. Lester Jenkins, the youngest person in the group at age twenty-eight, was on drums. Ellington veterans Al Sears on tenor sax and bassist Al Lucas augmented the group, in addition to baritone saxophonist Elwyn Fraser. Four titles were recorded: "Rinky Dink," "Please Give Your Love to Me," "Block Rock," and "Percy Speaks." Some discographies and releases have listed Kenny Burrell as a second guitarist, but that isn't accurate. Burrell confirmed he never recorded with Williams.[9]

These 1957 RCA recordings firmly established that Cootie Williams was aligned with the rhythm and blues market. *Variety* reported "Williams plans to aim more at the regular pop market rather than the jazz clientele with whom he has been a standard name for decades."[16]

The rhythm and blues stylings continued on Cootie's May 15 session. This marked the debut of a new vocalist for Williams, Wini Brown. Chicago-born Winifred "Wini" Brown (1927–1978) got her start as a vocalist with Lionel Hampton in 1946. She started singing with the Williams band sometime in the spring of 1955.[17] The four songs recorded at this session all focused on vocals. Three of the four were released with Cootie's name in second place: "Now That You've Loved Me," "Blue Sunday," and "Available Lover" (both credited as Wini Brown with Cootie Williams), and "It's All in Your Mind" (credited as Wini Brown and Larry Dale with Cootie Williams). *The Billboard* said of the last title: "The slow down-to-earth song co-cleffed by Otis Blackwell, is most appealingly presented by the vocalists with great band backing. Spins should prove highly acceptable as something 'different.' On the flip, 'Available Lover,' Miss Brown turns in a fine solo vocal with more of the same listenable backing by Williams."[18]

Cootie made his third (and last) R&B session on July 10, recording three titles: "Rangoon," "Boomerang," with "It Hurts Me" released as Larry Dale with Cootie Williams. "Rangoon" was released as a single, paired with "Block Rock" from the March date. In its advice to disk jockeys, *The Billboard* described

Cootie Williams with Everett Barksdale on guitar in the background at his May 15, 1957, RCA recording session. (Author's collection)

"Rangoon" as a "[s]mooth, slow instrumental blues with usual fine trumpet by Williams against organ and ork backing[;] should attract jockey whirls. Danceable side can go." "Block Rock" is a "[m]edium-tempo dance side[,] features a baritone sax solo in addition to fine trumpet by Williams. Solid orking helps sell side. Rates deejay spins." "Block Rock" was scored at 74 and "Rangoon" at 73, which both translated to a "B" grade rating. (The jazz press, such as *Metronome* and *Down Beat*, declined to review these recordings.)

Besides a newly rejuvenated recording career, there was more to be optimistic about. Cootie received news that he would be booked into the Savoy Ballroom "at least five times yearly for three weeks each time for the next four years."[19] But the types of shows Williams was playing were grossing peanuts compared to those of Elvis Presley.[20]

♪

Despite his new life in the studio, Cootie's fans in the press weren't satisfied with the music that was being recorded; Nat Hentoff and John Hammond weren't the only critics to decide that Cootie was overdue for a jazz date.

Writer George T. Simon got the idea to record Williams with a true jazz group, but to his surprise Cootie wasn't enthusiastic saying, "I made some of those jazz dates nine years ago and I didn't like the way they were run. They did me more harm than good." It's unclear which records from that time period would have been harmful to Williams, since at the time he referenced, he was already recording R&B material. Simon decided to deputize Rex Stewart to win over the reluctant Williams. Williams also stipulated that he didn't want a jam session, saying "Don't just put us in the studio and tell everyone to blow—please!" So structure was imposed with arrangements by Ernie Wilkins and Joe Thomas.[21]

Cootie wanted a good rhythm section and got one with Hank Jones, piano, Billy Bauer, guitar, Milt Hinton, and a former member of Cootie's band, Gus Johnson on drums. Eventually, it was decided that the horn section would include pairings on each horn. Besides the pair of Williams and Stewart, Hawkins was matched with Bud Freeman, and Lawrence Brown and J. C. Higginbotham were on trombones.

On May 7, in between the RCA rhythm and blues session of March 29 and May 15, Cootie returned to his jazz roots with this all-star session. Of the seven tracks, two are by Ellington, befitting a session with three star alumni from the band. Though they didn't know it at the time, Brown and Williams were just a few years from returning to the Ellington fold.

In reviewing the album *The Big Challenge* for *Down Beat*, Ralph J. Gleason wrote that Cootie and Rex supplied "delightful moments" and overall said the musicians were "all great men in jazz." Like several other critics, he was of the opinion that the Ellington musicians are lesser-than when outside the band, writing, "this LP reinforces my suspicion that many of the stars of the Ellington band shone brighter somehow in the Ducal universe than they do when disengaged." Despite the misgivings Gleason gave the album a four out of five-star rating.[22] The album stands up today as a great example of classic jazz, with swing, heat and competitive, yet respectful jousting between the soloists.

Cootie also performed as a sideman with an RCA label mate, Ronnie Gilbert. Gilbert (1926–2015) was a member of the Weavers, a popular folk quartet. Gilbert recorded *The Legend of Bessie Smith* in 1958 backed by Williams and an illustrious group of veterans that included trombonist Bennie Morton, clarinetist Buster Bailey, and pianist Claude Hopkins. Bailey had recorded with Smith several times during the period of 1924 to 1927. The band sounds great on the album. "Her backing is excellent, especially by Cootie Williams, who is [in] rare form."[23] However, Ronnie Gilbert's vocals are problematic. She had no feeling for the blues and delivers the lyrics as if she were performing Broadway show tunes. One reviewer quipped that the album makes as much sense as "The Legend of Louis Armstrong by Burl Ives."[24]

Cootie Williams in Hi-Fi was a favorite recording of Cootie and Catherine Williams.

Cootie nominally led a big band again for three sessions spread across March and April 1958 to produce the RCA Victor album *Cootie Williams in Hi-Fi*. (RCA also issued it as *Cootie Williams in Stereo*.) But there was a variation on the usual big band format of trumpets-trombones-saxophones and rhythm section—there was only one trumpet. Recording in stereo was a relatively new process. Stan Kenton was among those who thought it was a gimmick and a fad that would quickly pass.[25] Stereo helped sell a lot of audio equipment and record reviews of the day were slanted toward the audiophile.

Cootie called *Cootie Williams in Hi-Fi* his favorite of his own recordings and said Catherine was "crazy about it."[26] But the critics were not fond of it. Part of the harsh judgments came from the comparison to the Cootie of Ellington days: "Ellington sidemen seldom sound at their best when they are away from Duke." *Down Beat* was gave the album one and a half stars (out of a possible five) and called the record a "product of misguided management and mechanized minds, this LP is a shameful example of presenting an important jazzman in a ludicrous setting." They go on to call the arrangements of Bill Stegmeyer "either dreadfully dull or grossly imitative" and the session "a grotesque studio band date." Whatever one thinks of the arrangements, the stellar lead soprano saxophone playing on some of the pieces is perfection. *Metronome* took a wider view on the album saying, "If you are expecting the Cootie of old you will be disappointed; otherwise this is a pleasant album of good music very well played."[27] It was to be Cootie's last album under his RCA contract.

THE HOLY CITY

Cootie Williams and W. C. Handy were neighbors in St. Albans. They had formed a mutual admiration society and when Handy died at the age of eighty-four on March 28, 1958, he had made plans for Cootie to play at his funeral. The funeral was held on April 2 at Harlem's Abyssinian Baptist Church and presided over by its pastor, Rev. Adam Clayton Powell Jr. His funeral was one of the biggest Harlem had seen in years, of the same scope as those of Chick Webb and Bill "Bojangles" Robinson. More than 150,000 people were estimated to have lined the streets. The music included a brass band performing Handy's most famous composition, "St. Louis Blues."[1] Cootie had been designated to play Handy's favorite hymn, "The Holy City." A few seconds of Cootie's playing at the side of Handy's flower smothered casket can be seen on a British Pathé newsreel.[2]

Duke Ellington had fared better than Cootie Williams in the early 1950s, but he had nowhere near the same amount of visibility he had enjoyed in the previous two decades. But as a result of the near riot induced by Paul Gonsalves's heroic twenty-seven blues choruses at the 1956 Newport Jazz Festival, Ellington was thrust back into the limelight. The 1958 edition of the Newport Jazz Festival was dedicated to him, with most of the participating artists programming their sets heavily with Ellington compositions in tribute, with the very characteristic exception of Miles Davis.

An all-star group of Ellington alumni were assembled specially for the festival. Under the nominal leadership of cornetist Rex Stewart, they included Cootie Williams on trumpet, Tyree Glenn trombone, Hilton Jefferson alto sax, Ben Webster tenor sax, Billy Strayhorn piano, Oscar Pettiford bass, and Sonny Greer on drums. Jefferson and Glenn were the only member of the band whose time hadn't coincided with Cootie's.

Cootie Williams playing at the funeral of W. C. Handy at Abyssinian Baptist Church on April 2, 1958. (Author's collection)

The reviews of the performance were mixed at the time; the group sounds under-rehearsed. Until a 2021 CD on the Sounds of Yesteryear label was released as *Le Grand Romp*, only two songs from the nine-song set had seen the light of day. They decided to start their set with Ellington's original theme song, 1926's "East St. Louis Toodle-oo."³ But the melody is barely present; it's almost as if the group was trying to unsuccessfully summon the old Cotton Club days. *Down Beat* called the set "a constant struggle to recapture the past" and blamed "the wages of years and economic pressures. Stewart's unfortunate valve-flicking, Williams's now-mild growl . . . and Greer's inconsistency marred the group's performance."⁴ *Metronome*'s review was pretty similar, saying that "[t]here was only faded elegance here as a general rule." They concluded that "[a]ll of it more or less confirmed our suspicion of longstanding, that Ellington without Duke (or, better said, Ellington musicians without Duke) are not impressive."⁵

George Gershwin's 1935 musical *Porgy and Bess* enjoyed quite a revival in the late 1950s due to the release of a film version directed by Otto Preminger and starring Sidney Poitier and Dorothy Dandridge. The 1959 movie prompted a veritable glut of soundtrack recordings of wildly different approaches and quality. Simon decided to get Cootie Williams and Rex Stewart to jump into the fray and colead a soundtrack album released as *Porgy and Bess Revisited*. There are no singers on the album; the novel idea for this project was to portray the roles instrumentally. Cootie was cast in the role of Porgy with Simon writing that his open horn work was "one of the most soulful, at times mournful trumpeters I've ever heard. What an ideal sound for the songs of the crippled Porgy!"[6] The other parts were Hilton Jefferson (Bess), Rex Stewart (Sportin' Life), Lawrence Brown (Serena and Clara), and Pinky Williams (no relation) playing Jake on baritone saxophone. Except for Pinky Williams, the soloists were all ex-Ellingtonians and four of the group had participated in *The Big Challenge*. The arrangements were written by Jim Timmens (1920–1980), who would spent his last decade in charge of the music for *Sesame Street* and *The Muppet Show*.[7]

The reviews for the album were very good. The *Cleveland Call and Post* said the solos "range from very good to excellent." They added that Cootie "is at his best on "I Got Plenty of Nothin.""[8] *Metronome* ran a single-page review comparing a selection of the many Porgy and Bess albums on the market. A total of nine LPs were rated, produced by artists like Miles Davis and Gil Evans, Louis Armstrong and Ella Fitzgerald, Sammy Davis Jr. and Carmen McRae, and Mundell Lowe. The Williams-Stewart effort was deemed the "best of the whole collection.... The casting is excellent—Cootie in particular in brilliant, and his duet with Hilton Jefferson is a high point of the album. Almost any jazz fan will find this an unusually pleasant album."[9]

♪

Art Ford's Jazz Party was a live television show featuring some of the best musicians who have ever lived. It only ran for a short time—May to December 1958. Coleman Hawkins and Lester Young made a historic joint appearance on the show and some of the other musicians on the soundstage included Pee Wee Russell, Charlie Shavers, Willie "The Lion" Smith, Sonny Greer, Rex Stewart, and Tyree Glenn. A few kinescope video examples survive, but unfortunately, Cootie's two appearances on the show only exist in audio form. His first appearance was on the August 28 broadcast. Besides Cootie, the band consisted of Basie alumnus Buck Clayton on trumpet; Rolf Kuhn, a young German clarinetist; Georgie Auld, Cootie's bandmate from his Goodman days, on tenor sax; Harry Sheppard on vibraphone, Roland Hanna piano, Mundell Lowe guitar, Vinnie Burke bass, and Roy Burnes drums.

Less than two months later, on October 16, Cootie was back on the show. The Adderley brothers, Cannonball and Nat, rising stars in the jazz world, were part of the band. Their father, Julian Adderley Sr., was Cootie's section mate in the Eagle Eye Shields band back in the 1920s.

Two of the songs, "Fine and Dandy" and "Air Mail Special," were taken at very brisk tempos. Without the video, it's not possible to tell who set the pace, but Cootie doesn't fare well at this speed. "Cootie's Big Time Blues," however, is a different story. A themeless medium tempo blues in the key of F, it lets Cootie shine in a way the first two songs don't allow. Across nine choruses, an unusually long stretch, he builds a plunger muted solo of increasing intensity. After solos by pianist Billy Taylor and guitarist Roy Gaines, Cootie returns, this time on open trumpet to build to a roaring finale after another four choruses. Vibraphonist Harry Sheppard was present on both of Cootie's *Jazz Party* appearances and recalled: "I jammed with Cootie several times in the 1950s. He was a sweet man, played a very original style, was always ready to play, and loved hangin' out with his old buds!"[10]

These weren't Cootie's first television appearances. Cootie appeared on Eddie Condon's early television show that ran on CBS from 1949 to 1950. Entitled *The Eddie Condon Floor Show*, it was a half hour show featuring jazz musicians like Sidney Bechet, Pee Wee Russell, Gene Krupa, and Bobby Hackett.[11] Condon was credited with the first jazz concert on American television, in 1942.[12] Perhaps Cootie Williams appeared on the show because he would have known Condon through their joint appearance at 1947's Front Page Ball. *Floor Show* ran on Saturday nights from 8:30 to 9:00 p.m. Williams appeared on the January 29, 1949, edition of the show. Unfortunately, no known audio or video recordings survive from that show. The *Chicago Defender* wrote, "Cootie Williams . . . has added another laurel to his list of musical achievements—success on television." Williams's appearance went over well; he "stole the show" and he "was immediately resigned for an encore appearance Feb. 5."[13] The new medium of television did require a learning curve in filming African Americans. While trying to make the adjustments to film the mixed group (four white musicians, with Teddy Wilson and Cootie) on this television broadcast, at one point "they had Cootie the lightest one in the bunch."[14]

EUROPEAN TRIUMPH

The Savoy Ballroom had been on life support for much of the 1950s. Cootie said, "Things was bad there. I stayed there till they tore it down, with seven pieces."[1] On March 12, the Savoy Ballroom held its annual birthday party, with entertainment provided by the bands of Cootie Williams and Dick Vance.[2] This celebration of thirty-two years in business would turn out to be the last. After struggling for years, the property was sold to the city, and the Savoy Ballroom closed in October 1958. The next year, it was demolished, and a housing project went up on the site.[3] In 2002, a plaque was installed to memorialize the spot where "the Home of Happy Feet" brought great times to so many.[4]

Cootie met his wife Catherine at the Savoy Ballroom in the early days of its existence. He was playing there when it was shut down by the authorities in 1943 and was chosen to play there when it reopened a few months later. Over the course of two decades, Cootie played there more than any other musician. And he was there to close it down on its final day of operation. Yet, he is hardly connected with the Savoy Ballroom in the minds of fans and critics. Most seem to think the Savoy Ballroom only existed as Chick Webb's domain.

♪

Cootie Williams's early 1959 European tour was born in July 1958, when Williams was approached by French jazz promoter Daniel Filipacchi at the Savoy. Filipacchi was formerly a photographer of some renown, but his love of jazz led him to pursue concert promotion. Cootie was interested, telling Filipacchi, "Of course I want to return to Europe. Organize a little tour and I'll arrive as soon as possible." Cootie hadn't been to the continent since his 1939 tour with the Duke Ellington orchestra.[5]

Cootie Williams and tour promoter/guide Frank Tenot reunited during the Cootie's visit to France as part of the Ellington band's 1964 European tour. (Photograph by Jean-Pierre Leloir, Copyright owned by the Estate of Jean-Pierre Leloir)

Frank Tenot (1925–2004), French jazz fan, critic, and promoter, was assigned to chaperone the group through the tour. He wrote of his experiences in a two-part, 7,500-word article, in the April and May 1959 issues of the French publication *Jazz Magazine* and in *Frankly Speaking*, a collection of his writings. Tenot was a huge Cootie Williams fan and couldn't imagine that he'd be in the company of a childhood hero, one whose recordings he played repeatedly.

The tour almost didn't happen. The day before the musicians were to leave America, one of the involved promoters had said the tour was canceled for "obscure reasons." Somehow, it was misunderstood that a gentleman speaking for only his venue was speaking for all the various site promoters. Filipacchi knew that there were still commitments from venues in enough of the other cities to make the tour viable. Tenot was only partially persuaded, saying he didn't breathe normally until he saw the band disembark from their flight at Paris' Orly Airport on January 27, 1959. The group was billed as "Cootie Williams and His Orchestra" but the "orchestra" was really just a quintet. Besides Cootie, the band members were George Clarke on tenor saxophone, Larry Dale vocalist and guitarist, Arnold Jarvis organ and piano, and Lester Jenkins on drums. They were about to start on a jam-packed tour—thirteen cities in fourteen days.[6]

Poster for the January 30 concert in Brussels. (Author's collection)

WEDNESDAY, JANUARY 28 – LYON, FRANCE

Lyon hosted the first concert of the tour, and it was a huge success. The audience was enthusiastic, and the band was inspired by the crowd response, playing with "astonishing inspiration, warmth and swing."[7]

THURSDAY, JANUARY 29 – LIMOGES, FRANCE

In some of the cities, tour logistics were eased with the help of various European "Hot Clubs," which were jazz fan clubs. A welcoming reception was held at the Limoges home of Jean-Marie Masse, who was one such hot club member. As various albums played on the stereo system, Masse served the appreciative musicians red beans and rice. Cootie enjoyed this dish immensely. He didn't find European fare appealing as it wasn't hearty enough for him.

The group traveled to Paris by train that same night, arriving the next morning at 7:00 a.m. From Paris's Gare d'Austerlitz, they transferred to the train that would take them to Brussels. Their liaison in Brussels was Carlos de Radzitzky, another huge jazz fan, who also happened to be Belgian royalty, the Baron Radzitzky of Ostrowick.

38. EUROPEAN TRIUMPH

Lester Jenkins, Cootie Williams, and George Clarke performing in Europe, 1959. Jenkins and Clarke are sporting the objectionable "rock and roll" band uniforms. (Author's collection)

Advertisement for the January 31, 1959, Paris show. (Author's collection)

FRIDAY, JANUARY 30—BRUSSELS, BELGIUM

During the day, the band recorded for television.[8] The Brussels broadcast was equally successful, save one detail. Carlos de Radzitzky felt the band's red checkered jackets were too showy and too reminiscent of Bill Haley and the Comets. (To some, Cootie's music reminded them of rock and roll, not understanding that he played rhythm and blues. The jackets didn't help.)[9] Fortunately, the band also had a more sedate blue uniform to change into, much to the relief of the concert organizers. (The *Pittsburgh Courier* had predicted in 1956 that the rock and roll "craze is dying out and will be long gone in a few months.")[10]

SATURDAY, JANUARY 31—PARIS, FRANCE

The sets performed this night are described as a mixture of straight jazz and R&B. Again, some heard R&B and thought rock and roll. Cootie's ex-sideman, tenor saxophonist Sam "The Man" Taylor (1916–1990), didn't see rock and roll as something exotic: "Actually, this Rock and Roll is just the same as swing in the 30s except that they've added a tinkling piano and a backbeat on the guitar and drum. It's just another flavor to the music. Any true musician, if he's a true musician, and the music's got a beat and moves, he likes playing it."[11] Writing for *Jazz Hot*, Aris Destombes said:

> Not everyone was enamored of what they saw of the "new" Cootie. It's in old problem; critics don't always like change or evolution in their favorite artists. The artist is also criticized if they *don't* change. Personally, I was struck by the difference between the "plunger" and the "open" sound of Cootie. Muted, he becomes almost like himself twenty years before: "Echoes of Harlem," "Mood Indigo" have given us fairly conclusive testimonies. On the other hand, one gets the impression that by removing the mute, it opens the way to bad taste and triviality. All-around phrases without flight or consistency, hackneyed clichés, drawn from the worst, free effects, all the low cost of "Middle Jazz" goes there, without nuance, and it looks almost without shame. Is it the influence of rhythm and blues that makes one think it's not the climate for intelligent choruses? Is it the desire to excite at all costs? Is it weariness? I do not know.[12]

Trumpeter Nelson "Cadillac" Williams (1917–1973), no relation to Cootie, sits in for "We Remember Duke" and "Perdido." Besides sharing a surname, the Williamses also shared Alabama origins, with Nelson having been born in Montgomery. Nelson Williams was also an Ellington alumnus, having played several stints with the orchestra starting in 1949. He had moved to Paris in 1951. Fortunately, the Paris concerts were recorded and released on the French Decca label, allowing one to evaluate the offerings for themselves. They can't be without merit—the following year, the Academie du Disque awarded the recording the prize for "The Best Jazz Recording of 1959."[13]

Next, the band was off to Geneva via plane.

SUNDAY, FEBRUARY 1–GENEVA, SWITZERLAND

Tenot notices Cootie is pretty grumpy—he's not liking the European food and he's not getting enough sleep. While in Geneva, Tenot is informed by the hotel's proprietor that "one of the Americans is seriously ill." The hotelier said two doctors came and gave the patient drugs. Rushing upstairs, Tenot discovers that the patient is Williams. The vaccinations he had received in New York prior to his departure had exacted an allergic reaction and his arm was hugely swollen. Cootie also had pain in his shoulder from this condition.

"What did the doctors tell you?" Tenot enquires.

"It was normal! Well, I find it abnormal that a doctor is paid to say that what you have is normal! Now, let me suffer and sleep this off," Cootie grumpily responded.

Tentatively and perhaps unwisely, Tenot reminds Williams that he has a concert later this evening, which provoked an angry response from Cootie. Williams replies, "What do you mean? . . . Of course, I'm playing tonight. I'm not dying yet . . . But if you want me to play, let me sleep . . . I want, I have to sleep . . ." More than likely, Tenot didn't know about Williams's "the show must go on" attitude.

The next stop on the tour, Constance, Germany, required the band to wake up at the ungodly (at least for musicians) hour of 5:00 a.m. It would require changing trains twice and the last train, a "small country railcar" seemed to stop "twenty times every five minutes."

MONDAY, FEBRUARY 2, CONSTANCE, GERMANY

Before the evening concert, Tenot noted that Williams still didn't look very good. It's winter and it's "polar cold" in the hotel. Tenot went down to the front desk and asked the clerk to raise the temperature on the central heating system for Williams's benefit. The clerk responded, "That's the problem with you French. You're just like the Negroes. You French need a cozy atmosphere to live. Dear sir, when you travel, you need to breathe the clean mountain. The heat makes one soft!" Fortunately, Tenot had the presence of mind to mention that the request was not for him, but for the American band performing in an official concert that very evening. Upon receiving this information, the clerk's demeanor softened and he "almost stood at attention." "Of course, the temperature will be raised," he said, adding "we are friends with the Americans. They are the reason why there is jazz. During the Third Reich, there was no jazz, no cinema. Jazz and cinema weren't allowed for young people."

The Constance concert was organized by the critic and disk jockey Joachim-Ernst Berendt (1924–2000), and it was broadcast by Südwestfunk, the German radio station. Constance didn't have a big population, only about 30,000, but the concert drew over 1,000 people, in the dead of winter no less. Tenot attributes this partly to the prestige that Berendt's involvement brought to the event.[14]

Larry Dale brought down the house singing a song Joe Williams popularized with Count Basie, "Alright, OK, You Win." The fans and critics were impressed with the variety of Cootie's repertoire—traditional ("Basin Street Blues," "When the Saints Go Marching In"), swing ("Air Mail Special"), and the rhythm and blues pieces. Again, the band was enthusiastically received. Afterward, they signed autographs for a crowd so enamored that many even ask for a puzzled Frank Tenot's autograph. A local chef brought 120 postcards for Cootie to sign for him and his family.

There was an exuberant after-party in San Stefan's Keller, one of the historic cellar clubs in the city. Exhausted, a drowsy Williams left the festive after-party early; they had to leave at 6:00 a.m. for Zurich. Tenot returned to the hotel at about 2:00 a.m. and came across drummer Lester Jenkins, dejected and slumped in a lobby chair.

"What's wrong?" Tenot asked.

"I can't find my passport," replied Jenkins.

Tenot was immediately seized by panic. To be in Germany at that time without a passport was a major problem. They were scheduled to make borders crossings on the next leg of their journey. Panicked calls were made to the American Consulate and to New York. At 6:00 in the morning, Cootie appeared and asked for a "hearty" breakfast. (The typical light European "continental breakfast" wouldn't do.) Tenot explained the dire straits they were in due to Lester Jenkins' lost passport. At that point, a smiling Cootie Williams theatrically pulled out Jenkins' missing passport.

"If you had it all this time, why didn't you let us know?" Tenot asked.

Cootie replied, "I wanted to teach him a lesson about being careful with his papers!"

Tenot was not amused.[15]

TUESDAY, 3 FEBRUARY—BASEL AND ZURICH, SWITZERLAND

The band traveled to Basel via local rail. It was small and looked more suited to agriculture than personnel transport. They nicknamed it "Milk Train II." Once they arrived at Basel, they found themselves on the same platform as Count Basie and his orchestra, which was also on a European tour. The Basie organization was headed in the opposite direction. Tenot said, "We only had six minutes to change trains in Zurich; it was barely sufficient but, in any event, the schedules were not respected that day, because at the moment when the Cootie orchestra was passing from platform 3 to platform 13, the Basie orchestra, then in tour in Switzerland, completed the same route in reverse! The melee was general. The whole world kissed: The suitcases were dropped. Cootie and the Count roared with joy. [They were old friends and lived near each other in St. Albans.] I went to find a station manager, explained the problem to him and the flags were not lowered for the departure of the two trains until after the effusions had ended."

The scheduled activity was an afternoon radio show performance. At Basel, there was another hitch—customs officials refused to release Jenkins's drums, believing that they are a vessel for smuggling contraband. Cootie grabbed one of the drums and beat on it furiously and said, "You see, it's a drum, just a drum." The drums were released after "the vigor of this intervention caused a certain panic in the [customs] offices."

After the radio show, it was a relatively short train ride of approximately fifty miles to Zurich, where there was an evening concert. The concert went well until Larry Dale got whistled at during one of his songs; the audience was demanding that he play jazz. (Whistling is the European equivalent of booing.) Cootie switched his set list to accommodate the crowd.[16]

Tenot and Williams conversed a lot during the course of the tour. Williams chided Tenot's publication, *Jazz Magazine*, for not paying enough attention to King Oliver. He added that Oliver was a cautionary tale: "Poor King! He was the greatest of trumpeters and he died in misery. Me, I will not die in misery. I put money aside for my old age." He talked about his life's story and also gave Tenot some advice, saying, "if you're going to New York, Frank, don't eat in Harlem. It's the most expensive place in town. This is funny. You would think that, because there are broke people in this area, everything should be cheap; well, it's the opposite. It is the most expensive area. Me, I always take my wife to lunch or dinner at the restaurant in the other districts. It's much cheaper and we eat just as well . . ." He also volunteered: "You see, Frank, I'm seriously allergic to two things: pork makes me sick, and when I see snow my body swells and I get goose bumps. That's the only thing I can't stand in life: pork and snow."

On the train ride to Megève, Lester Jenkins was intrigued by the scenery, asking "What are those bits of wood for?," pointing to symmetrically arranged structures along the hillside. Cootie replied, "They are vines. Vineyards!" Jenkins says, "But where are the grapes?" Everyone laughed, because it was February and nothing was growing that time of year. Cootie explained to Tenot: "This guy never left New York before coming here. Once upon a time you would have searched in vain for someone this ignorant about the country side of life; now they believe that the milk is made by milk bar waitresses and that the ham is produced by the Detroit factories."[17]

WEDNESDAY, FEBRUARY 4–MEGEVE, FRANCE

Cootie went to bed as soon as he arrived and Tenot found that waking him up in order to prepare for the evening was not an easy task, "it requires firmness and flexibility." But overall, he said, "there is no musician more conscientious of his duties and he is always on time."

THURSDAY, FEBRUARY 5 AND FRIDAY, FEBRUARY 6–BARCELONA, SPAIN

To the great joy of the musicians, the weather was springlike in Barcelona. "This is Florida," said Cootie. And even better, the band had the day off. The next day, there were two concerts at 7:00 and 11:00 p.m. The enthusiasm of the Spanish fans surprised both Tenot and Williams. Cootie told Tenot "he never thought he was so famous." Tenot said, "it was really amazing to see the crowds following Cootie from his hotel to the concert hall."[18]

Cootie was interviewed by a Spanish publication, *La Vanguardia*. Tenot purchased a copy on the day of publication, the day after the concert, but was loathe to show it to Williams since he didn't feel the accompanying drawing of Williams was flattering or even a good likeness. But Williams insisted on seeing the newspaper. Even if he couldn't understand the language, he could at least see the caricature. Reluctantly, Tenot handed over the journal. Williams studied it for a moment while Tenot braced for the worst. To his amazement, after a few moments studying the likeness, Cootie "puffed out his chest and with a joyous face announced to his stunned musicians, 'They took me for a diplomat. They made me look like a diplomat, I'm a diplomat.'" The band traveled from Barcelona to Paris and for the rest of the trip to Paris, Cootie took on the air of a diplomat, saying to any inquiry, "I'll speak to you like I'm [John] Foster Dulles!"[19]

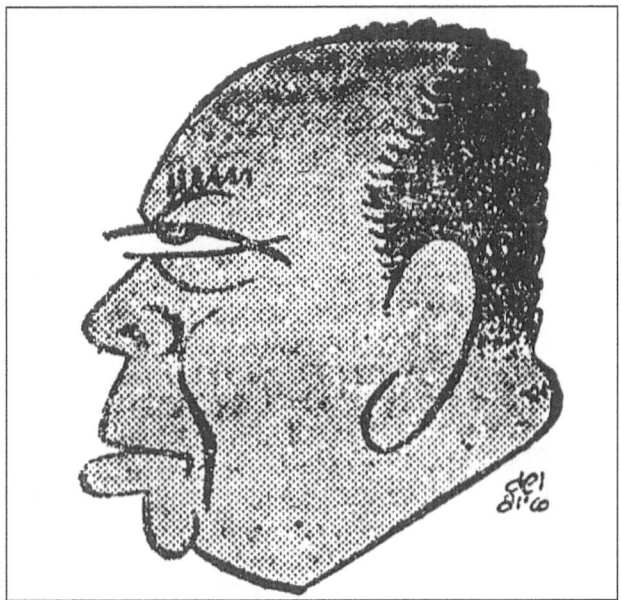

The drawing from *La Vanguardia*—Cootie Williams, "the diplomat." (Courtesy of Jazz Magazine)

Poster from the February 8 concert in Bordeaux. (Author's collection)

SUNDAY, FEBRUARY 8 – BORDEAUX, FRANCE

The band took a train from Paris to Bordeaux. In Bordeaux they once again encountered good weather. Counterintuitively, Tenot didn't think this a good thing and was apprehensive at drawing a crowd here. He knew that when the weather is good in Bordeaux, the population deserts the city. Fortunately, Tenot's fears turned out to be unfounded as the fans turned out in large numbers. As a bonus, they were a receptive and enthusiastic audience.

MONDAY, FEBRUARY 9 – POITIERS, FRANCE

Jazz concerts were rare at this time in Poitiers. But in 1997, long after Cootie's visit, the city became the site of regular concerts via the Jazz à Poitiers organization.

TUESDAY, FEBRUARY 10 – TOULOUSE, FRANCE

After their concert in Toulouse, a jump of 300 miles from Poitiers, the band returned to Paris.

WEDNESDAY, FEBRUARY 11 – PARIS, FRANCE

While back in Paris, Cootie "indulged in the joys of shopping," presumably for Catherine. The last concert was a cause for reflection, for Cootie was genuinely surprised by the reception he received on this whirlwind European tour, thinking that he was a forgotten figure. He was impressed by the knowledge possessed by the fans, telling a reporter that "at a concert in Europe, there are 70% connoisseurs. In the United States, there are only 20% [connoisseurs]."[20]

The band returned to New York on February 13, 1959, on TWA Flight 801.[21] This tour was a much-needed career boost for Cootie Williams. It turned out to be the last summit he would reach in his life as a bandleader.

39

BACK HOME

In early 1959, Cootie was able to tout his "smash European Tour" in his advertising. (*Intelligencer Journal*)

For a few months after the tour, Cootie's advertising carried the boast "Direct From His Smash European Tour, The Great Cootie Williams Orchestra."[1] (A lot of Cootie's advertising post 1947, the last year he led a big band, generously used the word "orchestra" for his combos.) But a few months into 1959, his agency began booking him as a "single." (A single is a musician who travels to a city without a group, using an ensemble of local musicians.) It's a very cheap way to provide entertainment but can be very risky if the locale can't supply good musicians. It also meant Cootie was "playing in places where I didn't like to play."[2] In October 1959[3] and February 1960,[4] Cootie played as a single at the Westover Hotel in Toronto, Canada. He was backed by the band of Cliff McKay, a reed player who also happened to be a Canadian television pioneer. Williams found it odd that they wanted him to sing, tell jokes, and entertain over playing the trumpet. "I was a trumpet player. I wasn't no singer." Still the audience would exhort him—"Come on, Cootie, sing. Sing. Sing." "Don't care how much trumpet I can blow, they want me to entertain them, singing and dancing, and telling jokes."[5] Perhaps the audiences were familiar with his *Around Midnight* album, which featured a lot of Williams vocalizing, sometimes in tandem with Wini Brown, and very little trumpet work. At the time, *Variety* reported that Williams was focusing on vocals: "After all these years, he's laying aside the horn and doing a ballad turn, and with exceptional results."[6] The change in direction was apparently short lived and a little odd because Williams wasn't too fond of his own vocal efforts, telling the Smithsonian Jazz Oral History Project, "I don't like my singing."[7] But he recorded songs like "Lover" and "That Old Black Magic" in vocal duets with Wini Brown in a manner that was very reminiscent of Louis Prima and Keely Smith.

Williams didn't like the single regimen and found it stressful, during one week's stint he lost fourteen pounds. He said, "I'd be playing, maybe, "Do Nothing Till You Hear from Me," and they'd be playing something else. You have to learn that in this business. See, the public is very funny. You're standing in front of the public out there; they don't want to know nothing about John Doe back there." Further galling to Williams—sometimes the band couldn't read music and was ignorant of chord structure and progressions![8] "I had to learn to close my ears." He called working as a single "the hardest musical experience I ever had."[9] Despite his unhappiness, Williams was ever the professional. One Canadian's review was titled "Cootie Proves He's One of [the] Best" and raved that Williams "was the best jazz trumpeter I have heard in the flesh, at Basin Street or anywhere else." Preferring Williams's work on open trumpet, he said it could only be bested by Louis Armstrong "at his finest."[10]

Once again, Cootie found himself recording for another small record company when he made the *Around Midnight* album for the Jaro International label. Like most small record labels, discography details are almost nonexistent, and it can only be dated to being recorded sometime in 1959. "Gone Again" was a hit record for Wini Brown when she recorded it with Lionel Hampton in 1947. Her *Around Midnight* version with Cootie was released as a single (with "Johnny with the Gentle Hands" on the other side) in 1960 and rekindled a spark of fame for her; she was billed as "The Gone Again Girl" during her appearances as part of an R&B revue.[11] But like Eddie Mack and Robert Merrill before her, she faded from the limelight and was largely forgotten by the time of her death in 1978. When Williams's recording of "On the Sunny Side of the Street," from *Around Midnight* was played for Ruby Braff in a *Down Beat* Blindfold Test, Braff said "the singer doesn't seem too comfortable about that song, or else he's

Cootie's album for the Jaro International label, *Around Midnight*. (Author's collection)

Released in 1960, *Do Nothing Till You Hear From . . . Cootie* was recorded on the small Warwick label. (Author's collection)

trying too hard. It's kind of forced." But Braff had praise for Williams's horn, even though he couldn't name the player: "I enjoyed the trumpet solo—it sounded very, very good."[12]

Although the European tour had put some wind in the sail of Cootie's career, it was short lived. In September, he was relegated to backing status, with small font billing, for rising singing star Jackie Wilson, who was riding the pop charts with the Top Ten hit "I'll Be Satisfied."

With the Savoy Ballroom out of the picture as a study source of work, Cootie found himself a regular at the Roundtable starting in the fall of 1960 and continuing until the end of 1961. The Roundtable, located at 151 East 50th Street in Manhattan, was described by the New York Times as "a large, high-ceilinged, oval room with a graciously spacious air" and "vast and austere."[13] It was a mob-owned joint, a "wiseguy hangout" under the control of notorious mobster Morris Levy.[14]

Sometime in 1960, Cootie recorded for Warwick, yet another small record label. Released that same year, it was titled *Do Nothing Till You Hear From . . . Cootie*. Six of the nine selections are Ellington compositions and again there are almost no details available. The recording date is unknown and the band, besides Williams on trumpet and vocal, is uncredited but consists of baritone sax, vibraphone, piano, guitar, bass, and drums.[15]

Wini Brown went on her own way during the summer of 1960, leaving Cootie without a vocalist other than himself. Whether the idea came from Cootie or Mortie Craft, the president of Warwick Records, the call went out to hold auditions for "a pretty Negro songstress who can belt out a song like Keely Smith for a week long engagement at The Roundtable with Cootie Williams and Bill 'Mr. Inkspot' Kenny." The winner would also get a demonstration recording test.[16] A female singer was hired by Cootie in July[17] but she walked out of the job for unknown reasons, which cost Cootie a $350 reduction in his contract.[18]

At this point in his career, Cootie Williams wasn't always the star, but he was working. One such gig inspired a reporter's pity in June 1961: "A depressing sight these nights is to watch Cootie Williams, the famous old Duke Ellington trumpet man, finish his stint at the Roundtable with his quartet—and then sit in, as a mere sideman, in the band that backs up Adam Wade's amiable singing, Wade being the show's star."[19] Adam Wade (1935–2022) was able to break out as a singer star in 1961 with three singles on the Billboard Top Ten.[20] He was later to become the first Black game show host on the television show *Musical Chairs* in 1975. "A giant of jazz and still in great form, Cootie looks highly out of place as a straight man to a young singer who undoubtedly would be the first to admit that Cootie knows more about music than he does or will."[21]

During the summer of 1961, he also could be found at the Metropole Café, a venue catering to traditional and mainstream music. But at the Metropole, the bands found themselves in competition with the loud audiences.

Belle Barth In Person was recorded live at the Roundtable in New York City. Cootie and his group can be heard in their limited supporting role on this album.

Metronome gave the group a short favorable review: "Cootie served up good sounds, proving once again that the men of the swing generation have a staying power which will be hard to match. It is a great pity that men like Roy [Eldridge] and Cootie can't be heard in those New York clubs which cater to a listening audience. They could provide plenty to hear."[22] Despite playing in venues where the music was secondary to the food, Cootie "plays with such rich, full-toned beauty that the attention of even the most casual listener is caught."[23]

But this was not the last of Cootie's bad gigs. Starting in March, he would share the bill at the Roundtable with Belle Barth. Eventually, he would become her musical director. Barth (born Annabelle Saltzman, 1911–1971) was a bawdy comedienne and regular act at the Roundtable. She had numerous encounters with the law because of her "blue" language, like other "blue" comedians of the day (such as Lenny Bruce and Mort Sahl). This type of law enforcement activity was typical of the time, forcing tests to the limits of the First Amendment. She would sometimes use double-entendre and Yiddishisms instead of cursing to evade censor scrutiny.[24] In what was most probably a gimmick, the management of the Roundtable installed a red light on stage that would flash if Barth needed to tone her act down.[25]

Barth played a midnight show at Carnegie Hall on November 25, 1961. Carnegie Hall had fallen on hard times and like the Savoy Ballroom before it, was in danger of being demolished. The master of ceremonies for the show was Mercer Ellington, who at this time was also a disk jockey for Harlem's WLIB.[26] The younger Ellington also wrote arrangements for Barth, to the dismay of some.[27] The performance was a "flop." Barth said, "Plainclothesmen came in just before the show and said if I told one dirty joke or used any blue lyrics they'd turn off the mike and close the curtain. They even threatened me with arrest."[28] This forced Barth to change her act on the fly, which wasn't an easy adjustment on such little notice. Fans were angry that they didn't get the show that they were expecting. Poor Cootie only got one mention in *Variety*'s review, saying his group had "worked better elsewhere."[29] Ironically, Duke Ellington and his orchestra played New York City's Town Hall only three days earlier. The reviewer lamented that because of personnel problems, the only veteran trumpeter in the section was Cat Anderson, who had to take on the growl duties "formerly performed by Ray Nance, Cootie Williams and Bubber Miley."[30] Despite the Carnegie Hall failure, Barth was hot enough to land an open-ended engagement in the Miami's Copa City nightclub. She hired Cootie Williams as her musical director—after an absence of thirty-three years, Cootie Williams returned to Miami.

On November 10, 1961, Cootie and Catherine sold their St. Albans residence. The timing suggests that with Cootie taking an indefinite job in Miami, it was time to downsize residences. The buyer turned out to be singer James Brown (1933–2006), later to be known as "The Godfather of Soul" and "The Hardest Working Man in Show Business." At the time, he was an up-and-coming singer and about to rise even higher as the sixties progressed. Williams and Brown were both booked by Universal Attractions Agency and had the same manager, Ben Bart. Bart facilitated the sale between the two musicians. Brown said in his autobiography that "[t]he house in St. Albans needed a lot of work—the basement was full of water, things like that—so I hired a bunch of people to work on it while I went on tour."[31] The house had also seen a fire in early 1953, but fortunately it was "discovered before it became too serious."[32] Brown spent $65,000 to repair and remodel the home.[33]

The 1956 *Guide to After Dark Miami* described Copa City as "cost[ing] a million dollars about eight years ago. It has since been redesigned in ultramodern decor by Franklin Hughes. Largest café in the whole Miami area, it's one of the few clubs here dishing out complete floor shows along with name performers."[34] It was a large club, boasting 750 seats. Only a few years before this glowing description was written, Copa City was a segregated venue. When Josephine Baker was booked there in 1951, she refused to perform unless the audience was integrated. Management acquiesced and from that point, Copa

City was an integrated venue. The Black entertainers who visited Miami usually stayed at the Sir John Hotel (formerly the Lord Calvert), so it's likely that was where Cootie was based during his four-month stay in Miami. It was only about six miles from Copa City.

The Jewish Floridian described the act as "well-balanced, with Cootie Williams' great quartet backing Belle." The trio of Frank DiFabio and singer Bobby Milano completed the bill of fare.[35] Fried chicken, sirloin steak, and red snapper dinners were served for $3.95, with a two-drink minimum required.[36] Business must have good; within a few weeks, ads were touting "Belle's Packing 'Em In!!!" The admission policy had been changed to require buying dinner for an increased price of $4.95 or taking in the show from the bar for a three-drink minimum instead of the previously required two drinks.[37]

Barth recorded several live albums of her comedy routines. While very risqué by the standards of the early 1960s, her jokes would seem just a little beyond the mainstream today. But she would sometimes deliver her bluest punchlines in Yiddish in order to stay ahead of the police. She would banter with the audience as part of the act. When a woman exclaimed, "I never heard such words in my life," Barth shot back, "So how do you know what they mean?" Cootie wasn't immune from being included in the act. Barth said, "I'm gonna make Cootie do this [act] and I'm gonna blow the horn. If I could blow like you, I'd be retired by now."[38]

Williams didn't like these backing gigs,[39] but they were gigs nonetheless. As a top-notch musician who was used to working with equally talented musicians, he didn't like her inability to follow song form. "She wasn't a very good musician. She would jump the meter, and wherever we were playing I would get headaches from the musicians. During rehearsal I would tell them, 'Please, watch me at all times. This is the way we ordinarily do it. If she don't get high.' She might sing eight bars, jump to two in the channel [bridge], come back right in here, and end up somewhere else. The musicians would be tearing out their hair. I got no chance to blow, either." On Barth's *In Person* album, recorded live at the Roundtable, Cootie is heard introducing Barth, but musically only heard playing a few bars of "Night Train" and "When the Saints Go Marching In." Another headache for the ever-punctual Williams was his pianist. "Each night the piano player came in five or ten minutes late. And I got tired of having the boss on my neck."[40] But that candid admission came years after he was done working with her. To the public, he put a good face on the gig, saying that he was happier as her musical director than running his own band, particularly since the pay was "more regular."[41]

Billboard reported that the "Moodsville label will have a new set recorded by Cootie Williams in Miami. The album was cut by Sid Wayman while Williams was playing the show with Belle Barth."[42] The Moodsville imprint (a short-lived

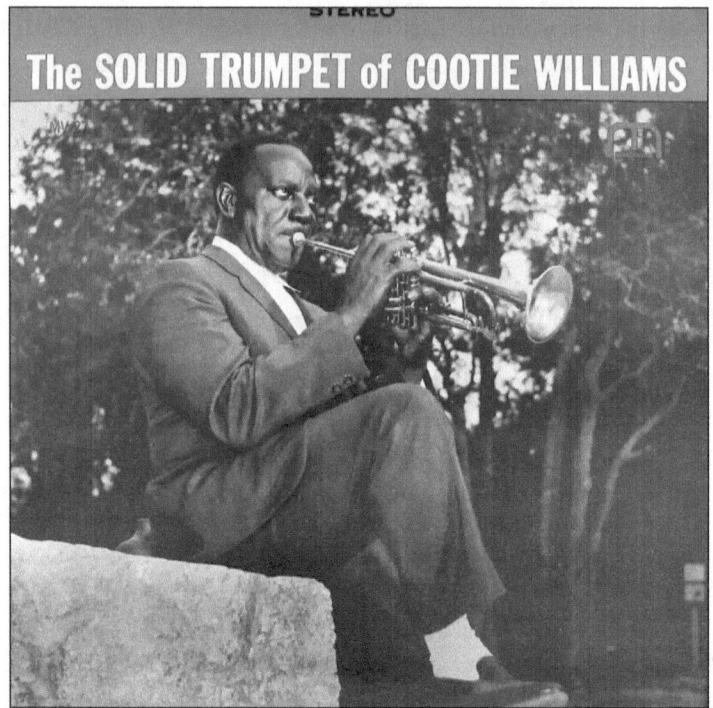

The Solid Trumpet of Cootie Williams, Cootie's last recording session as a bandleader.

subsidiary of Prestige Records) was designed to carry "mood music," which could be defined as non-obtrusive background music, but Cootie's open and plunger trumpet sounds were too assertive to be considered aural wallpaper. The liner notes were by LeRoi Jones[43] (1934–2014), later known as Amiri Baraka.

On April 4, Cootie Williams took his working group into the studio. Although it was impossible to know at the time, this would turn out to be Williams's last recording session as a leader. The group consisted of Williams on trumpet, with no vocals this time. The rhythm section of pianist Nat Jones, bassist Harold Dodson, and drummer Bill Peeples, were all Florida-based musicians. The results were released as *The Solid Trumpet of Cootie Williams*. Another version of "Concerto for Cootie," which by this time was really "Do Nothing Till You Hear from Me," starts off the album. Taken at a leisurely pace, it covers only two choruses of the song in a little over four minutes. The group is a solid working combination. While there is no new ground broken here, this is an album reflecting the work of a mature musician. "Night Train" was a big seller for tenor saxophonist Jimmy Forrest in the late 1940s and was based on Duke Ellington's "Happy-Go-Lucky Local." Played at a bouncy medium tempo, the recording shows Cootie's use of the "set" solo (a solo that sounds improvised but in reality is played almost the same night after night). After a vigorous block chord solo from Jones, Williams returns to play three blues choruses that he would recycle into his solo routine on his Ellington showcase "Tootie for Cootie" (aka "Tutti for Cootie"). Ironically, Williams covers "Sugar Blues," which was a big hit for trumpeter Clyde McCoy in the mid-1930s. McCoy also used plunger effects on his trumpet throughout his career, but he was considered "corn" (a la Guy Lombardo and Lawrence Welk) instead of real jazz. Benny Goodman said way back in 1939, that, "Only an ear which has heard a Clyde McCoy can appreciate the true quality of a 'Cootie' Williams."[44]

There were few reviews of the album, and perhaps that was a good thing as the critics weren't kind. *Down Beat* gave the album a rating of three (good) out of a possible five (excellent) stars. The review spends its first half scolding Cootie for his career path choices. The rest of the review isn't much better, calling his improvising "repetitive" and "there is a deadening sameness evident on these tracks. It is unfortunate that his talent has wasted these years on things like this."[45] Another reviewer said Williams seemed intent "recreating the sound of Jonah Jones instead of his own . . . with little, if any, of the bite and drive that once were his trademarks."[46] Perhaps the lack of "bite and drive" could have been deliberate since the intent behind the Moodsville label was "mood music"? The confusion might be blamed on Cootie himself. In the liner notes, Jones said that "here the word *mood* does not mean sleep, as is so often the case with other so call 'mood music.' But it does occasionally mean a relaxed, though always purposeful kind of music. It would be impossible to go to sleep on Cootie . . ."[47]

At the completion of the long residency at Copa City, Barth and Williams did a short tour focusing on the Midwest. Cootie was given the role of opening the shows "with a couple of nifty trumpet solos," but again his part in the show was minimal.[48] It was hardly the best use of his talents. By the early sixties, it was hard for swing era musicians to make a living. Several jazz styles had succeeded swing (bop, cool, the nascent avant-garde) and rock had surpassed overall jazz in the popular imagination. Not to mention that their fan base had become middle-aged like the musicians themselves.

PART VI *Duke Ellington (1962)*

40

DRIFTING RIGHT BACK

> No one leaves the Ellington Institution. Some drift away now and then.
> And they drift right back—now and then.
> —DUKE ELLINGTON[1]

After Benny Goodman returned from his 1962 State Department sponsored tour of Russia, he once again asked Cootie Williams to join his band. For a performance at Chicago's Ravinia Highland Park on August 1, the King of Swing had assembled another big band especially for this occasion, with a trumpet section made up of Cootie Williams, Flea Campbell, George Trifton, and Harold Lieberman. Long-time Goodman alumnus, the great Teddy Wilson, held down the piano chair. Over 7,000 enthusiastic fans gave the band a rousing reception.[2]

Benny Goodman played a weeklong engagement (August 11 through 16) at Freedomland USA, a short-lived New York theme park centered on American history. Instead of a big band, Goodman used a small group, which included Cootie. Critic and writer Stanley Dance recalled running into Cootie a day after one of these shows. Dance noticed there was no bass player that night. Cootie told him that Goodman had fired the bassist the previous night and forgot to get another one. "Cootie was one guy that really admired Benny," said Dance. Goodman intimidated a lot of musicians, but Dance said, "I don't think [Cootie] was afraid of anybody."[3] (But as a youngster during his time with the Fletcher Henderson band, Cootie admitted to fearing Big Green.) Cootie's last Goodman gig occurred on Friday, September 7 at College Park, Maryland. It was a benefit performance for the University of Maryland's scholarship fund. Goodman performed with an orchestra that included Wilson and drummer Ed

Shaughnessy. Although the local newspaper had promoted the bassist would be Israel Crosby, he had died of a heart attack the previous month.[4]

Williams enjoyed working with Goodman, but Williams's gripe with Goodman was that he didn't keep a regular orchestra; he would assemble one based on an upcoming gig and then take a layoff until the next big festival or concert booking. By this time in his life, Goodman was well-off enough for this type of arrangement to work for him. "He doesn't keep a band. He'll just organize one for maybe two or three months, then he disbands."[5]

Sometime during the summer of 1962, Cootie had contacted Harry Carney in order to get his job back with the Duke Ellington orchestra. Williams's return to the Ellington orchestra amounted to a tacet admission of failure as a leader. There were many factors—luck, changing musical tastes, management, and something that isn't comfortable to discuss: racism. In a 1962 *Down Beat* interview, organist Jimmy Smith said in 1962 that Blacks were beginning to get "an even break. If things had been different, Duke Ellington would not have had to scuffle so hard. Cootie Williams could have made it. Satchmo wouldn't have had to 'Tom,' and Duke would be a millionaire today."[6] When Roy Eldridge retired, he summed up the limitations placed on his career: "I played fifty years, and that was long enough. Anyway, I found out the main doors were always locked. The color thing. I also found out I'd never get rich."[7] In his 1976 interview for the Jazz Oral History Project, Williams talked about fellow bandleader Buddy Johnson's (1915–1977) lack of fame and success, but his words applied to him, also: "[Buddy Johnson] never did break the white field open. Once you were identified in the white field, then you were established forever." Cootie's contemporaries like Duke Ellington, Louis Armstrong, Cab Calloway, and Count Basie come to mind as examples of artists who were able to cross over.

Cootie didn't record frequently when he was on his own and even then, about half of them reached the current marketplace. As a result, many of his personnel changes and song choices were never documented. John Coltrane recorded prolifically during his last years while on the Impulse! label, which forced his producer Bob Thiele to battle upper management on Coltrane's behalf. Duke Ellington had his own solution to the problem. Starting in the late 1950s he recorded the band at his own expense. He referred to the recordings as "the stockpile."

The orchestra had been through a lot during the twenty-two years Williams was away. Ellington had had his own series of Carnegie Hall concerts starting in 1943, where he premiered his tone parallel to the history of the American Negro, "Black, Brown and Beige." (Cootie was one of the honorary sponsors of that concert.)[8] The band survived the late 1940s nadir of the big bands. Lawrence Brown, Harry Carney, Johnny Hodges, and of course, Duke himself were still there from Williams's 1940 departure. Harry Carney had never left, but Johnny Hodges had left the Ellington orchestra to go out on his own in 1951, taking Lawrence Brown and Sonny Greer with him. Hodges found out being a leader wasn't all it was cracked up to be and returned to the fold in 1955. Unlike Williams, Hodges didn't feel the need to become a showman, saying "I've never been the emotional sort and it's too late for me to change now. I've never jumped around. I don't think a good showman is necessarily a good player." But like Williams, Hodges had struggled as a bandleader: "I had to scuffle and when you scuffle you can't play what you like. When you are famous and popular, you can."[9] Brown came back in 1960, after first playing in Hodges's band until he folded it and then working in the CBS studios. Greer's heavy drinking meant he wasn't on the best of terms when he left, so there was no push to bring him back.

Whitney Balliett probably described the stability of the Ellington band personnel best: "'Duke Ellington's band has something in common with the Supreme Court: its members tend to stay put for life. Thus when one of Ellington's sidemen quits, seismographs pick up the tremors." Cat Anderson also had a similar opinion: "Most musicians, I think, have the ambition, at one time or another, to play with this band. So it's quite an honor for us to be here. There's so many other guys that want to play, and [for] there [to] be time for them. There won't be a seat for them, because the guys that are here—they're not going any place."[10]

Five days after his last gig with Benny Goodman, Cootie Williams was back with Duke Ellington, recording on a September 12 "stockpile" session. Unlike his departure nearly twenty-two years earlier, there was no grand press announcement or a welcome back party when Cootie Williams returned to the Duke Ellington band. Trombonist George "Buster" Cooper (1929–2016), who had joined the band in June, said he had heard some rumors about Cootie returning, but didn't know he was back until he heard someone grumbling behind him. He turned around at saw it was Cootie.[11]

The first thing recorded was "Tutti for Cootie," a blues that alternated between A♭ major and C minor keys, credited to Duke Ellington and Jimmy Hamilton. Unfortunately, this first recording of this Williams showcase has not been released as of this date, but it is circulating among collectors. It's taken at a tempo notably faster than later recordings. A lot of times, songs get faster performances as time goes on. For "Tutti for Cootie" that wasn't the case; it got slower and slower with time. Vocalist Kurt Elling set words to Cootie's trumpet solo and recorded the song on his 2012 album *1619 Broadway—The Brill Building Project*. The remaining three titles were "Broadstream," "To Know You Is to Love You," and an impromptu D♭ blues jam dubbed "September 12th Blues." For this last title, following statements by Johnny Hodges, Lawrence Brown, Harry Carney, Jimmy Hamilton, Buster Cooper, and Paul Gonsalves, Cootie gets the honor of the climactic last solo on this effort with Ellington vocally egging on Williams in the background. The last three titles weren't released until 1987, a quarter century after their creation.

The addition of Williams brought the trumpet section up to five members. Ray Nance, Cootie's "replacement," was still there from 1940. Bill Berry (1930–2002), one of the rare white musicians to play with the band, William "Cat" Anderson, and Jamaican Roy Burrowes (1930–1998) were the rest of the section. September 1962 would become a memorable month in Ellington history. Besides the return of Cootie Williams on the 12th, Ellington would record a trio album (*Money Jungle*) with bassist Charles Mingus and drummer Max Roach on September 17. And just nine days later, Duke's encounter with the controversial saxophonist John Coltrane was waxed.

While the return of Cootie Williams to the Duke Ellington band in 1962 didn't get as much press as his 1940 departure, there was still critical notice. Critic Ralph Gleason noted that "Williams's return adds another episode to the curious history of the Ellington sidemen of the early years."[12] At the time Williams left, the Ellington band was in a remarkable burst of creative activity. The orchestra of the period of 1939–1942 has been dubbed the "Blanton-Webster Band" and many critics and fans consider it a musical summit not just for the band, but one of the highest artistic peaks for any musical act. In 1962, just before the arrival of Williams, Carney took issue with that judgment. He said, "A lot of people come up and start talking about the 1940 band and say, 'Gee, that was *the* band.' For the most part, they've stopped going where the band's playing. Then they come out one night and say, 'Oh, this band is nothing like the band of 1940.' And they actually haven't heard enough or absorbed enough of the current band's playing to say that. In 1940 there was something that did something to them, and that's all they remember."[13]

Williams was philosophical about his time as a leader: "I think it was a very good idea for me to have the experience of going out on my own when I was younger, though, because you can see some parts of the world and look on life a little differently than when you were with a man [Ellington] for so many years. They say that one-nighters are always the same, but when you're on your own you look at the concert halls differently and the people differently, everything."[14] Williams described the differences from the time he left: "My name is still on some of the parts in the arrangements, and that makes me feel especially good. Oh, the band have [sic] changed some. Jimmy [sic] Blanton, he's gone, and Sonny Greer and Ben Webster and Tricky Sam Nanton, and I think Duke builds the band more around arrangements now than around soloists. Of course, he had a lot of soloists to work with when I left."[15] Williams wasn't too thrilled at the prospect of revisiting the old repertoire, however: "It doesn't improve you. I always look forward to something new. Before I came back with

Duke this time, I told him, 'I don't want to play Black and Tan [Fantasy] and those things I did forty years ago.' My mind is different now. The public doesn't understand that when you've played a thing for six months, it may be finished for you."[16] Williams might have made his thoughts known on the subject, but "Black and Tan Fantasy," "The Mooche," and other numbers from his early days with the band were still in the performance rotation throughout his second tenure. He didn't have to worry about soloing on those songs initially—they were assigned to Ray Nance.

"One reason I came back with Duke is he's the greatest man I ever knew."[17] "But I wouldn't work for Duke Ellington unless I was satisfied musically. I wouldn't work for nobody. It's not the money part of it because I can get out in the street and hustle enough to make a living for myself, I'm not that damn stupid."[18] While publicly saying it wasn't about the money, he would go on to have financial disputes with Ellington.

Ellington was glad that Williams had returned and said that his chair had always been open during his twenty-two-year absence. He said, "It's done for my ear health. I am addicted to certain zesty sounds, of which Cootie's is certainly one. My ear health is very important. It is so near my mind and that gets a little diluted by the wrong sound."[19] "Cootie is a valuable man. We have always maintained a friendly relationship since he has been away. His place has been open to him any time he wanted. He said he wanted to be back in the band and he is back." Ellington thought that the reason for the return was Cootie being tired of the small-group setting and it not offering the same characteristics of a big band. "The guy gets his setting in here with us and we write to the man, what he is doing and playing. We write what we consider the most fitting framework for his talent. It's like the difference between the tailor made and the ready-made suit. You get a small combination and a guy plays just as good a solo but the design behind it is not the same. It's a case of custom tailoring."[20] Billy Strayhorn added that Cootie's new material wouldn't be ready immediately. "Since Cootie's return, we have been hectically touring. Soon we shall be getting round to some new writing just for him."[21]

The first public performances with prodigal son Williams produced great reviews, with the *Los Angeles Times* saying Cootie "preach[ed] such a powerful trumpet sermon that the roof nearly fell in."[22] His section mate, Cat Anderson, raved about his playing and said: "Cootie sounds great as ever now. It's phenomenal, with that powerful plunger work he does. He just knocks us out when he starts playing. We just sit back there and crack our jaws, because we're so happy that he's doing these things with as much talent as he ever had."[23]

But Williams's return meant that the band now had three plunger specialists—Williams, Nance, and Cat Anderson. William Alonzo Anderson was born on September 12, 1916, in Greenville, South Carolina. Both of his parents died when he was young and he was placed in the Jenkins Orphanage in Charleston. It was here that his fighting style earned him the nickname "Cat," although it's been said that he acquired the tag because of his green eyes. He joined the Duke Ellington orchestra in the fall of 1944. He was a masterful trumpeter, capable of playing the "jungle-style" plunger muted style, playing the lead trumpet role and in duplicating the half-valve style of Rex Stewart. But where he excelled, in a territory all of his own, was in the trumpet's stratospheric upper register.

Cootie's return coincided with Ellington's departure from Columbia Records, his recording home since 1956. Duke had had several stints with them, but this would be this last one. He was dropped for "not selling records." Ellington replied, "Well I think you have it turned around. I write the music, you're supposed to sell the records."[24] His next label stop came courtesy of Frank Sinatra when he signed Ellington to his Reprise Record label and additionally made him head of Reprise's jazz catalog. Sinatra gave Ellington large latitude in what he could record.[25] In November of 1962, Ellington made his first recordings with the label and Cootie's first commercially available recordings with the band were released on *Will the Big Bands Ever Come Back?* (Enough material was recorded for two albums, but the second album, *Recollections of the Big Band Era*, didn't hit the market until 1974.) The first track on the album, Erskine Hawkins's "Tuxedo Junction," features Cootie as the first solo voice heard on the album. Cootie's hero, Louis Armstrong, had his theme song, "When it's Sleepy Time Down South," covered, but it was Ray Nance and clarinetist Russell Procope taking the solo duties, not Cootie.

♪

"[A] guy would come in the saxophone section, a new man come in there, and he'd just be setting there. A guy wouldn't tell him what he'd be playing next or nothing. He'd just be sitting there. He'd be lost. By the time he'd be getting into the number, he'd be looking for the music, we'd be done finished." Williams said they never helped the new guy out because "they never felt like it was their duty." Partially, this was because "Duke didn't write all of the music out. He would give you certain notes, and you'd play a certain part like this, on the piano, note for note, and it wasn't written out. And when the new guy come in there, he'd have a piece of music, and he'd have a great big blank space, and things, and the guy wouldn't know what to be playing, you know. And the guys would keep on playing their parts. They wouldn't even [give him a clue] or nothing. And the guy'd just be sitting there, till he'd catch on."[26]

The Ellington band had a reputation for not welcoming newcomers. Dizzy Gillespie, Clark Terry, and Al Sears have spoken of being left to fend for themselves on the bandstand. Although Williams said the saxophone section were the guilty party in this regard, the trumpet section did it, too. Dizzy Gillespie got called to substitute for Ray Nance at a recording session. In his autobiography, *To Be or Not to Bop*, Gillespie got the full treatment from the trumpet section:

> The guys in Duke's band weren't too nice . . . They didn't help anyone. In rehearsal, they wouldn't tell me that you had to jump from "A." I'm supposed to remember all that, that you jump from "A," to the first three bars of "Z," and then jump back to "Q," and play eight bars of that , and then jump over to the next part, and then play the solo. Nobody would tell you anything. Cootie Williams, Rex Stewart and Wallace Jones were sitting up there, as silent as high priests in a temple. I had to guess what it was.[27]

While Cootie was guilty of this behavior at times, in the incident Gillespie describes, he was innocent; he wasn't even in the Ellington band at the time and was busy leading his own band. Stewart and Jones were there along with Taft Jordan. Jordan might need to be given some grace in this case since he had only been in the band about six months at the time.

The practice extended into the 1960s. Swedish trumpeter Rolf Ericson (1922–1997) was hired into the band on the recommendation of Clark Terry in 1963. It was an interesting experience:

> I was mystified at first. Duke had this huge library, with just fragments of paper; I couldn't find any music, and I'd ask the other trumpeters.[28] I asked Cootie Williams but he just turned his back on me and grunted something. So I asked Ray Nance what the last tone was supposed to be. He said: "Anything, you'll hear what it shall be." Then I asked Cat Anderson, who gave me a great smile and said: "B-flat." Then Cootie suddenly said: "Don't listen to that asshole, it should be E♭!" So things were not exactly easy. The only way to work things out was to construct my own book. I sat in the evenings and wrote out my own parts, made my own music out of those notes and fragments. So after about a month I had a good grip of everything. But the situation within the trumpet section was still the same. When I showed up in the evening and said hello to Cootie he would turn his back on me and grunt and Cat just smiled and showed his white teeth. It went on like that night after night. When we started and when we closed it was always the same procedure. But then we went on a tour to the Middle East [1963].[29] Suddenly one

evening Cootie turned to me and said: "Hey Rolf, let's go get the girls." With those words it was like the ice broke up and we have been the best of friends since then.[30]

Richard Williams (no relation) subbed for Mercer Ellington for a short period and described it as "quite an experience" sitting between Cat and Cootie.[31] But for some reason, trombonist Julian Priester didn't receive that kind of treatment when he joined in 1970. He said Cat Anderson was "a nice guy, really a nice guy. When I first joined the band, he was the one that first took me into a corner and said, 'Look, this band runs this way and this is what is expected of you and don't get too excited, don't be too quick . . .' and just to be careful not to change the character."[32]

Even the great drummer Elvin Jones, fresh out of John Coltrane's groundbreaking quartet, was not immune to the band's frosty receptions. The orchestra was on tour in Europe at the time he was recruited. When he arrived, to his chagrin, he saw that there was a second drummer. The two drummers clashed rhythmically and personally and to boot, Jones' style was quite different from what the band had been used to. According to Jones, the key members of the band complained to Duke about his playing. Jones singled out Cootie's behavior saying, "I don't know whether Cootie, who kept giving me the fisheye, wanted me to call him Mr. Williams and shine his shoes or what."[33] Jones wound up leaving after only a few days with the band.[34]

THE ROAD

When the band traveled by bus, there were a set of rules to be followed, based on seniority. "Duke occupies the first seat by the door, and Harry Carney sits next to him; but because they generally ride together separately from the band in dad's Lincoln, Cootie Williams often occupies the front seat. We call him 'the pretender to the throne.' Although Johnny Hodges could bump Cootie, he generally takes the second seat from the front by the window. And just as in international law, air rights go with each seat—meaning the storage rack."[1] When band boy Frank Racette and bassist Jeff Castleman were "newbies," Racette said "we always joked that as new guys, as well as being the only white guys with the band, we ended up in the 'back of the bus.'"[2]

Singer Toney Watkins had a battery-operated portable record player that he used to keep himself amused during the long periods of time on the bus. Frank Racette, who was the "band boy" from 1968 to 1974, recalled that during one trip, Castleman "began a long lecture to us about some recording he liked on which he claimed that the musicians were playing 'so in tune.' I remember that Cootie Williams walked down the aisle of the bus at this moment and interrupted Jeff's lecture by stating that 'If it's in tune, it ain't jazz!' That certainly brought Jeff's lecture to an abrupt conclusion!"[3]

The Ellington band had its own ideas on intonation. Racette shared that

> among us younger members of the troupe, as well as among fellow students at Berklee, the Ellingtonian concept of playing "in tune" was a frequently discussed subject. There was virtually NO tuning or warming up prior to any performances at which I was present. There are many stories in print about the egos of these musicians, and I think they would have resented the idea of having to tune their instruments

A smiling Cootie Williams graces the cover of the April 1963 issue of the Canadian jazz magazine *Coda*. (Author's collection)

This photograph is from the collection of jazz aficionado Timme Rosenkrantz (sitting at the front right side) and was taken in Sweden in 1963. Bus seating with the Ellington band was by seniority with the longest tenured musicians in the front. Harry Carney, looking out the window on the left side, was the most senior musician and usually didn't ride the bus. Instead, he would chauffeur Duke Ellington in his Chrysler Imperial. Mercer Ellington referred to Cootie Williams as "the pretender to the throne" because he insisted on sitting towards the front despite his long absence from the band. Jimmy Hamilton is directly behind Cootie. (Courtesy of University Press of Southern Denmark)

to a fellow band member's pitch. "Let the other guy tune his horn to ME," would have been the dynamic in play. The trumpet section might eventually get in tune with each other during the first number, but the saxes and trombones were all welcome to find their own tonality quite independently. Although the "Ellington sound" of course evolved from the various distinctive timbres and musical personalities of each member, I think it also resulted from their idiosyncratic and egocentric concept of tuning!⁴

Buster Cooper recalled a particularly turbulent bus trip. "It was about 2 in the morning. We had just got through with one job and going to another. So Cootie was sitting in front of Cat. And so Cat got up to go to the toilet at the end of the bus." Cat came back to find his window open. "Cat stood up in the middle of the bus and said, 'Who opened my window?' Cootie didn't say nothing, you know."

"Cat said it again, 'Who opened up my window?'"

Finally, Cootie said, "I opened it up because it was getting kind of warm in here."

Cat was still standing in the aisle, when all of a sudden he punched the seated Cootie Williams. Cootie couldn't get up right away because Cat was on top of him, swinging away. When Williams was finally able to get up, the scuffle continued in the aisle as the bus traveled on to its destination. "The bus driver looked in the rear-view mirror, he saw the fighting and put on [the] brakes. When he put on the brakes, that made Cootie fall on top of Cat. When Cootie fell on top of Cat, then Cootie started choking him. Cat's tongue was hanging out. Cat was saying 'Somebody stop him, somebody stop him.'"

"I was kind of new to the band, I was 32 years old, and I was strong at that time. I was starting to pull Cootie's hands a loose. Cootie said, "I'm gonna kill this so-and-so."

As Buster tries to pry Williams away, some of the members of the band said, "Turn him a-loose, Buster." Cooper decided against naming those who wanted to see the fight continue.

Cooper stated, "After you talk to Cat Anderson, you understand what he came through, he came through pure hell."⁵ But Jimmy Hamilton noted that "Cat Anderson had a personality that nobody liked[.]"⁶

Buster also said, "The incidents with Cat, it was like a jealous[y] thing. Because see, if I had a man in my group of Cootie's caliber, I'm going to feature him all the time also. Because people come to see him. They come to see Johnny Hodges, because that goes along with the band. You know, Johnny Hodges, Cootie Williams and Paul Gonsalves, guys like that. Well, Cat Anderson was jealous of that. But it wasn't Cootie's fault because he didn't instigate none of it.

Definitely. He couldn't care less because he didn't want to play no way—only on his featured tunes. Cootie didn't care."[7]

Buster Cooper summed up his view of Cootie, by saying "he was a nice guy. Believe me and I'm not saying that just because he's dead. If you're not nice when you're living you're still not nice when you're dead. So that's how that goes . . . He was a good dude, man. Believe me and I really liked him, you know, and he liked me, too. He used to swing on everybody except me, and I was the only one who could talk to him. I mean really, I don't know why, but I was only one who could cool him down in the heat of his argument."[8]

THE STATE DEPARTMENT TOUR

> If one is not socially aware, it is very easy to be caught in a position where one's chauvinistic shirttail is showing.
> —DUKE ELLINGTON, *MUSIC IS MY MISTRESS*[1]

> When Ray Nance left Duke Ellington nobody wrote a song about it like they did when Cootie Williams first left the band, yet the loss of the trumpeter, violinist and singer-dancer was a heavy one.
> —VALERIE WILMER[2]

It wasn't long before Cootie was back to international travel with the Ellington band. Excluding a few trips to Canada, Cootie's 1959 European tour was the only time he traveled outside of the United States as a bandleader. On January 9, 1963, the Duke Ellington Orchestra left New York to begin a two-month series of shows in Europe. The first stop was in London, where the return of Cootie Williams was eagerly awaited. "Clap hands, here comes Cootie!" was a headline in the British music magazine *Melody Maker*.

The following month, they were in France. One of the band's best latter-day live recordings can found on *The Great Paris Concert*. On this album, Ellington revisits "Echoes of Harlem" of course as a feature for Cootie, taken at a leisurely 74 beats per minute, a far cry from the peppy 105 BPM on the original 1936 recording. The slower tempo gives the piece a brooding atmosphere. After Ellington starts the tune, Cootie can be heard to say to no one in particular "Old man now, man. Can't play all those fast numbers—outta air!" Fast tunes were never Cootie's forte, but he's definitely not out of air. He plays with force, authority and perhaps a bit of menace, sculpting each note with his plunger. "Echoes of Harlem" would stay in the Ellington band repertoire sporadically until almost the end of Ellington's life.[3] Mercer Ellington would have liked it to be a regular feature for the newly returned Williams, but Cootie "didn't feel like it."[4]

Even though this international travel was just getting started, Williams found the travel taxing; he was no longer the young man he was during his first time with Ellington. In a 1963 interview, Cootie said, "You don't have no proper time to go to sleep, proper time to eat. Up early, run to the airport, get on the plane. Sitting around the airport all day, you get into a different country to sit at the airport only to go play the concert, and you play two concerts and you get to bed around twelve, one o'clock and you're up about six the next morning and you grab a hot dog or a hamburger, and try and blow your horn, sometimes you don't have time to get a meal and you don't live right."[5]

♪

In 1956, the US State Department began sending American jazz musicians abroad in a propagandistic effort to win the Cold War fight against the Eastern Bloc.[6] The first in the group was trumpeter Dizzy Gillespie, leading a big band that he described as "a complete 'American assortment' of blacks, whites, males, females, Jews, and Gentiles in the band."[7] Other "jazz ambassadors" included Louis Armstrong, Benny Goodman, and Dave Brubeck. The use of jazz as a means to win allies and support was not a guarantee of success. The Soviets countered with their own propaganda that highlighted the mistreatment of Blacks in the United States. The touring musicians were given the guidance by the State Department that they should be honest in their responses to foreign media about America's civil rights issues.[8]

In 1963, it was Duke Ellington's turn to represent the United States abroad. On September 6, Duke Ellington and his orchestra embarked from New York City for their fourteen-week State Department–sponsored tour. After a layover in Rome, the band reached their destination of Damascus, Syria, the site of their first concert. Over 17,000 patrons attended this concert on September 9, and the band's performance was well received.[9] All told, the Ellington band would spend 174 days of 1963 overseas, the most of its existence.[10] Unlike their usual tours, this one did allow time for sightseeing, which the band appreciated. Another plus was that all the hotel accommodations were nice, and the food was "just about the best you could get."[11]

Accompanying the Ellington orchestra were various government liaison personnel, agents, and other support personnel, including one Tom Simons. Simons, twenty-four years old at the time, was new to the State Department and his official title was Escort Officer. Simons's career eventually included ambassadorships to Poland and Pakistan. Although he grew up in a diplomatic family and had spent part of his early years in British India, traveling with a group of older (and quirky) Black jazz musicians was a different experience. "Cootie was one of the two guys in the band that were sort of toughest on me in little ways. The other one was Cat Anderson," said Simons. The two men knew that they couldn't be overt in their mistreatment of Simons since he was with the government. Simons related that someone, most likely Billy Strayhorn, told him that Williams was a bitter man to explain his behavior.[12] Benny Goodman observed that "[l]eaders don't want to be sidemen again."[13] It was indeed quite a change going from sideman to leader and back to sideman, and to paraphrase what Williams told Charlie Holmes, "Duke's name is in the lights downstairs, not the sideman's. Nobody wants to hear you. The people come in here to hear him."

Williams had returned to Ellington after a very high career trajectory and a precipitous fall at the end. Johnny Hodges had returned, after a four-year absence, in 1955. His experience as a leader hadn't been as high profile or nearly as long as Cootie's twenty-two years. And most importantly, he didn't experience the difficulties Cootie encountered during the last half decade before his return to the fold.[14]

As an outsider, Simons also found the concept of two musicians sharing a hotel room to be unusual and parsimonious.[15] But it was an old practice designed to reduce the expense of traveling with a large group. Cootie Williams was assigned to room with Ray Nance, the musician who replaced him in 1940. Ray's wife, Gloria, thought Ray and Cootie being booked together was a "stupid idea." "There were many guys on the band who barely spoke to each other. Cootie Williams had a number of serious health problems and consequently was never good company. Ray on the other hand, generally got along with everyone, with the exception of Cat Anderson. . . . There was no personality clash between Ray and Cootie. It was simply a matter of life going on and time taking its toll."[16] The members of the orchestra knew that Cootie pretty much kept to himself, and they also knew it wasn't a good idea to approach him before he had his first cup of coffee in the morning. Most of them said they had no problem with him.[17]

On the night of September 11, 1963, the band played a second concert in Damascus. In remembering his time there, trombonist Buster Cooper recalled, "It was hard to sleep. I never heard so much car horns blowin' in all my life, like it was a toy, three or four o'clock in the morning." Cooper continued, "Ray Nance had been out all night drinking. He was drinking because he couldn't get to his stuff, you know what I'm saying? [Nance was a heroin addict.] What happened was, Cootie Williams was sleep. [Nance] came back to the hotel and pounded on the door. 'Bam, bam, bam. Open this door!' Ray Nance was [agitated], and Cootie was [agitated] so he started yelling at Cootie and so they had a fight. But that wasn't no fight, he hit Ray Nance." It was one hit—more of a slap—but it affected Nance mentally more than physically.[18]

Describing the incident years later, Ray's widow, Gloria Nance, said, "[I]t seems that Cootie pretty much forgot the incident by the next day—but not Ray Nance. Ray could neither resolve nor understand the episode. He thought about it constantly, minute by minute, hour by hour, actually brooding. And then he found himself unable to play (a) because one of his idols disrespected him to such a marked degree and (b) because he began to think that he should have defended himself and not allowed Cootie to slap him as if he were little more than a pussy!"[19] However, the second point omitted a very important fact: Cootie was a large, solid man, and Ray was slight and 5'3"[20]—a defense would not have been a smart move.

The next tour stop was Amman, Jordan. The Crown Prince of Jordan was in attendance at that night's performance. During the first portion of the concert, a brooding Ray Nance sat with his legs crossed, unable to play due to the harm done to his psyche. This posture was a cultural taboo—it's considered rude to display something as dirty as the soles of your shoes. This and other do's and don'ts had been covered in the State Department briefings, but "Ray was showing his foot to the Arab crowd." Offended, the audience began to boo and hiss. Besides displaying his soles, they viewed Nance as disrespectful for refusing to play for a paying audience. He was wagging his feet, occasionally walking around in back of the band, and just making a spectacle of himself. "At the break, I got a message from the chief public affairs officer and he came up to me and said, 'the ambassador wants you to get him out of here, if you have to take him out in chains.' So I got him, and he went him back to the hotel with me before the second half. He was chagrined and embarrassed at what he had done. I commiserated with him at the bar. He was a sweet person . . ." Tom Simons recounted. "What to do? By the next morning, we agreed he needed to go home," he continued. Ellington got the consensus of the band that Ray Nance, a band veteran of over twenty years, would have to leave. It was decided that Herbie Jones would be sent for as his replacement.[21] Ironically, the departure of Ray Nance coincided with the first anniversary of Cootie's return with the band.

There is a tendency to be circumspect when describing someone's addiction in the media. Privacy and the possibility of a wrongful accusation are amongst the reasons for this.[22] *Jet* magazine said no drugs were involved in Ray Nance's departure from the band. Technically, they were right, drug abuse was not the problem; it was the *lack* of drugs that was the issue.[23] The band's two addicts (Ray Nance and Paul Gonsalves) used a common remedy for deprived addicts: an overuse of alcohol. Mercer Ellington wrote of an incident in 1961 that got the band blacklisted from Las Vegas for several years: "[S]everal of the guys in the band had been raided while carousing and were being brought up on a narcotics [marijuana] charge. Ray Nance and Paul Gonsalves were the most renowned, and they suffered the most publicity. I think the incident would have passed over fairly quietly, but Ray thought he had been manhandled and brutally treated by the police, and he made quite a scene, which boomeranged on him. As a result, he went to prison, whereas the charges against Paul were more or less dropped and he was let off on probation."[24] In his Jazz Oral History Project interview, neither Cootie nor his interviewer, Helen Oakley Dance, mentioned Ray Nance. Cootie said, "If there was anybody to be fired it would have been Paul Gonsalves . . . Paul was a great saxophone player. When Paul was straight, I think he was one of the greatest tenor saxophone players around . . . When you'd catch him straight, he was something else."[25]

Snippets of video from the 1963 State Department can be found on the internet, but a nearly complete concert video exists from their November 14, 1963, date at Baghdad's Khuld Hall. Released under the title *Le Roi du Jazz Americain—Duke Ellington et son Orchestre* (*The King of American Jazz—Duke Ellington and his Orchestra*), this video is owned by the National Archives and Records Administration and is distributed for free at their website.[26] The occasion was also broadcast on live television at the time. Duke can be seen periodically checking to someone off-camera to see if he needs to insert a break in the proceedings. The sound and video have a few imperfections here and there, but overall, it's the music that counts—and it's a great performance by the band. All the stalwarts—Cootie, Johnny Hodges, Lawrence Brown, Jimmy Hamilton, and Paul Gonsalves—get turns to display their solo wares. Williams is featured on "Tutti for Cootie," a medium-tempo blues that alternates between minor and major keys for the plunger-muted and open trumpet, respectively. Cootie prowls the stage, and despite his trumpet pointing toward the floor and being away from the microphone, his huge sound is clearly heard. (Williams explained his playing stance in a later interview—". . . [B]ecause I get the best result playing like that. Actually, you are more relaxed in that position with certain notes and moving the plunger back and forth; in this way I can get more sensitivity.")[27] In his playing posture, despite his profession of relaxation, it seems like every muscle in his body is contracted; this feeling of tension is confirmed by his almost explosive uncoiling of his body at the conclusion of some of his phrases. His instrumental seriousness is in stark contrast to the mugging he does during the band's interlude between his solo passages. He's dancing, eyes cast skyward, hand wagging—it borders on embarrassing. Fortunately, his solo role resumes, and we again realize that we're in the presence of a master musician. At the conclusion of the piece, Cootie returns to his seat and takes repeated bows to a loud and enthusiastic ovation, complete with foot stomping, and Duke gestures toward him, repeating "Cootie Williams! Cootie

Relations between trumpet-men Williams (l) and Nance deteriorated during Ellington band's Middle East good will tour.
Nance Leaves Duke's Band Over Tiff With Cootie

The October 24, 1963, issue of *Jet* magazine carried an account of the Williams/Nance State Department tour incident. (Photograph by Isaac Sutton for *Jet* magazine, Johnson Publishing Company Archive. Courtesy J. Paul Getty Trust and Smithsonian National Museum of African American History and Culture)

Williams!" into the microphone. (Another concert highlight is a rare on-stage appearance by Billy Strayhorn, playing a solo version of his iconic torch song, "Lush Life." Following this, the video ends with Strayhorn leading the full band in a performance of his composition "Take the 'A' Train.")

Just a few days later, on November 22, 1963, while the band was Ankara, Turkey, the State Department personnel on the tour heard the news that President John F. Kennedy had been assassinated. The State Department officials debated over who was to inform Duke Ellington. It was decided that young Tom Simons would be the one. Simons said, "I told Duke and his inclination was to continue with the tour."[28] Despite the wishes of Ellington, the State Department thought it best to abort the tour and send the band home with remaining dates in Turkey, Cyprus, Egypt, and Greece unfulfilled.[29]

In his autobiography *Music Is My Mistress*, Duke Ellington described the State Department tour but avoided any mention of the incident that reconfigured his band and almost caused an international incident. But Nance's absence turned out to be temporary. He would return on an intermittent basis starting in January 1965.

43

THE BOOKENDS

Cootie Williams, Buster Cooper, and Cat Anderson on the cover of the March 1964 issue of *Crescendo*, a British jazz magazine. (Author's collection)

Even though Williams had been back with Ellington for almost two years, a 1964 *New York Times* review ("Ellington is Back") carried the subheading "A Solid Band, Including Cootie Williams, Plays Old and New at Carnegie Hall."[1] "One is not apt to realize how much he has been missed until one hears him playing his prominent role in the band once again. The traditional opening medley, for example—'Black and Tan,' 'Creole Love Call' and 'The Mooche'—has been played well while Mr. Williams was away. But now that he is back it has its old authority and flair. And when he steps out on 'Caravan,' this piece, which had become something of a warhorse, takes on all kinds of bright new hues."[2] As a result of the departure of Ray Nance, Cootie inherited the solo role on "Take the 'A' Train."

♪

During a 1964 matinee gig at Tin Pan Alley in Redwood City,[3] the band started their set with everyone present save Anderson and Williams. Duke noticed their absence and asked their whereabouts. He was told by the band that the two brassmen were outside fighting. Duke kept playing. When the battling trumpeters came in and took their seats, the fact that they had been fighting again was apparent from their disheveled appearance. In the heat of it all, Cootie had hit Cat on the side of his head with trumpet, resulting in an instrument that looked like the bent horn of Dizzy Gillespie.[4]

Cootie Williams and Cat Anderson refused to sit next to each other in the trumpet section, so the other two trumpeters were always in the middle. Bass trombonist Chuck Connors dubbed Anderson and Williams "The Bookends," a nickname that stuck.[5] (Connors [1930–1994] was classically trained at the Boston Conservatory. He wasn't able to obtain a job in the classical realm because the field wasn't open to him as an African American. Joining the band in 1961, he stayed on after Duke's death. He would continue with Mercer until his own death in 1994. His time with the band, thirty-four years, is not given the prominence it deserves when it comes to mentioning long time Ellingtonians due to the fact that twenty years were under Mercer's baton.)[6] Mercer Ellington said, "[Cat and Cootie] never spoke a word to each other when they came off [the stage]. They just hated each other's guts, and there were several people in the band who really did not like [Duke] Ellington himself. They hated each other, but they had to admire the talent that existed in the person who sat next to them." Mercer felt comfortable airing these thoughts while both men were alive because "Cat and Cootie . . . I'm close to, so I can talk about them if I want to. It's like family!"[7] Frequent Ellington collaborator Jimmy Jones said, "I think it was the most unique outfit that I've ever seen, you know, as far as the personnel. [T]hey were very courteous to everybody that wasn't in the band, but when they got on the stand to play, they were quite together, you know? And Ellington had to be a great politician to keep those guys, all of those drunks, in the band, and to keep them playing."[8]

As a general rule, the fighting and quirks of the band weren't discussed publicly. Ironically, Anderson credited Williams for the Ellington job: "Cootie is the reason [for] me being in the band. He talked me into it, originally. I was with Erskine Hawkins, then Lionel Hampton, and I kept telling him: 'Yes, I'll probably go over there and take the job.' One day he cornered me—I couldn't get out of the house. He called Duke and accepted the job."[9]

Frank Racette said, "Off stage Cootie may have engaged in rough activities, but he treated the stage as a place for professionalism. For the most part, Cootie apparently never got caught up in any of those atrocious antics while he was with Ellington. I have read that at some [point] when he was leading his own band he may have become a drinker, but during my period with the band, from 1968–1974, his behavior was consistently professional. It was obvious he took great pride in his several nightly solo spots. He strolled down to the front of the stage and performed with complete professionalism. His posture, his stance, and all his gestures demonstrated a show-biz flair that had been developed and polished meticulously, dating back to his days at the Cotton Club."

♪

Occasionally, the Ellington sidemen would participate in sessions led by one of the other sidemen. Most of these "extracurricular" sessions were led by Johnny Hodges. They were a continuation of the practice started in the mid-1930s, but not as structured—that is, they weren't confined to a certain label and the personnel wasn't always drawn from the pool of the Ellington band. During his second stint with the Ellington band, Cootie participated in only one such project, the album *Joya Sherrill Sings Duke*. One of Ellington's better vocalists, Joya Sherrill (1924–2010) sang with the band in the mid-1940s, so her tenure didn't overlap Cootie's. The session was done in two parts with two slightly different groups. Cootie was teamed up with Johnny Hodges and Paul Gonsalves and a rhythm section of John Lamb on bass and Sam Woodyard on drums. The pianist was Ernie Harper, a Chicago-based musician. Of the six Ellington tunes recorded by the group, only "Mood Indigo" and "Sophisticated Lady" were from Cootie's 1929–1940 time with the band. It's unknown why Cootie picked this session to participate in, but as for doing more, Buster Cooper said it was hard enough to get Cootie to do anything other than his solo features; why would he want to do outside sessions?[10]

Joya Sherrill, Duke Ellington, and Cootie Williams, 1962. (Photograph by G. Marshall Wilson for *Jet* magazine. Johnson Publishing Company Archive. Courtesy of J. Paul Getty Trust and Smithsonian National Museum of African American History and Culture)

Cooper said Cootie "played when he wanted to play, you know parts and everything. He'd just lay out until he got ready. But Duke would never say nothing. Of course Duke wouldn't say anything to nobody. He wasn't that type of boss."[11]

During his periodic returns to the band, Nance didn't get his solo on "Take the 'A' Train" back. Mercer Ellington explained the Ellington rules: "The only way a man can be separated from his property is by leaving the band. When this happens, the number is given over to someone else and it becomes the permanent property of its new owner. It can never revert once it has changed hand. It's just tradition and in most cases musicians are as jealous about their numbers as Duke is strict in enforcing their apportionment. If you asked Nance in Cootie's presence today to play *A Train*, he wouldn't do it. A number must be formally released by its owner before another man will play it. To do otherwise would be discourteous."[12]

Cootie was not exempt from this rule, either. His "Concerto for Cootie," was retired when it became "Do Nothin' Till You Hear from Me." When Cootie was asked "whether he'd like to play 'Concerto [for Cootie]' again" he shrugged his shoulders and said "'Ask the boss.' Ask the boss why Williams never plays it, and he'll say, 'We still do; [Lawrence] Brown does it.' Then he will move on to another subject."[13]

Benny Goodman was highly regarded as a musician, but as a person, he was not always kindly thought of. But Cootie and Benny got along well and enjoyed each other's company and musicianship. They had another reunion when the Benny Goodman Quintet, the Duke Ellington Orchestra, along with vocalist Joe Williams, and flutist Herbie Mann played the first portion of the two day Boston Globe Jazz Festival on January 15, 1966. *The Boston Globe* reported that Goodman "greeted old friends from the Ellington band. Two or three times, he would stroll over to his old band alumnus, Cootie Williams, and talk over old times."[14] Goodman's set went particularly well, so well that "[t]hey wouldn't let [Goodman] off the stage. He returned with Cootie Williams" to play an encore.[15]

At the end of July 1966, the Ellington band along with Ella Fitzgerald performed several concerts at Juan-les-Pins in the south of France. The format featured sets by the Ellington band, Ella Fitzgerald accompanied by her trio and then accompanied by the Ellington band. Most of the Ellington band/Fitzgerald feature trumpet obligati by Cootie, perhaps as a rekindling of their many tours in the mid-1940s. It marked a rare instance of Cootie taking on extra horn duties. During this tour, Ellington is filmed with a trio playing for artist Joan Miró. One of the selections was a fast minor blues that became "The Shepherd Who Watches Over the Night Flock." This composition became a Williams showcase that he would wind up playing until his retirement in 1980. He described how it came to be:

> It was a funny thing. First [Duke] was playing it on the piano. He wasn't playing it; he was just running it over. He called me and said, "Hey, Coots, come here." He said, "How do you like this number? Do you think you would like to play this number?" I said "Yeah." I said, "I'll play it." So he wrote a lead sheet out on it. So I started messing around with it. He said, "What do you think of it?" I think it was about a week. I said, "Give me a chance. Give me time to feel the thing, so I can get something out of it." So we made an arrangement on it. So I started to playing it. He said, "Yeah, uh-huh. Yeah." "You're right." And that's how that number come about.[16]

"The Shepherd" was an up-tempo piece when Ellington played it in his trio format, but when he passed it over to Williams, it became a lot slower, almost a dirge. The piece can be heard developing in a rehearsal tape from the Juan-les-Pins engagement.

Steve Little, who played drums in the Ellington band in the late 1960s, said, "At that time most of the guys there were old enough to be my father. You know, Paul Gonsalves was closer to my age, so he was a guy I used to hang with." Although there was an age gap between Little and most of the band, he said "It was no problem at all." The only generation gap–related problem, perhaps, lay in the conception of the beat.

> I don't know if it's if it's an age thing or whatever a style think that different ages, but [Cootie] would lay so far back [on the beat]. I remember sometimes we'd play "The Shepherd." He would lay so far back in the time and those breaks that sometimes you had to wonder where to come in. Especially since at that time Bebop was very prevalent and they played way up on the time, you know, and Cootie and Johnny Hodges the like from that school at laid back on the time, if you know what I mean. But that stands out in my mind on that one tune that he would always play those pickups with the rhythm section stopped and it was unbelievable. So I always looked at [bassist] Aaron Bell [to see] when he was going to play it down because you know, he's doing it so long and it was it was really rather remarkable that everybody could come in after it.[17]

("Slicing the Beat: Jazz Eighth-Notes as Expression Microrhythm," a 2006 paper by Fernando Benado of American University, is just one of the studies describing the complex relationships possible with the beat.)[18] British filmmaker Russell Davies quipped that Cootie played so far behind the beat that it "sometimes sounded as if he were keeping time with another band [that was located] across the street."[19]

"The Shepherd" would later be incorporated in Ellington's 1968 "Sacred Concert" program. Even when performed in as mundane a setting as a midwestern high school gymnasium in Burlington, Iowa, Cootie's performance of "The Shepherd" moved the crowd: "Cootie, employing a rubber mute and his familiar body gyrations, held the audience spellbound. His efforts rated a standing ovation."[20]

♪

Although Williams could be volatile, at the end of the day, those who knew him said he was a cool guy and great to hang out with. Perhaps Buster Cooper summed up the varying reactions to Cootie best—"if he didn't like you, he didn't hide it."[21]

Bassist Jeff Castleman joined the band in 1967. He recalled that "the first night, in the first set, they played 'In a Mellow Tone.' And I didn't know [the song]. Cootie yelled across the bandstand at me 'Rose Room! Rose Room!' meaning it has the same chord changes as 'Rose Room'. But I didn't know 'Rose Room' either!"[22]

John Lamb said that Cootie would sometimes confer with him about what he wanted in the way of accompaniment: "Some people would say he was a bad guy, but actually he was not. He was really a nice guy. He was very complimentary to me. I mean if you wanted me to do something behind him, he would come up to me and tell me in that gravel voice of his, he would say 'Hey, look here, when I play that certain thing here, I want you to drag a little bit you and I want you to do this and do that. Nobody else [in the band] would say anything but he'd come up and tell me exactly what he wanted—and I did it." Lamb's wife was a big fan of Cootie's playing and requested that Cootie's music was to be played at her funeral when the time came. "She said, 'I want you to play something of Cootie's music for my funeral.' I played some of Cootie's things, you know, and it was very, very effective. Out of all the cats in the band, she dug Cootie! She was a West Indian girl, and she didn't care that much about American music, but she dug Cootie."[23]

Lamb told another story of Cootie's popularity: "We were either in Spain or Portugal and this little, short woman walked up to me and says, 'Are you in the band?' And I said yes I am. She says 'Well, is Cootie back there?' I said yeah, he's back there somewhere. 'Well, I'm Ava Gardner.' How about that. Out of all the people in the band, they would ask for Cootie." While some might imply some romantic intent, that was apparently not the case.[24] Gardner was well known as a fan of jazz.

Duke Ellington was known for his many female companions on the road. He never divorced his wife, Edna Ellington, and thus was able to string them along by claiming she wouldn't give him a divorce. Several members of the band also had companions during their travels. Valerie Wilmer, a noted British photographer and journalist, wrote that Johnny Hodges and Cootie Williams "carried themselves like lords, effortlessly producing elegant women to accompany them on out-of-town trips." Cootie told her about film star conquests by name. He said, "All great jazz musicians, every one of them, have had many loves and girls in their lives. People don't read about these things in books, but a girl *is* jazz music. They throw something into the mind to make you produce jazz."[25]

Lamb noted Cootie's appetite: "Cootie liked to *eat his food*. I used to sit down and watch him eat. I used to watch it off in the distance and he would sit down, and he would take a few bites and then he would pat his foot. He always patted his foot when he ate. That's something, that's really something, enjoying that food so much, it becomes a ritual. It's more than just something to sustain the body, it's something else."[26] Trombonist Art Baron said Cootie would make sure he ate on *his* schedule: "Cootie had this other job. A very important job when you're riding the bus. And it's an old, old tradition—the guy who's sitting opposite the driver, his job is to always be awake and make sure that the driver is safe. Cootie did that [job]. [And] as soon as he got hungry, he'd yell "Eat Stop! Eat Stop!"[27]

Jeff Castleman: "I found Cootie to be a remarkable musician. Cootie would create a solo and I mean literally create a solo to a piece and then his game or thrill was to try and play that same solo better the next night. And then the next night better than that; constantly improving on a solo that sounded like it was improvised, but in reality it was preconceived. And it got better every time he played it. That was an amazing talent. My experience with Cootie was that he was very kind to me. He was very understanding that I was young. It probably brought back the time when he was a young man in the band. It took him a while to warm up to me personally but after he saw the way the rest of the guys had warmed up to me he was right there and very friendly with me. He was a very special musician. In a league of his own."[28]

Books have been written describing and defining what actual improvisation consists of. Most agree that pure improvisation is almost impossible since a musician is going to play what's in their vocabulary. Eddie Lambert wrote that "[v]ery few jazz soloists have been able (or even wanted to) improvise constantly, and most stick to more or less set patterns in their solos. Much of their success has depended on making these solos sound as if the phrases were newly minted, in just the same way that a good actor will enunciate familiar lines and convince an audience that they are the natural and impromptu speech of the character he is portraying."[29] Another consideration would be the closed nature of most big band arrangements, with some allotting solos of just eight bars.

By the mid-1960s, Williams's stage demeanor was usually described as "dour" or "grumpy." He would sit on stage and sometimes not even play his parts, only putting his horn to his lips when it came time for his solos. Williams pushed back on this saying, "Well no, I'm not grumpy! That's music itself. Sometimes there's different moods in music and I'm with every mood that music has."[30] He also explained his mien as what could be described as a Zen state: "I've learned to control myself. I tell myself now that it doesn't matter much. If you've [got] high blood pressure, like I have, you must gain control. A lot of times people see me sitting up there on the [band]stand by myself, and probably think I'm acting real mean. Not everyone knows I've a health problem to face. I've learned to cut everything off, close my ears to the noise, drinking, and everything else. You can take medicine for blood pressure, but keeping calm is the thing."[31] Ellington would explain Cootie's behavior to outsiders by saying, "He is a senior citizen of our company. He has that privilege."[32]

Instead of a "dour" person, John Lamb saw Cootie's persona as something developed over the years. "We were together every night for three years.

Yeah, that's a lot of interaction and I accompanied all of his solos during that time. Of course, you learn a lot about an individual by the way they perform. And Cootie was definitely unique and different, and I liked him as a person although he had that crust about him after having been around for so many years and having been a good bandleader and all that stuff. You know, you have to develop something to ward off all the nonsense. Once I got to talking with him and got to know him a little bit, I found him to be a very personable person. Very nice person. In other words, I liked Cootie."[33]

Art Baron said, "Some people thought he was mean, evil. But he wasn't, he had a real big heart of gold. Cootie was a straight-ahead guy." Cootie was honest about being tired or not wanting to be bothered, one of the effects on being on the road for fifty years.[34]

Art Baron and Vince Prudente do impressions of Cootie's deep, raspy voice. Baron described an instance where this skill got him in trouble. On stage, at an outdoor concert, Mercer was doing an introduction explaining one of Duke's last pieces, "The Three Black Kings." Mercer hears a deep raspy voice say, "The Three Black Boys." Mercer thought it was Baron doing his impression, so he lashed into Baron. But it was really Cootie, and with getting Baron blamed he's "having a fit, he's laughing so hard." "He loved to start shit" and watch the after-affects. "He was a very funny guy."[35]

Although Williams constantly protested against playing the old music, Ellington knew that he could never abandon it. While he loved creating new music, he knew he couldn't disappoint the fans who didn't know or care about his extended works. The medley of hits that he played at his concerts may have provoked groans from the hardcore fans and critics, but it helped satisfy the general public. In 1966, he released *The Popular Duke Ellington*, an album that except for one new item ("The Twitch") consisted of material from the 1920s through the 1940s. But it wasn't an exercise in nostalgia as this wasn't a re-creation of the old repertoire. Instead, we hear the songs as a statement of what the band sounded like in the mid-1960s, with the benefit of stereo sound reproduction. Williams is at his ferocious best on "The Mooche," "Black and Tan Fantasy," and "Creole Love Call," all plunger vehicles he inherited from Bubber Miley. His open solo work is highlighted on "Take the 'A' Train," fidelity-wise probably the best recorded version of his work on this song.

THE ROAD MANAGER

After his longtime road manager Al Celley quit in 1963, Duke Ellington found himself needing a replacement for this demanding job. Cootie Williams suggested Mercer Ellington, remembering that he had performed well for him back in the 1940s.[1] Mercer said of the role:

> I have the most important job I ever had in my life. . . . In a sense, it's difficult for me, because here I am directing certain people to do things—and they raised me. We have Harry Carney, Lawrence Brown, Cootie Williams, Johnny Hodges, and these are people who, in 1927, were leading me around New York by the hand, showing me zoos and buying me ice cream cones. So I really can't jump up and say: 'All right, it's time now for you to move from here to there.' And yet I must get them to do this. You have to find your way around and do what you can. The difficulty is to be able to set myself on their level, because of the great regard in which I've held them all these years. It's quite a job. Then you realize you're dealing with men who have a terrific reputation, and ability to match under conditions which are extremely difficult. We're averaging a country a day, with two concerts per day. In most instances, it means you start at seven or eight at night, and you finish at one. So, for the first two weeks, we average four or five hours sleep a night. So the men are obviously fatigued—and yet they still manage to have a verve when that spotlight goes on. There's all time magic when that light hits. And you have to recognize that they're doing the impossible already, before you ask them to do more.[2]

That was Mercer's public stance on the job. The true story was Mercer found the road manager job as "work I detested doing." Maybe it would have been easier to do if it wasn't the Duke Ellington orchestra. In a more candid variation on the previous response, he said, "It was a very difficult band to handle. The problems of drunkenness and all that were very slight in comparison to one other that I had to face. I had Johnny Hodges, Harry Carney, Cootie Williams, and Lawrence Brown. In the thirties these were the people who took me to the beach, hold me by the hand, take me to the movies, buy me lollipops, whatever. And suddenly I was in a position wherein I had to ask them to be on-stage at a certain time, get up when they were sleepy, get on the bus when it was time to leave and so forth. That was the most difficult part of the job, was to go back to these people who you knew loved you and to scream and holler at them and insult them. You know, I could get them to do it, but it called for some very stringent things in order to get them to do it. And I had to sacrifice our relationship in order to get the job done."[3] Knowing that Duke Ellington sometimes had a difficult time with Cootie, one can only imagine the extent of the problems Mercer must have faced with him. In a bit of wordplay, the younger Ellington dubbed the band "the world's greatest musical aggravation."[4]

As the 1960s rolled on, the band was starting to show signs of mortality in its ranks. The death of longtime smoker Billy Strayhorn on May 31, 1967, from throat cancer deeply affected Ellington. Strayhorn's contributions to the Ellington orchestra are still being evaluated and reevaluated to this day. In the fall of 1967, the band recorded a collection of Strayhorn compositions that were released as the album . . . *And His Mother Called Him Bill*. Cootie takes notable and authoritative solos on the album, most notably on "Snibor" and "Rock Skippin' at the Blue Note."

Despite the ticking clock, Ellington refused to stand still and kept adding new achievements to his oeuvre. Later in the year, in between routine gigs at an NCO club in Lompoc and a fairgrounds dance in Santa Maria, Duke Ellington and Frank Sinatra teamed up to make their only joint recorded appearance in Los Angeles. Sinatra had a slight cold and was a little off from his top form, but it wasn't enough to postpone the session. Sinatra's cold is one of the reasons the resulting album isn't held in high esteem, but perhaps the biggest fault of this album is that it's not one of the Sinatra/Basie collaborations. Those comparisons are meaningless because Ellington isn't Basie and Basie isn't Ellington. *Down Beat* gave the album four stars, saying that "[a]t first hearing, this much heralded summit meeting is a bit disappointing, but it grows on you."[5] There was only one Ellington composition, "I Like The Sunrise," from 1947's "Liberian Suite," on the album. Still the album has many wonderful moments and has been unfairly maligned and marginalized in the canon of both stars. Arranger Billy May had provided the charts to the band in advance of the session. Although some accounts say that the band hadn't bothered to look at them before the session, Jeff Castleman, the sole surviving participant from that date, says that isn't true. He said, "Billy May flew up to Seattle" with the charts and met the band at a club called DJ's, "which is where I first joined the band." The "rehearsal" consisted of playing them that night at the gig. Some have maligned the Ellington band for being poor sight-readers, but Castleman said "they were better readers than they were given credit for."[6]

Johnny Hodges, Paul Gonsalves, and Lawrence Brown solo on the album, with Hodges stealing the show during "Indian Summer." Cootie is the only trumpet soloist heard on the date. As the senior member of the brass and a distinctive voice, it made sense. But it wasn't a policy that made other trumpet players happy. Eddie Preston, who played in the band in 1963 and 1971, found that trumpet solos were rare "unless you were Cootie . . . I guess Duke just has certain people he wants to present and it happens I'm not one of them."[7]

Jeff Castleman said, "Cootie was really quite unique and quite adaptable. He played some backgrounds on the Sinatra album that are just absolutely gorgeous. In that situation, I know he didn't have time to work out [his solos]; he just played. And what he played was beautiful."[8]

♪

On December 27, 1967, fifty-one-year-old bandleader Harry James married a twenty-seven-year-old former showgirl in Reno. The James band was playing at Harold's Club, while the Ellington band was holding forth at Harrah's.[9] The two bands combined at the champagne reception.[10] James was delighted to see Cootie after so many years; he grabbed his trumpet and decided to play by his side.[11] Like Strayhorn's death earlier in the year, the Harrah's gig was another reminder that the band was mortal. While there, Lawrence Brown, now sixty years old, was hospitalized for a heart ailment. Harry Carney and Sam Woodyard were absent due to illness. And Cootie Williams wasn't present for the whole run of the engagement, having to leave for some unspecified minor surgery.[12]

45

MORTALITY

Duke Ellington's seventieth birthday was celebrated at the White House at a party hosted by President Richard Nixon on April 29, 1969. The double LP released as *Duke Ellington's 70th Birthday Concert* was actually recorded months later in the fall of that same year during another European tour and it's one of their best late efforts. Cootie gets to play yet another version of "'A' Train," and his "Tootie for Cootie" shows how markedly the piece had slowed since its 1962 introduction. This album would turn out to be one of the last appearances of longtime alto saxophonist Johnny Hodges.

Johnny Hodges died unexpectedly from a heart attack on May 11, 1970. in the midst of Ellington's recording sessions for the *New Orleans Suite* album, just a few months after the 70th Birthday Concert. He was Ellington's most popular star and that he was the highest paid member of the band certainly reflected that. Cootie said, "Me and Johnny was good friends. We was good pals."[1] Like the death of Strayhorn, the passing of Johnny Hodges deeply affected Ellington. Cootie said, "That was a very close relationship there, between those two. Always, you know. Johnny was real close to him, you know. They was real tight."[2]

Hodges was to play soprano saxophone, an instrument he had abandoned in 1940, for an Ellington-composed tribute, "Portrait of Sidney Bechet." Instead, it was played on tenor saxophone by Paul Gonsalves.[3] Hodges was an obvious choice for the Bechet tribute since the New Orleans reedman was an immense influence on his playing. Similarly, "Portrait of Louis Armstrong" could have gone to no one but Cootie Williams. The performance was an homage, not an imitation, with Cootie unmistakably playing himself. Williams also shone on "Second Line" and the "portraits" for two other Crescent City honorees, Ellington bassist Wellman Braud and gospel singer Mahalia Jackson. the *New Orleans Suite* is considered by some to be Ellington's last major release in his lifetime.

♪

There were many tributes to Louis Armstrong on the occasion of what was thought to be his seventieth birthday. *Down Beat* dedicated the July 9, 1970, issue of the magazine to him with a banner at the top of the cover proclaiming, "SATCHMO AT 70: A BIRTHDAY SALUTE TO THE KING." A tribute section boasted a who's who of jazz from Louis's early collaborators (Zutty Singleton, Lil Armstrong, Earl "Fatha" Hines) to musicians from the avant garde (Ornette Coleman, Archie Shepp, Sun Ra). Cootie, of course, weighed in, saying "Louis Armstrong and Charlie Parker are the two most important jazzmen that ever lived. Louis Armstrong is the greatest jazz trumpet player I ever heard in my life. No more needs to be said."[4]

♪

There weren't any vacations for the Ellington band as a whole; it never shut down. Russell Procope said, "If Duke could work 365 days a year, he'd do it."[5] If a musician in the band wanted to take a vacation, it would be with a substitute in place, the exception being a summer hiatus featuring a small group from during the summers of 1967–1973 at New York City's Rainbow Grill. Cootie did not participate in these small group gigs.[6]

Cootie didn't always see eye to eye with Ellington. In a draft of his not yet published manuscript *Ellington the Composer: Caught in the Act*, Dr. Jack Chambers tells the story of Cootie's evolving role in the orchestra: [Arranger Ron] Collier said[,] "I wanted to do 'A Taste of Honey,' as a solo for Cootie. [I thought] Gee, this will work great, a plunger solo." He phoned Ellington with his plan. "Duke said, 'Cootie's not in the band anymore, but don't worry I'll have a good plunger man there.' When I got there for the recording, I said, 'Have you got a good plunger man?' He said, 'I've got Cootie.' I said, 'What? I thought he wasn't in the band anymore.' Duke goes, 'Oh, Cootie. Oh, Cootie. More money, more money. All he wants is more money. I told him, 'We're both going to end up in the same place, but I'll be driving the bus.'" As it turned out, Ellington seems to have struck a deal to give Williams release time instead of more money. RCA Victor's producer Ben Young says, "During the *Reader's Digest* sessions, Williams wrought miracles in solo and melodic statements on 'A Taste of Honey' and 'Spanish Flea,' but he often did not play a trumpet section part in the ensemble." Apparently in his negotiation with Ellington, Williams won the right to sit silent (and no doubt wryly amused) while studio fill-in Lloyd Michels played his ensemble parts.[7]

Another example of Cootie's pick-and-choose behavior involved singer Ann Henry. She had composed a piece of music for the dedication of Mount

Angel Benedictine Abbey's new library, located in Portland, Oregon, and Ron Collier had orchestrated it for the Ellington band. Collier said, "She has written this music and as we get to the end, I'm almost finished, there's a very slow piece, a very melodic piece. [He asked her,] 'Well, who's gonna play this?' She said, 'Cootie's gonna play it.' It's in B major, which is like five sharps, and I said, 'Most jazz musicians aren't used to playing in that key. I said maybe if you move it up a half-tone or something.' Well we'll give it a try. But two days later she came back and said, 'No it has to be in B.' I said, 'Ann, Cootie won't play this.' And she said, 'Cootie will do it for me.'" (Going a half step up to C or a half step down to B♭ would have put the piece in more manageable and customary territory.)

While the band was in Chicago, they were convened to go over Ann Henry's piece. Collier said, "We were in a hotel [ball]room. Cootie's a little late. He comes in and takes his place. Cootie takes one look at the music, closes the book, puts his trumpet in the case, and walks out of the hall. C♯ for the trumpet, and that's like seven sharps, and that's like ridiculous. He's never seen that many sharps in his life. So Cat [Anderson] played the solo."[8] The young man who played in any key for Fletcher Henderson was no more.

Buster Cooper said Cootie "played when he wanted to play . . . it was no argument." Cooper saw the relationship between Ellington and Williams as complex because they "grew up together, so to speak" in the 1920s and 1930s. "I could compile five books about that band. They were something else."[9] But even the apparently unflappable Duke Ellington sometimes reached his limit. Mercer Ellington said, "One night, when we were in the middle of a rehearsal in Providence, Cootie Williams said something, or didn't do exactly what he wanted, and Ellington took a bottle of Coke off the piano and threw it at him."[10] Another instance of Cootie's misbehavior resulted in Ellington throwing a series of empty ash trays stacked on the piano at him.[11]

Ellington had sly ways of diffusing situations with people and Cootie was no exception. When the band was boarding an airplane, Cootie protested when Ellington turned to take his seat in first class while the rest of the band went to their seats in economy. Ever the wit, Ellington replied, "Cootie, you wouldn't want to work for a leader who didn't ride first class."[12]

It's hard to imagine any other bandleader putting up with the behaviors of his sidemen that Ellington did. Cooper confessed to sitting on stage during the last set of a gig and not putting his trombone to his lips. He didn't think Ellington noticed or even cared at the time. However, Ellington strategically recalled the incident a few days later in order to humble Cooper.[13]

Trombonist Vince Prudente joined the band in March 1972, and found the Ellington-Williams dynamic startling. He said, "Six weeks after I joined the band, [I saw] Cootie and Duke cussing each other out on the bandstand. It's quiet, but I'd be thinking 'Are they gonna fight?' [Ellington would say,]'Play your part' [and Cootie would say,] 'I don't play on that.'"[14]

♪

The Ellington band started a three-month European tour in September 1971. Ellington was seventy-two years old, and Cootie had just turned sixty. The number of long-serving veterans was dwindling, and Cootie was the only senior trumpeter left. The only other "old" soloists left were Procope, Gonsalves, and Carney. The tour started in Russia, where they were well received. Cootie said, "How did I find it in Russia? It was very cold, both indoors and out, but we enjoyed the visit. I only wish we could go back." Given some of the other band members' opinions (Procope—"I wouldn't like to go back there"; Mercer Ellington—"They don't like blacks or Jews over there"), Cootie may have been just being diplomatic in his response.[15]

The tour took the band from Russia to England, Belgium, France, Poland, and more European countries. From Spain, they flew directly to Brazil. They played dates in South America, Central America, and Mexico before returning to the USA on December 11. It was a grueling itinerary at any age.

The University of Wisconsin, located in the city of Madison, hosted a "Duke Ellington Week," a series of seminar and concerts with the band, starting on July 17, 1972. Everybody but Cootie, Mercer Ellington, and Harold Minerve did instrumental clinics. Cootie felt that the students should find what they needed on their own.[16] A few years earlier, he had talked about writing a book to help the next generation, saying "Maybe in three or four months I'll write a book on the trumpet. I see so many young musicians [that] don't even stand properly, [and] don't know how to breathe. My power comes from breathing properly, from using my chest and my abdomen."[17] When asked for trumpet tips by *Down Beat* in 1955, Cootie said, "[F]or phrasing, your teacher can give you the correct and legitimate way to phrase. But for jazz playing you can't be biased or set in your methods. It's entirely up to yourself and how far you think you can or ought to go. In a section you should always try to phrase like the lead trumpeter. Solo phrasing is entirely an individual matter."[18] But by 1972, he wasn't interested in such pursuits.

46

WE LOVE YOU MADLY

In 1973, the increasing honored and celebrated Ellington was the subject of an elaborate all-star tribute, *Duke Ellington, We Love You Madly*, the brainchild of Quincy Jones. The show included Count Basie, Ray Charles, Sammy Davis Jr., Peggy Lee, Aretha Franklin, and Joe Williams. The song selection was heavy on vocals, but during the Ellington medley near the end of the show, Cootie was featured for sixteen bars on "Do Nothing 'Till You Hear from Me." A huge band, drawn from the Ellington band and the best of Los Angeles's studio musicians, played for the show.[1] Ellington band alumni Louie Bellson, Clark Terry, and Cat Anderson were included. But out of the current band, only the "old-timers" Cootie Williams, Harry Carney, Paul Gonsalves, and Russell Procope were used for the show. Vince Prudente said, "there were some ill feelings [from the rest of the band] about that, and I always felt that it was a little bit of a slap in the face" to those left behind. Norris Turney was particularly incensed. Prudente also thought it was a bit of an insult to Duke as it implied his current band wasn't good enough.[2] The CBS show was an amazing tribute, but taping required many grueling hours. Ellington was ill with the flu at the time with a fever of 103 degrees and was admitted to the hospital the following day.

On June 7, 1973, Duke Ellington and His Famous Orchestra started a two-week gig at the Shamrock Hotel in Houston, Texas. It was becoming an annual tradition; they had similar bookings there in 1971 and 1972. Long-term bookings like this had become fairly uncommon; it had been almost six months since they had been able to stay put for so long. Time was continuing to take a toll on the orchestra. Road weariness and death left only Cootie and saxophonists Russell Procope, Paul Gonsalves, and the ever-dependable Harry Carney as the long-standing veterans of the band. Because of his addictions and the resulting health problems, Gonsalves became increasingly unreliable, forcing Ellington to carry a sixth saxophonist as a backup. Clarinet star Jimmy Hamilton left in 1968 after being refused a raise in pay. Trombonist Lawrence Brown said good-bye in 1970. He moved to Los Angeles, put his trombone case behind his sofa, and never played again. High-note trumpeter Cat Anderson also left in 1970 and had also moved to Los Angeles. But instead of retiring, he became a busy and very in-demand session player.

Cootie's health wasn't the best. Besides suffering from hypertension, he was also a diabetic. The sedentary life of a musician on the road had caused his weight to increase steadily over the years. At the Houston gig, Cootie suffered a serious health scare. Cootie related, "I went out to play [Take] the 'A' Train. I come [sic] back to my seat, and they wanted me to take a bow, and I couldn't hardly get up to take a bow." Things weren't right, but he didn't know anything beyond feeling that it was something serious. He thought, "Something's wrong. I got to go back home. I got to go home. There's definitely something wrong with me." Cootie and the rest of the band were taken to San Jacinto Medical Center in nearby Baytown for testing. The entire orchestra, many of them smokers and all victims of exposure to secondhand smoke, failed the test screening for emphysema. The doctors at the medical center thought Duke Ellington and Harry Carney tested so badly that they recommended follow-up examinations with their own physicians. Williams was diagnosed with tuberculosis. Despondently, Williams realized that lung problems meant he "wasn't going to play anymore." For someone who had played trumpet for over half a century, this was devastating news. "I had to give it up. No, I said, this is it. So the band went to Europe. I was only in the hospital . . . about three or four weeks. I had a private room. [Then t]hey sent me home. But I had to take the medicine for a year."[3] With that, Williams retired. It would turn out to be the first of several retirements.

The band continued its globetrotting ways unabated and at the end of October embarked on a tour of Europe and Africa. This would turn out to be Ellington's last trip abroad, and notably included the premiere of *The Third Sacred Concert* in London. While the band was in Europe, Ellington called Williams twice to plead with him to continue with the band. In his Jazz Oral History Project interview, Williams related the conversation:

Ellington: "Are you ready to come back to go to work?"
Williams: "No, man. I ain't thinking about working no more."
Ellington: "Ah, don't do that, man. I miss you so much. Come on back. You don't have to blow. Just sit up there and hold on."
Williams: "Okay, I'll do it for you. Nobody else in the world I would do this for but you . . . He missed looking at me, seeing me."

Williams reported, "[A]fter I took my medicine for a year, they took me off the medicine. I had to go back every two months. Then they started every three months, like that. Every six months. Now I go back once a year for a checkup." While Williams was away on his medical leave, there was a serendipitous encounter for Duke Ellington. Tenor sax great Arnett Cobb, a saxophonist Williams had unsuccessfully tried to recruit into his orchestra in the forties, went to see the Ellington band. A serious auto accident in 1956 had left him unable to walk without crutches, let alone drive. He enlisted the services of a young Texas Christian University trumpet player named Barrie Lee Hall Jr. to drive him to the concert. After the concert, Cobb and Hall visited Ellington backstage. Cobb introduced Hall to Ellington and told him Hall was a fine trumpet player. Ellington asked sharply, "Why aren't you playing in my band?" With that, Hall became one of the last players recruited to join the orchestra of Duke Ellington.

Succumbing to Ellington's power of persuasion, Williams returned to the fold in February 1974, after an eight-month absence. (Hall had been with the band about four months at that time.) Hall recalled coming into work one day and being surprised to see Williams back on the bandstand. He described Williams as real jolly, in contrast to the demeanor observed by others. Williams only played when it was time for his solos on "Take the 'A' Train" and "The Mooche." Hall said, "Cootie was royalty. Cootie didn't play no parts! There were five trumpets." The fifth trumpet was needed to cover the notes Cootie didn't play. "He didn't play parts; he was Cootie Williams! He was used to being a star, every group he had been in, he was a star. He had his own group, he was with Benny Goodman for a minute, and he was the star in that group, too."[4]

Not knowing all the history and background, the press had a problem with this behavior: "Although there were not too many solos in the band during the entire concert, we noticed, when veteran trumpet-star Cootie Williams wasn't blowing solos he just sat in his section holding his horn (not teaming or reading music with the other three trumpets) and looking towards the audience, sometimes, back stage. He did this on several occasions . . . [W]e didn't dig Williams's strange behavior."[5]

The old timers were important to Ellington. In the early 1970s, Ellington tried to lure Juan Tizol back on the road many times, and offered him the same arrangement that Cootie had, telling him he wouldn't even have to play. "I'll pay you—just sit there and hold your horn." Tizol couldn't do it—"I can't be supposed to be playing and not playing. How can I be on the bandstand holding my horn?"[6]

Ellington himself was experiencing failing health. In the fall of 1973, he was diagnosed with lung cancer. In early December of that same year, his thyroid gland was removed. As 1974 unfolded, he was increasingly forced to cancel gigs or use a supplemental or a substitute pianist. Even as Ellington's health was fading, the band's 1974 schedule took them to Illinois, Indiana, South Dakota, Missouri, Iowa, Connecticut, New York, and Ohio—and that was just in the first two months of the year!

At a February concert in Michigan, the reviewer singled out Williams for his "exuberant" solos and Carney for his "superb" work on baritone sax and bass clarinet. Although Ellington played, he had a backup pianist, the highly versatile Jaki Byard (1922–1999). Paul Gonsalves was out and Ray Nance, back in the band, appeared in a drunken state, wearing clothes that were too big for him with a bottle visible in his coat pocket. Instead of playing cornet and violin, he played random outbursts on a tambourine.[7] Sunday, March 17 found the band in Minneapolis, playing at the Guthrie Theater. Cootie Williams "frowned every now and then, but he actually participated with his fellow trumpeters in the section work instead of amusing himself between solo spots by glowering unwaveringly at the audience."[8] Ellington was described as "looking a bit fragile," while Gonsalves as someone "whose best years, I suspect, are behind him."[9] Sadly, he was right—there were less than two months left for Gonsalves.

On March 22, 1974, Duke Ellington played two concerts with his Famous Orchestra at the Sturges-Young Auditorium in Sturgis, Michigan. That was the last time that combination was ever heard in person. Cootie said it was apparent that Ellington was really sick on "[t]hat last trip we was on. See, he was working night by night. And I know he was sick. He was just barely making it. He told Mercer don't take the bus too far away from him, because he may have to leave any minute to come home. That's when he left to come home."[10] Ellington flew home to New York City, and after a few days of resting at home, he checked in to Columbia Presbyterian Hospital. Although confined to a hospital bed, he continued to work until the very end. A portable electric keyboard was brought into his room to allow him to work on new compositions. Ellington also reviewed selections of recordings to use for the album release of *The Third Sacred Concert*. There were also bookings for Duke Ellington and His Famous Orchestra that needed to be fulfilled once he got out of the hospital.

Williams didn't visit Ellington in the hospital. "No. I didn't get a chance to go up there. They didn't want any visitors. I used to send a message by Mercer. I didn't want to disturb him. I used to tell Mercer to tell him I'm saying a prayer for him every day."[11] Harry Carney was hospitalized for a few days with pneumonia around the same time Ellington entered the hospital. While he was there, Ellington called him to see if *he* was all right.[12]

Down Beat dedicated a large portion of its April 25, 1974, issue to the celebration of Duke Ellington's seventy-fifth birthday. A smiling Ellington is depicted on the cover, with a large caption saying, "Love You Madly!" Fans were given an address to send birthday wishes to The Maestro. There was nothing in the magazine to hint that Ellington lay dying in the hospital. Music luminaries such as Frank Sinatra, Leonard Bernstein, and Quincy Jones are represented in the tribute. Former and current members of the Ellington band were also quoted. Cootie Williams said, "Musically, you are a very wise man. Other than musically, you are a very wise man. There is something for everyone to learn by working for you."[13]

Ellington's star tenor soloist Paul Gonsalves passed away on May 14, and his former trombonist Tyree Glenn died of cancer a few days later. Because of his fragile health, the decision was made to not inform Duke of these deaths. On Friday, May 24, 1974, Edward Kennedy "Duke" Ellington succumbed to lung cancer at the age of seventy-five. His remains were taken to the Walter B. Cooke Funeral Home, where it joined those of Gonsalves and Glenn. Ellington's funeral was held the following Monday. Cootie Williams said of Ellington: "He was the greatest guy I ever met in life. Musician and man. He really was. I never met a greater man than him."[14]

PART VII *Mercer Ellington (1974)*

NOW MORE THAN EVER

> I think that Mercer needed me more than ever, so that's the reason why I'm with the band.[1]
> —COOTIE WILLIAMS

On May 27, one day after Duke's funeral, the organization now billed as the Duke Ellington Orchestra under the direction of Mercer Ellington, played their first gig, a twelve-day booking at an IBM convention at the Southampton Princess Hotel in Bermuda. It was a booking that Duke had arranged prior to his death and Mercer knew that he would have been okay with the band proceeding without him. Russell Procope, a twenty-eight-year veteran of the orchestra, decided to end his tenure with the band and not make the trip. That left Cootie Williams and Harry Carney as the only veterans of Duke Ellington and His Famous Orchestra during the glory days of the 1920s. Carney was the only member of the band with more seniority than Cootie.

Cootie went out due to a sense of loyalty and obligation: "I went out with the band for that reason, the main reason, on account of Duke. Because I thought [Mercer] needed me, and he really needed me at that time."[2] He also felt that he had a unique and special role, saying, "Mercer don't understand yet about the old music. I play things now which I wouldn't play with Duke, all that old music! I don't like old music. but he has requests, I imagine, for it, and no trumpet player in the band knows these things but me, so who else gonna play them?"[3]

Comparisons of the senior and junior Ellington were inevitable and unavoidable. Cootie said, "Mercer's not created like his father, to write things. I don't know, but I think he will come around because you have to have new music in order to keep the band going. And I might be talking to him to try to tell him that you got to keep creating in jazz. You can't go backwards, you want to go forwards."[4] The paradigm established by the elder Ellington was immense and daunting—constant travel, non-stop composition, nearly daily performances, and more. It would be a hard load for anyone to carry; Duke was even composing on his deathbed. Mercer had only written four original pieces two years into his stint as the leader and none of them had been publicly performed.[5]

Mercer observed, "It was fateful that our first job without Pop is an easy one. We only work two hours a night, and the surroundings are relaxing. When Pop passed, I had to rehearse the band in the daytime and go over to the funeral parlor at night." Duke Ellington didn't leave a will and all his instructions to Mercer were implicit. "Pop never talked about my taking over. He'd been told several times that he was in terrible shape, but he refused to give up hope," said Mercer.

Critic Leonard Feather wrote an article about the Bermuda gig but did not review the performances themselves. Under the byline "Duke's Band Alive, Swinging," he noted that "Of the old-line Ellington stars, only trumpeter Cootie Williams remains." Although he was still a member of the band, Harry Carney wasn't there because he was recuperating from phlebitis complicated by pneumonia. When he later rejoined the band, it was against his doctor's wishes. Pianist Billy Taylor was deputized as a temporary replacement until a more permanent solution was found. Soon Lloyd Mayers, at forty-five years of age and a veteran of the bands of Eddie "Cleanhead" Vinson and Dinah Washington, two musicians Cootie had worked with in the 1940s, was eventually hired as the band's piano player.

But no one could deny that Duke Ellington was irreplaceable. Cootie said, "Duke used to say, 'I'm no good without the band.' And I used to tell him the band is no good without him. Just his appearance and calling the tunes, and things, made a whole world of difference."[6]

John S. Wilson of the *New York Times* reviewed the band's first New York performance after Duke's death. In an article headlined "Full Ellington Band Performs with Cootie Williams as Star," he wrote, "The occasion was a personal triumph for Cootie Williams, the brilliant growl trumpeter who is the last of the colorful early Ellington stars still playing with the orchestra." Cootie was one of the stars of the Duke Ellington Orchestra. After Duke's death, he became *the* star.

Mercer Ellington inherited a band that would need a large amount in order to bring it back to working shape. Because the personnel was constant for so many years, a lot of music parts resided solely in the heads of the musicians. And who could fill the piano chair? Besides a pianist, the band also needed a piano book since all the piano parts were in Duke's head. And since neither Ellington nor Strayhorn wrote drum parts, there was no drum book either.

A few members of the band, one of them being Barrie Lee Hall, were set to the task of transcribing the old Ellington records to fill out the band's library.[7]

Mercer had plans to change the band. He said, "I want a band Pop would be proud of." Leonard Feather wrote that in conversation with Mercer, "the faceless figures who had begun to inhabit the bandstand when Duke became too old, tired and sick to care would be replaced by men steeped in the Ellington tradition." It's unclear which of them thought the band consisted of "faceless figures."[8] But Cootie was enthusiastic about the new players: "We have a whole lot of new players. The bass player, he's 18 years old, is terrific, out-of-sight, he's something else! We have a tenor player, he's 20, terrific. We have a very nice crop of musicians. When I was young, coming up, the older musicians didn't like the younger musicians, but they, I think they keep jazz alive. They have new ideas, and they're coming up with the world the way the world is and they play to their feeling. And if a musician is not set in his ways and mind, he can travel along with them but in his way."[9] However, he did find that they had a different energy: "The band keeps going, but you see, what's happening is that the younger guys come in and play this old music like it's new music. And sometimes I get kind of peeved about it and they want to know 'What's the matter, Cootie? What's the matter?' And I say 'Man, I've been playing this music for 50 years. You've just come here.'"[10]

Mercer said, "We pick the guys on their ability to get along with each other, their gentility and their respect for the people they are with and play for. Sometimes, we might have a very good musician, but he isn't able to get along—out he goes."[11] Duke wouldn't have had much of a band if he had followed that philosophy!

During the summer of 1974, Mercer Ellington told the press that Lawrence Brown would be rejoining the band. Ellington even had grand plans for the occasion: "I feel that the day Lawrence Brown enters the band should be a smart affair; I'd like to time it so it is during some gala occasion."[12] Unfortunately, when Brown (1907–1988) put down his trombone in 1970, he never picked it up again. After his retirement from the instrument, Brown was emphatic that his playing days were in the past: "I like beautiful music, but no, not for me to participate in, I don't think. No, I don't think I could ever develop enough interest in it."[13] Mercer also mused about getting former Basie tenor saxophonist Paul Quinichette (1916–1983), but that, too, didn't pan out.[14]

Young Ricky Ford had taken the tenor sax chair vacated with the death of Paul Gonsalves. "I met Mercer Ellington at a reception and Alma Lewis said that I was one of the most promising students in Boston."[15] Based on that endorsement, Ford was hired. "I was very close to Cootie Williams. We would always eat together. He would give me advice on how to play. He told me about how he grew up. He used to study with Lester Young's father. He told me all kinds of crazy stories. [Cootie felt he] had like an obligation to let you know about the music business, the pitfalls, etc."[16]

Ford characterized Williams as someone who "had quite a few conflicts with many great musicians." Ford related that the piano player irritated Williams when "he did "A" Train and he didn't play the intro correctly. He did some improvisation on it. After the gig, Cootie said, "Hey, you didn't play the intro to "A" Train very well. You did something different." And the cat said, 'Oh, Coo . . .'" Before he could finish the second syllable of the name, "Cootie slapped the shit out of him. We had to break up the fight. He was cut under his eye. He slapped him so hard. . . ."[17]

Cootie decided to tutor Ford on the horses, and he had some rookie's luck in betting on the horses. Williams asked Ford to meet him at the Belmont racetrack for some additional pointers. Ford was late for his meeting with Williams. "Ricky, I missed my daily double because you wasn't on time. Where you been, man?" Cootie said. Knowing Williams's temper, Ford thought to himself, "Man, if he slaps the shit out of me, I'll die."[18] Cootie took his horse racing seriously. And he was good at it, too. Clark Terry said, "I knew I'd never be as lucky as Cootie Williams, who went to the racetrack daily just like he was going to work. He took his lunch with him and would go home every night with money."[19] Bob Udkoff said, "Cootie . . . was pleasant, nice, but all he could talk about was horses. He was a big horse player."[20] Freddie Redd played piano in Cootie's band in the early 1950s. He said, "But Cootie was beautiful, as a person and as a musician. He has done so well financially because he's a great gambler, too. Probably if he hadn't been a musician, he'd have been the world's best gambler."[21]

Cootie had been a patron of the Belmont Park racetrack for many years and was well known to his fellow horse enthusiasts. The Duke Ellington orchestra was booked to play the track on Sunday, July 6, 1975. The band had played a short twenty-minute set, which included Cootie's feature, "Take the "A" Train." At the conclusion, "Cootie's walking off of the bandstand and this cat comes up to him and says, 'Cootie! Man, I didn't know you played the trumpet!'"[22]

Ford said that "[t]here was a giant memorial service for the first anniversary of Duke's death at [the Cathedral of] Saint John the Divine in New York. [Charles] Mingus sat in with us and played solo 'In a Sentimental Mood.' We were all in the bandstand and he realized I was there. Then at the reception, someone came up to me and said: 'Someone's gonna steal you from the Duke Ellington Orchestra.'"[23] That someone was Charles Mingus. Cootie heard about the Mingus job offer. "Cootie liked my playing and wanted a chance to talk me into staying, so he invited me to his home for lunch."[24]

By this time, Cootie and Catherine Williams lived at 144-24 181st Street in Queens. Ford described the home as modest and not showy. In the fashion of the time, the living room furniture was covered with plastic slipcovers. What was most notable was there was only one award displayed in the house. The *Down Beat* plaques, *Esquire* statuettes, and other honors gathered over the years were nowhere to be seen. Occupying a place of honor in the Williams home was the key to the city of Mobile he received in 1946. Williams told Ford that this was the only award he got in his entire career, saying "I want you to see this recognition I got. One day, you'll get some recognition, too." Williams also told Ford, "Don't ever stop playing music, don't get discouraged," along with other pieces of advice for the young musician.[25] One could interpret that the civic recognition, coming from a place where he was marginalized as a child, meant more than being honored by critics or fans. Ultimately, despite Williams's efforts, Ford moved on to the Mingus band. He was to be the last saxophonist employed by Charles Mingus, who soon developed ALS and passed away in 1979.

The younger Ellington brought the band to the studio for the first time on July 16 and 17, less than two months after the death of their longtime leader. Harry Carney had been in and out of the band due to bouts with phlebitis and pneumonia.[26] Carney's robust baritone saxophone was featured in a new arrangement of "Drop Me Off in Harlem," an Ellington *père* composition dating back to 1933. Sadly, this would be his swan song. He died less than three months later, at the relatively young age of sixty-four. Some said he had never recovered from the death of Duke Ellington.

The question facing Mercer Ellington was: What kind of band was this to become? A tribute band, frozen in time, or a more youthful vision with young musicians and new material? At the time of Duke Ellington's death, there were still plenty of alumni who were actively playing—trumpeters Cat Anderson, Bill Berry, and Clark Terry; trombonists Buster Cooper, Britt Woodman, and Quentin Jackson; saxophonists Marshal Royal, Jimmy Forrest, and Russell Procope; bassists John Lamb and Aaron Bell; and drummers Sonny Greer, Louie Bellson, and Sam Woodyard. While these older players brought experience and name recognition to the table, they were hard to recruit due to their lack of desire for life on the road. Mercer Ellington: "So what we must do now is go out there and really shock them with the strength of the band, so that the tradition not only will live but will be enhanced." At least for the short term, the tribute aspect had to dominate because the death of Duke Ellington was so recent. Duke Ellington was scheduled to appear at the Ravinia Festival in Highland Park, Illinois, on August 13, 1974. Instead of canceling the gig, the Ravinia Festival Association decided to use the band in what was billed as "A Tribute to Duke Ellington." The orchestra added guest vocalist Sarah Vaughan, a singer blessed with one of the most versatile instruments in jazz.[27]

Again, by this point in his career, Williams was not playing section parts at all, only putting the trumpet to his lips for his solo turns. Sometimes he didn't even appear to be up for that. To the chagrin of Ellington, Cootie would point to Barrie Lee Hall to let him know that he was to take it. But Hall understood what was going on. Cootie knew he wasn't going to be there forever, and it was his way of passing the torch to the younger musician.[28]

Mid-December 1974 found the band in Bayside, New York, to perform the American debut of Duke's *Third Sacred Concert*, his last major work. The *New York Times* noted the orchestra's revitalization and once again Williams merited special recognition: "Cootie Williams' trumpet specialty was a particular hit." After the Bayside date, the band embarked on a tour of the West Coast. On December 21, they played a gala at Donte's, a jazz club located in the North Hollywood area of Los Angeles. Whenever the band played at a place where their alumni lived, the old veteran would come by to check them out. At Donte's, high-note trumpet king (and Cootie Williams nemesis) Cat Anderson was in the house. At one of the breaks, Anderson took young Barrie Lee Hall aside and told him, "Now you be sure you listen to Cootie. I wish I had."[29]

Williams saw himself as a mentor to the younger members of the band. Mercer said, "A large majority of the band people have passed away and the bulk of the big numbers were in the minds of the people who died, not on paper. Mr. Williams would tell how the new men should use an inflection. The parts that were missing he would hum." Once, Mercer Ellington said, Williams told the group, "You all sound like a band that's trying to play like Duke Ellington instead of being the Duke Ellington band."[30]

While the band was in Chicago, Mercer Ellington and the orchestra were honored at a luncheon hosted by John Johnson of Johnson Publishing. The company produced magazines like *Ebony*, *Jet*, and *Essence*, designed to cater to the African American market. At the event, Prudente related, "Cootie stood up and he made a beautiful tribute to Duke saying how much he learned from the man, not just as a musician, but as a human being. He taught me about the world." Despite some of the rancor that Prudente saw between Ellington and Williams, he knew deep down there was love and respect between them. Prudente was amazed. "It was incredible. [Cootie] was a deep guy." Prudente said, "Duke was this very sophisticated guy, but he never forgot about pattin' your foot and snappin' your fingers and enjoying yourself."

48

CONTINUUM

Super Bowl IX was held at Tulane Stadium in New Orleans on January 12, 1975. The event was supposed to be played indoors at the brand-new New Orleans Superdome, but the arena wasn't completed in time. Instead, the game was played in Tulane Stadium, an open-air stadium. The competing teams were the Pittsburgh Steelers and the Minnesota Vikings.

Given the pop music–oriented halftime shows of today, it's hard to imagine jazz being featured. But the recently deceased Duke Ellington was saluted in the Super Bowl IX halftime extravaganza. (The death of Louis Armstrong had inspired a similar tribute in 1972.) The band had arrived in New Orleans the day before, and according to Barrie Lee Hall, the temperature outside had been "about 75 degrees" the previous day. But when the band "took the field [for the game the next day], it was 28 degrees." "[A]ll we had on were those flimsy [dinner] jackets. It was absolutely miserable," he lamented. Vince Prudente was extremely happy that his hometown Pittsburgh Steelers were in the Super Bowl and looked forward to viewing the game in person. There was a problem. When the band arrived at Tulane Stadium, Mercer informed the band that there would be no seats for them for the first half and only the potential for seats in the second half. "Mercer, that's my team there. If I don't get to see the first half, I'm not playing at halftime," said Prudente. More than half the band felt the same way. A solution was reached—the band was allowed to stand on the sidelines next to the team. The band was more than happy with that arrangement.

At halftime, the Pittsburgh Steelers were leading the Minnesota Vikings by a score of 2–0. The Grambling marching band started off the halftime show, entering the field from the end zones, while the announcer intoned, "Ladies and gentlemen, the National Football League proudly presents a Super Bowl halftime spectacular!" After a long pause, the Grambling band finally played some quick-tempo music to march/run to center field position. As they began to play, it was clear the cold weather was affecting their intonation. Anyone who has played a musical instrument can tell you that it's hard to stay in tune in cold conditions. After Grambling's overture, the Duke Ellington band took over. The band was crowded onto a relatively small float and as they played, Ellington-themed cupcakes surreally swirled around the field. They were dressed in white dinner jackets and Mercer wore a Pepto-Bismol-colored suit. Cootie Williams, the last of the old guard, received a significant amount of solo time on "Take the 'A' Train" and "C-Jam Blues," putting him in fine spirits, even though increasing health problems would make this his last year with the band (for the time being).

Fortunately, they didn't fall prey to the same intonation problems. Prudente confessed "we might have had a little anti-freeze" (in the form of vodka) to help against the cold, damp weather. After a rubato introduction from Grambling, the stadium announcer enthusiastically called out, "All aboard the 'A' Train!" as a salute to "one of America's greatest jazz artists, Duke Ellington." As Williams got in solo position, he again called out, "And here's Cootie Williams and his trumpet and a solo we all know so well." (The casual fan would be unaware that the famous solo was originated by Ray Nance.) Watching the performance on YouTube in 2012, Barrie Lee Hall remarked that "[Cootie] was doing his show biz thing. He didn't look like he was cold at all! He was having a good time." After "'A' Train," the band launched into "Things Ain't What They Used to Be," featuring tenor saxophonist Harold Ashby, followed by "It Don't Mean a Thing (If It Ain't Got That Swing)" sung by Anita Moore. With his plunger-muted trumpet soloing over "C-Jam Blues," Williams concluded the performance. Cootie impressed in this outing—"Franco Harris was good, but I would have voted for trumpeter Cootie Williams (terrific solo on 'A Train') as the Most Valuable Player in the Super Bowl."[1] (It was a low scoring game—the final score was Steelers 16, Vikings 6.)

There was some irony in Williams being acclaimed for this solo. First of all, it was a variation on Ray Nance's 1941 solo. Second, Williams had quit the band over playing "'A' Train" too many times ("The 'A' Train used to run out of my ears!"). During a 1972 engagement at Atlantic City's Steel Pier, Cootie implored Duke to give him some solo space besides "'A' Train." Ellington ignored Williams and started yet another set with the song. Cootie had enough, "I said 'Bye!' I [took] my horn, went upstairs and put it in the case, and went to New York, just like that." After three weeks, Ellington asked for Williams to return. "I thought it over and I went back and he let me play something else that time. But things like that can get to you."[2]

♪

Continuum, the first album by the Duke Ellington Orchestra under the direction of Mercer Ellington. Mercer is flanked by the last of the old guard Ellingtonians, Harry Carney and Cootie Williams. The album is autographed to the author by Mercer Ellington. (Author's collection)

A lot of the Ellington sound is built on the clarinet. "[S]o much of this music depends on clarinet work and a clarinet soloist."³ Mercer eventually found Bill Easley to carry the legacy of Bigard, Procope, and Hamilton. He was from Memphis and joined the orchestra in early 1975. He initially found Williams to be gruff and aloof. He said, "After a month with the band, we hadn't had much dialogue." On February 16, 1975, the band played an engagement for the Left Bank Jazz Society in Baltimore. After the gig was over, while the band was changing into their street clothes, "Cootie looks over at me and says, 'Easley. Easley. I been meaning to tell you, you're a fine musician.' I'll never forget it as long as I live. That's I call it one of my Mountaintop Moments." Easley jokingly added, "I think I peed myself!"⁴

On May 12, 1975, Cootie Williams participated in what would be his last studio session with the Duke Ellington Orchestra. Only one number, "Happy-Go-Lucky Local," was recorded. It was included in the first album released under Mercer's baton as *Continuum* (on the Fantasy record label) with the rest of the material drawn from July 1974 and January 1975 sessions. The reviews for the album were mixed. The biggest problem Mercer faced was expectations.

Whose band was this? *What* band was this? Aside from a tribute song, "Carney," written by 1950s former band member Rick Henderson, the program was all compositions that had been recorded by Duke Ellington. When the album was reissued in compact disc form in 2001, four songs were added that space didn't allow to be included on the original album. One of these, 1940's "Harlem Air Shaft," featured Cootie Williams reprising his original role. The power was still there, but there were fewer notes than in days of old. While Mercer and the band were targets of the critics, it seems that senior veteran Cootie Williams was immune: "Cootie Williams is present and playing with all the fire and authority one could wish"[5] and he "sounds as fresh as when he took over Bubber Miley's chair in the trumpet section back in 1929."[6]

Mercer was able to promote the album on radio on shows like that hosted by Gerald Wilson on Los Angeles's KBCA. He even appeared on the *Mike Douglas Show* with the full band, playing selections from the album—"Jeep's Blues," "Black and Tan Fantasy," both heavily featuring Cootie, and "Happy-Go-Lucky Local," a showcase for tenor saxophonist Ricky Ford.

Another television program derived from the band's engagement as part of a jazz-themed festival at sea called Showboat 3. From June 7 through 14 in 1975, the SS *Rotterdam* voyaged from New York City to Nassau, Bermuda. The festival featured a stellar array of talent: Earl "Fatha" Hines, Carmen McRae, Lionel Hampton, Dave Brubeck, The World's Greatest Jazz Band, Dizzy Gillespie, and more. Writing for the *Los Angeles Times*, critic Leonard Feather said of the Ellington group, "The Ellington orchestra today, just a year after the maestro's death, is in far better shape than it was during Duke's last years." Williams was singled out for praise in the review: "Cootie's searing, growling trumpet, the last reminder of the old guard, lent an authentic early-Ducal flavor to 'Jeep's Blues,' 'The Shepherd' and several other pieces." The cruise was filmed and turned into a BBC television series, *Jazz Ship*. The show aired eleven episodes in two seasons (1975 and 1976).[7]

♪

Cootie decided to quit the musician's life for the second time in 1975. "The doctor told me to retire because I got pneumonia in South America," said Cootie. Catherine, his wife of forty-seven years, had retired in June from her job and Cootie didn't want her at home by herself. He found retired life extremely enjoyable—a regular schedule, good meals, and time spent with his wife.[8]

UNRETIREMENT

The retirement of Cootie Williams didn't last very long. He was lured out of retirement again for a special tribute to Duke Ellington at the Newport Jazz Festival by promoter George Wein. Williams recalled, "I had retired for a year, and this is what brought me back. I hadn't touched my trumpet in that time, but George Wein talked me into coming back as he said I was the only person around today who knew anything about Ellington's music in the 1920s and 1930s. I thought it over and in my mind I decided I would do it for Duke Ellington's sake. I did two concerts in Carnegie Hall with the New York Jazz Repertory Company, playing Duke's music of the twenties, thirties and forties and doing the solos."[1] Wein was proven right. The critical consensus was that the re-creations were stiff and inauthentic; Cootie Williams's playing was considered the only thing that brought them to life. "[H]e played this concert with a strength that scared the whole trumpet section. When Cootie blew, his section-mates—trumpeters like Joe Newman, Jon Faddis, and Doc Cheatham—just looked around at each other in not-so-mock disbelief," Wein recounted in his autobiography.[2]

Wistfully looking back on his nine months of retirement, Cootie said, "I never lived so good until that one year [sic] of retirement. My wife and I love horse-racing, and we would go to the races nearly every day and then go out to dinner. I enjoyed that. When I was with Duke in the early years my wife used to go everywhere we went, but now she don't want to travel. I was really happy being retired, living life like a human being, not having to grab a hot dog and rush onto the bandstand, not having proper meals, not getting proper sleep—it's not good for your health. When I was retired I was in bed by about eight o'clock and waking up at 6 a.m."[3]

Cootie Williams performing at the 1976 Newport Jazz Festival. (Keith Sipes Photography)

Ricky Ford would occasionally cross paths with Williams after their time together in the Ellington fold. They both were playing at this edition of the Newport Jazz Festival. Williams explained to Ford that he wasn't playing in the section, he was only taking solos: "I told George Wein I ain't playin' no fuckin' parts."[4] He didn't need to—"He played with such exquisite fire, finesse, and urgency that the rest of the band receded into the ether. Cootie's magnificent performance reminded us that on the original recordings, every musician was an individualist, a vital contributor."[5]

Trombonist James "Trummy" Young (1912–1984), a contemporary of Cootie who came to fame with the Jimmie Lunceford band, had strong feelings against re-creations of this type. He said, "First thing, how can you recapture spirit? When you copy, there may be spirit, but it's a different spirit, and usually the copy is too precise. Even the tempos aren't the same. When people work together for a long time, they feel each other. Like Duke: how in the world would you ever record something like Duke's old band with Cootie (Williams), Tricky Sam, Barney and Sonny (Greer)? You might get technically better men, but how in the world could you get that sound on the old stuff Duke did? Man, the band will never see the day that could do it. It might play the notes, but Duke had a band of *individuals*."⁶

A few weeks after the New York Ellington tribute concerts, Wein brought a version of his Newport Jazz Festival to Nice, France. It was an eleven-day affair (July 8 through 18) featuring performances by Count Basie, Dizzy Gillespie, Bud Freeman, Sarah Vaughan, and many more, with the acts spread across three different venues.⁷ A group billed as "Cootie Williams and the Newport All Stars" had promoter George Wein on piano with Ellington alumni—trombonist Mitchell "Booty" Wood and drummer Sam Woodyard—as part of the group.

At an interview conducted during the Nice Festival engagement, Cootie pondered his next move. "When I get back home [from France] I don't know what my mind is going to be because throughout my life I have traveled all over and been away from home. . . . I think I may do some recordings before I retire again as I've had three or four offers. I would like to do something with a big band, something like the RCA-Victor *Cootie in Hi-Fi*. That's my favorite own recording and my wife is crazy about it."⁸ While Cootie didn't get his desire to realize a big band project, he made his last known studio recordings for the French Black and Blue label with an appearance in a Barcelona recording studio. Wood and Woodyard, participants at the Nice festival performance, returned for the studio session. Instead of George Wein, the pianist is Frenchman Raymond Fol. Fol was heavily influenced by Duke Ellington and adds a ducal flair to "Las Tres Senoras," a slow, dark blues. Overall, Cootie's playing is strong but there are more fluffed notes than in years past. So far, the complete results of that session, consisting of seven songs, have not been released. Only one song ("C Jam Blues") was released in Cootie's name as part of a Grande Parade du Jazz anthology series. Three songs were released under the name ("You Talk a Little Trash," "Finger Poppin' at the Popcorn," "Las Tres Senoras") of the date's tenor saxophonist, Gerard Badini.

Cootie's European tour continued with an appearance at the tenth edition of the Montreux Jazz Festival, which paid tribute to the Newport Jazz Festival on the night of July 11. Sarah Vaughan, the Preservation Hall Jazz Band, and the Newport All Stars represented George Wein's stable of talent. Next, the Williams group played at the North Sea Jazz Festival on Friday, July 16. Ted Easton's Jazz Band followed Williams. Cootie had recorded with Easton on May 13, 1976, for the group's *Salute to Duke Ellington* album, performing "Creole Love Call." Williams is only heard briefly, playing one chorus and playing over the ending, but he sounds like the Cootie of old.

The Ellington band continued to tour the world, but without Cootie. On October 2, 1976, they recorded an audiophile album, *Ellington Fresh Up*, while in Japan. The band didn't record as much as they did when Duke was alive, so this was a fairly rare snapshot of the band at work. The album consisted of nine Ellington standards like "Mood Indigo," "Solitude," and "Satin Doll." Barrie Lee Hall took the trumpet spot on "Take the 'A' Train" and made it all his own—there is no reference whatsoever to Ray Nance's classic solo or Cootie's variation on it.

The ranks of Ellington veterans had thinned considerably only two years after Duke's death. There were just a few remaining members that played with Duke. Even though he had retired, people still asked about Cootie. The band's road manager Charlie Harrison wasn't delicate when he said, "Cootie Williams is still alive, but he's old now." At the time, Williams was all of sixty-five years old.[9] But part of the reason for the Cootie inquiries may have been that most of the band's newspaper articles, from some outdated press release, still listed Williams as a member of the Duke Ellington orchestra. But this wasn't the most egregious error. The late Harold "Money" Johnson was still on the band's active roster![10]

♪

On April 23, 1977, a little over thirty years after receiving the key to the city, Williams received another honor from his hometown—the Mobile Music Award. The presentation of the award is a highlight of the annual American High School Jazz Festival. The *Mobile Register* published a picture of a leisure suit–attired Williams holding the certificate, flanked by local officials. At the state level, Cootie wasn't inducted into the Alabama Jazz Hall of Fame until 1991, six years after his death.[11] Although he is more than worthy, Williams is not a member of *Down Beat*'s Hall of Fame at the time of the publication of this book.[12]

50

THE LAST TENURE

Under Mercer Ellington, the band continued to tour on a regular basis. Mercer said, "A band is like a traveling salesman or gypsy. If you don't have the desire to travel, you don't belong."[1] Cootie continued to be a standout, and not just because he was the last of the "old guard." He continued to do "beautiful trumpet solos" in his concert appearances.[2] And only trumpet solos—no section work!

Cootie Williams made a cameo appearance at Carnegie Hall during singer Teresa Brewer's concert on April 5, 1978, just a little over forty years after his first time there as a guest artist with Benny Goodman. She was accompanied by an all-star big band with guest soloists. Brewer had enjoyed a successful singing career facilitated by Bob Thiele, her high-powered record company executive and producer, who opened up many avenues for her. Cootie took a chorus on "Mood Indigo," before trading phrases with another plunger specialist, trombonist Al Grey. As of this writing, these are the last commercially released notes from Cootie Williams's trumpet until some recordings from the Australian tour turn up.

Cootie and Russell Procope sat down for an interview with documentary film maker Gary Keys in 1978 that was released in 1980 as part of the movie *Memories of Duke*. Typical of musicians of their generation, they're both sharply attired in suits. Their reminisces about Ellington, their bandmates, and their time in the band are distributed in segments at various points in the film.

In October 1979, Cootie left retirement and for the last time rejoined the Duke Ellington orchestra. A veteran of the 1950s edition of the band, trombonist Britt Woodman, had also signed back on.[3] The permanence of personnel that marked the Duke Ellington band was no longer present under Mercer Ellington. Five years after Duke's death, the only musicians left under his tenure were bass trombonist Chuck Connors, saxophonist Harold "Geezil" Minerve, singer Anita Moore, and trumpeter Barrie Lee Hall.[4] "People still want to see the band. Everyone loved Duke," Cootie said.[5] He came out of retirement yet again "because Mercer asked me to. Mercer said the fans kept asking for me. It's good to be back playing again but these tours sure are tough on me, not because of my age, but because I've been retired and learned what it is to live like a human being."[6]

Cootie usually stole the show with his solo spots and was singled out in the reviews with such accolades as "Jazz Hall of Famer"[7] and "Ellington superstar trumpeter."[8] It was also noted that "[o]nly Cootie Williams, the 70-year-old [sic] trumpeter is a recognizable part of the Ellington legacy."[9] Cootie was featured on all his previous vehicles: "The Shepherd (Who Watches Over The Night Flock)," "Things Ain't What They Used to Be," "Mood Indigo," and "Take the 'A' Train." Hall had the solo duties on the latter during Cootie's latest retirement, but it passed back to Cootie. The Ellington rule of solos not changing hands apparently did not apply to Cootie at this point in time. Interestingly, Mercer reinstated "East St. Louis Toodle-oo," as the band's theme song.[10]

In Asheville, North Carolina, Cootie even participated in a post-concert jam session.[11] It was unusual for a man who often confined himself to featured solo spots at this point in his career to take part in extracurricular activities. Cootie continued to be the standout. "Williams was the show stealer. He stepped out for four numbers: 'The Shepherd [Who] Watches over the Night Flock,' 'Take the "A" Train,' 'Things Ain't What They Used to Be,' and 'Mood Indigo.'"[12]

Cootie enjoyed increased attention as the elder statesman in the band and earned standing ovations "out of respect for his age and in admiration of his brilliant ability."[13] Cootie said, "You know, I enjoy a good ovation more now than I did in those old days. It means a lot to me. Maybe I took them too much for granted, or maybe I realize they're numbered for me."[14] At the time Cootie expressed these sentiments, he was just shy of his sixty-ninth birthday. So many of his past colleagues, like Chick Webb, Jimmie Blanton, Joe "Tricky Sam" Nanton, Bud Powell, Charlie Parker, Dinah Washington, and Charlie Christian had died tragically young. But at sixty-nine, Cootie had achieved an age that had eluded confreres Harry Carney (sixty-four), Ben Webster (sixty-four), Johnny Hodges (sixty-two), Rex Stewart (sixty), and Wini Brown (fifty).

THE LAST TOUR

Continuing their touring ways, the Ellington band undertook a South American tour in May, which included Brazil, Argentina, and Chile.¹ While in Chile, Cootie contracted pneumonia and had to be sent home.² This was the second time he had contracted pneumonia in South America. The band took part in a night of nostalgia called "Big Bands '80s" at the Inglewood, California Forum on June 14. The evening featured the big bands of Tex Beneke, Ray Anthony, and Duke Ellington. The critic for the *Los Angeles Times*, Leonard Feather, panned the entire event. He noted the Cootie was not present due to illness and called the orchestra "a shell of its former self" and deemed the pianist, Onzy Matthews, "adequate."³ It's only speculation, but perhaps Cootie was "ill" because he didn't deem the show at the Forum worthy of his participation. Because the next day, Cootie was back on the bandstand when the band played at the Catamaran Hotel in San Diego. Reporting on the gig, Stanley Dance wrote, "Cootie Williams sounded very much as he did while Duke was alive, and his humorous vocal greatly enhanced "Things Ain't [What They Used To Be]."⁴ The next day, the Ellington band left San Diego to start a ten-day, eight-city tour of Australia, sponsored by the Australian Elizabethan Theatre Trust. This was a momentous event and perhaps, as the last of the Old Guard, Cootie didn't want to disappoint Mercer, the band, and the fans Down Under. The billing for the Australian concert tour was "The Internationally Famous Duke Ellington Orchestra." In slightly smaller print, the publicity materials said, "Featuring Mercer Ellington, Cootie Williams, Harold Minerve, Anita Moore (vocalist)."

As usual, the itinerary was grueling, and the band suffered jet lag enough for it to be noticeable in their performances. They started with two concerts at the famous Sydney Opera House on June 18. From there it was on to the capital

Advertisements from the Australian concert tour of June 1980. (Author's collection)

city of Canberra (June 19), Melbourne (two concerts on June 21), Adelaide (June 22), Darwin, Townsville (June 25), Brisbane, Newcastle, and a return to Sydney (July 1).

"Jeep's Blues" had been a longtime feature for Johnny Hodges before it passed on to Cootie Williams for the *Continuum* album. By the time of the Australian tour it was an alto saxophone piece again, played by Kenny Garrett. Now an influential saxophonist, Garrett started his career in jazz with the Mercer-led Duke Ellington Orchestra in 1978 at just seventeen years of age. He viewed Cootie as his "friend, mentor and protector." By this time, Williams was diabetic, and Garrett had a habit of bringing a large bag of cookies on the band bus. Garrett recalled that "[w]hen Cootie's sugar would go down, he would look over and say, 'Give me some of those cookies.' I'd heard all these stories about how rough he was, but he was a nice guy to me. He was always telling me to write my own songs."[5]

Cootie found time to record an interview with 2MBS-FM while in Sydney, which aired on Wednesday, July 23, about a month after the band had returned to America. He was said to have talked about "his work and life" on the show. Unfortunately, attempts to track down a copy of this show have proven to be futile, and it is unknown if a recording of it exists.[6] As a sidenote, it's not unusual to find bootleg concert recordings of a tour like this, but if they're out there, they are hiding well.

The band's last concert circled them back to Sydney. This time, instead of the Opera House, they played Sydney's Capitol Theatre on Tuesday, July 1. The

Capitol Theater was opened in 1928 and this beautiful theater was added to the New South Wales State Heritage Register in 1999. This was a venue that seats a little over two thousand people. The critic reviewing the concerts, Eric Myers, had an overall negative opinion of what he saw. He considered the offerings overly commercial, found Mercer Ellington to be "something of a comic figure," and thought that "nowhere did he indicate that he is in touch with the real meaning of his father's music." To say Mercer Ellington was "not in touch with the real meaning of his father's music," a music he heard since he was in the womb, a music he heard develop incrementally over his entire lifetime, is a gross insult.

But Myers had high praise for Cootie Williams: "Cootie Williams, now 71 [sic] played a solo spot in each concert. He still has that gorgeous and powerful trumpet sound, and he managed some memorable blues lines which were reminiscent of the great years. These flashes of the old spirit were enough to make his visit worthwhile. My heart went out to him. Surrounded by buffoonery, Cootie kept his dignity and his artistic integrity intact."[7] The review for the rest of the band was so harsh that Mercer was moved to write a rebuttal. He was particularly stung by the critic's charge that the band's overriding rationale for existence was for commercial reasons—the review even ran under the title "Overriding commercial element." Instead, Mercer argued that it existed "to extend the memory of [Duke] Ellington until he becomes a matter of history. He's not well enough embedded in history to my satisfaction and I personally am subsidizing the promoter in an attempt to accomplish this end."[8]

In July, the band was on the other side of the globe to play George Wein's Nice Festival in the south of France. It was a ten-day event featuring artists like Art Pepper, Joe Williams, and Dave Brubeck. Mercer Ellington and the band continued to be compared unfavorably to Duke's legacy in reviews. One reviewer dubbed the Ellington band "the greatest disappointment" of the festival—"Not only were the arrangements poor but precious little of Duke's music was played and then it was done badly." Once again, Cootie was praised for his work—"Cootie Williams, with his plunger muted trumpet, came on at the end to play 'The Shepherd' which was the only worthwhile number heard."[9] Cootie understood Mercer's situation, telling an interviewer that, "Now it was to be expected that the person who took over the Ellington Band would have other ideas than Duke himself. We have—in contrast to the earlier Ellington Band—now no longer any influence on the music. Mercer is the boss and what he does is his decision."[10]

52

PAJJING THE TORCH

In the fall of 1980, Mercer Ellington was part of a team that was working on conceptualizing *Sophisticated Ladies*, a musical revue celebrating the music of Duke Ellington. At that time, shows featuring the music of Eubie Blake (*Eubie!*) and Fats Waller (*Ain't Misbehavin'*) were very successful, so an Ellington-themed show was an obvious thing to do. Mercer decided to use the Ellington band onstage to perform instrumental numbers and backup for dancers and singers. This would take the band off the road and give them a period of steady employment. But for someone like Cootie, who only wanted to play his few featured solos, this concept doesn't sound like it would have appealed to him. Given his general health and advancing age, Cootie decided to retire in 1980 after the band's summer European tour.[1] Cootie said in a 1980 interview that he would be able to live comfortably in retirement, with money from "all sorts of thing, like engagements, records and especially royalties."[2] (One wonders how significant the royalty payments from "'Round Midnight" were to Cootie's portfolio.) Tenor saxophonist Al Sears said, "Cootie and his wife go to the race track every day, and [they] just enjoyed life and relaxed . . . he doesn't work because he doesn't want to, and he's doing very well."[3]

Now that Cootie Williams had retired for his fourth and final time after nearly sixty years in music, he decided to pass the torch, or in this case, the trumpet, to his protégé, Barrie Lee Hall Jr. Hall said, "We did a documentary at Mercer's apartment one day. A film crew out of England filmed everything. Cootie came over and to my surprise they called me to join in with Cootie's interview where Cootie presented me with his last horn. I was happy to get it, but everyone in the apartment was in tears. It was a great moment. . . . We were good friends."[4]

The trumpet was a Conn Model 2B.[5] When Hall was interviewed for this book in January of 2012, he stated that the trumpet was in his closet and in need of work since it hadn't been played since Cootie gave it to him. The interview became a reminder to take the trumpet to be restored so that it didn't seize up completely. Sadly, Hall passed away sixteen days after the interview.

Cootie Williams was a marvelous student of the trumpet and made his teachers proud. Charlie Lipscomb, his first teacher back in his Mobile youth, bequeathed his trumpet to Cootie when he died in 1949.[6] William Costello did the same when he passed on in 1956. Rather than wait until he was gone, Cootie decided to pass the torch while he was still around.

Lawrence Brown said that "you get to a certain period in life [where] I think you should sort of sit down and let the rest of the world carry on."[7] Certainly, Cootie Williams, along with Brown, was at this point in life. Williams was one of the rare high-profile musicians who was able to ply his trade and not die in the saddle (as did Ellington, Carney, Hodges, Armstrong, and so on).

Any mentions of Cootie Williams in the early 1980s were all in the past tense and usually reviews of new Duke Ellington recordings reissues. Although the movements of Cootie and Catherine Williams are not known past this point, it's a good bet that he spent his retirement years as he described in his 1980 interview with *Jazz Podium*, a German magazine: "Our daily routine looks like this: I usually get up around 6 a.m., take a shower, then make myself a cup of tea and it makes so much noise that my wife wakes up . . . We're going to have breakfast together, then to the racetrack. Around noon we have our lunch—I love hot dogs more than anything—then we walk back to the racetrack. In the evening there is dinner again and finally we go home tired. I like to go to bed early." In the same interview, he also said, "I just expect more [out] of life before it's over for me."[8]

When asked to name his favorite trumpeters for *Music and Rhythm* magazine in 1941, Harry James included Cootie Williams, saying "Cootie Williams is probably the greatest 'growl' artist there ever has been. But more than this Cootie has a fine range, an exceptional beat and does a lot of nice open work."[9] Four decades later, in 1982, Dizzy Gillespie was asked to name his favorite trumpeters. He listed only four: 1) Louis Armstrong, 2) Miles Davis, 3) Cootie Williams, 4) Clifford Brown.[10] Coming from fellow trumpet masters, this high praise, while he was still alive, showed the heights Cootie reached as a professional musician.

Charles Melvin Williams was admitted to Long Island Jewish Hillside Medical Center on August 21, 1985. After a stay of nearly a month, he passed away on Sunday, September 15 at 4:18 a.m.[11] The cause of death was reported as a kidney ailment. Most newspapers reported Williams's age at death as seventy-seven, which presumed the incorrect 1908 date of birth. Many of the obituaries also erroneously stated that he died at home. However, an important detail that was reported correctly was that Williams was the last of the band members from the 1920s. (Juan Tizol, who joined the Ellington band the same year as Williams

Cover and Order of Service for the funeral of Charles "Cootie" Williams, held at St. Peter's Church on September 18, 1985. (Rutgers University Institute of Jazz Studies)

[1929], had passed away in 1984.) "Cootie Williams and his fellow musicians gave America the roots of a proud musical form that will endure forever, even though its practitioners will not," said an editorial tribute.[12]

The funeral service for Cootie Williams was held on Wednesday, September 18 at Saint Peter's Church, located at 54th and Lexington in Manhattan. The dedicatee of the Ellington composition and longtime Williams feature "The Shepherd Who Watches Over the Night Flock," Rev. John Genzel, conducted the ceremony.

The Daily News reported that, "To say goodby[e] to Cootie Williams they came to St. Peter's early. They filled the wooden pews and once those seats were gone, they stood in the doorways and then at the end of aisles. Finally, when there was no other space, they stood along the walls in the balcony. The church had the look of a theater in the round." Benny Goodman was one of the many mourners in attendance.[13] He would pass away just nine months after Cootie, another reminder that the era that spawned them was losing its giants.

The service started with Mercer Ellington leading the Duke Ellington Orchestra through "The Shepherd Watches Over the Night Flock." Barrie Lee Hall Jr., Cootie's protégé, played the solo role of his mentor. Anita Moore sang "'Round Midnight" and trumpeter Joe Newman played "Echoes of Harlem." (Cootie's brother Leroy Barney Williams had helped Newman get

Headstone of Cootie and Catherine Williams at Woodlawn Cemetery in the Bronx. (Photo by Susan A. Olsen—Director of Historical Services, Woodlawn Cemetery)

his professional start with Lionel Hampton.)[14] Another trumpet giant, Roy Eldridge, gave a eulogy that praised Cootie's style. "You hear Louis Armstrong, and you know it's him," he said. And then he looked down at the casket and he said, "That's what Cootie did."

Williams was buried at Woodlawn Cemetery in the Bronx. Many jazz greats are interred at this cemetery—W. C. Handy, Lionel Hampton, Coleman Hawkins, Miles Davis, and Duke Ellington are just a handful of the names to be found there. Other Ellingtonians laid to rest there include Sonny Greer, Arthur Whetsel, and Clark Terry.

Catherine Williams passed away on August 5, 2000, and was buried next to her husband. Below their names is the inscription "In God's Loving Care." The left side of the headstone, next to Cootie's name, has an engraving of a trumpet.

The great singer Tony Bennett (1926–2023) said, "I think that [Duke Ellington is] timeless and so avant-garde. Each guy in his legendary orchestra was an artist: Paul Gonsalves, Johnny Hodges, Harry Carney, Ray Nance, Cootie Williams. All these guys were part of an era of individualism."[15] Ellington was able to take these great singular voices and mold them into something timeless and everlasting. Since 1995, the Essentially Ellington program has spread the gospel of Ellingtonia through a distribution of free transcribed Ellington/Strayhorn arrangements to high schools around the US and Canada. Cootie's work is probably not familiar to the younger generation, so there are performance notes that give tips on the art of playing trumpet with a plunger, even specifying a preferred brand—"Kirkhill is a very good brand, especially if you can find one of their old rubber ones." But most importantly, they say "Listen carefully *many times* [emphasis added] to the Ellington recording of these pieces."

Cootie believed in the power of music and felt it could be a force for peace. "Music is the language that honestly springs from people's souls and it is therefore sincere. That's why it is so very easy to learn and comprehend the meaning of folk music from other lands. Music is the product of an honest mind and therefore free access to [the] music of different people would aid in gaining mutual understanding of peoples thereby the quicker winning of understanding between people. It is the language of peace, why not make full use of it in attempting to gain that end?"[16]

ACKNOWLEDGMENTS

I've always found it odd that author spouses are put at the end of an acknowledgments section as "last but not least." I'd like to start *my* acknowledgments with love and gratitude to my wife Julie Swayze. Her advice, support, and encouragement for this project was invaluable.

As every author knows, no matter the merits of your project, it's meaningless unless you can make it through the hurdles to actual publication of your work. Craig Gill of the University Press of Mississippi approved this proposal by a first-time author and there are no adequate words to express my thanks for this. UPM's Katie Turner provided great assistance and guidance through the publication process.

Steven Lasker is a font of jazz knowledge and has an amazing trove of recordings, books, and photographs that are in many cases one of a kind. His generosity in sharing his unique assets helped immeasurably in making this a better project. He also proved to be a keen proofreader in the early stages of this book. If any errors crept in afterwards, they are mine alone.

Tom Samuels seems to have found every online newspaper and informational database on the internet! His generosity in sharing that knowledge was extremely valuable, especially during the pandemic, when there were no other research opportunities available.

David Palmquist's website "The Duke, Where and When" (www.tdwaw.ca) details the daily activities of Ellington and his musicians. Despite its immense size, it will probably never be complete as new Ducal activities are constantly being added. It's a great resource, as is David.

Jazz film expert and author Mark Cantor provided me with a great copy of Cootie's 1943 film short *Film Vodvil*. He also generously gave me permission to post it on YouTube. The Rutgers Institute of Jazz Studies provided access to their files, which included Cootie Williams's funeral program. Dr. Jack Chambers graciously gave me access to his unpublished manuscript and allowed me to use material on Cootie Williams from it.

While I could have done the solo transcriptions for this book (eventually), for me, it's a slow and time-consuming process. I would have liked to have included transcriptions of Cootie's solos in the manuscript but obtaining copyright permissions would have unacceptably extended the book's publication timeline. Thanks to Bryan Wendell Bennett for allowing the use of transcriptions from his 2009 PhD thesis *Cootie Williams, Rex Stewart, and Ray Nance—Duke Ellington's Trumpet Soloists 1940–1942*. Transcription of Cootie's solos on "Rumpus in Richmond," "Harlem Air Shaft," "In a Mellotone," and "Concerto for Cootie" and other performances can be found there. A link to the document can be found at www.EllingtonReflections.com on the "Recommended Reading" tab.

I commissioned Curtis Swift at saxsolos.com for additional transcription work—Cootie's improvisations on "Airmail Special," "House of Joy," "He Flip'd When He Shoulda Flop'd," "That's the Lick," and "Typhoon." Please check out his website at www.saxsolos.com; he has a large and varied inventory of quality work available!

I'd also like to thank the many people who helped me in ways large and small. It may have been a factoid, an email contact, an introduction, or simply much appreciated encouragement. I hope I have included everyone, and I deeply apologize if I haven't. Heartfelt thanks go out to Abigail Herrera, Alessandro King, Alexandre Villemaire, Benjamin Shepard, Bill Crow, Bo Haufman, Bob "Ironside" Hunt, Bobbi Merrill, Brian Priestley, Camryn Mickan, Carl Woideck, Con Chapman, Dan Weinstein, Darlene Chan, David Creek, David Fletcher, David Hazard, David Sherr, Desmond Polk, Donald McGlynn, Dwayne Clemons, Ellen Shimomura, Eric Facon, Eric Shultz, Eric Wright, Fred Goaty, Henry Besser, Ian Bradley, Jan Evensmo, Jeanne Andersen, James Garfinkel, James Zollar, Jane Meditz, Jean-François Pitet, Jean-Marie Juif, Joe Bebco, Joe Hagan, John Wilby, Jon-Erik Kellso, Joo Rhee, Joseph Cavaseno, Josh Welchez, Keith Sipes, Ken Steiner, Kenny Burrell, Kevin O'Neal, Kristen Gardner, Kurt Dietrich, Laurence McFalls, Leor E. Gamzo, Lewis Porter, Marilyn Lester, Marion Leloir, Mark Cantor, Mark Miller, Mboya Nicholson, Michel Macaire, Mike Stephenson, Nan Lee, Nick Rossi, Noah Weinbaum, Patricia Willard, Paul Ellington, Paul Watts, Quentin Bryar, Quinton Carr, Randolph Anderson, Renee J. LaPerriere, Robert Shegog, Ryosuke Sano, Scott Wenzel, Shane Philen, Sherwin Dunner, Steve Boisen, Steve Voce, Ulf and Brigitte Lundin, Val Wilmer, Vickie Wilson, Vincent Pelote, Yoshiya Inoue, Yves Francois.

Last but certainly not least, this biography would not be what it is if not for the documentation left by the Black newspapers of America. The struggles and triumphs of the African American communities were not deemed noteworthy by the white (aka "mainstream") news media. *The Pittsburgh Courier, Baltimore Afro-American, Detroit Tribune, The New York Age, The People's Voice,* and *The Chicago Defender* are some of the newspapers that left stories that would have disappeared from memory without their work. Writers such as Ted Yates, Billy Rowe, and Fredi Washington told stories that Walter Winchell, Earl Wilson, and other white writers of the time couldn't be bothered to tell. There are many more Black biographies that can be written from these valuable and largely unmined resources.

NOTES

1. MOBILE BLUES

1. *Collected Works*, Balliett, 207.
2. Author interview with Barrie Lee Hall Jr.
3. "Meet Cootie Williams, The Guy the Tin Can Brought to Music," *Chicago Defender*, February 3, 1945, 13. There are about a dozen Black churches that are still around that were active at the time of Cootie's birth, but none of them had birth records.
4. "Memories of Duke" documentary.
5. "Sur La Route Avec Cootie II," Frank Tenot, *Jazz Magazine*, May 1959, 17. (A 1940 article ("'Cootie' Flies From Chicago to New York to Join Goodman Ork," *Pittsburgh Courier*, November 16, 1940, 21) quotes Williams saying the origin of his nickname is unknown.
6. "How Cootie Williams got his band," Skippy Adelman, *PM's Sunday Picture News*, July 8, 1945, m4.
7. "'Cootie' Flies from Chicago to New York to join Goodman Ork."
8. 1880 federal census, Montgomery County, Alabama.
9. Ike Williams 1959 death certificate.
10. In 1850, only 0.65 percent of Alabama's 345,000 African Americans were free, according to the 1850 US federal census.
11. "Slavery in America, The Montgomery Slave Trade," Equal Justice Initiative, 33.
12. "Montgomery County, Alabama, Largest Slaveholders from 1860 Slave Census Schedules and Surname matches for African Americans on 1870 Census," Tom Blake (https://freepages.rootsweb.com/~ajac/genealogy/almontgomery.htm).
13. "Idol of Two Continents, Duke Ellington and 'Jazz,' Music Born Out of Tyranny," *Irish Times*, July 1, 1933.
14. Rutgers Jazz Oral History Project, 1976 Interview of Cootie Williams by Helen Oakley Dance. Subsequent references to the source in the footnotes will be abbreviated "JOHP."
15. Isaac Williams's 1959 death certificate.
16. "On the Road with Cootie, part II," Frank Tenot, *Jazz Magazine*, May 1959, 17.
17. Ike Williams SSN application.
18. 2020 US federal census.
19. There is a possibility that Melvina Frost may have been born in 1879. For the 1880 census, the Frost family lists a one-year-old named "Viney" Frost. It may be that "Viney" is a nickname for "Melvina."

20. The source for the 1881 year of birth is the 1910 census. She's reported as thirty-five years old on her 1917 death certificate, which implies a birth year of 1882. In the 1880 census, her parents report a daughter, born in 1879, named "Vina." This may be her if they used it as a nickname for "Melvina."

21. 1867 Alabama Voter Registration.

22. 1859 federal slave census. In true southern fashion, Huckabee was known as "The Colonel." But his title was legitimate, earned in the Alabama Militia.

23. The source of the name Baalam can be found in the Bible's Old Testament. Baalam was a soothsayer whose story is told in the book of Numbers.

24. Williams JOHP.

25. 1910 Federal Census for Alabama.

26. "Forest Products Industry in Alabama," Encyclopedia of Alabama, http://encyclopediaofalabama.org/article/h-3021.

27. Williams JOHP.

28. Williams JOHP.

29. Williams JOHP.

30. Williams JOHP.

31. Williams JOHP.

32. "How Cootie Williams got his band."

33. *Satchel: The Life and Times of an American Legend*, Tye, 5.

34. I was only able to find one reference to Cootie playing piano as an adult. The band was recording a rehearsal tape for the Alvin Ailey dancers. While performing "The Vortex," Ellington stayed in the control room while "trumpeter Cootie Williams played the few piano notes called for. Once, when Williams improvised a bit, Ellington said, 'All right, Cootie, cool it.' He quickly took any sting out of the abrupt sentence by adding, 'You're apt to play something I won't be able to find. Somebody will ask me to play it sometime and say, 'What's the matter? You wrote it.' You're apt to stumble up on something good.'"—"Duke Ellington Composes Ballet Music," Mary Campbell, [Albany] *Times-Union*, July 5, 1970.

35. Williams JOHP.

36. "On the Road with Cootie, part II," Frank Tenot, *Jazz Magazine*, May 1959, 17.

37. Williams JOHP.

38. Williams JOHP.

39. Williams JOHP.

40. Melvina Williams death certificate.

41. Text message from author Paulette Davis-Horton, August 5, 2023.

2. BOY MEETS HORN

1. "Cootie," *Whitney Balliett Collected Works*, 207.

2. Williams JOHP.

3. The 1920 federal census shows Lipscomb and his parents were all born in Alabama.

4. 1940 federal census.

5. 1924 and 1926 Mobile city directories.

6. Williams JOHP.

7. Williams JOHP.
8. Williams JOHP.
9. Williams JOHP.
10. *The Davis Avenue Story*, Paulette Davis-Horton, 69.
11. Cootie's entries in *New Grove Dictionary of Jazz*, the *Encyclopedia Britannica*, and the liner notes to the 1940s Mercury Sessions box set are examples.
12. Williams JOHP.
13. Williams JOHP.
14. "Cootie Speaks," Bradley and Failows, 1963, 2.
15. "Reminiscing with Cootie," Eric Townley, *Storyville*, June-July 1977, 172.
16. Williams JOHP.
17. "Cootie," *Whitney Balliett Collected Works*, 207.
18. *King Joe Oliver*, Rust and Allen, 14.
19. Williams JOHP.
20. *Swing, Swing, Swing*, Firestone, 33.
21. Williams JOHP.
22. Death certificate of Melvina Williams.
23. "Maternal Mortality in Black and White: Seeking lifesaving solutions for an enduring disparity," *UAB Medicine Magazine*, https://www.uab.edu/medicine/magazine/spring-2021/maternal-mortality-in-black-and-white-seeking-lifesaving-solutions-for-an-enduring-disparity.
24. Williams JOHP. Williams's memory is off on the age of his oldest brother. At the time of the 1910 census, Isaac Jr. is listed as three years old, implying a birth year of 1907. In his 1940 draft registration, Isaac gives his date of birth as February 24, 1907. So there is an age difference of four years, not seven.
25. 1920 federal census, Marengo County, Alabama.
26. 1930 federal census, Marengo County, Alabama.

3. A YOUNG PROFESSIONAL

1. "Lee Young Dies at 94," Douglas Martin, *New York Times*, August 9, 2008, page x.
2. Williams JOHP.
3. Williams JOHP.
4. "Marching To a Different Drummer," J. Lee Anderson, *Mississippi Rag*, December 1992, 1.
5. Williams JOHP.
6. *Lester Leaps In*, Douglas Henry Daniels, 70.
7. Williams JOHP.
8. Williams JOHP.
9. *Lester Leaps In*, Daniels, 118.
10. Williams JOHP.
11. Williams JOHP. Elbert Williams's later life is unknown. The other three brothers are mentioned in records, sometimes in connection with Cootie, but not Elbert.
12. "Cootie," Whitney Balliett, 208.
13. *The Davis Avenue Story*, Davis-Horton, 153.
14. *The Davis Avenue Story*, Davis-Horton, 69.

4. FLORIDA

1. "No Blue Notes for Jazzman Hall," *Corpus Christi Caller-Times*, June 25, 1967.
2. Williams JOHP.
3. Williams JOHP.
4. "The Adventures of Edmond Hall," J. Lee Anderson, *Mississippi Rag*, August 1993, 3.
5. Williams JOHP.
6. Florida certificate of death for Calvin Anthony Shields, State File No. 19613.
7. Federal census records, Jacksonville city directories, Calvin Shields death certificate.
8. "Cootie," Balliett, 207. Although the Balliett renders the name as "Coin," it's spelled more likely spelled "Coyne." There are a handful of Coynes in Jacksonville records of the time, but no one with the name Coin. The author was unable to find any documentation of Son Coyne's demise.
9. "Cootie," Balliett, 207.
10. "Nat Adderley Interview," Alwyn and Laurie Lewis, *Cadence*, March 1992, 6.
11. "Ride," *New Grove Dictionary of Jazz*, Kernfeld, 1046.
12. "The Adventures of Edmond Hall," J. Lee Anderson, *Mississippi Rag*, August 1993, 3.
13. "Coy Cogitates," Coy Herndon, *Chicago Defender*, October 23, 1926, 7.
14. "The Adventures of Edmond Hall," J. Lee Anderson, *Mississippi Rag*, August 1993, 3.
15. "Syncopators Depart," *Miami Herald*, April 6, 1927, 3.
16. "Steward's Stewings," Billy Steward, *Chicago Defender*, April 16, 1927, 6.
17. "The Musical Bunch," Dave Peyton, *Chicago Defender*, May 7, 1927, 6.
18. "Steward's Stewings," Billy Steward, *Chicago Defender*, May 14, 1927, 6.
19. "The Adventures of Edmond Hall," J. Lee Anderson, *Mississippi Rag*, August 1993, 4.
20. "Cootie Speaks," Bradley and Failows, 1963, 2.
21. "The Musical Bunch," Dave Peyton, *Chicago Defender*, September 24, 1927, 6.
22. "Recommended Disk Records," *Variety*, November 30, 1927, 54.
23. Though out of print, used copies of *Florida Rhythm* (Jazz Oracle BDW 8011) are still floating around. The very knowledgeable (and valuable!) liner notes were written by Mark Miller, with assistance of researchers John Wilby, Sherwin Dunner, Lawrence Gushee, et al.
24. *Florida Rhythm* liner notes, Mark Miller, 1999.
25. "The Musical Bunch," Dave Peyton, *Chicago Defender*, October 22, 1927, 6.
26. "Syncopators Depart," *Miami Herald*, April 6, 1927, 3.
27. Williams JOHP.
28. Williams JOHP.
29. "The Adventures of Edmond Hall," J. Lee Anderson, *Mississippi Rag*, August 1993, 4.

5. NEW YORK

1. Ross De Luxe Syncopators, *Storyville*, 1996-97, 225.
2. "The Adventures of Edmond Hall," J. Lee Anderson, *Mississippi Rag*, August 1993, 4.
3. Williams JOHP.
4. "Haskell Proper, etc., Among Eagle Air Features," *Brooklyn Daily Eagle*, February 15, 1925, 41.
5. 1928 New York City radio listings.

6. National Weather Service, Past History, https://www.weather.gov/wrh/climate.
7. "The Adventures of Edmond Hall," J. Lee Anderson, *Mississippi Rag*, August 1993, 4.
8. "The Musical Bunch, Dave Peyton, *Chicago Defender*, March 10, 1928.
9. *Duke Ellington*, Barry Ulanov, 80.
10. Williams JOHP.
11. "Dance to be held at Trianon," *Fort Lauderdale Daily News*, July 6, 1935, 3.
12. 1950 federal census and 1966 death certificate of Alonzo Ross.
13. *Duke Ellington*, Barry Ulanov, 86.
14. Conservatively, Ike Williams must have lost or spent about $6,000 of his son's money, which would be over $100,000 in today's dollars!
15. Williams JOHP.
16. Williams JOHP.
17. *Duke Ellington*, Barry Ulanov, 86.
18. "New Orleans Clarinets: Edmond Hall," Herman Rosenberg and Eugene Williams, *Jazz Information*, August 9, 1940, 12.
19. "The Adventures of Edmond Hall," J. Lee Anderson, *Mississippi Rag*, August 1993, 4.
20. Williams JOHP.
21. "How Cootie Williams got his band."
22. "How Cootie Williams got his band."
23. Williams JOHP.
24. "The Adventures of Edmond Hall," J. Lee Anderson, *Mississippi Rag*, August 1993, 4.
25. Williams JOHP.
26. Williams JOHP.
27. *Music Is My Mistress*, Ellington, 94.
28. "Cootie Speaks," Bradley and Failows, 1963, 2.
29. *Hendersonia*, Allen, 99.
30. *The Uncrowned King of Swing*, Magee, 59.
31. *Rhythm Man*, Crease, 64.
32. *Rhythm Man*, Crease, 328.
33. *Hendersonia*, Allen, 225.
34. Williams JOHP.
35. Williams JOHP. There's a story in Walter Allen's *Hendersonia* that gives a different reason for Chick Webb being on the outs with the union from the November 24, 1928, issue of the *New York Age*. According to that newspaper, Webb is standing outside the Alhambra Dance Hall, where the orchestras of H. G. DeLeon and Bill Brown alternated sets. Webb was accused of heckling one of the bands and at some point he went to the ballroom's proprietor and said, "A good orchestra [Webb's] and ham fat bunch working." He needn't have bothered since the Alhambra Dance Hall closed on November 13 after barely six weeks of operation.
36. Williams JOHP.
37. Williams JOHP.
38. *The World of Duke Ellington*, Dance, 104.
39. "Webster: 'Rex could say a lot of things on cornet,'" Max Jones, *Melody Maker*, September 23, 1967, 20.
40. Williams JOHP.
41. "Reminiscing with Cootie," Eric Townley, *Storyville*, June-July 1977, 172.
42. Williams JOHP.
43. *Boy Meets Horn*, Stewart, 93.

44. "Cootie," Whitney Balliett *Collected Works*, 207.
45. *Boy Meets Horn*, Stewart, 93.
46. *Boy Meets Horn*, Stewart, 112.
47. Williams JOHP.
48. Williams JOHP.

6. DUKE ELLINGTON

1. *Ellington, The Early Years*, Tucker, 208.
2. Williams JOHP.
3. Williams JOHP.
4. Williams JOHP.
5. Williams JOHP.
6. *The World of Swing*, Dance, 160.
7. *The Song of the Hawk*, Chilton, 360.
8. *Music Is My Mistress*, Ellington, 119.
9. Williams JOHP.
10. Williams JOHP.
11. Williams JOHP.
12. *Ellington, The Early Years*, Tucker, 101.
13. *Reminiscing in Tempo*, Nicholson, 89.
14. *New Grove Dictionary of Jazz*, 892.
15. "Cootie Williams," Gudrun Endress, *Jazz Podium*, September 1980, 6.
16. Juan Tizol JOHP interview, 24.
17. *Duke Ellington, A Listener's Guide*, Lambert, 34.
18. *Duke Ellington*, Ulanov, 90.
19. Cootie Williams interview, *Memories of Duke* documentary.
20. Duke Ellington on *The Dick Cavett Show*, February 10, 1971.
21. *Duke Ellington in Person*, Mercer Ellington, 25.
22. Bob "Ironside" Hunt email, January 2018.
23. *The Duke Ellington Reader*, Tucker, 465.

7. CATHERINE

1. Wedding certificate; 1930 federal census.
2. "The Duke Where and When," www.tdwaw.ca.
3. *Duke Ellington Day by Day and Film by Film*, Strateman, 5.
4. "Dance Halls," Levi H. Jolley, *Baltimore Afro-American*, June 21, 1930, 9.
5. "Cootie Speaks," Bradley and Failows, 1963, 2.
6. "Reminiscing with Cootie," Ric Townley, *Storyville*, June-July 1977, 173.
7. *A Listeners Guide*, Lambert, 43.

8. BUGLE CALL RAG

1. *Buck Clayton's Jazz World*, Clayton, 38, 39.
2. "My Favourite Things: Buck Clayton chooses Cootie Williams," *Melody Maker*, July 1, 1967, 6.
3. *Buck Clayton's Jazz World*, Clayton, 64.
4. "My Favourite Things: Buck Clayton chooses Cootie Williams."
5. "Reminiscing with Cootie," Eric Townley, *Storyville*, June-July 1977, 172.
6. *Duke Ellington*, Collier, 149.
7. "What is Swing?" *The Big Book of Swing*, Treadwell, 8.
8. *Beyond Category*, Hasse, 150.
9. Williams JOHP.
10. Williams JOHP.
11. "Major Holley," Bob Rusch, *Cadence*, July 1989, 8.
12. *Reminiscing in Tempo*, Nicholson, 293.

9. THE FIRST EUROPEAN TOUR

1. *Duke's Diary, Part I*, Vail, 80.
2. Williams JOHP.
3. "Reminiscing with Cootie," Eric Townley, *Storyville*, June-July 1977, 174.
4. Williams JOHP.
5. *Reminiscing in Tempo*, Nicholson, 144.
6. *Duke's Diary, Part Two*, Vail, 86.
7. Hugues Panassie, "Duke Ellington at the Salle Pleyel (1946)," *The Duke Ellington Reader*, Tucker, 83.
8. "Duke Ellington a la Salle Pleyel," Hugues Panassie, Jazz Tango Dancing, August 1933, 5.
9. "The Case [for] Cootie," Hugues Panassie, *Hot-Revue*, December 1945, 9.
10. *Duke's Bones*, Dietrich, 186.
11. Author interview with Vince Prudente.
12. Author interview with John Lamb.
13. Author interview with Art Baron.
14. "The Case for Cootie," Hugues Panassie, *Hot-Revue*, December 1945, 10.

10. WILLIAMS, WHETSEL, AND STEWART

1. *The Duke Ellington Reader*, Tucker, 234.
2. Williams JOHP.
3. *The World of Duke Ellington*, Dance, 106.
4. "On the Road with Cootie, part II," Frank Tenot, *Jazz Magazine*, May 1959, 17.
5. Williams JOHP.
6. "Cootie Speaks," Jack Bradley and Jeann Roni Failows.
7. *Duke's Diary, Part One*, Vail, 105.

8. *Jazz from the Beginning*, Bushell, 121.
9. Bill Berry interview, JazzProfessional.com, 1980.
10. Author interview with Claire P. Gordon.
11. "In Duke's Head," Michael Zirpolo, *IAJRC Journal* 33, no. 3 (Summer 2000): 21.
12. Liner notes, *The Complete 1932–1940 Ellington*, Lasker, 18.
13. "A Survey of Recent Jazz Recordings—with a Digression on Native 'Swing,'" John Hammond, *Brooklyn Daily Eagle*, May 5, 1935, 37.
14. *John Hammond On Record*, Hammond, 132.

11. ECHOES OF HARLEM

1. A working title for "Echoes of Harlem" may have been "Black Misery" per a John Hammond column ("A Review of Recent Disks," *Brooklyn Daily Eagle*, March 8, 1936).
2. "Best Record Sides of 1936," Gordon Wright, *Metronome*, January 1937, 23.
3. "Colored Musicians Not Always Given Credit Due Them—Star in '36," Paul Eduard Miller, *Down Beat*, January 1937, 10.
4. "Swing," Lionel Hampton, *Baltimore Afro-American*, April 29, 1939, 10.
5. Catalog of Copyright Entries, part 3, Musical Compositions, 1936, 991.
6. "Reminiscing with Cootie," Eric Townley, *Storyville*, June-July 1977, 170.
7. "Praise and Criticism," Porter Roberts, *Pittsburgh Courier*, July 18, 1936, A7.
8. Steven Lasker email, June 2023.
9. *Duke Ellington*, Collier, 215.
10. "Hi Hattin' in Harlem," Allan McMillan, *Chicago Defender*, October 3, 1936, 19.
11. "Swingin' around Manhattan," B. Y. Stander, *Tempo*, August 1936, 2.
12. "Duke Ellington at the Apollo," HMG, *Metronome*, October 1936, 45.
13. "Duke Ellington at the Apollo."
14. "165 Sides Waxed as Mills Starts; 75 Every Month," *Variety*, March 24, 1937, 59.
15. "Review of Records," *Variety*, May 15, 1937, 13.
16. "Reminiscing with Cootie," Eric Townley, *Storyville*, June-July 1977, 172.
17. *Duke Ellington*, Ulanov, 187.
18. *The World of Swing*, Dance, 273.
19. In popular music, Bloomsbury Publishing has produced the 33 1/3 Series of books, in which each volume takes a deep dive on a particular album. Works like Captain Beefheart's *Trout Mask Replica* and the Isley Brothers' *3+3* have been given a thorough examination in this series.
20. The other "bridge fiends" in the band were Barney Bigard, Arthur Whetsel, and Fred Guy.
21. "The Duke Ellingtons—Cotton Clubbers En Mass," *Metronome*, April 1937, 19.
22. *Ellingtonia: The Recorded Music of Duke Ellington and his Sidemen*, Timner, 28.
23. *The Jazz Years: Earwitness to an Era*, Feather, 63. While the account in this book dates the recording to 1938, Steven Lasker and David Palmquist say there are a few other plausible dates. See "The Duke Where and When" website entry for February 24, 1938, for details.

12. CARNEGIE HALL

1. *Benny Goodman and the Swing Era*, Collier, 216.
2. Liner notes to *The Duke Ellington Carnegie Hall Concerts, January 1943*, Feather.
3. "Good Music . . . that's all!," Gretchen Weaver, *Band Leaders*, November 1944, 65.
4. "Benny Goodman, The Famous 1938 Carnegie Hall Jazz Concert," Hancock, 95.
5. "Benny Goodman, The Famous 1938 Carnegie Hall Jazz Concert," Hancock, 97.

13. THE SECOND EUROPEAN TOUR

1. "And a gay time was had by all, all though parting, now or then, is such sweet sorrow," *Pittsburgh Courier*, April 1, 1939, 24.
2. *Duke's Diary*, Vail, 162.
3. Steven Lasker, TDWAW, www.tdwaw.ca.
4. *Boy Meets Horn*, Stewart, 185.
5. Juan Tizol JOHP interview, 24.
6. "Ellington Gave Concert in Bomb-Proof Hall!," Duke Ellington, *Metronome*, June 1939, 10.
7. *Rhythm Man*, Crease, 85.
8. "Cootie Calls Chick Greatest Leader," Ulanov, *Metronome*, July 1941, 21.
9. *Duke Ellington—A Listener's Guide*, Lambert, 88.
10. "While unusual, it was hardly new. Records featuring a single soloist go back to Herbert L. Clarke and other classical soloists. In jazz, Johnny Dunn recorded Hawaiian Blues on 8/18/22. Solo almost from start to finish. On Clarence Williams's Wild Cat Blues/Kansas City Man Blues (recorded 7/30/23), Sidney Bechet solos from start to finish on both sides."—Steven Lasker via email, June 2023.
11. Williams JOHP.
12. Williams JOHP.
13. "Cootie Speaks," Bradley and Failows, 1963, 2.
14. Williams JOHP.
15. "Billy Strayhorn Interviewed by Bill Coss," *The Duke Ellington Reader*, 502.
16. "Record Reviews," *Down Beat*, June 1, 1940, 12.
17. *Jazz: Its Evolution and Essence*, Hodeir, 77.
18. *Jazz: Its Evolution and Essence*, Hodeir, 95.
19. "Why I Quit Duke Ellington After 11 Years," Cootie Williams, *Music and Rhythm*, December 1940, 9.
20. "Edward Green: Delighting in the Duke," Douglas Groothuis, September 2, 2019.
21. Transcription of Cootie's solos on "Rumpus in Richmond," "Harlem Air Shaft," "In a Mellotone," and "Concerto for Cootie" can be found in Bryan Wendell Bennett's excellent 2009 doctoral thesis for the University of Iowa, "Cootie Williams, Rex Stewart, and Ray Nance: Duke Ellington's trumpet soloists 1940–1942." A link to the document can be found at www.EllingtonReflections.com on the "Recommended Reading" tab.
22. Liner notes for *Classic Columbia and OKeh Benny Goodman Orchestra Sessions*, Loren Schoenberg, 7.

14. BENNY GOODMAN

1. *Swing, Swing, Swing*, Firestone, 281.
2. *Swing, Swing, Swing*, Firestone, 287.
3. *John Hammond on Record*, Hammond, 116.
4. Williams JOHP.
5. Interview with Berger.
6. "Duke Ellington," Green, 47.
7. *Boy Meets Horn*, Stewart, 192.
8. "Rabbit's Blues," Chapman, 162. But in a review of "Jump for Joy" in the October 1941 issue of *Metronome* magazine, George T. Simon says, "Hodges came through with some marvelous soprano saxing."
9. Williams JOHP.
10. *The World of Duke Ellington*, Dance, 106.
11. *Swing, Swing, Swing*, Firestone, 288.
12. "Ellington 'Fixture' Leaves Duke for BG," *The Billboard*, October 26, 1940, 9. Juan Tizol confirmed this in his 1978 JOHP interview with Patricia Willard.
13. "Cootie Williams to Leave Duke Ellington," Billy Rowe, *Pittsburgh Courier*, October 26, 1940, 21.
14. "Cootie Williams Joins Benny Goodman," *Jazz Information*, October 25, 1940, 4.
15. "Duke Suggests Jitterbug Hop to Cure Hitler," *Winnipeg Free Press*, November 5, 1940, 3.
16. "Orchestra Notes," *The Billboard*, November 23, 1940, 10.
17. "Cootie Williams Joins Benny Goodman," *Jazz Information*, October 25, 1940, 3.
18. *Roy Eldridge, Little Jazz Giant*, Chilton, 102.
19. "Swingin' the News," Al Monroe, *Chicago Defender*, November 9, 1940, 20.
20. *Duke's Diary, The Life of Duke Ellington 1927–1950*, Vail, 189.
21. "'Cootie' Flies from Chicago To New York To Join Goodman Ork," *Pittsburgh Courier*, November 16, 1940, 21.
22. "Nance Takes Cootie Spot with Duke," Jimmy Gentry, *Down Beat*, November 15, 1940, 1.
23. *BG on the Record*, Connor and Hicks, 281.
24. *BG on the Record*, Connor and Hicks, 285.
25. "Hear Count Basie May Join Benny Goodman's Band," *Chicago Defender*, November 9, 1940, 21.
26. *A Biography of Charlie Christian, Jazz Guitar's King of Swing*, Goins and McKinney, 176.
27. "Charlie Christian Tried to Play Hot Tenor," *Metronome*, March 1941, 16. The Ellington band passed through Oklahoma City in November 1933, July 1935, February 1936, and November 1939 per the David Palmquist website "The Duke Where and When" www.tdwaw.ca. One or all of these dates could be the occasion for Williams and Christian to have previously met.
28. *New Grove Dictionary of Jazz*, 209.
29. "Benny Goodman Tries Mixed Orchestra on First College Date," *Pittsburgh Courier*, November 9, 1940, 20.
30. "Cootie Williams Joins Benny!" *Metronome*, November 1940, 1.
31. "BG Grabs Cootie for Hot Chair," Dave Dexter Jr., *Down Beat*, November 1, 1940, 1.

32. "Cootie and the King," *Metronome*, November 1940, 22.
33. "You're Telling Us," Arthur Zinkin Jr., *Metronome*, December 1940, 22.
34. "Should Negro Musicians Play in White Bands?" *Down Beat*, October 15, 1939, 1.
35. "Benny Should Be Congratulated for His Courage—Jimmy Dorsey," *Down Beat*, October 15, 1939, 1.
36. "Benny Should Be Congratulated for His Courage—Jimmy Dorsey."
37. "Notes on Records," *San Antonio Express*, November 10, 1940, 9A.
38. "After 6 months with Benny G, Cootie Williams Likes it Fine." *Baltimore Afro-American*, March 8, 1941, 13.
39. "Air Ya Listenin?" *Mason City Globe-Gazette*, November 9, 1940, 11.
40. "All Ears," Bill Chase, *New York Amsterdam News*, November 2, 1940, 13.
41. "Is the Duke's Band Corny?" Charles Gant, *Tempo*, January 1937, 3.
42. *Those Swinging Years*, Barnet, 122.
43. "All Ears," Bill Chase, *New York Amsterdam News*, November 2, 1940, 13.
44. "Rowe's Notebook," Billy Rowe, *Pittsburgh Courier*, November 9, 1940, 7.
45. "Why I Sold My Half of *Down Beat*," Carl Cons, *Music and Rhythm*, May 1942, 49.
46. "Trombone Ace Is 2d Highest Salaried Star," Dan Burley, *New York Star & Amsterdam News*, January 18, 1941, 21.
47. "Brother, Can You Spare a Dime? The 1940 Census: Employment and Income," National Archives website.
48. "Why I Quit Duke Ellington After 11 Years," Cootie Williams, *Music and Rhythm*, December 1940, 9.
49. "Why I Quit Duke Ellington After 11 Years."
50. "Why I Quit Duke Ellington After 11 Years."
51. *BG on the Record*, Connor and Hicks, 286.

15. BENNY RIDES AGAIN

1. "Why I Quit Duke Ellington After 11 Years."
2. "Basie, Cootie Airs with Goodman," *Atlanta Daily World*, December 21, 1940, 2.
3. "Benny Goodman May Make Motion Picture," *Baltimore Afro-American*, December 21, 1940, 15.
4. "For Your Information," M. Oakley Christoph, *Hartford Daily Courant*, January 8, 1941, 7.
5. "Benny's New Band Is Too Much Like Benny's Old Band," George Frazier, *Down Beat*, March 15, 1941, 6.
6. "I Had the Craziest Dream," Forrest, 76.
7. *Jazz Anecdotes Second Time Around*, Crow, 227.
8. *Jazz Anecdotes Second Time Around*, Crow, 289.
9. *Sing, Sing, Sing*, Firestone, 296.
10. Jimmy Jones JOHP.
11. *The World of Duke Ellington*, Dance, 108.
12. *The World of Duke Ellington*, Dance, 107.
13. *The World of Duke Ellington*, Dance, 108.

14. Williams JOHP.

15. "Benny Goodman Band Debuts," *Swing: The Guide to Modern Music*, December 1940, 5.

16. "New Goodman Band Potentially Greatest of BG's Whole Career," *The Billboard*, M. H. Orodenker, December 14, 1940, 10.

17. *BG on the Record*, Connor and Hicks, 298.

18. Williams JOHP.

19. "Cootie Williams Discusses the Trumpet," Cootie Williams, *Music and Rhythm*, October 1941, 29.

20. "Popular Record Reviews," *The Billboard*, January 13, 1945.

21. *Trumpet Blues*, Levinson, 27.

22. "Phil Harris, Harry James Reminisce Three Nights," Carole Kass, *Richmond Time-Dispatch*, January 27, 1980, 131. The copyright credits the words and music to Ben Pollack and Harry James. It was published by Mills Music.

23. *Duke Ellington in Person*, Ellington and Dance, 59.

24. "Greatest Band of All Time Records for Musicians' Charity," *Metronome*, February 1939, 1.

25. "Hot Off the Platter," Carl Steger, *Honolulu Advertiser*, December 3, 1939, 32. As an example, Cootie was far down at sixteenth place on *Down Beat*'s 1939 poll. Steger wondered if winner and Goodman trumpeter Ziggy Elman was really better than Cootie, Rex Stewart, Bobby Hackett, and others. The move to Goodman was proving to be a great way to boost Cootie's visibility, as predicted by Steger.

26. "All-Stars Spotted Goodman, Dorsey Men," *Metronome*, February 1941, 10.

27. "Duke, Benny, Artie Top 1941 Discs," *Metronome*, January 1942, 18.

28. "*Down Beat*'s 1940 All-American Swing Band," *Down Beat*, January 1, 1941, 1.

29. "N.Y.—Hollywood," Charles G. Sampas, *Lowell Sun*, January 9, 1941, 6.

30. "'Old Gold' Goodman on Fitch Show Tomorrow," *Down Beat*, February 15, 1941, 2.

31. "Feature Race Stars for Third Time on Fitch Bandwagon," Billy Rowe, *Pittsburgh Courier*, February 22, 1941, 20.

32. *The Swing Era*, Schuller, 38.

33. "Birthday Ball Celebration Will Be Broadcast Tomorrow Night," *Index-Journal*, January 29, 1941, 8.

34. "The First Lady Greets BG," *Down Beat*, April 1, 1941, 19.

35. "Record Reviews," Dave Dexter Jr., *Down Beat*, October 1, 1941, 14.

36. "Popular Records," Alfred D. Charles, *Baltimore Sun*, November 16, 1941, M13.

37. "New BG Radio Show from Chi," *Down Beat*, June 15, 1941, 3.

38. Williams JOHP.

39. *Swing, Swing, Swing*, Firestone, 289.

40. *Hamp*, Hampton, 65.

41. *Jazz Anecdotes Second Time Around*, Crow, 153.

42. "Good Vibes, Lionel Hampton is all set to swing," Owen McNally, *Hartford Courant*, August 2, 1984, 92.

43. "Good Vibes, Lionel Hampton is all set to swing."

44. *Swing, Swing, Swing*, Firestone, 289.

45. "Rowe's Notebook," Billy Rowe, *Pittsburgh Courier*, November 22, 1941, 20.

46. *Roy Eldridge*, Chilton, 148.

47. *Luck's in My Corner*, Weeks, 151.

48. "Theatrically Yours," Eddie Colston, *Ohio State News*, September 23, 1944, 22.

49. *Piano Jazz*, 1986. NPR radio show, Marian McPartland, host, with guest Roy Eldridge.

50. "Mickey Finn," *The Tower*, February 27, 1941, 4. (In the same issue, they saw no irony with a column titled "It's Great to be an American.")

51. "Mixed Bands 'No Bed of Ease' Says Teddy Wilson," *Chicago Defender*, January 31, 1942, 20.

52. Williams JOHP.

53. *Down Beat*, May 7, 1952, 6.

54. "Benny's New Band Is Too Much Like Benny's Old Band," George Frazier, *Down Beat*, March 15, 1941, 6.

55. "Swingin' the News," Al Monroe, *Chicago Defender*, May 24, 1941, 21.

56. "After Six Months with Benny G., Cootie Williams Likes It Fine," *Baltimore Afro-American*, March 8, 1941, 13.

57. "Benny Goodman Employs Third Negro Musician," *Variety*, June 18, 1941, 38.

58. John Simmons JOHP.

59. "Goodman Adds Fourth Sepia Musician," *New Journal and Guide*, August 2, 1941, 15.

60. "The Clever Mr. Goodman Adds Bass Fiddler John Simmons To Orchestra," *Detroit Tribune*, August 16, 1941, 9.

61. *Jazz Anecdotes, Second Time Around*, Crow, 152.

62. "Democracy in Entertainment," *New York Age*, August 23, 1941, 6.

63. "Swingin' the News," Al Monroe, *Chicago Defender*, August 9, 1941, 20.

64. "Night Life Note Book," *Chicago Daily Times*, August 3, 1941, 88.

65. "Mixed Bands May Be Rule," *Baltimore Afro-American*, September 6, 1941, 13.

66. "Paul Robeson, Benny Goodman And Colored Stars Delight Big Robin Hood Dell Crowds," J. W. Poindexter, *Philadelphia Tribune*, July 17, 1941, 11.

67. "Swing on the Upswing," James J. Nagle, *New York Times*, July 13, 1941, X8.

68. "Hep Cats Hail Benny Goodman at Grant Park," Don Newton, *Chicago Daily News*, August 12, 1941, 4.

69. "Goodman Rouses Stadium Audience," *New York Times*, July 15, 1941, 22.

70. "King of Swing on WCAX," *Burlington Daily News*, September 12, 1941, 11.

71. "New Yorker Hotel, New York," *The Billboard*, October 18, 1941, 19.

72. Williams JOHP.

73. *Pittsburgh Courier*, June 17, 1939, 11.

74. "Swinging the News," Al Monroe, *Chicago Defender*, August 8, 1942, 22.

75. "Cootie Soon to Have His Own Band," *Down Beat*, October 1, 1941, 1. For a publication date of October 1, the story would have to have been sourced sometime in September.

76. "Talent and Tunes on Music Machines," Harold Humphrey, *The Billboard*, October 25, 1941, 65.

77. Simmons JOHP.

78. "Goodman to Be Left Without Sepia Stars," *Pittsburgh Courier*, October 25, 1941, 21.

79. "Benny Goodman Drops Two: Keeps His 'Cootie,'" Harold Jovien, *Chicago Defender*, 20.

80. "Encores and Echoes," E. Billingsworth, *Baltimore Afro-American*, November 1, 1941, 13.

81. "Barnet Gets Hectic; Hires Two Sepia Musicians—May Use Third," *The People's Voice*, February 21, 1942, 29.

82. "Inside Stuff—Orchestras," *Variety*, November 19, 1941, 47.

83. *Roy Eldridge, Little Jazz Giant*, Chilton, 123.

16. BUILDING A BAND

1. Williams JOHP.
2. "How Cootie Williams got his band," Skippy Adelman, *PM's Sunday Picture News*, July 8, 1945, m4.
3. "Does Blackout Loom for Negro Bands?" Dan Burley, *New York Amsterdam News*, November 23, 1940, 16.
4. "Good Music, That's All," Gretchen Weaver, *Band Leaders*, November 1944, 41.
5. "How Cootie Williams got his band," Skippy Adelman, *PM's Sunday Picture News*, July 8, 1945, m4.
6. "Good Music, That's All," Gretchen Weaver, *Band Leaders*, November 1944, 41.
7. "How Cootie Williams got his band," Skippy Adelman, *PM's Sunday Picture News*, July 8, 1945, m4.
8. "How Charles Williams Got the Tag, 'Cootie,'" Fredi Washington, *The People's Voice*, September 16, 1944, 22.
9. "Good Music, That's All," Gretchen Weaver, *Band Leaders*, November 1944, 41. This statement implies that Williams didn't have investors, yet other interviews and articles say he did.
10. Syndicated Walter Winchell column, *Philadelphia Inquirer*, February 27, 1945.
11. *Duke Ellington in Person*, Ellington, 70.
12. "John Hammond says," John Hammond, *The People's Voice*, October 24, 1942, 36.
13. "Rowe's Notebook," Billy Rowe, *Pittsburgh Courier*, 6 December 1941, 20.
14. Arnett Cobb JOHP interview.
15. Williams JOHP.
16. Williams JOHP.
17. Death certificate of William Luper, Missouri State Board of Health.
18. "How Cootie Williams got his band," Skippy Adelman, *PM's Sunday Picture News*, July 8, 1945, m4.
19. John Simmons JOHP.
20. "Out of Billy Rowe's Harlem Note Book," Billy Rowe, *Pittsburgh Courier*, December 11, 1937, 20.
21. "An Autobiography of Black Jazz," Travis, 418.
22. Holmes died on September 19, 1985, just four days after Cootie.
23. In the 1930 US census, Holmes was listed as a lodger with Harry and Dorothy Carney's apartment at 235 W. 146th Street.
24. Charlie Holmes JOHP interview, (11/29)–21.
25. Holmes JOHP.
26. Williams JOHP.
27. Williams JOHP.
28. Holmes JOHP.
29. "Portrait: Butch Ballard," *Modern Drummer*, June 1982.
30. "Cootie Williams's New Band Impressive in Harlem Rehearsal Hall," *Down Beat*, February 1, 1942, 2.
31. "'Unity and Lincoln' Air Topic," *Pittsburgh Press*, February 11, 1942, 20.
32. "The Duke Where and When," www.tdwaw.ca.
33. "Tapping the Wires," Harold Jovien, *Cleveland Call and Post*, December 20, 1941.
34. "'Cootie' Williams Stars on Discs Made by Jack Leonard," *Chicago Defender*, December 27, 1941.

35. "That Hot Horn Is Cootie's!" *Down Beat*, December 15, 1941, 15.
36. "Williams to Play," *Evening Bulletin*, November 29, 1941, 2.
37. "Tapping the Wires," Harold Jovien, *Cleveland Call and Post*, December 20, 1941, 9B.
38. "Cootie's Silence Worries His Fans," *Chicago Defender*, December 20, 1941, 21.
39. "Cootie Kills Him," *Music and Rhythm*, January 1942, 41.
40. "Cootie Kills Him."
41. "The Duke Where and When," www.tdwaw.ca.
42. Like Cootie, Walton was born in Mobile. It's unknown if they knew each other in their early years.
43. "I Tried to Team New & Old Stars," Cootie Williams, *Music and Rhythm*, May 1942, 31.
44. Holmes JOHP interview, 29.
45. "I Tried to Team New & Old Stars," Cootie Williams, *Music and Rhythm*, May 1942, 31.
46. "Benny Goodman, Glenn Miller Voted Champs!" *Down Beat*, January 1, 1942, 1.
47. "'Home Team' Loses to Benny Goodman Band," Herbert Elwell, *Cleveland Plain Dealer*, January 5, 1942.
48. "Swing Band, Symphony Orchestra 'Clash' Tonight In Unique Concert At the Mosque," *Pittsburgh Press*, January 6, 1942, 21.
49. "Benny Goodman Gets Ovation at Symphony," Donald Steinfirst, *Pittsburgh Post Gazette*, January 7, 1942, 4.
50. "Pittsburgh Upper Crust Knocks Itself Out at Goodman Concert," *The Billboard*, January 17, 1942, 11.
51. "Goodman's Drummer Stars as Swing Band Plays with Symphony," J. Fred Lissfelt, *Pittsburgh Sun-Telegraph*, January 7, 1942, 9. Lissfelt's review angered a number of readers, prompting letters of rebuttal. In reply to the letter writers, Lissfelt doubled down on his critique and amongst other things said: "I always contend that jazz is like a bad relation. He must have some good in him and so let us keep him in the family, maybe marry him off to a sturdier person who will eventually make a man of him."
52. Besides Cootie Williams, the band includes Benny Goodman, Benny Carter, J. C. Higginbotham, and Charlie Barnet.
53. "National Grapevine," Charley Cherokee, *Chicago Defender*, February 7, 1942, 15.
54. "Goodman's 'Swing' Thrills Audience at Concert Here," *Evening Star*, January 26, 1942, B-9.
55. "On the upbeat: Starting again at 72," T. J. Ryder, *Des Moines Register*, May 27, 1980, 13.
56. "Fresh Perspectives on the D.A.R.'s Rebuff of Marian Anderson," William H. Honan, *New York Times*, May 18, 1993.
57. "U.S. Jive Jottings," *Melody Maker*, April 11, 1942, 5.
58. "B.G. D.C. Concert Smash Success," *Metronome*, March 1942, 9.
59. "*Down Beat*, 60 Years of Jazz," 54.
60. Advertisement, *Music and Rhythm*, August 1942, 49.
61. "Cootie Williams's New Band Impressive in Harlem Rehearsal Hall," *Down Beat*, February 1, 1942, 2.
62. *The World of Earl Hines*, Dance, 251.
63. *The World of Earl Hines*, Dance, 251.
64. "Joe Doesn't Talk Much Even at a Party in His Own Honor," *New York Amsterdam News*, January 17, 1942.

17. FLY RIGHT

1. *The World of Earl Hines*, Dance, 92.
2. "Swingin' the News," Al Monroe, *Chicago Defender*, January 31, 1942.
3. "Ellington right at home in Chicago," Lloyd Sachs, *Chicago Sun-Times*, April 4, 1999, xx.
4. "Tab Cootie Williams' Band for Future Delivery, Gang," *Chicago Defender*, February 14, 1942, 21.
5. "On the Stand, Cootie Williams reviewed at Earle Theater, Philadelphia," *Variety*, July 15, 1944, 14.
6. "Swingin' the News," Al Monroe, *Chicago Defender*, February 14, 1942, 20.
7. "Benny Goodman Praises 'Cootie' Williams' New Band at Broadcast," *Chicago Defender*, February 21, 1942, 21.
8. "Benny Goodman Praises 'Cootie' Williams' New Band at Broadcast."
9. Holmes JOHP.
10. Holmes JOHP interview, 28.
11. *World of Swing*, Dance, 256.
12. "Detroit Topics," Rollo S. Vest, *Chicago Defender*, May 16, 1942, 23.
13. Holmes JOHP interview, 27.
14. "Williams, Waller Broadcasting," Harold Jovien, *New Journal and Guide*, February 14, 1942, A15.
15. "What's on the Air," *Wisconsin State Journal*, February 20, 1942, 16.
16. *World of Swing*, Dance, 74.
17. "Cootie Williams Given Trophy," *Chicago Defender*, March 28, 1942, 22.
18. "Theatricals," *Pittsburgh Courier*, March 28, 1942, 21.
19. "Rowe's Notebook," Billy Rowe, *Pittsburgh Courier*, March 14, 1942, 20.
20. "How Cootie Williams got his band," Skippy Adelman, *PM's Sunday Picture News*, July 8, 1945, m4.
21. The composer of "Sleepy Valley" is listed as unknown in its various reissues, but according to a review in the June 1942 issue of *Metronome*, it was written by Cootie Williams.
22. Composed by Victor Schertzinger, "Marcheta" was written in 1913.
23. "Cootie Cuts Four Sides on Okeh," *Down Beat*, April 15, 1942, 5.
24. "Cootie's "Flying High" Despite Short Shellac," *Baltimore Afro-American*, April 25, 1942, 13.
25. "Cootie Williams cuts for [sic] Sides for Okeh," *Atlanta Daily World*, April 27, 1942.
26. "Holdouts," Ulanov, *Metronome*, September 1943, 14.
27. "Eddie Lockjaw Davis," Bob Rusch and Kathy Joyce, *Cadence*, January 1988, 13.
28. "Jam Concerts Successful; Booked Ahead Next Year," *Pittsburgh Courier*, April 11, 1942, 21.
29. "D.A.R. Ices Condon, Jazz Is Too Impudent," Willie Weed, *Down Beat*, March 11, 1946, 2.
30. "I Tried to Team New & Old Stars," Cootie Williams, *Music and Rhythm*, May 1942, 31.
31. "I Tried to Team New & Old Stars."
32. "Coot Band on Upbeat," Bob Locke, *Down Beat*, April 15, 1942, 8.

18. BACK TO NEW YORK

1. "How Cootie Williams got his band," Skippy Adelman, *PM's Sunday Picture News*, July 8, 1945, m4.
2. "How Cootie Williams got his band."
3. "How Cootie Williams got his band."
4. "The Negro Makes Advances," *The Billboard*, January 2, 1943, 28.
5. "On the Upbeat," *Variety*, May 13, 1942, 42.
6. "Cootie to Apollo; Then Hits Road," *The People's Voice*, May 16, 1942, 27.
7. "House Reviews," *Variety*, May 20, 1942, 23.
8. "Band Reviews," *Variety*, June 10, 1942, 42.
9. "Cootie, Woody, Jimmy Click on Stage," Ulanov, *Metronome*, June 1942, 20.
10. "Cootie, Woody, Jimmy Click on Stage."
11. "Cootie, Woody, Jimmy Click on Stage."
12. "Billy Rowe's Notebook," *Pittsburgh Courier*, May 30, 1942, 20.
13. "Billy Rowe's Notebook," *Pittsburgh Courier*, June 27, 1942, 21.
14. "Let's Buy a Band," *Music and Rhythm*, April 1942, 45.
15. *Music and Rhythm*, May 1942, 30.
16. "Band Rating," *Music and Rhythm*, May 1942, 31.
17. Williams JOHP.
18. "Solid Meddlin," *The People's Voice*, June 20, 1942, 25.
19. "Original Duke Ellington music top priority for son," Luaine Lee, *Fort Worth Star-Telegram*, May 10, 1982, 25.
20. "I Was Jealous of My Father," Mercer Ellington, *Negro Digest*, May 1951, 56.
21. "New York Beat," *Jet*, June 24, 1954, 47.

19. THE IMPACT OF WAR

1. *BG On the Record*, D. Russell Conner and Warren W. Hicks, 329.
2. "War's Progress to Determine Extent of Coffee, Tea Rations," Alexander B. George, *Standard-Star*, June 4, 1942, 4.
3. National Archives website, https://www.archives.gov/research/guide-fed-records/groups/219.html.
4. "Busses Yanked, Leaving Negro Bands Jim-Crowed on One-Night Stands," *Variety*, June 24, 1942, 41.
5. "Uncle Sam Nabbed Leaders' Buses . . . But Not These," *Music and Rhythm*, August 1942, 13.
6. "Band Leaders Scribe for PV," *The People's Voice*, June 13, 1942, 28.
7. "Future Looks Gloomy Says Cootie Williams," Cootie Williams, *The People's Voice*, June 20, 1942, 27.
8. "Future 'Looks Bad' For Race Bands Says Cootie Williams in Interview," *Philadelphia Tribune*, August 8, 1942, 15.
9. "Future 'Looks Bad' For Race Bands Says Cootie Williams in Interview."

10. "Around Boston," Paul Rhone, *Chicago Defender*, July 18, 1942, 22.
11. "Bands on Tour," *The Billboard*, July 4, 1942, 24.
12. "Dartmouth Green Key to hold Prom August 8," *Yale Daily News*, July 27, 1942, 6.
13. "Encores and Echoes," E. Billingsworth, *Baltimore Afro-American*, August 1, 1942, 10.
14. "Sweet and Low-Down," George Frazier, *Boston Herald*, July 14, 1942, 11.
15. "Orks Drop Like Flies," *The Billboard*, July 18, 1942, 19.
16. "Negroes to Get a Break," *The Billboard*, June 6, 1942, 6.
17. "CBS Wants Scott to Lead Combo Ork," *The Billboard*, July 11, 1942, 6.
18. "'Powerhouse' Re-order," *Variety*, May 6, 1942, 31.
19. If you're not familiar with "Powerhouse" from the title alone, find it on YouTube and it's guaranteed you'll recognize it instantly.
20. "Ray Scott back to Columbia," *Variety*, July 8, 1942, 41.
21. The Ellington band recorded four songs in their July 28, 1942, Chicago recording session, their last before the recording ban took effect. This is most likely the date that Vinson missed. (It was also the last studio session for Ivie Anderson and Barney Bigard.)
22. "The Stepin Fetchit of The Blues," *Metronome*, September 1943, 20.
23. "Swinging the News," Al Monroe, *Chicago Defender*, August 1, 1942, 22.
24. "Filling Chairs Not Easy," *Variety*, August 5, 1942, 48.
25. "Cootie Williams Won't Go for CBS Offer of Peanuts," *The Billboard*, August 8, 1942, 21.
26. "Bebop and the Recording Industry: The 1942 AFM Recording Ban Reconsidered," Scott DeVeaux, University of California Press on behalf of the American Musicological Society, 128, 131.
27. "USO Shows a Must for Negro Bands," *Metronome*, October 1942, 5.
28. "Cab Headed Toward Long Theatre Tour," *Jackson Advocate*, September 26, 1942, 6.
29. "Cootie Williams and Band at Camp Edison," *New Journal and Guide*, September 26, 1942, B19.
30. "Cootie Williams 'King of Swing,'" *Pittsburgh Courier*, June 26, 1943, 21.
31. U.S. WWII draft cards, 1940–1947. Ancestry.com.
32. "Music," *Billboard*, November 6, 1943, 14.
33. "Inside Stuff—Orchestras," *Variety*, May 26, 1943, 42.
34. "Bands Down to Bedrock," Elliott Grennard, *The Billboard*, January 2, 1943, 47.
35. "Rowe's Notebook," Billy Rowe, *Pittsburgh Courier*, April 17, 1943, 20.
36. Advertisement, *The People's Voice*, October 17, 1942, 29.

20. MOE GALE AND THE SAVOY BALLROOM

1. "Frankie Manning, Ambassador of Lindy Hop," Manning, 61.
2. "Negro Tootlers Get Call from NBC for Permanent Berths," *The Billboard*, October 3, 1942, 19.
3. "How Cootie Williams got his band," Skippy Adelman, *PM's Sunday Picture News*, July 8, 1945, m4.
4. "How Cootie Williams got his band," Skippy Adelman, *PM's Sunday Picture News*, July 8, 1945, m4.
5. *To Be or Not to Bop*, Gillespie and Fraser, 63.

6. Williams JOHP.

7. "Meet Bill Kenny, First Tenor of the Ink Spots," Michael Carter, *Baltimore Afro-American*, December 2, 1944, 1.

8. "Meet Bill Kenny, First Tenor of the Ink Spots."

9. "'Fatha' Hines Comments on Race Future," Russ J. Cowans, *Michigan Chronicle*, December 2, 1944, 14.

10. *Rhythm Man*, Crease, 77.

11. *Grove Dictionary of Jazz*, 901.

12. Advertisement, *New York Age*, March 13, 1926, 6.

13. "Fletcher Henderson, Eddie Rector, Other Stage Stars at Savoy," *New York Age*, March 6, 1926, 6.

14. *Rhythm Man*, Crease, 56.

15. "Orchestra Grosses," *Variety*, September 2, 1942, 46.

16. "Louis Armstrong set to record . . . ," Onah L. Spencer, *Down Beat*, January 1939, 4.

17. Barney Bigard JOHP.

18. "Band Briefs," *Pittsburgh Courier*, October 10, 1942, 21.

19. "Cootie's Crew Worthy of Its Leader," Barry Ulanov, *Metronome*, October 10, 1942, 10 and 24.

20. Band Reviews, *Variety*, May 19, 1943, 34.

21. "'Cootie dated enough to draw tears,' says Hallock," Ted Hallock, *Down Beat*, April 4, 1952, 8.

22. 3-A was assigned for Hardship Deferment, while 4-F meant not qualified for military service. Selective Service website, www.sss.gov.

23. "Cootie's Crew Worthy of Its Leader," Barry Ulanov, *Metronome*, October 10, 1942, 10 and 24.

24. House Review, Apollo, *Variety*, January 27, 1943, 39.

25. *Ain't Nothing Like the Real Thing*, Carlin and Conwill, 100.

26. Williams JOHP.

27. Williams JOHP.

28. *The Raw Pearl*, Bailey, 33.

29. *The Raw Pearl*, Bailey, 33.

30. "Business humming in Baltimore," *Metronome*, November 1942, 27.

31. "Back to the Piano, Nat," Harold Jovien, *Chicago Defender*, March 20, 1943, 18.

21. TRUMPET STUDENT

1. "Concerto for Cootie," John Hammond, *Down Beat*, 7 May 1952, 6. Recalling the story nearly ten years after it happened, Hammond got the gist of the story correct, but missed a lot of details. According to Cootie's trumpet teacher at the time, William Costello, Cootie was actually scheduled to perform the piece, but it conflicted with other gigs. Williams asked Costello for a recommendation for a substitute. Costello suggested another one of his students, a sixteen-year-old named Johnny Vohs, who performed at the concert with "smoothness and dispatch." And the trumpet he used that night had come from "an Eighth Avenue hock shop"! (According to Costello, the F trumpet Cootie was to use "belonged to

"Mr. [Arturo] Toscanini.") "Slide Trumpet History Again; A Kid Find," William Costello, *Metronome*, May 1943, 26. Vohs (1927–1980) would go to play with Hal McIntyre, Charlie Barnet, Claude Thornhill, and Glen Gray, to name a few.

2. "Tan Manhattan," Maurice Dancer, *Chicago Defender*, October 19, 1941, 20.

3. "Why I Quit Duke Ellington After 11 Years," Cootie Williams, *Music and Rhythm*, December 1940, 9.

4. "Jazzman Just Can't Stop Blowing That Horn," *Journal Times*, September 26, 1972, 9.

5. Origin of the Stevens-Costello Embouchure Studios for Brass Players (http://www.stevens-costellochops.com/History.html).

6. "Cootie Speaks," Bradley and Failows, 1963, 2.

7. "A Lot of Brass," William Costello, *Metronome*, December 1937, 42.

8. "Doubling in Brass," John O'Donnell, *Down Beat*, April 1, 1942, 17.

9. The Vocabell provided the "first true bell given to a band instrument. The first to provide against disturbing vibration factors which muffle and distort tone" resulting in "glorious new tonal beauty which will thrill you as it has thrilled every artist who has blown the CONNQUERER."

10. Advertisement, *Metronome*, June 1932, ii.

11. Ad for Rudy Mück trumpets, *Down Beat*, December 15, 1940, 6.

12. Barrie Lee Hall interview with author.

13. "Cootie Williams Discusses the Trumpet," Cootie Williams, *Music and Rhythm*, October 1941, 29.

14. "Reminiscing with Cootie," Eric Townley, *Storyville*, June-July 1977, 173.

15. "On the upbeat: Starting again at 72," T. J. Ryder, *Des Moines Register*, May 27, 1980, 13.

22. CLOSING AT THE SAVOY

1. "Platterbrains," *Metronome*, March 1943, 15.

2. "The Lighter Side," Ann Petry, *The People's Voice*, January 2, 1943, 26.

3. *The Duke's Diary, Part One*, Vail, 227.

4. "The Lighter Side," Ann Petry, *The People's Voice*, January 2, 1943, 26.

5. "Solid Meddlin'," Marienne Boyd, *The People's Voice*, January 2, 1943, 24.

6. "The Listening File," *The People's Voice*, December 26, 1942, 35.

7. "Count Basie," *Music and Rhythm*, June 1942, 45.

8. "Eddie Lockjaw Davis," Bob Rusch and Kathy Joyce, *Cadence*, January 1988, 13.

9. Charlie Holmes JOHP.

10. "Radio Reviews—Duke, Disciple Shine," Will Roland, *Metronome*, May 1943, 18.

11. "Cootie Williams and Band Score at N. Y. Savoy," Ted Yates, *Chicago Defender*, April 3, 1943, 18.

12. "Krupa Admits One Charge; Savoy Closed," *Metronome*, May 1943, 7.

13. "Stompin' at the Savoy," *Metronome*, June 1943, 5.

14. "Vice Charges Against Savoy 'Lies,' Walter White Tells LaGuardia," Grant O'Neal, *Baltimore Afro-American*, May 1, 1943, 8.

15. "Mixed Dancing Closed Savoy Ballroom!" *New York Amsterdam News*, May 1, 1943, 1.

16. "Savoy Closing Puts 3 Bands Out of Work," *Down Beat*, May 15, 1943, 1.

23. FILM VODVIL

1. "'Cootie', Band to Make Short," *New York Amsterdam News*, June 19, 1943, 17.
2. "Cootie Williams and his Orchestra," Mark Cantor, https://www.jazz-on-film.com/cootie-williams-and-his-orchestra/.
3. *To Be or Not to Bop*, Gillespie and Fraser, 168.
4. Holmes JOHP.
5. "The Douglas Brothers of Harlem Tops," *Chicago Defender*, April 10, 1943, 18.
6. "Cootie Williams and his Orchestra," Mark Cantor, https://www.jazz-on-film.com/cootie-williams-and-his-orchestra/.
7. "Yankee Jazz Beat," George A. Borgman, The *Mississippi Rag*, June 2001, 8.
8. "Band Reviews," *Variety*, May 19, 1943, 34.
9. While Russell Williams and Leon James started their dancing careers as members of Whitey's Lindy Hoppers, this foursome was not that group (Cantor).
10. "Cootie Williams and his Orchestra," Mark Cantor, https://www.jazz-on-film.com/cootie-williams-and-his-orchestra/.
11. "'Cootie,' Band to Make Short," *New York Amsterdam News*, June 19, 1943, 17.
12. Dave Penny, liner notes to the album *Billy Eckstine and Cootie Williams 1944*, August 1988.
13. "How Cootie Williams got his band," Skippy Adelman, *PM's Sunday Picture News*, July 8, 1945, m4.
14. "Short Reviews," *Showmen's Trade Review*, October 23, 1943, 37.
15. "Short Reviews, Novelty," *The Exhibitor*, October 6, 1943, 1383.
16. "Short Subjects Reviews," *Motion Picture Daily*, October 25, 1943, 3.
17. "Encores and Echoes," E. B. Rea, *Baltimore Afro-American*, April 29, 1944, 20.
18. "House Reviews, Apollo, NY," *Variety*, August 4, 1943, 41.
19. "Cootie Williams Still Sending 'Em," *New York Amsterdam News*, July 17, 1943, 15.
20. "Williams Plays Tonight," *Chattanooga Times*, September 24, 1943, 3.
21. "Business on Upsurge Among 'Name' Bands," *Pittsburgh Courier*, July 24, 1943, 21.
22. "'Cootie' Williams, Billy Eckstein [sic] Featured on Fays Theatre Stage," *Philadelphia Tribune*, October 16, 1943, 14.
23. "Cootie Nixes BG Booty," *Metronome*, September 1943, 7.
24. "How Cootie Williams got his band," Skippy Adelman, *PM's Sunday Picture News*, July 8, 1945, m4.
25. "Music of Cootie Thing of Beauty," Leonard Feather, *Metronome*, September 1943, 24.
26. "Band Reviews," *Variety*, May 19, 1943, 34.
27. "Reminiscing with Cootie," Townley, *Storyville*, 172.
28. "Savoy Reopens: Scale Raised," *Metronome*, November 1943, 7.
29. "802 Hikes Savoy Scale to $50; Ends Old Feud," *The Billboard*, November 6, 1943, 14.
30. "Savoy "Premiere" Draws Capacity; Turn Away 5,000," *The People's Voice*, October 30, 1943, 36.
31. "'Cootie' Williams, Sultans Score at Savoy Reopening," *Pittsburgh Courier*, October 30, 1943, 19.
32. "On the Stand: Cootie Williams," *The Billboard*, November 13, 1943, 17.
33. "House Reviews," Apollo, *Variety*, December 1, 1943, 18.

24. A RETURN TO THE STUDIO

1. "*Esquire*'s All-American Jazz Band," Robert Goffin, *Esquire*, February 1944, 29.
2. "*Esquire*'s All-American Band," Robert Goffin, *Esquire*, February 1943, 74.
3. "I've Been Around," Ted Yates, *New York Age*, December 11, 1943, 11.
4. "Bands Dug by The Beat," TAC, *Down Beat*, February 15, 1944, 12.
5. "Cootie Gets Break; Long Theater Tour," *The People's Voice*, December 4, 1943, 29.
6. "Ink Spots Heading New $9,500 Package," *Variety*, December 1, 1943, 39.
7. "Kenny of Ink Spots Banks on Brain as well as Vocal Chords," *Chicago Defender*, July 21, 1945, 14.
8. "Moe Gale Plans Unit for Ella, Ink Spots and Savoy Hoppers," *Pittsburgh Courier*, February 24, 1940, 20.
9. *Ella Fitzgerald, 1935–1948*, Vail, 52.
10. "Swing the News," Al Monroe, *Chicago Defender*, January 22, 1944, 8.
11. "The Petrillo Ban of 1942–'44: Past & Future at War," John McDonough, *Down Beat*, August 16, 2022, https://downbeat.com/news/detail/the-petrillo-ban-of-194244-past-future-at-war.
12. "Hollywood Periscope," *Metronome*, December 1943, 10.
13. "The Music Whirl," *St. Louis Globe-Democrat*, February 3, 1944, 9.
14. "Madriguera, Williams to Wax for Oberstein," *Variety*, January 5, 1944, 112.
15. "Oberstein Signs Bands," *Down Beat*, June 15, 1944, 16.
16. "Discs cut in Mexico, Says Eli," *Down Beat*, November 1, 1942, 1.
17. "Eddie Lockjaw Davis," Bob Rusch and Kathy Joyce, *Cadence*, January 1988, 13.
18. "Record Reviews," Feather and Ulanov, *Metronome*, August 1944, 34.
19. "Record Reviews," Feather and Ulanov, *Metronome*, August 1944, 34.
20. *Variety* describes her new act at the Village Vanguard and says she's "formerly with Cootie Williams" in the February 10, 1943, issue of *Variety*. But later reviews show her singing with the band up until mid-May 1943. During the last week of December 1943, she opened as part of a show at a new but short-lived incarnation of the Cotton Club.
21. *The Raw Pearl*, Bailey, 33.
22. "Recorded Music News and Reviews," Cliff Bradt, *Knickerbocker News*, February 11, 1944, 9.
23. *Pop Memories 1890–1954*, Whitburn, 457.
24. "Night Club Reviews: Four Queens, Las Vegas," *Variety*, February 17, 1988, 175.
25. Oddly, the label on the Williams version credits the song to someone named "Haggart"; could it be bassist Bob Haggart?
26. *The Autobiography of Malcolm X*, Haley, 89. (Malcolm X misremembered part of the lyrics as the title.)
27. "Radio: WOV's Lily White Disc Policy K.O.'s 'Red Blues,' Done So Jive'll Thrive," *Variety*, November 29, 1944, 23.
28. *Pop Memories 1890–1954*, Whitburn, 457.
29. "How Cootie Williams got his band," Skippy Adelman, *PM's Sunday Picture News*, July 8, 1945, m4.
30. *The Billboard Book of Top 40 R&B and Hip-Hop Hits*, Whitburn, 623.
31. "One God—One People," Ben Richardson, *The People's Voice*, July 8, 1944, 22.

32. *Pop Memories 1890–1954*, Whitburn, 457.
33. "Billy Rowe's Notebook," Billy Rowe, *Pittsburgh Courier*, May 30, 1942, 20.
34. "Rating the Records . . . ," Frank Marshall Davis, *New Journal and Guide*, February 27, 2943, B22.
35. "The Rhythm Section," Miller and Feather, *Esquire*, July 1944, 94.
36. "Inkspots, Ella Fitzgerald Score with Williams at Temple," George L. David, *Rochester Democrat and Chronicle*, January 8, 1944, 7.
37. *Ella Fitzgerald*, Nicholson, 36.
38. *Rhythm Man*, Crease, 280.
39. "Exploding the Myth in Sat Eve Post About Negro Artists," Charlie Michelson, *Music and Rhythm*, November 1941, 18.
40. "Gale Vaudeville Unit Rated Tops on Tour," Izzy Rowe, *Pittsburgh Courier*, February 5, 1944, 17.
41. "Moke & Poke Jammed on Reefer Charges," *Variety*, January 12, 1944, 55.
42. "Moke & Poke Jammed on Reefer Charges."
43. "Out in Front . . . with E. B. Radcliffe," *Cincinnati Enquirer*, January 15, 1944.
44. "Bobbing Along with Bob Williams," Bob Williams, *Cleveland Call and Post*, February 12, 1944, 10B.
45. Williams Family Tree, Ancestry.com.
46. "Bands Dug by the Beat," Clyde Lucas, *Down Beat*, March 1, 1944, 4.
47. "Notes for You," William L. Doudna, *Wisconsin State Journal*, March 1, 1944.
48. "Ink Spots-Williams and Fitzgerald Up 'World' to Boff $25,000, Mpls.," *Variety*, February 23, 1944, 14.
49. Charlie Holmes JOHP interview, 40.
50. On February 12, 1944, the second day of the show's time in Omaha, the low temperature for the day was -19 degrees Fahrenheit. (www.weather.gov).
51. "Ella-Spots-Cootie Terrific on Road," *Pittsburgh Courier*, February 26, 1944, 15.
52. "In the Groove," *Central High Register*, February 18, 1944, 2.
53. "What the Critics Say," *Quad-City Times*, March 19, 1944, 27.
54. "Odds and Ends," Fredi Washington, *The People's Voice*, April 8, 1944, 31.
55. "All-Negro Show Draws Crowd," *Hanford Sentinel*, April 22, 1944, 2.
56. "Night Clubs-Vaudeville," *The Billboard*, May 6, 1944, 27.
57. "Cocktail-Band Vaude Grosses," *The Billboard*, May 13, 1944, 21.
58. "Cootie Williams," *Metronome*, June 1944, 30.
59. "'Ink Spots' Acclaimed at Orpheum," Neil Rau, *Los Angeles Examiner*, April 26, 1944, 3.
60. "The Encyclopedia of Old-Time Radio," Dunning, 376.
61. "Coast-to-Coast," Walter Winchell, *Daily Times*, July 8, 1944, 8.
62. "Swinging the News," Al Monroe, *Chicago Defender*, May 6, 1944, 8.
63. "Odds and Ends," Fredi Washington, *The People's Voice*, June 17, 1944, 26.
64. "Odds and Ends," Fredi Washington, *The People's Voice*, June 3, 1944, 26.
65. "Odds and Ends," Fredi Washington, *The People's Voice*, July 1, 1944, 26.
66. "Headlines Footlights," Fredi Washington, *The People's Voice*, June 10, 1944, 21.
67. "Norman Granz, the man who used jazz for justice," Hershorn, 212.
68. An example includes the Colored June German dance in Rocky Mount, North Carolina, in 1954.

69. "Keynotes," Alyce Key, *Los Angeles Sentinel*, April 4, 1946, 20.

70. *Rhythm Man*, Crease, 224.

71. "Exploding the Myth in Sat Eve Post about Negro Artists," Charlie Michelson, *Music and Rhythm*, November 1941, 18.

72. "Ella Fitzgerald and Ensemble Perform for Soldiers at Tuskegee," *New York Age*, July 1, 1944, 10.

73. "Ella, Ink Spots, Cootie Headline TAAF Theater Opening," *New Journal and Guide*, June 17, 1944, B17. (The photos in the article were official US Army Air Force documents. Unfortunately, Smithsonian National Air and Space Museum and the National Archives could find no trace of them.)

74. "The Tuskegee Airfields," Daniel L. Haulman, 2014, https://www.airandspaceforces.com/article/0614tuskegee/.

75. "Stark Patients Hear Musical Ink Spots," *Charleston Evening Post*, June 3, 1944, 5.

76. "Good Music . . . that's all!" Gretchen Weaver, *Band Leaders*, November 1944, 40.

77. House Review, Stanley, Pitt, *Variety*, June 21, 1944, 22.

78. "The New Film," Harold V. Cohen, *Pittsburgh Post Gazette*, June 17, 1944, 12.

79. "Ray Brown Interview," Alwyn and Laurie Lewis, *Cadence*, September 1993, 14.

80. *Ella Fitzgerald*, Nicholson, 80.

81. Holmes JOHP interview, 41.

82. *Ella Fitzgerald*, Nicholson, 81.

83. "Our Stars Reap Golden Harvest In '44," George F. Brown, *Pittsburgh Courier*, December 30, 1944, 13.

84. "Billie Holiday Breaking Records," *Chicago Defender*, August 25, 1945, 14.

85. "Benny Carter," *Philadelphia Tribune*, September 23, 1944, 14.

25. 'ROUND MIDNIGHT

1. Holmes JOHP interview, 42.

2. "He Knows Why He Got in the Business," Calvin Ahlgren, *San Francisco Examiner*, May 1, 1983, 226.

3. "Cooling Off Hot Trumpet," *Philadelphia Tribune*, August 12, 1944, 15.

4. *Duke's Diary, Part One*, Vail, 257.

5. "Swinging the News," Al Monroe, *Chicago Defender*, August 19, 1944, 6.

6. Cummings Guest House, National Park Service website, https://www.nps.gov/places/cummings-guest-house.htm.

7. "Old Orchard Beach Socko with Stars," *Metronome*, September 1940, 10.

8. "Louis Jordan: Son of Arkansas, Father of R&B," Koch, 37.

9. Williams JOHP.

10. Thanks to bassist Kevin O'Neal for bringing this item to my attention.

11. *Boy Meets Horn*, Stewart, 124.

12. *Thelonious Monk*, Kelley, 450.

13. "Pop Record Reviews," *Billboard*, January 27, 1945, 64.

14. "Round Midnight," Jazz Standards, https://www.jazzstandards.com/compositions-0/roundmidnight.htm.

15. "Bill Doggett, 80, Keyboard Player and Rhythm-and-Blues Innovator," Peter Watrous, *New York Times*, November 20, 1996, 21.

16. *Wail*, Pullman, 5.

17. Williams JOHP.

18. *Reminiscing in Tempo*, Reig with Berger, 21.

19. Williams JOHP.

20. Williams JOHP.

21. "Good Music, That's All," Gretchen Weaver, *Band Leaders*, November 1944, 41.

22. "Lockjaw Davis—a musician who matters," *Jazz Journal*, September 1970, 10.

23. *Wail*, Pullman, 402.

24. *Wail*, Pullman, 43.

25. Williams JOHP.

26. Holmes JOHP.

27. *Wail*, Pullman, 49.

28. Williams JOHP.

29. Williams JOHP.

30. "Cootie May Get a Role," *Pittsburgh Courier*, January 16, 1943, 21.

31. "In the Big City," Richard Dier, *Baltimore Afro-American*, March 3, 1945, 5.

32. "'SYWA' and Raphaelson Play Main Events of Boston Week," *Hollywood Reporter*, September 26, 1944, 10.

33. "Lena Grabbing 45G's," *Hollywood Reporter*, September 27, 1944, 2.

34. "'SYWA' and Raphaelson Play Main Events of Boston Week," *Hollywood Reporter*, September 26, 1944, 10.

35. "Music: More $$ for Negro Musickers," Paul Secon, *The Billboard*, February 3, 1945, 13. (*The Billboard* gives a partial list of over forty cities played on this tour. In addition to the four earlier, they are —Johnson City, TN; Gary, IN; Akron, OH; Dayton, OH; Cincinnati, OH; Knoxville, TN; Asheville, NC; Charleston, WV; Bluefield, WV; Raleigh, NC; Greensboro, NC; Columbia, NC; Charlotte, NC; Durham, NC; Camp LeJeune, NC; Savannah, GA; Charleston, SC. In Florida, there was Jacksonville, Tampa, Ft. Lauderdale, Miami, Bartow, St. Petersburg, Orlando, Pensacola. New Orleans, LA. In Texas—Beaumont, Galveston, Houston, Port Arthur, Ft. Worth, San Antonio. Oklahoma City; Kansas City, MO; St. Louis, MO; Louisville, KY; Lexington, KY.)

36. "Music: More $$ for Negro Musickers."

37. "House Review, RKO, Boston," *Variety*, September 27, 1944, 40.

38. "'Ink Spots' Highlight New Stage Show at the Stanley," Dick Fortune, *Pittsburgh Press*, June 17, 1944, 8.

26. PERSONNEL CHANGES

1. "Here's How Your Favorite Entertainers Will See Action During the Holidays," *Chicago Defender*, December 23, 1944, 7.

2. "Swing the News," *Chicago Defender*, December 23, 1944, 7.

3. World War II US Army enlistment records, 1938–1946. Ancestry.com.

4. *Reminiscing in Tempo*, Reig, 13.

5. "Goodbye Mr. Cleanhead," Tim Porter, TravelingBoy.com.
6. Cootie would go to nightclubs and attend jam sessions to scout for talent. One such jam session, held at the Heat Wave (266 W. 145th St.) on January 21, included Cootie Williams and drummer Chris Columbus billed as featured guest stars. The other musicians included Franz Jackson on tenor, Leo Guarnieri (brother of pianist Johnny) on bass, and Charlie Parker on alto sax. "Back Door Stuff," Dan Burley, *New York Amsterdam News*, January 27, 1945, 12A. (In 1942, the New York Musicians' Union, Local 802 attempted to police jam sessions in which their member musicians weren't paid. Often the names of "top-flight Negro jazz men" like "Cootie Williams, Cosy [sic] Cole, Albert Ammons . . . [etc.]" were "often used as bait" to attract other musicians and audiences.) "802 Cracks Down on Jam Sesh Gag," *The Billboard*, November 7, 1942, 21.
7. Williams JOHP.
8. Williams JOHP.
9. Holmes JOHP.
10. *Collected Works*, Balliett, 209.
11. "All-American Jazz Ballot, 1945," Leonard G. Feather, *Esquire*, February 1945, 28.
12. "Cops Esquire Award," *Pittsburgh Courier*, April 14, 1945, 13.
13. "Shaw will sing with new firm," *Down Beat*, December 15, 1945, 6.
14. Advertisement, *The Billboard*, December 23, 1944, 15.
15. "I've Been Around," Ted Yates, *New York Age*, March 4, 1944, 11.
16. "Midnight Curfew Causing Howl," *Victoria Advocate*, February 20, 1945, 1.
17. "That Time the US Government Made All Bars in America Close at Midnight," Sabrina Doyle, *Smithsonian Magazine*, February 2014, https://www.smithsonianmag.com/smart-news/that-time-the-government-made-all-bars-in-america-close-at-midnight-180949915/.
18. "Business Is Lousy and Town Is Blue as Curfew Rings," *Daily News*, February 27, 1945, 1.
19. "Earl Wilson," *Daily News*, February 23, 1945, 38.
20. "On Broadway with Dorothy Kilgallen," *Pittsburgh Post-Gazette*, March 27, 1945, 22.
21. "How Cootie Williams got his band," Skippy Adelman, *PM's Sunday Picture News*, July 8, 1945, m4.
22. "Tops in their World," *Pittsburgh Courier*, March 17, 1945, 13.
23. "That Time the US Government Made All Bars In America Close At Midnight," Sabrina Doyle, *Smithsonian Magazine*, February 2014, https://www.smithsonianmag.com/smart-news/that-time-the-government-made-all-bars-in-america-close-at-midnight-180949915/.
24. "House Reviews, Paramount," *Variety*, March 7, 1945, 25.
25. "Picture Grosses: 'Affairs' Great 31G in Philly," *Variety*, May 16, 1945, 32.
26. "The Drama Desk," *Pittsburgh Post-Gazette*, May 15, 1945, 20.
27. "Ink Spots, Ella Fitzgerald Share Honors as Stanley Returns Briefly to Stage Shows," Dick Fortune, *Pittsburgh Press*, May 5, 1945, 6.
28. "House Review," *Variety*, May 16, 1945, 49.
29. "Ella Fitzgerald Fails to Show Up Opening Day at Howard, Wash." *Variety*, May 23, 1945, 48.
30. "Dan Burley's Back Door Stuff," Dan Burley, *New York Amsterdam News*, May 26, 1945, 14A.
31. Advertisement, *Hartford Courant*, May 25, 1945, 5.

27. CAPITOL RECORDS

1. "Cootie & Ella on the Cover," *Down Beat*, July 15, 1945, 2.
2. "What's New on Disking Front," *The Billboard*, June 16, 1945, 65.
3. "Majestic Loses Cootie Williams to Capitol Disks," *The Billboard*, June 9, 1945, 33.
4. *Capitol News*, May 1945, 1.
5. "Billy Rowe's Notebook," Billy Rowe, *Pittsburgh Courier*, June 9, 1945, 9.
6. "Playback," Dave Dexter, 85.
7. "Classic Capitol Jazz Session," Mosaic Records, liner notes by Dan Morgenstern.
8. "Juice Head Baby" was used as part of the soundtrack for *L.A. Noir*, an elaborate 2011 video game set in 1947 Los Angeles.
9. Daylie would go on to become a disk jockey and use the name "Daddy-O" Daylie. Cannonball Adderley named the song "One for Daddy-O" in his honor.
10. World War II Hospital Admission Card Files, Ancestry.com.
11. "Cootie Williams Has Sensational Hit," *Omaha Star*, August 3, 1945, 6.
12. "'Mood for Coot' New Disc Hit," *New Journal and Guide*, July 21, 1945, 13.
13. "Orchestra Leader Has Sensational Hit," *New York Age*, July 21, 1945, 10.
14. "House Review, Apollo, NY," *Variety*, September 18, 1946, 49.
15. "Stage Show Reviews," *Metronome*, September 1945, 28.
16. "On the Records," Dewey Dunn, *Capital Times*, September 16, 1945.
17. "4 Ink Spots, Blues Singer Applauded," *Michigan Chronicle*, December 9, 1944, 15.
18. "Cootie Williams Pleases Crowd at Nightingale Club," *Cleveland Call and Post*, November 23, 1946, 3B.
19. "Dan Burley's Back Door Stuff," *New York Amsterdam News*, January 6, 1945, A12.
20. "Cootie's 'House of Joy' Is Too Much for Harlem Hall," *Baltimore Afro-American*, February 23, 1946, 10.
21. "Savoy Likes 'Joy,' Not Name," *Chicago Defender*, June 15, 1946, 10.
22. "Odds and Ends," *The People's Voice*, September 8, 1945, 25.
23. "Vaudeville Reviews, Chicago, Chicago," *The Billboard*, July 7, 1945, 35.
24. "Sudden Hike in Humidity Didn't Keep 'Em Away from Apollo Show," *New York Amsterdam News*, June 23, 1945.
25. "Charlie Holmes—Interview," Shirley Klett and Al Vollmer, *Cadence*, August 1979, 8.
26. "Eddie Vinson Puts Emphasis on Youth," *Detroit Tribune*, January 15, 1949, 15.
27. "Best of Luck,' Eddie!," *Baltimore Afro-American*, September 8, 1945, 10.
28. "Cootie Williams talks to Valerie Wilmer," *Jazz Journal*, August 1967, 4.
29. "House Reviews, Apollo, New York," *Variety*, March 27, 1946, 28.
30. Robert Alphonso Merrill World War II draft registration.
31. Emails to author from Bobbi Merrill, granddaughter of Bob Merrill.
32. "Bandleaders Head Group Seeking Own Radio Outlet," *Baltimore Afro-American*, December 29, 1945, 6.
33. "New Radio Station to Open Tomorrow," C. W. Greenlea, *Atlanta Daily World*, October 2, 1949, 1.
34. "Ownership of WLIB Is Passing into Blacks' Hands," Albin Krebs, *New York Times*, June 27, 1972, 83.

35. "Cootie Williams Asks for Telephone in Car," *Detroit Tribune*, April 12, 1947, 13. It is unknown if Cootie got his phone. The FCC records from 1947 have not been digitized or indexed yet. They exist in paper form only and a manual search would cost "hundreds, if not a few thousand dollars."

36. "Cootie Applies for Wave License," *Ohio State News*, April 19, 1947, 23.

37. "Cootie Williams May Open Terrace," *Chicago Defender*, April 27, 1946, 16.

38. "Cotton Club May Return To New York Scene Negotiations My Go Through C. Williams," *New York Age*, March 1, 1947, 10.

28. MAINSTREAM PRESS ATTENTION

1. "Cootie Williams," *Look*, May 15, 1945, 78.
2. "Hot Trumpeters," *Look*, August 6, 1946, 32.
3. "In the Big City," Richard Dier, *Baltimore Afro-American*, July 21, 1945, 14.
4. "*Esquire*'s All-American Jazz Band, 1946" Leonard G. Feather, *Esquire*, February 1946, 56.
5. "Be-Bop a Flash," *Baltimore Afro-American*, May 1, 1948, 6.
6. "On the upbeat: Starting again at 72," T. J. Ryder, *Des Moines Register*, May 27, 1980, 13.
7. "That Guy Condon Is All Over Esky Jazz Book!" *Down Beat*, January 29, 1947, 17.
8. "*Esquire* passes out of the jazz picture," Barry Ulanov, *Metronome*, March 1947, 22.
9. "34 Musicians Quit Jazz-Book Board," *Baltimore Afro-American*, April 5, 1947, 6.
10. *The Jazz Years*, Feather, 92.
11. *The Jazz Years*, Feather, 92.

29. A CHANGE IN MANAGEMENT

1. "St. Louis—1945," Lynn [*sic*, Linton] Foersterling, *Jazz Music*, 11.
2. "St. Louis Swing Pic Looking Better," *Down Beat*, November 15, 1945, 15.
3. "Negro Preacher to Stand Sunday Anti-Dance Vigil," *Tulsa Daily World*, October 20, 1945, 7.
4. "Looks Like Cool Sunday for Negro Hep-Cats, Chicks," *Tulsa Daily World*, October 19, 1945, 3.
5. "Negro Dance Goes On; Starts After Midnight," *Tulsa Daily World*, October 21, 1945, 2. (One wonders how Rev. Mitchell would have reacted to the tap dancing of Bunny Briggs in "David Danced Before the Lord" in Ellington's "Concert of Sacred Music.")
6. "Ella Fitzgerald, Cootie Williams Next Week," *Gruber Guidon*, October 19, 1945, 1.
7. "Cootie Williams Follows the Duke into NY Zanzibar," *Capitol News*, October 1945, 1.
8. "Cootie Williams at Zanzibar for Ten Long Years," *Detroit Tribune*, December 8, 1945, 5.
9. "Famed Zanzibar Folds on B'way," *Baltimore Afro-American*, May 17, 1947, 6.
10. "The Bronzeville Scene," Russell A. Jackson, *Ohio State News*, March 1, 1947, 22.
11. Advertisement, *Pittsburgh Courier*, December 22, 1945, 29.
12. "Odds and Ends," Fredi Washington, *The People's Voice*, December 22, 1945, 39.
13. "Zanzibar's Greatest Show Is 'Theatre' In A Night Club," Joe Bostic, *Chicago Defender*, December 15, 1945, 14.

14. "Zanzibar Gives Talent Real Broadway Home," Fredi Washington, *The People's Voice*, December 15, 1945, 26.

15. "PV Probes NY Taxicab Bias," Rick Hurt and George Lawrence, *The People's Voice*, January 26, 1946, 2.

16. "New York Show Front," Don de Leighbur, *Chicago Bee*, January 8, 1948, 13. The column starts by asking "Is the Big Name Band Era coming to an end?"

17. "Classic Capitol Jazz Session," Mosaic Records, liner notes by Dan Morgenstern.

18. Liner notes, Johnny Mercer, *Mosaic Select* (CD box set), Billy Vera, Mosaic Records.

19. "Mercer Joins Cootie in Recording Date," *Cleveland Call and Post*, February 16, 1946, 12B.

20. "Johnny Mercer Paired on New Record with Cootie Williams," *California Eagle*, February 7, 1946, 17.

21. "New Negro Film Features Songs by Crippled Boro Girl," *New York Amsterdam News*, July 26, 1947, 13.

22. "Bojangles Pays Bonus to Cootie's Band," *New Journal and Guide*, July 20, 1946, 21.

23. *Encyclopedia Britannica* online, https://www.britannica.com/biography/Bill-Robinson.

24. "Announcing Look's All-American Amateur Swing Band," *Look*, November 12, 1946, 70.

25. "Swinging the News," Al Monroe, *Chicago Defender*, May 13, 1944, 8.

26. "Final Note: Wally Holmes," AFM newsletter, Richard Simon and Cynthia Crosby, https://www.afm47.org/press/final-note-wally-holmes/.

27. "Tampa Bay CL," https://www.cltampa.com/music/on-this-day-in-1974-the-hues-corporations-rock-the-boat-became-the-first-disco-song-to-top-the-charts.

28. "What's Next?" *Down Beat*, July 15, 1946, 20.

29. "Cootie Settles Artistic Feud," *Chicago Defender*, June 29, 1946, 10.

30. "House Reviews: Apollo, NY," *Variety*, September 18, 1946, 49.

31. "Williams Begins Tour of Dixie," *Baltimore Afro-American*, November 2, 1946, 6.

32. "Southern U. Students Name Cootie's Ork 'Band of Year,'" *Baltimore Afro-American*, November 16, 1946, 8.

33. "Fort Polk to be Renamed for New York Guardsman Henry Johnson," https://www.army.mil/article/266813/fort_polk_to_be_renamed_for_new_york_guardsman_henry_johnson.

34. "Officer Group at Texas Base Breaks Precedent for Cootie," *Ohio State News*, November 30, 1946, 24.

35. "Former 'Bad Boy' Of Mobile Given Warm H'coming," *Cleveland Call and Post*, December 14, 1946, 7B.

36. "Andy Kirk Fills Washington Dates," *Philadelphia Tribune*, August 8, 1942, 15.

37. Alabama Deaths and Burial Index 1881–1974, Ancestry.com.

38. *The Davis Avenue Story*, Davis-Horton, 149.

39. "Jazzman Just Can't Stop Blowing That Horn," *Journal Times*, September 26, 1972, 16.

40. "Cootie Plans to Glorify Race in 'Jazz Cavalcade,'" *Cleveland Call and Post*, March 15, 1947, 7B.

41. "Cootie Goes Longhair!!: Bandleader Writes Trumpet Concerto; Lasts Six Minutes," *New Journal and Guide*, October 5, 1946, 14.

42. "Cootie Williams Hits DAR Policy," *Chicago Defender*, June 1, 1946, 10.

43. "Williams Berates DAR; Fears KKK Endorsement," *Baltimore Afro-American*, June 1, 1946, 6.

44. *Encyclopedia Britannica* online, https://www.britannica.com/topic/Fair-Employment-Practices-Committee.

45. "Cootie Williams Wires FEPC Aid," *Detroit Tribune*, March 16, 1946, 13.

46. Their FBI files can be found at https://vault.fbi.gov/reading-room-index.

47. Letter to the author from the US Department of Justice regarding FOIA request 1149151-000.

48. *Encyclopedia Britannica* online, https://www.britannica.com/topic/Fair-Employment-Practices-Committee.

49. "'Seaman' Cootie Ordered Off Ship," *Chicago Defender*, September 14, 1946, 10.

50. "'Seaman' Cootie Ordered Off Ship."

51. Emails to author dated August 25, 2020, and September 2, 2020.

52. "Cootie's Band Breaks Barrier in S. C. Hotel," *Philadelphia Tribune*, September 3, 1946, 9.

53. "Cootie's Band Breaks Barrier in S. C. Hotel."

54. The hotel's next band booking was Guy Lombardo, a safer (and sweeter) choice.

55. Defined, a "race man (or woman)" is "a loyal member of the Black Race who dedicate their life to directly contributing to the betterment of Black people."—Assata Shakur.

56. "Cootie Williams to Visit Biggest Insurance Firms," *New Journal and Guide*, November 17, 1945, 17.

57. "Scuffle Jails Cab Calloway," *Columbus Daily Enquirer*, December 24, 1945, 9.

58. "Musicians Need Protection in Jim-Crow Cities," *Pittsburgh Courier*, January 5, 1946, 17.

59. "Million Dollars in Talents Support Benefit for Vet," *New York Amsterdam News*, August 10, 1946, 26.

60. "Blind Vet Receives $22,000 From Rally," *Omaha Star*, August 30, 1946, 1.

61. "Cootie's Cue Costs Band Leader $100," *Baltimore Afro-American*, October 9, 1948, 6.

30. A YEAR OF CHANGE

1. "Cootie Williams to Play for Front Page Ball," *Los Angeles Sentinel*, January 9, 1947, 20.

2. "N.Y. Newspaper Guild Picks Cootie Williams and Ork," *California Eagle*, January 2, 1947, 17.

3. "The Town Crier," *Rock Island Argus*, April 30, 1947, 17.

4. "Cootie is Victim of Cowpox, does 'Cowpox Boogie,'" *Cleveland Call and Post*, May 3, 1947, 13B.

5. "The Laugh is on Maestro Cootie," *Baltimore Afro-American*, May 3, 1947, 6.

6. "'Cootie' Ork to Aid Europe's Starving," *Chicago Defender*, May 18, 1946, 10.

7. "Cootie Williams' Band Starts Food Fund," *Cleveland Call and Post*, May 11, 1946, 6B.

8. "DPs To Benefit from Williams' Tardiness Fund," *Ohio State News*, January 8, 1949, 18.

9. "Cootie, Ella, 'Inkies' Thrill B'way With Season's Topper," *Baltimore Afro-American*, February 8, 1947.

10. "Cootie, Ella, 'Inkies' Thrill B'way With Season's Topper."

11. "How Cootie Williams got his band," Skippy Adelman, *PM's Sunday Picture News*, July 8, 1945, m4.

12. "To Court We Will Go, Cry Tenants of Swanky '555,'" *The People's Voice*, March 23, 1946, 4.

13. World War II draft registration for Charles Melvin Williams. In the 1939 passenger list for the Ellington band's European tour, Williams listed his address as 470 W. 159th Street. (Note: Paul Robeson also lived at 555 Edgecombe Avenue. The apartment building was designated a National Historic Landmark on December 8, 1976, as "The Paul Robeson Residence.")

14. "Swinging the News," Al Monroe, *Chicago Defender*, May 18, 1946, 10.
15. *St. Albans*, Serant, 39.
16. "The Chronicler," Lillian Scott, *Michigan Chronicle*, February 22, 1947, 6.
17. *St. Albans*, Serant, 43.
18. "Know your Boroughs: Orchestra Men Talk About Show Business," *New York Amsterdam News*, April 30, 1949, 15.
19. "Around 'n' About," Gerry Major, *New York Amsterdam News*, November 13, 1948, 12.
20. "The Long Island Scene," Sylvia Bartley, *New York Age*, October 1, 1948, 8.
21. "Duke's Kingdom Lives On and On," Stuart Troup, *Cincinnati Enquirer*, March 6, 1983, 92.
22. "Odds and Ends," Fredi Washington, *The People's Voice*, March 15, 1947, 27.
23. Williams JOHP.
24. Holmes JOHP interview, 36.
25. Williams JOHP.
26. Williams JOHP.
27. *The World of Duke Ellington*, Dance, 112.
28. *The World of Duke Ellington*, Dance, 112.
29. *The World of Duke Ellington*, Dance, 107.
30. "Joe Louis Marries a Business Woman; Rose Morgan Calls Ex-Champion 'Boss,'" *New York Times*, December 26, 1955, 12.
31. "Party Fare," *Jet*, November 25, 1954, 43. The party's $150 in booze costs is $1,632 in 2023 dollars, which averages to be only about $11 per person! There must not have been many musicians in attendance. The 1954 guest wealth of $10 million equates to $109 million in 2023 dollars.
32. "Cootie Offers Help for Joe," *Cleveland Call and Post*, May 29, 1948, 8B.
33. Ike Williams was living in Bakersfield, California, per the 1950 US federal census.
34. Williams JOHP.
35. Marriage license of Ike Williams and Truda Clabon, July 3, 1926. In some records, her name is spelled "Truda," which is most likely a reflection of how "Trudy" is pronounced with a southern accent.
36. 1930 federal census.
37. "Work to be resumed at docks today," *Houston Post*, October 5, 1931, 1.
38. Williams JOHP. In his Oral History interview, Cootie says that after his father got shot, he quit strike breaking and became a minister. The shooting occurred in 1931, yet in the 1940 census, Ike Williams still lists his occupation as longshoreman.
39. 1940 federal census.
40. California death certificate for Trudy Williams, dated September 17, 1943.
41. Williams JOHP.
42. Williams JOHP.
43. Williams JOHP.
44. Death certificate for Leroy B. Williams, New York, 1990.
45. *Jazz Magazine*, May 1959, 17.
46. Texas Death Certificate No. 65471, Ike William [sic].
47. "Mr. 1-2-5 Street," *New York Amsterdam News*, November 7, 1959, 11.
48. Texas Death Certificate No. 65471, Ike William [sic].
49. "6 Suits for Cootie on Wager," *Chicago Defender*, July 6, 1946, 16.

50. "'Frame' Costs Cootie Eight Fight Tickets," *Pittsburgh Courier*, April 24, 1948, 4.

51. Author interview with Randy Anderson, Jarvis's nephew.

52. "Cootie's 'Rainstorm' Deal Results in Bigger Profits," *Ohio State News*, March 23, 1946, 22.

53. "Florida Dancers Get Extra Music on Cootie's Bet," *Cleveland Call and Post*, December 21, 1946, 12B.

31. END OF AN ERA

1. "Horse Runs Away on Cootie's Music, Owner Tries Suit," *Cleveland Call and Post*, July 5, 1947, 6B.

2. "Cootie Williams, Ellington Trumpeter, Dead," C. Gerald Fraser, *New York Times*, September 16, 1985, 8.

3. "Cootie Williams Sued for Broken Ear Drum," *Jackson Advocate*, July 17, 1948, 3.

4. "Grow Trumpet Swingster Sets Savoy Record," *New Journal and Guide*, January 25, 1947, 5.

5. "Blizzard Socks Stem B.O.," *The Billboard*, March 8, 1947, 37.

6. "Cootie Williams Goes Great With 'Open the Door,'" *Cleveland Call and Post*, February 15, 1947, 6B.

7. *Pop Memories 1890–1954*, Whitburn, 564.

8. "Capitol Dropping Cootie Williams," *The Billboard*, January 11, 1947, 14.

9. "Playback," Dave Dexter, 117.

10. "Open the Door, Richard, The Story of a Showbiz Phenomenon," liner notes, Paul Watts.

11. "Cootie Williams Leads Diskery's Ork Sales," *Pittsburgh Courier*, March 1, 1947, 19.

12. "Majestic Coup Pulls in Cootie," *Baltimore Afro-American*, March 29, 1947, 6.

13. "Jimmy Walker Gets Job with Records Firm," *New York Herald Tribune*, February 14, 1945, 21.

14. "Strictly Ad Lib," *Down Beat*, March 1, 1945, 5.

15. "Eli Oberstein returns to RCA-Victor," *Variety*, July 25, 1945, 41.

16. "Cootie's disc of "Can't Get Started" Rivals Berigan's," *Cleveland Call and Post*, April 5, 1947, 11B.

17. "Majestic Coup Pulls in Cootie," *Baltimore Afro-American*, March 29, 1947, 6.

18. "New Singing Star Is Product of 'Sidewalks of New York,'" *Baltimore Afro-American*, June 21, 1947, 13.

19. "Record Reviews and Possibilities," *The Billboard*, May 24, 1947, 30.

20. "How Great a Jazzman Was Bunny Berigan," *Down Beat*, March 12, 1947, 12.

21. *Heart Full of Rhythm*, Riccardi, 288.

22. "Historical Parallels to Today's Inflationary Episode," White House Blog, https://www.whitehouse.gov/cea/written-materials/2021/07/06/historical-parallels-to-todays-inflationary-episode/#:~:text=In%201947%2C%20inflation%20jumped%20to,%2C%20and%20pent%2Dup%20demand (page discontinued).

23. "Cootie Williams to Incorporate," *New York Amsterdam News*, March 29, 1947, 24.

24. "Record Reviews," *Hollywood Reporter*, November 6, 1947, 6.

25. "Cootie's Ork Men Get Two Day Vacation After Cleveland Date," *Ohio State News*, April 26, 1947, 22.

26. "Bulletin!" *Sunday Courier and Press*, April 27, 1947, 1.

27. "Williams, Ork Race for Shelter as Leathernecks Greet 1947," *Ohio State News*, January 11, 1947, 23.
28. "Music—As Written," *The Billboard*, March 15, 1947, 30.
29. "Williams Sets Attendance Mark at Regal," *Chicago Defender*, May 17, 1947, 18.
30. "A Break for Dixie Junior Trumpeters," *Baltimore Afro-American*, May 17, 1947, 6.
31. "Handy's Impassioned Trumpet Dedicates New Negro Theater," William Clay McKee, *Commercial Appeal*, May 12, 1947, 14.
32. "Williams Sets Attendance Mark at Regal," *Chicago Defender*, May 17, 1947, 18.
33. Historic Memphis website, https://www.historic-memphis.com/memphis-historic/movietheaters/handy.html.
34. Historic Memphis website.
35. "Swinging the News," Al Monroe, *Chicago Defender*, May 24, 1947, 18.
36. "Cootie Uses 8 Horns," *Los Angeles Sentinel*, July 31, 1947, 20.
37. "Voice of Broadway," Dorothy Kilgallen, *Cincinnati Enquirer*, April 3, 1945, 3.
38. "'Cootie' Wars on Long Skirts," *California Eagle*, September 25, 1947, 19.
39. "Record Reviews," *Hollywood Reporter*, October 22, 1947, 11.
40. "Record Reviews," *The Billboard*, October 25, 1947, 134.
41. "Record Reviews," *Metronome*, November 1947, 49.
42. "Billy Rowe's Notebook," *Pittsburgh Courier*, November 22, 1947, 16.
43. "Cootie Williams Moves to Universal Agency," *Pittsburgh Courier*, November 29, 1947, 17.
44. "Whither Blows the Gale; So Goes Cootie Williams," *The Billboard*, November 22, 1947, 23.
45. Williams JOHP.
46. "Bard [sic] Buys Out Univ Partner," *The Billboard*, February 14, 1948, 18.
47. "Sur La Route Avec Cootie II," Frank Ténot, *Jazz Magazine*, May 1959, 17.
48. *Collected Works*, Balliett, 208.
49. Williams JOHP.
50. "How Cootie Williams got his band," Skippy Adelman, *PM's Sunday Picture News*, July 8, 1945, m4.
51. "Final Bar," *Down Beat*, September 17, 1970, 8.
52. "Know your Boroughs: Orchestra Men Talk About Show Business," *New York Amsterdam News*, April 30, 1949, 15.
53. "Cootie Williams/Erskine Hawkins," *The Swing Era*, Schuller, 403.
54. "Good Music . . . that's all!," Gretchen Weaver, *Band Leaders*, November 1944, 40.
55. "Cootie Williams/Erskine Hawkins," *The Swing Era*, Schuller, 405.

32. THINGS AIN'T WHAT THEY USED TO BE

1. "House Reviews, Apollo, NY," *Variety*, March 10, 1948, 56.
2. "House Reviews, Apollo, NY," *Variety*, September 15, 1948, 53.
3. "Swinging the News," *Chicago Defender*, 14 June 1947, 19.
4. "Ray McKinley Band Quits Majestic Disks Over Production Beef," *Variety*, October 29, 1947, 44.

5. "The Mighty Monarch of the Air: A Short History of the Short Life of Majestic Records," David N. Lewis, *ARSC Journal*, Spring 2013.

6. "It's all under one tent," Leonard Feather, *Metronome*, August 1949, 18.

7. *Top 40 R&B and Hip-Hop Hits*, Whitburn, 609.

8. "Teen-agers," Howard B. Woods, *Chicago Defender*, December 13, 1947, 18.

9. "The Man Who Crippled the Recording Industry, James Caesar Petrillo and the American Federation of Musicians Recording Bans (1942—1948)," Allan Sutton, https://78records.wordpress.com/2021/10/29/the-man-who-crippled-the-recording-industry-james-caesar-petrillo-and-the-american-federation-of-musicians-recording-bans/.

10. "Dusty and Cootie Involved in Melee," *Baltimore Afro-American*, May 1, 1948, 1.

11. "Capital Spotlight," Louis Lautier, *New Journal and Guide*, May 8, 1948, 5.

12. "Beyond Category," Hasse, 214.

13. "Cootie Announces He'll Take on Comers for Trumpet Jam," *Pittsburgh Courier*, May 15, 1948, 17.

14. "Cootie Williams Goes to Prison but to Play Date," *Chicago Defender*, May 22, 1948, 8.

15. "New Jazz Foundation to Honor Cootie Williams On Dixie Tour," *Chicago Defender*, June 19, 1948, 9.

16. "Billy Rowe's Notebook," Billy Rowe, *Pittsburgh Courier*, August 14, 1948, 22.

17. "'Cootie' Williams on Tour of the Seaboard," *Chicago Defender*, September 11, 1948, 9.

18. "Cootie Williams to Tour Mexico," *Chicago Defender*, August 14, 1948, 9.

19. "Cootie to Mix Business," *New York Amsterdam News*, August 14, 1948, 24.

20. "'Cootie' Williams on Tour of the Seaboard," *Chicago Defender*, September 11, 1948, 9.

21. "House Reviews, Apollo," *Variety*, September 15, 1948, 53.

22. "Some Bocce—No Insurance, Execs Advise Williams," *New Journal and Guide*, September 18, 1948, D24C.

23. "Cootie Williams to Visit Biggest Insurance Firms," *New Journal and Guide*, November 17, 1945, 17.

24. "Cootie Williams to Visit Biggest Insurance Firms."

25. "News," *Down Beat*, August 11, 1948, 19.

26. "Concerto for Cootie," John Hammond, *Down Beat*, May 7, 1952, 6.

27. Not to be confused with the Los Angeles–based magazine of the same name, which was published from 1933–1940.

28. "Trumpeter Cootie May Set Precent [sic] In Indies Trip," *Ohio State News*, November 20, 1948, 25.

29. "Bands Once Luke Warm To Dixie, Now Claim It Fertile Territory," Rob Roy, *Chicago Defender*, October 2, 1948, 9.

33. GATOR

1. "Cootie Signs Tenor Sax Ace," *Pittsburgh Courier*, October 16, 1948, 20.

2. "You Can Always Put Him in a Musical Straight Jacket," *Los Angeles Sentinel*, 24 February 1949, C5.

3. "Jacquet Defeated in Tenor Battle," *Cleveland Call and Post*, February 11, 1950, 8B.

4. "When Ballyhoo Backfires: 'Sax Battle' Leads to Verbal 'Brick Battle,'" *Baltimore Afro-American*, February 18, 1950, 19.

5. *On the Road*, Kerouac, 238.

6. Premieres Impressions d'Amerique," Hugues Panassie, *La Revue du jazz*, April 1949, 11.

7. *The Billboard Book of Top 40 R&B and Hip-Hop Hits*, Whitburn, 479.

8. "Encores and Echoes," E. B. Rea, *Baltimore Afro-American*, December 4, 1948, 6.

9. "Cootie Williams, Three Musicians Hurt in Wreck," *Pittsburgh Courier*, April 9, 1949, 19.

10. "Theater in Brief," *New Journal and Guide*, April 23, 1949, E20.

11. "People," *Jet*, February 25, 1954, 47.

12. "Fined in Magistrate Court," *Gasconade County Republican*, May 20, 1954, 1. Cootie's bus was described as a 1949 Beck, so it is presumed it was the replacement for the bus that got totaled in the April 1949 accident.

13. "Cootie Keeps Date the Hard Way—Afoot," *Chicago Defender*, August 3, 1946, 10.

14. "Know your Boroughs: Orchestra Men Talk About Show Business," *New York Amsterdam News*, April 30, 1949, 15. The newspaper article spotlighted musicians from the New York boroughs. Cootie was chosen to represent Queens. Tenor saxophonist Joe Thomas (Manhattan), pianist and composer Eubie Blake (Brooklyn), and saxophonist/composer/arranger Edgar Sampson (The Bronx) round out the quartet. Staten Island wasn't represented.

15. "How Charles Williams Got the Tag, 'Cootie,'" Fredi Washington, *The People's Voice*, September 16, 1944, 24.

16. "Society World," Gerri Major, *Jet*, July 1, 1954, 41.

17. "Midnight Snack of the Week," *Jet*, February 3, 1955, 29.

18. "Out of Billy Rowe's Harlem Notebook," Billy Rowe, *Pittsburgh Courier*, January 28, 1939, 11.

19. "On the Avenue," Al Monroe, *Chicago Defender*, January 28, 1939, 17.

20. "Cootie Williams Seeks Entry in Indianapolis Race," *Los Angeles Sentinel*, May 23, 1946, 10.

21. The first African American participation in a NASCAR event occurred in 1955. The driver was Elias Bowie, a cousin of the author.

22. World War II draft card. According to Social Security, he was born in 1913.

23. "Apollo Records Ink New Blues Singer," *New Journal and Guide*, April 15, 1950.

24. "Ink Spots Head Earle Bill; 'Deputy Marshal' on Screen," *Philadelphia Inquirer*, December 31, 1949, 15.

25. "House Reviews, Apollo, NY," *Variety*, February 22, 1950, 55.

26. "House Reviews, Apollo, NY," *Variety*, May 23, 1951, 56.

27. "House Reviews, Apollo, NY," *Variety*, Feb 22, 1950, 55.

28. "Cootie Williams Will Not Increase His Ork," *Chicago Defender*, August 21, 1948, 8.

29. "On the Upbeat, Hollywood," *Variety*, June 14, 1950, 62.

30. "Screen And Footlights," *Gulf Informer*, May 13, 1950, 6.

31. "Willis Jackson Due To Form His Own Band," *Variety*, May 31, 1950, 40.

32. Liner notes to Willis Jackson, *Call of the Gators*, Bob Porter, Delmark CD.

33. "Cootie Traps A Weasel," *California Eagle*, September 21, 1950, 17.

34. "Cootie Williams Signs Sax Ace 'Weasel' Parker," *Chicago Defender*, September 9, 1950, 20.

35. "Cootie Williams Sees Another Lush (Blues) Era That Is," *California Eagle*, September 28, 1950, 17.

34. SAVOY BALLROOM CHAMPION

1. "Cootie Williams Savoy Veteran," *Philadelphia Tribune*, September 19, 1950, 12.
2. "Rhythm and Blues Notes," *The Billboard*, January 6, 1951, 21.
3. "The Shotgun Boogie," Wikipedia, https://en.wikipedia.org/wiki/The_Shotgun_Boogie.
4. Advertisement for "Shotgun Boogie," *Cash Box*, March 24, 1951, 24.
5. "Hot in Other Cities," *Cash Box*, March 10, 1951, 19.
6. "Hot in Other Cities," *Cash Box*, March 24, 1951, 35.
7. "Divorce Me C.O.D.," Wikipedia, https://en.wikipedia.org/wiki/Divorce_Me_C.O.D.
8. In 2001, Blue Moon Productions released Eddie Mack, *The Complete Recordings 1947–1952* (BMCD 6026). Mack's entire recorded output fits on a single compact disk.
9. Death Certificate #23370 for Matthew Edmondson, State of Texas, filed March 17, 1984.
10. "Capsule Comments," *Down Beat*, February 10, 1950, 7.
11. "'Bargain' Deals Seen as Drawback to Big Bands," *Baltimore Afro-American*, June 2, 1951, 8.
12. "2-Act Package Getting Criticism," *Philadelphia Tribune*, May 22, 1951, 12.
13. "Voice of America to Carry Jazz," Jack Gaver, *Odessa American*, March 23, 1951, 16.
14. "Cootie Williams' Orch Off on Southern Tour," *Variety*, June 14, 1950.
15. "Providence Nitery Debuts Name Bill," *Detroit Tribune*, September 16, 1950, 15.
16. "The Celebrity Club: Best Jazz in Providence," Yuanyuan Dai, https://rhodetour.org/items/show/39.
17. *Pop Memories 1890–1954*, Whitburn, 128.
18. "House Reviews, Apollo, NY," *Variety*, August 27, 1952, 55.
19. "Cootie Williams at Latin Quarter," *The Gazette*, November 4, 1953, 13.
20. "Cootie Williams to Change Band Style," *Chicago Defender*, August 16, 1947, 10.
21. Williams JOHP.
22. "You're Great, Basie tell British audiences," Max Jones, *Melody Maker*, April 13, 1957, 8.
23. "Swinging the News," Al Monroe, *Chicago Defender*, January 3, 1953, 22.
24. Advertisement, *Arizona Sun*, January 4, 1952, 3.
25. "Jazz Gets Lift in Frisco as Flip Phillips Swings In," Ralph J. Gleason, *Down Beat*, March 21, 1952, 16.
26. *More Than Words Can Say*, Goldberg, 239.
27. "Cootie Williams' Ork Welcomes New Year Over MBS," *Chicago Defender*, January 2, 1954, 18.
28. "Swinging the News," Al Monroe, *Chicago Defender*, July 31, 1948, 9.
29. "The Automatic Lifestyle: Consumer Culture and Technology: The History of Television," https://www.cs.cornell.edu/~pjs54/Teaching/AutomaticLifestyle-S02/Projects/Vlku/history.html.
30. "Night Club Reviews, Birdland," *Variety*, January 27, 1954, 59.
31. Liner notes for Various Artists, *The 1940s Mercury Sessions*, Lorenzo Thomas.
32. "Apollo Theater Cards, Frank Schiffman Apollo Theater Collection (Set 2)."
33. "'Cleanhead' image here for taking," Bob Claypool, *Houston Post*, July 12, 1980, 38.

35. THE HOUSE BAND

1. Williams JOHP.
2. "No Rock and Roll for Savoy Ballroom," *Alabama Tribune*, August 2, 1957, 5.
3. *The Night People*, Wells, 114.
4. "Harlem Speaks Honors Lonnie Youngblood," All About Jazz, https://www.allaboutjazz.com/news/harlem-speaks-honors-lonnie-youngblood-september-28-at-the-jazz-museum-in-harlem-630pm-800pm/.
5. "No Rock and Roll for Savoy Ballroom," *Alabama Tribune*, August 2, 1957, 5.
6. The ProQuest Black newspaper database reports 1,014 mentions of "Cootie Williams" during the 1940s. For the 1950s, it's 246, less than 25 percent. There are only five mentions of Cootie for all of 1957.
7. "Record Notes," Dillon O'Leary, *Vancouver Sun*, May 14, 1955, 31.
8. "Concerto for Cootie," John Hammond, *Down Beat*, May 7, 1952, 6.
9. "A Flack of Anecdotes," Sam Wall, *Los Angeles Mirror*, August 13, 1955, 5.
10. "Feather's Nest," Leonard Feather, *Down Beat*, March 9, 1955, 8.
11. "Musician's Musicians" Poll, Leonard Feather, *The Encyclopedia Yearbook of Jazz*, 74.
12. "Musician's Musicians" Poll, Leonard Feather, *The Encyclopedia Yearbook of Jazz*, 56.
13. "Adlai Tours N.E. Cities After Game," John Harris, *Boston Globe*, October 5, 1956, 1.
14. Advertisement, *New York Age*, October 6, 1956, 9.
15. "Behind the Headlines," Robert M. Radcliffe, *Pittsburgh Courier*, 6 October 1956, 7.

36. BACK TO THE STUDIOS

1. "Counterpoint," *Down Beat*, April 4, 1957, 30.
2. "Strictly Ad Lib," *Down Beat*, March 21, 1957, 8.
3. "Cootie's back," *Melody Maker*, May 18, 1957, 6.
4. *Ride, Red, Ride*, Chilton, 193. It's not really clear what Allen means when he says Williams and Fitzgerald "were having a scene together." Did he mean they were having an affair?
5. "Sholes' Life Reads Like History Lesson in A.&R.," *Billboard Music Week*, March 20, 1961, 4.
6. "Sholes Dies; Trade Catalyst," *Billboard*, May 4, 1968, 70.
7. "RCA-Victor Signs Cootie to Top Pact," *New York Amsterdam News*, May 11, 1957, 13.
8. Williams JOHP.
9. Kenny Burrell interview by author.
10. "How the 45 RPM Single Changed Music Forever," *Rolling Stone*, March 15, 2019, https://www.rollingstone.com/music/music-features/45-vinyl-singles-history-806441/.
11. Smith, *Notable Black American Women: Book II*, 51.
12. "Those Crazy Sounds You'll Hear, Mean 'Rinkeydinks' Are Near," *New York Age*, October 25, 1952, 25.
13. "Izzy Rowe's Notebook," *Pittsburgh Courier*, May 11, 1957, A18.
14. "Tele Turntable's Top 10," *Pittsburgh Sun-Telegraph*, June 1, 1957. https://sites.google.com/site/pittsburghmusichistory/pittsburgh-music-story/radio/bill-powell.
15. "Review Spotlight on R&B Disk Jockey Programming," *Billboard*, April 20, 1957, 60.

16. "Cootie Williams to RCA," *Variety*, April 10, 1957, 66.
17. "After Dark," *Detroit Free Press*, April 19, 1955, 22.
18. "R&B Disk Jockey Programming," *The Billboard*, July 8, 1957, 56.
19. "R&B Ramblings," *Cash Box*, May 18, 1957, 36.
20. "Rock 'n' Rollers Keep Defying the Critics," George E. Pitts, *Pittsburgh Courier*, April 20, 1957, A21.
21. Liner notes for Cootie Williams and Rex Stewart, *The Big Challenge*, George Simon.
22. "Record Reviews," Gleason, *Down Beat*, December 12, 1957, 36.
23. "Moods and Music," *Daily Journal*, April 21, 1958, 11.
24. "Needle Talk," *Oakland Tribune*, April 13, 1958, B-15.
25. "Kenton Sour-Notes Stereo; Sees Only a 'Fiasco' Future," *Variety*, July 1959, 66.
26. "Reminiscing with Cootie," Eric Townley, *Storyville*, June-July 1977, 173.
27. "Record Reviews," Bill Coss, *Metronome*, April 1959, 28.

37. THE HOLY CITY

1. "150,000 Say Farewell to W. C. Handy," Robert McCarthy, *New York Daily News*, April 3, 1958, 4.
2. "Thousands Attend W. C. Handy Rites," *Cleveland Call and Post*, April 12, 1958. A two-minute newsreel by British Pathé can be found at https://www.britishpathe.com/video/VLVA1T9722BDXUDPVKUJ8R5RP2HVE-USA-WCHANDY-FUNERAL/query/handy+funeral.
3. Although many versions use double o's in "Toodle-oo," the original 1926 copyright, sheet music, and 78 rpm recording used "East St. Louis Toodle-o."
4. "Newport Jazz 1958," Don Gold and Dom Cerulli, *Down Beat*, August 7, 1958, 16.
5. "The Newport Jazz Festival," Bill Coss, *Metronome*, September 1958, 14.
6. Liner notes, Stewart-Williams and Co., *Porgy and Bess Revisited*, George Simon.
7. "Jim Timmens," Muppet Wiki, https://muppet.fandom.com/wiki/Jim_Timmens.
8. "Bob Snead's Jazz Corner," Bob Snead, *Cleveland Call and Post*, March 21, 1959, 8.
9. "Porgy and Bess," *Metronome*, July 1959, 35.
10. Harry Sheppard email to author, January 2, 2012.
11. "Eddie Condon Floor Show," Classic TV Archive, https://ctva.biz/US/MusicVariety/EddieCondonFloorShow.htm.
12. Photo caption, *Metronome*, May 1942, 8. (Fats Waller appeared on British television in 1938.)
13. "Theatre in Brief," *New Journal and Guide*, February 12, 1949, E16.
14. "Adventures in Race Relations," *Chicago Defender*, March 5, 1949, 7.

38. EUROPEAN TRIUMPH

1. Williams JOHP.
2. "Theatricals," Jesse H. Walker, *New York Amsterdam News*, March 15, 1958, 12.
3. "Around Town," *Daily News*, October 26, 1958, 6.
4. "History of the Savoy," https://ilindy.com/blog/history-of-the-savoy-ballroom/.
5. "On the Road with Cootie, part I," Frank Tenot, *Jazz Magazine*, April 1959, 32.

6. "Cootie Williams i Europa 1959," Bo Scherman, *Duke Ellington Society of Sweden Bulletin*, January 2015, 6.

7. "On the Road with Cootie, part I," Frank Tenot, *Jazz Magazine*, April 1959, 32.

8. It's unknown if a recording of the television show exists. "Cootie Williams and his quintet to play in 12 European Cities," *Jazz Magazine*, March 1959, 12.

9. "On the Road with Cootie, part I," Frank Tenot, *Jazz Magazine*, April 1959, 33.

10. "Behind the Headlines," Robert M. Ratcliffe, *Pittsburgh Courier*, October 6, 1956, A3.

11. "Rock and Roll: Is it Music?," Charles Gruenberg, *New York Post*, October 10, 1956, 64.

12. "Sic Transit Gloria Cootie," Aris Destombes, *Jazz Hot*, February 1959, 37.

13. "The grand prizes of the Academie du Disque," *Le Courrier Australien*, February 25, 1960, 4.

14. "On the Road with Cootie, part I," Frank Tenot, *Jazz Magazine*, April 1959, 34.

15. "On the Road with Cootie, part I," Frank Tenot, *Jazz Magazine*, April 1959, 35.

16. "On the Road with Cootie, part II," Frank Tenot, *Jazz Magazine*, May 1959, 16.

17. "On the Road with Cootie, part II," Frank Tenot, *Jazz Magazine*, May 1959, 17.

18. "Cootie Williams on Tour," Felix Manskleid, *Metronome*, October 1959, 35.

19. "On the Road with Cootie, part II," Frank Tenot, *Jazz Magazine*, May 1959, 18.

20. "On the Road with Cootie, part II," Frank Tenot, *Jazz Magazine*, May 1959, 37.

21. New York State passenger and crew list 1917–1967. Ancestry.com.

39. BACK HOME

1. Advertisement, *Intelligencer Journal*, March 20, 1959, 42.

2. "Ellingtonians Talking," *Crescendo*, February 1965, 32.

3. "Ad Lib," *Down Beat*, November 12, 1959, 54.

4. "Ad Lib," *Down Beat*, February 1960, 47.

5. Williams JOHP.

6. "Night Club Reviews," *Variety*, September 14, 1961, 52.

7. Williams JOHP.

8. Williams JOHP.

9. "Collected Works," Balliet, 209.

10. "Cootie Proves He's One of Best," Patrick Scott, *Globe and Mail*, January 16, 1960, 14.

11. Advertisement, *The State* (Columbia, SC), May 7, 1961, 8.

12. "Ruby Braff, the Blindfold Test," Leonard Feather, *Down Beat*, January 21, 1960, 38.

13. "Jazz Becoming Music to Eat By," John S. Wilson, *New York Times*, December 22, 1960, 18.

14. *Peppermint Twist*, Johnson, Selvin, Cami, 127.

15. The earliest Warwick ad I could find for this album was from the October 1960 *Metronome* magazine.

16. "Hey You Singers! Here's Your Chance," *New York Amsterdam News*, September 3, 1960, 15.

17. "Izzy Rowe's Notebook . . ." Izzy Rowe, *Pittsburgh Courier*, July 9, 1960, 23.

18. "Izzy Rowe's Notebook . . ." Izzy Rowe, *Pittsburgh Courier*, July 30, 1960, 22.

19. "My New York," Med Heimer, *Kane Republican*, June 6, 1961, 6.

20. *The Billboard Book of Top 40 R&B and Hip-Hop Hits*, Whitburn, 612. Before his singing career, Wade worked as a lab assistant for Dr. Jonas Salk.

21. "My New York," Med Heimer, *Kane Republican*, June 6, 1961, 6.

22. "The Jazz Scene," *Metronome*, July 1961, 5.

23. "Jazz Becoming Music to Eat By," John S. Wilson, *New York Times*, December 22, 1960, 18.

24. "Show Scene," Herb Kelly, *Miami News*, April 1, 1961, 9.

25. "Sip and Sup," Frank Ross, *Daily News*, April 14, 1961, 558.

26. "A Grandchild of Ellington to Dance on TV," *Chicago Tribune*, September 14, 1963, 128.

27. "Life with Feather," Leonard Feather, *Valley Times*, October 7, 1961, 14.

28. "Belle Blames the Cops," *Daily News*, December 2, 1961.

29. "Bell Barth Sluffs Her Buffs at Carnegie Hall 'Class' Recital," *Variety*, November 29, 1961, 60.

30. "Ellington's Band in Program Here," John S. Wilson, *New York Times*, November 23, 1961, 51.

31. *James Brown: The Godfather of Soul*, James Brown with Bruce Tucker, 143.

32. "Izzy Rowe's Notebook," *Pittsburgh Courier*, January 24, 1953, 17.

33. *The One*, Smith, 124.

34. Cuban Information Archives, https://cuban-exile.com/doc_176-200/doc0189.html.

35. *Jewish Floridian*, 26 January 1962, B-12.

36. *Miami Herald*, 18 January 1962, 38-E.

37. *Miami Herald*, 6 March 1962, 4B.

38. *Belle Barth in Person*, side 1.

39. "Cootie Williams," *The World of Duke Ellington*, Dance, 111.

40. "Cootie Williams," *The World of Duke Ellington*, Dance, 113.

41. "Izzy Rowe's Notebook," Izzy Rowe, *Pittsburgh Courier*, July 28, 1962, 14.

42. "Prestige Names Ozzie Cadena A.&R. Director; Signs Artists," *Billboard*, October 13, 1962, 6.

43. His first name is misspelled as "LeRoy" on the back of the album.

44. "New Crop of Books on Elusive Theme of Jazz Music Appears," Frederick Yeiser, *Cincinnati Enquirer*, May 21, 1939, 2.

45. "Record Reviews," Gilbert M. Erskine, *Down Beat*, March 14, 1963, 28.

46. "Trumpet Still Sounds in Recording Studio," Patrick Scott, *Globe and Mail*, November 3, 1962, 16.

47. Liner notes, Cootie Williams, *The Solid Trumpet of Cootie Williams*, LeRoy Williams.

48. "Night Club Reviews: Freddie's, Mpls," *Variety*, May 16, 1962, 59.

40. DRIFTING RIGHT BACK

1. "Jazz—Written and photographed by Gordon Parks," Gordon Parks, *Esquire*, December 1975, 143.

2. "7,097 Swing to Goodman at Ravinia," William Leonard, *Chicago Tribune*, August 2, 1962, 46.

3. "Stanley Dance," film interview, American Masters Digital Archive (WNET). March 11, 1993, https://www.pbs.org/wnet/americanmasters/archive/interview/stanley-dance/.

4. "Goodman to Do Concert," *Evening Sun*, August 20, 1962, 20.

5. "Ellingtonians Talking," *Crescendo*, February 1965, 32.

6. "Jimmy Smith: Reaching the People," Barbara J. Gardner, *Down Beat*, July 5, 1962, 17.

7. "Collected Works," Balliett, 733.

8. "LaGuardia, Stokowski are Duke Ellington Concert Chairmen," *Cleveland Call and Post*, January 9, 1943, 5. Besides Williams, the other honorary sponsors include Jack Benny, Count Basie, Aaron Copeland, Bing Crosby, Benny Goodman, Fletcher Henderson, Oscar Levant, Jimmie Lunceford, and Adam Clayton Powell.

9. *Rabbit's Blues*, Chapman, 118.

10. "Ellington—by the Ellingtonians," *Crescendo*, March 1965, 4.

11. Author interview with Buster Cooper.

12. "Another Famed Sideman Returns to Ellington Fold," Ralph Gleason, *Des Moines Register*, October 6, 1962, 4.

13. "Double Play," Don DeMichael, *Down Beat*, June 7, 1962, 21.

14. "Cootie Williams Talks to Valerie Wilmer," *Jazz Monthly*, August 1967, 2.

15. *Collected Works*, Balliett, 207.

16. "Cootie Williams," *The World of Duke Ellington*, Dance, 107.

17. "Cootie Williams," *The World of Duke Ellington*, Dance, 107.

18. "Cootie Williams talks to Valerie Wilmer," *Jazz Monthly*, August 1967, 4.

19. "Cootie's good for my ear health," *Melody Maker*, January 26, 1963, iii.

20. "Cootie's good for my ear health," *Melody Maker*, January 26, 1963, iii.

21. "Cootie's good for my ear health," *Melody Maker*, January 26, 1963, iii.

22. "Ellington Concert Enjoyable," Mimi Clar, *Los Angeles Times*, November 17, 1962, B6.

23. "Ellington—by the Ellingtonians," *Crescendo*, March 1965, 4.

24. "Tony Bennett in an Ellington Mood," Bill Milkowski, *JazzTimes*, December 1999, 67.

25. *Duke Ellington, A Listener's Guide*, Lambert, 239.

26. Williams JOHP.

27. *To Be or Not To Bop*, Gillespie, 185.

28. "Rolf Ericson: A Legend with a Future," Leonard Feather, *Los Angeles Times*, May 30, 1990, F6.

29. Ericson joined the band at the end of May 1963 and the Middle East tour started in September of that year. So Cootie's cold shoulder treatment lasted almost four months.

30. "Rolf Ericson Interview," Martin Westin and Lars Westin, *Duke Ellington Society of Sweden Bulletin*, August 2018, 9.

31. "Duke, Basie, and now Thad," Richard Williams, *Melody Maker*, September 13, 1969, 19.

32. "Julian Priester Interview," Mack Crooks and Bob Rusch, *Cadence*, April 1978, 15.

33. "Profiles: A Walk to the Park," Whitney Balliett, *New Yorker*, May 18, 1968, 46.

34. In a 2003 interview for the Smithsonian, which was nearly forty years after the event, Jones said: "I was right near the bass player, and Duke was right in front of me so it was very comfortable for me. And I knew most of the men in the band. Paul Gonzalez [*sic*] is a good friend, Cootie Williams, all them guys. It was a great experience; I enjoyed that."

41. THE ROAD

1. "Inside Ellington," John McDonough, *Down Beat*, July 25, 1968, 20.
2. Frank Racette email to author, September 12, 2012.
3. Frank Racette email to author, September 12, 2012.
4. Frank Racette email.
5. Author interview with Buster Cooper.
6. *Reminiscing in Tempo*, Nicholson, 341. (Hamilton describes Cootie as "kind of touchy.")
7. Author interview with Buster Cooper.
8. Author interview with Buster Cooper.

42. THE STATE DEPARTMENT TOUR

1. *Music Is My Mistress*, Ellington, 301.
2. "Jazzscene," Valerie Wilmer, *Melody Maker*, July 3, 1971, 30.
3. *Ellingtonia: The Recorded Music of Duke Ellington and His Sidemen*, Timner, 443.
4. "Inside Ellington," John McDonough, *Down Beat*, July 25, 1968, 21.
5. *Reminiscing in Tempo*, Nicholson, 341.
6. *The Jazz Ambassadors*, PBS television documentary.
7. *To Be or Not to Bop*, Gillespie, 414.
8. *The Jazz Ambassadors*, PBS television documentary.
9. *Duke's Diary—The Life of Duke Ellington 1940–1974*, Vail, 225.
10. *Beyond Category*, Hasse, 352.
11. Lawrence Brown JOHP.
12. Author interview with Simons.
13. "Goodman's the name—Benny Goodman," Richard Schwarze, *Journal Herald*, April 8, 1978, 27.
14. *Rabbit's Blues*, Chapman, 117.
15. Author interview with Simons.
16. "Setting the Record Straight," *DEMS Bulletin*, 10.
17. Author interview with Cooper.
18. Author interview with Cooper.
19. "Setting the Record Straight," *DEMS Bulletin*, 10.
20. Ray Nance's draft registration card.
21. Interview with Simons.
22. Interview with Simons.
23. "Nance Leaves Duke's Band over tiff with Cootie," *Jet*, October 24, 1963, 60.
24. *Duke Ellington in Person*, Ellington, 131.
25. Williams JOHP.
26. "Duke Ellington et son Orchestre," Archive.org, https://archive.org/details/gov.archives.arc.47984.
27. "Reminiscing with Cootie," Eric Townley, *Storyville*, June/July 1977, 172.
28. Interview with Simons.
29. *Duke's Diary—The Life of Duke Ellington 1940–1974*, Vail, 231.

43. THE BOOKENDS

1. "Ellington is Back," John S. Wilson, *New York Times*, March 20, 1964, 37.
2. "Ellington is Back," John S. Wilson, *New York Times*, March 20, 1964, 37.
3. Cooper was unable to remember the exact date of this performance. TDWAW show that the band played Redwood City on two occasions, both in 1964: June 7–11 and October 29–November 7, 1964.
4. Buster Cooper interview.
5. Buster Cooper interview.
6. Interview with Art Baron—He gave Art Baron the nickname of "Bydlo" (pronounced "beed-low") after Mussorgsky's *Pictures at an Exhibition*. Cootie enjoyed calling Baron by this nickname and after a while, it became "Meatball" and sometimes "Meatloaf" under his rendering. When the band traveled abroad, Cootie would find out how to say "meatball" in the local language and say "Hey, boulette" if they were in France, and so on.
7. Yale Ellington Project, Mercer Ellington interview with Dan Caine, July 22, 1979.
8. Jimmy Jones JOHP.
9. "Ellington—by the Ellingtonians," *Crescendo*, March 1965, 4.
10. Author interview with Buster Cooper.
11. Author interview with Buster Cooper.
12. "Ellington Explained," *Down Beat*, July 25, 1968, 21.
13. "Ellington Explained," *Down Beat*, July 25, 1968, 21.
14. "If You Call Working 35 Weeks a Year Semi-Retirement. . . ." Ernie Santosuosso, *Boston Globe*, January 16, 1966, 36.
15. "Great Performers Prove Again That Good Jazz Is Immortal," George McKinnon, *Boston Globe*, January 16, 1966, 36.
16. Williams JOHP.
17. Author interview with Steve Little.
18. "Slicing the Beat: Jazz Eighth-Notes as Expression Microrhythm," Fernando Benadon, *Ethnomusicology* (Winter 2006): 94.
19. "Ellington Forever: Russell Davies," Alison Kerr's Jazz Blog, jazzmatters.wordpress.com.
20. *Jazz Memories*, Bied, 23.
21. Author interview with Buster Cooper.
22. Author interview with Jeff Castleman.
23. Author interview with John Lamb.
24. An anonymous source: "I think [Cootie] implied that he knew Ava Gardner intimately, although, alas, I can't be sure."
25. "Mama Said There'd Be Days Like This," Wilmer, 147.
26. Interview of John Lamb.
27. Interview of Art Baron.
28. Interview of Jeff Castleman.
29. *Duke Ellington, A Listener's Guide*, Lambert, 255. Although Lambert wrote these words in reference to Johnny Hodges, they are equally appropriate for Cootie Williams.
30. "Cootie Williams talks to Valerie Wilmer," *Jazz Monthly*, August 1967, 2.
31. "Cootie Williams," *The World of Duke Ellington*, Dance, 106.
32. *Duke*, Jewell, 207.

33. Author interview with John Lamb.
34. Author interview with Art Baron.
35. Author interview with Art Baron.

44. THE ROAD MANAGER

1. *Duke Ellington In Person*, Ellington, 136.
2. "Speaking My Mind," Mercer Ellington, *Crescendo*, April 1966, 21.
3. *Reminiscing in Tempo*, Nicholson, 361.
4. "Inside Ellington," John McDonough, *Down Beat*, July 25, 1968, 20.
5. "Record Reviews," Dan Morgenstern, *Down Beat*, April 18, 1968, 32.
6. Author interview with Jeff Castleman.
7. "Preston: a leading question," Max Jones, *Melody Maker*, November 6, 1971, 24.
8. Interview of Jeff Castleman.
9. *Duke's Diary 1950–74*, Vail, 327.
10. "Harry James Marries Ex-Showgirl," *Reno Gazette Journal*, December 28, 1967, 13.
11. "Trumpet Blues," Levinson, 245.
12. *Duke's Diary 1950–74*, Vail, 327.

45. MORTALITY

1. Williams JOHP.
2. Williams JOHP.
3. *Rabbit's Blues*, Chapman, 162.
4. "Roses for Satchmo," *Down Beat*, July 9, 1970, 16.
5. Russell Procope JOHP.
6. Steven Lasker email, June 2023.
7. "Ellington the Composer: Caught in the Act," Jack Chambers, unpublished manuscript.
8. "Ellington the Composer: Caught in the Act," Jack Chambers, unpublished manuscript. Transposed for the B♭ trumpet, a piece in B major becomes C♯ major or seven sharps. A half step change in either direction changes the key to D major (two sharps) or C major (no sharps or flats).
9. Author interview with Buster Cooper.
10. *Duke Ellington In Person*, Ellington and Dance, 155.
11. *Reminiscing in Tempo*, Nicholson, 340.
12. *Music Is My Mistress*, Ellington, 469.
13. Author interview with Buster Cooper.
14. Author interview with Vince Prudente.
15. "Russia was great but . . . ," *Melody Maker*, November 6, 1971, 24.
16. Interview with Vince Prudente.
17. *Collected Works*, Balliett, 208.
18. "Tips for Wind Instrumentalists," *Down Beat*, October 5, 1955, 35.

46. WE LOVE YOU MADLY

1. *Duke's Diary 1950–74*, Vail, 428.
2. Author interview with Vince Prudente.
3. Williams JOHP.
4. Author interview with Barrie Lee Hall Jr.
5. "Believe Me . . . When I Tell You," Bob Womack Sr., *Indianapolis Recorder*, October 7, 1972, 10.
6. Juan Tizol JOHP interview.
7. "Duke Ellington at Hill Auditorium," Nathanael Charles, *Ann Arbor Sun*, February 8–22, 1974, 14.
8. "Spot-Check on The Duke," Kent Hazen, *Mississippi Rag*, April 1974, 5.
9. "Views and reviews," Michael Anthony, *Star Tribune*, March 19, 1974, 22.
10. Williams JOHP.
11. Williams JOHP.
12. Williams JOHP.
13. *Down Beat*, April 25, 1974.
14. Williams JOHP.

47. NOW MORE THAN EVER

1. Williams JOHP.
2. Williams JOHP.
3. "Cootie Williams tells Valerie Wilmer why he's sticking with Mercer and the Ellington band," Val Wilmer, *Melody Maker*, March 8, 1975, 47.
4. "Cootie Williams tells Valerie Wilmer why he's sticking with Mercer and the Ellington band," Val Wilmer, *Melody Maker*, March 8, 1975, 47.
5. "New Ellington Band Transforms Tradition," Leonard Feather, *Los Angeles Times*, August 15, 1976, 294.
6. Williams JOHP.
7. *Music Is My Mistress*, liner notes by Leonard Feather.
8. *The Jazz Years*, Feather, 240.
9. "Cootie Williams tells Valerie Wilmer why he's sticking with Mercer and the Ellington band," Val Wilmer, *Melody Maker*, March 8, 1975, 47.
10. "Cootie Williams tells Valerie Wilmer why he's sticking with Mercer and the Ellington band," Val Wilmer, *Melody Maker*, March 8, 1975, 47.
11. "Purring Ellington Cats Combine Old, New," Gene Grey, *Press and Sun-Bulletin*, May 13, 1977, 17.
12. "Duke's sib reassures Ellington fans," *Central New Jersey Home News*, August 4, 1974, C17.
13. Lawrence Brown JOHP interview.
14. "Mercer Ellington picks up Duke's baton," Harriet Choice, *Boston Globe*, June 13, 1974, 41.
15. Author interview with Ricky Ford.
16. "Ricky Ford, Five or Six Shades of Jazz," Jazz Hot https://www.jazzhot.net/PBCPPlayer.asp?ID=1463322.

17. Author interview with Ricky Ford.
18. Author interview with Ricky Ford.
19. *Clark*, Clark Terry, 146.
20. *Reminiscing in Tempo*, Nicholson, 340.
21. "Freddie Redd Interviewed," Valerie Wilmer, *Jazz Journal*, April 1961.
22. Author interview with Ricky Ford.
23. "Ricky Ford, Five or Six Shades of Jazz," Jazz Hot https://www.jazzhot.net/PBCPPlayer.asp?ID=1463322.
24. Author interview with Ricky Ford.
25. Author interview with Ricky Ford.
26. "Mercer Ellington picks up Duke's Baton," *Boston Globe*, June 13, 1974, 35.
27. Advertisement, *Chicago Tribune*, August 11, 1974, 117.
28. Hall interview by author.
29. Hall interview by author.
30. "Cootie Williams, Ellington Trumpeter, Dead," C. Gerald Fraser, *New York Times*, September 16, 1985, 8.

48. CONTINUUM

1. "You Can't Believe All the Things, You See, Hear," Stan Hochman, *Philadelphia Daily News*, February 3, 1975, 47.
2. "Cootie Williams tells Valerie Wilmer why he's sticking with Mercer and the Ellington band," Val Wilmer, *Melody Maker*, March 8, 1975, 47. (During Williams's second term with the band, they played the Steel Pier in 1964, 1966, 1969, and 1971–73. Williams doesn't specify the year in which he walked out of the Steel Pier gig, but 1972 and 1973 are the most likely dates.)
3. "Mercer Ellington Talking," *Crescendo*, March 1975, 6.
4. Interview of Bill Easley by the author.
5. "Reviews," Doug Murray, *Storyville*, April/May 1976, 157.
6. "Jazz," Owen McNally, *Hartford Courant*, September 28, 1975, 158.
7. Efforts to find a copy of *Jazz Ship* have proven futile so far. https://www.bbc.co.uk/programmes/m00211l4z.
8. "Reminiscing with Cootie," Eric Townley, *Storyville*, June-July 1977, 173. I was unable to determine where Catherine Williams worked and what she did. It was possibly secretarial work—a *Chicago Defender* from July 23, 1938, mentions that she and Dorothy Carney were potentially going to work at the New York offices of that newspaper in secretarial positions.

49. UNRETIREMENT

1. "Reminiscing with Cootie," Eric Townley, *Storyville*, June-July 1977, 174.
2. *Myself Among Others*, Wein and Chinen, 409.
3. "Reminiscing with Cootie," Eric Townley, *Storyville*, June-July 1977, 173.
4. Author interview with Ricky Ford.
5. "Newport Report," Gary Giddens, *Ann Arbor Sun*, August 12, 1976, 11.
6. *The World of Earl Hines*, Dance, 227.

7. "Nice Fest Showcases Top Array of Talent," Mike Hennessey, *Billboard*, July 31, 1976, 56.
8. "Reminiscing with Cootie," Eric Townley, *Storyville*, June-July 1977, 173.
9. "Ellington Keeping Pop's Sound Alive," Leigh Cook, *Asbury Park Press*, November 15, 1976, 9.
10. "Ellington Orchestra To perform At N.C. Wesleyan On Tuesday," *Nashville Graphic*, November 2, 1978, 15.
11. "Sloss smokes again," *Birmingham Post-Herald*, October 25, 1991, 50.
12. The following Ellingtonians are members of *Down Beat*'s Hall of Fame: Duke Ellington (inducted in 1956), Billy Strayhorn (1967), Johnny Hodges (1970), Ben Webster (1974), Clark Terry (2000), Jimmie Blanton (2008), Harry Carney (2008), and Oscar Pettiford (2009). Only Only Ellington and Terry were alive at the time they were inducted. Besides Cootie, some other prime Ellington associated candidates should include Mercer Ellington, Sonny Greer, Rex Stewart, Lawrence Brown, Sam Woodyard, Juan Tizol, Tricky Sam Nanton, Cat Anderson, Louie Bellson, Ray Nance, Jimmy Hamilton, and Paul Gonsalves.

50. THE LAST TENURE

1. "Purring Ellington Cats Combine Old, New," Gene Grey, *Press and Sun-Bulletin*, May 13, 1977, 17.
2. "The Duke's Band Is Going Strong," David B. Kozinski, *News Journal*, July 28, 1977, 38.
3. "Hot Notes," *San Francisco Examiner*, October 5, 1979, 23.
4. "They loved Ellington madly," Ernie Santosuoso, *Boston Globe*, April 29, 1979, 91.
5. "People," *Daily Sentinel*, October 31, 1979, 1.
6. "On the upbeat: Starting again at 72," T. J. Ryder, *Des Moines Register*, May 27, 1980, 13.
7. "Reese-Ellington, solid show," Bob Fixmer, *Capital Times*, March 8, 1980, 10.
8. "Ellington Orchestra shines on still," Welch D. Everman, *Wisconsin State Journal*, March 8, 1980, 28; "Ellington's Swing Heritage Alive and Well," Ralph V. Ellis, *Asheville Citizen*, March 26, 1980, 22.
9. "Mercer has trouble mixing old and new," Juan Rodriguez, *The Gazette*, April 1, 1980, 71.
10. "Reviews/Music," Ernie Santosuoso, *Boston Globe*, March 31, 1980, 30.
11. "Bits, Pieces," Tony Brown, *Asheville Citizen-Times*, March 30, 1980, 79.
12. "Ellington's Swing Heritage Alive and Well," Ralph V. Ellis, *Asheville Citizen-Times*, March 26, 1980, 22.
13. "What's happening," Eleanor Sussex, *Daily Chronicle*, August 9, 1975, 5.
14. "On the upbeat: Starting again at 72," T. J. Ryder, *Des Moines Register*, May 27, 1980, 13.

51. THE LAST TOUR

1. "Ellington Orchestra into South America," *Billboard*, May 17, 1980, 29.
2. "The Ellington Empire Strikes Back," Stanley Dance, *Jazz Times*, August 1980, 11.
3. "4 Big Bands and a Cloud of Dust," Leonard Feather, *Los Angeles Times*, June 18, 1980, 89.
4. "The Ellington Empire Strikes Back," Stanley Dance, *Jazz Times*, August 1980, 11.
5. "Kenny Garrett honor his mentors on new CD," *SFGATE*, May 3, 2012, https://www.sfgate.com/music/article/Kenny-Garrett-honors-his-mentors-on-new-CD-3528642.php.

6. "Worth Hearing," *Sydney Morning Herald*, July 21, 1980, 14.

7. "Overriding Commercial Element," Eric Myers, *Sydney Morning Herald*, June 20, 1980, 8.

8. "In Memory of Duke Ellington," Mercer Ellington, *Sydney Morning Herald*, June 27, 1980, 6.

9. "The Nice Festival," Eric Townley, *Mississippi Rag*, September 1980, 7.

10. "Cootie Williams," Gudrun Endress, *Jazz Podium*, September 1980, 5.

52. PASSING THE TORCH

1. "Ellington," Jack Garner, *Democrat and Chronicle*, September 5, 1980, 17.

2. "Cootie Williams," Gudrun Endress, *Jazz Podium*, September 1980, 6.

3. Al Sears via Patricia Willard in the Juan Tizol JOHP interview, 25.

4. "Barrie Lee Hall, Jr.—Conservator and Innovator," *Ellingtonia*, February 2007, 3. Attempts to track down the footage and the identity of the filmmaker before the publication of this book have been unsuccessful.

5. In December 1965, Cootie's trumpet was stolen from the band bus during a stop in Scranton, Pennsylvania. Fortunately, it was recovered in a trash can the next day. Apparently the thief probably thought they were stealing luggage. It's not known for sure if this is the same trumpet.

6. "Jazzman Just Can't Stop Blowing That Horn," *Journal Times*, September 26, 1972, 16.

7. Brown JOHP interview, 20.

8. "Cootie Williams," Gudrun Endress, *Jazz Podium*, September 1980, 6.

9. "My Ten Favorite Trumpeters," Harry James, *Music and Rhythm*, December 1941, 17.

10. "Armstrong heads Dizzy's list," James Stewart Thayer, *Seattle Times*, February 14, 1982, 117.

11. Death certificate of Charles Williams, filed September 17, 1985. Many of the newspaper obituaries reported that Williams died at his home. This was incorrect.

12. "Epitaph for an era," *Trenton Evening Times*, September 17, 1985, A14.

13. "Cootie Williams, 1908–85," John McDonough, *Down Beat*, February 1986, 13.

14. "It All Began with Louis Armstrong," *Melody Maker*, April 27, 1957, 8.

15. Tony Bennett interview, https://jazz.fm/tony-bennett-interview-1993-bill-king/.

16. "Cootie Williams Calls Music Peace Language," *New York Amsterdam News*, June 28, 1947, 25.

COOTIE WILLIAMS DISCOGRAPHY

This discography documents the known recordings of Cootie Williams. There are two notable and deliberate exclusions. Any recordings under the leadership of Duke Ellington and Benny Goodman are not included because thorough discographies already exist for these two musicians. *Ellingtonia: The Recorded Music of Duke Ellington and His Sidemen* by W. E. Timner (Scarecrow Press) is currently in its fifth edition. (Additionally, there is a free online Duke Ellington discography at www.ellingtonia.com.) *BG on the Record: A Bio-discography of Benny Goodman* by D. Russell Connor and Warren W. Hicks (Arlington House) and *Benny Goodman, A Supplemental Discography* by David Jessup (Scarecrow Press) provide exhaustive detail on the documented recording activities of Benny Goodman and his associates. The sources for this discography are the above-named references, numerous record/CD liner notes, and Tom Lord's online discography at www.lordisco.com. For years, Bo Haupman had been at work on his own Cootie Williams discography and generously shared his research with me. Compositions written or cowritten by Cootie Williams are noted in italics.

There's a four-CD set that's a companion to this book. *Concerto for Cootie: Selected Recordings 1928–62* was released on the Acrobat Music label in early 2024. The eighty-eight selections, selected by the author, cover key musical milestones in Cootie's career—his first recording session, his first plunger muted solo, his first recording sessions with Ellington and Goodman, and various showcase pieces, up until his return to Ellington in 1962. I also wrote the liner notes for the set. Many thanks to Paul Watts of Acrobat Music for making this project a reality. In the words of the company, "there have been very few products of this substance devoted specifically to Cootie Williams," making it "a welcome addition offering an insight into his music and a varied and fascinating showcase for his huge contribution to the genre."

♪

Concerto for Cootie CD—Discography

JIMMY JOHNSON AND HIS ORCHESTRA
18 JUNE 1928, NEW YORK CITY [COLUMBIA]

Cootie Williams, possibly Ward Pinkett—trumpet; possibly Garvin Bushell or Charlie Holmes—clarinet, soprano sax, alto sax; James P. Johnson, Fats Waller—piano; Joe Watts—bass; Perry Bradford—vocal.
    Chicago Blues (v—PB)
    Mournful Tho'ts

BARNEY BIGARD AND HIS JAZZOPATORS
19 DECEMBER 1936, LOS ANGELES [VARIETY]

Cootie Williams—trumpet; Juan Tizol—valve trombone; Barney Bigard—clarinet; Harry Carney—baritone sax; Duke Ellington—piano; Billy Taylor—bass; Sonny Greer—drums.
    Clouds In My Heart
    Frolic Sam
    Caravan
    Stompy Jones

COOTIE WILLIAMS AND HIS RUG CUTTERS
8 MARCH 1937, NEW YORK CITY [VARIETY]

Cootie Williams—trumpet; Joe Nanton—trombone; Johnny Hodges, Otto Hardwick, Harry Carney—reeds; Duke Ellington—piano; Hayes Alvis—bass; Sonny Greer—drums.
  I Can't Believe That You're in Love with Me
  Downtown Uproar
  Diga Diga Doo
  Blue Reverie
  Tiger Rag

THE GOTHAM STOMPERS
25 MARCH 1937, NEW YORK CITY [VARIETY]

Cootie Williams—trumpet; Sandy Williams—trombone; Barney Bigard, Johnny Hodges, Harry Carney—reeds; Tommy Fulford—piano; Bernard Addison—guitar; Billy Taylor—bass; Chick Webb—drums; Ivie Anderson—vocal; Wayman Carver—arranger.
  My Honey's Lovin' Arms (v—IA)
  Did Anyone Ever Tell You? (v—IA)
  Alabamy Home (v—IA)
  Where Are You? (v—IA)

TEDDY WILSON AND HIS ORCHESTRA
31 MARCH 1937, NEW YORK CITY [BRUNSWICK]

Billie Holiday—vocal; Cootie Williams—trumpet; Johnny Hodges—alto sax; Harry Carney—baritone sax; Teddy Wilson—piano; Allan Reuss—guitar; John Kirby—bass; Cozy Cole—drums.
  Carelessly (v—BH)
  Moanin' Low (v—BH)
  How Could You? (v—BH)
  Fine and Dandy

LIONEL HAMPTON
14 APRIL 1937, NEW YORK CITY [VICTOR]

Cootie Williams—trumpet; Lawrence Brown—trombone; Johnny Hodges—alto sax; Lionel Hampton—vibraphone, vocal;

Jess Stacy—piano; Allan Reuss—guitar; Billy Taylor—bass; Cozy Cole—drums.
    Buzzin' 'Round with the Bee
    Whoa Babe (v—LH)
    Stompology

JOHNNY HODGES AND HIS ORCHESTRA
20 MAY 1937, NEW YORK CITY [VARIETY]

Cootie Williams—trumpet, vocal; Barney Bigard, Johnny Hodges, Otto Hardwick, Harry Carney—reeds; Duke Ellington—piano; Fred Guy—guitar; Hayes Alvis—bass; Sonny Greer—drums; Buddy Clark—vocal.
    Foolin' Myself (v—BC)
    A Sailboat in the Moonlight (v—BC)
    You'll Never Go to Heaven (If You Break My Heart) (v—BC)
    Peckin' (v—CW and band)

COOTIE WILLIAMS AND HIS RUG CUTTERS
26 OCTOBER 1937, NEW YORK CITY [VOCALION]

Cootie Williams—trumpet; Juan Tizol—trombone; Barney Bigard, Otto Hardwick, Harry Carney—reeds; Duke Ellington—piano; Billy Taylor—bass; Sonny Greer—drums; Jerry Kruger—vocal.
    Jubilesta
    Watchin' (v—JK)
    Pigeons and Peppers
    I Can't Give You Anything but Love

LIONEL HAMPTON
18 JANUARY 1938, NEW YORK CITY [VICTOR]

Cootie Williams—trumpet; Johnny Hodges—alto sax; Edgar Sampson—baritone sax, arranger; Lionel Hampton—vibraphone, vocal; Jess Stacy—piano; Allan Reuss—guitar; John Kirby—bass; Sonny Greer—drums.
    You're My Ideal (v—LH)
    The Sun Will Shine Tonight (v—LH)
    Ring Dem Bells (v—LH)
    Don't Be That Way

COOTIE WILLIAMS AND HIS RUG CUTTERS
19 JANUARY 1938, NEW YORK CITY [VOCALION]

Cootie Williams—trumpet; Joe Nanton—trombone; Barney Bigard, Johnny Hodges, Harry Carney—reeds; Duke Ellington—piano; Fred Guy—guitar; Billy Taylor—bass; Sonny Greer—drums.
   Lost In Meditation (Have A Heart)
   Echoes of Harlem

JOHNNY HODGES AND HIS ORCHESTRA
19 JANUARY 1938, NEW YORK CITY [VOCALION]

Cootie Williams—trumpet; Lawrence Brown—trombone; Johnny Hodges, Otto Hardwick, Harry Carney—reeds; Duke Ellington—piano; Fred Guy—guitar; Billy Taylor—bass; Sonny Greer—drums; Mary McHugh—vocal.
   My Day (v—MM)
   Silvery Moon and Golden Sands (v—MM)

JOHNNY HODGES AND HIS ORCHESTRA
28 MARCH 1938, NEW YORK CITY [VOCALION]

Cootie Williams—trumpet, Lawrence Brown—trombone, Johnny Hodges, Otto Hardwick, Harry Carney—reeds; Duke Ellington—piano; Fred Guy—guitar; Billy Taylor—bass; Sonny Greer—drums; Mary McHugh—vocal.
   Jeep's Blues
   (What Would You Do) If You Were in My Place (v—MM)
   I Let a Song Go Out of My Heart (v—MM)
   Rendezvous with Rhythm

COOTIE WILLIAMS AND HIS RUG CUTTERS
4 APRIL 1938, NEW YORK CITY [VOCALION]

Cootie Williams—trumpet; Joe Nanton—trombone; Barney Bigard, Johnny Hodges, Otto Hardwick, Harry Carney—reeds; Duke Ellington—piano; Fred Guy—guitar; Billy Taylor—bass; Sonny Greer—drums; Jerry Kruger—vocal.
   A Lesson in C (v—JK)
   Swingtime in Honolulu (v—JK)

Carnival in Caroline (v—JK)
Ol' Man River (v—JK)

JOHNNY HODGES AND HIS ORCHESTRA
22 JUNE 1938, NEW YORK CITY [VOCALION]

Cootie Williams—trumpet; Lawrence Brown—trombone; Johnny Hodges, Harry Carney—reeds; Duke Ellington—piano; Fred Guy—guitar; Billy Taylor—bass; Sonny Greer—drums; Mary McHugh—vocal.
 You Walked Out of the Picture (v—MM)
 Pyramid
 Empty Ballroom Blues
 Lost In Meditation

JOHNNY HODGES AND HIS ORCHESTRA
1 AUGUST 1938, NEW YORK CITY [VOCALION]

Cootie Williams—trumpet; Lawrence Brown—trombone; Johnny Hodges, Harry Carney—reeds; Duke Ellington—piano; Fred Guy—guitar; Billy Taylor—bass; Sonny Greer—drums; Leon LaFell—vocal.
 A Blues Serenade (v—LL)
 Love in Swingtime (v—LL)
 Swingin' in the Dell
 Jitterbug's Lullaby

COOTIE WILLIAMS AND HIS RUG CUTTERS
2 AUGUST 1938, NEW YORK CITY [VOCALION]

Cootie Williams—trumpet; Barney Bigard, Johnny Hodges, Otto Hardwick, Harry Carney—reeds; Duke Ellington—piano; Fred Guy—guitar; Billy Taylor—bass; Sonny Greer—drums; Scat Powell—vocal.
 Chasin' Chippies
 Blue Is the Evening (v—SP)
 Sharpy (v—SP)
 Swing Pan Alley

JOHNNY HODGES AND HIS ORCHESTRA
24 AUGUST 1938, NEW YORK CITY [VOCALION]

Cootie Williams—trumpet; Lawrence Brown—trombone; Johnny Hodges, Harry Carney—reeds; Duke Ellington—piano; Billy Taylor—bass; Sonny Greer—drums; Mary McHugh—vocal.
    Prelude To a Kiss (v—MM)
    There's Something About an Old Love (v—MM)
    The Jeep Is Jumpin'
    Krum Elbow Blues

JOHNNY HODGES AND HIS ORCHESTRA
20 DECEMBER 1938, NEW YORK CITY [VOCALION]

Cootie Williams—trumpet; Lawrence Brown—trombone; Johnny Hodges, Harry Carney—reeds; Duke Ellington—piano; Billy Taylor—bass; Sonny Greer—drums.
    I'm In Another World
    Hodge Podge
    Dancing On the Stars
    Wanderlust

COOTIE WILLIAMS AND HIS RUG CUTTERS
21 DECEMBER 1938, NEW YORK CITY [VOCALION]

Cootie Williams—trumpet; Barney Bigard, Johnny Hodges, Otto Hardwick, Harry Carney—reeds; Duke Ellington—piano; Fred Guy—guitar; Billy Taylor—bass; Sonny Greer—drums.
    Delta Mood
    The Boys from Harlem
    Mobile Blues
    Gal-Avantin'

JOHNNY HODGES AND HIS ORCHESTRA
27 FEBRUARY 1939, NEW YORK CITY [VOCALION]

Cootie Williams—trumpet, Lawrence Brown—trombone, Johnny Hodges, Harry Carney—reeds; Duke Ellington—piano; Billy Taylor—bass; Sonny Greer—drums; Jean Eldridge—vocal; Billy Strayhorn—arranger.
    Like a Ship in the Night (v—JE)

Mississippi Dreamboat (v—JE)
Swingin' On the Campus
Dooji Wooji

COOTIE WILLIAMS AND HIS RUG CUTTERS
28 FEBRUARY 1939, NEW YORK CITY [VOCALION]

Cootie Williams—trumpet, vocal; Barney Bigard, Johnny Hodges, Harry Carney—reeds; Duke Ellington—piano; Billy Taylor—bass; Sonny Greer—drums.
Beautiful Romance
Boudoir Benny
Ain't The Gravy Good? (v—CW)
She's Gone (v—CW)

JOHNNY HODGES AND HIS ORCHESTRA
21 MARCH 1939, NEW YORK CITY [VOCALION]

Cootie Williams—trumpet; Lawrence Brown—trombone; Johnny Hodges, Harry Carney—reeds; Duke Ellington—piano; Billy Taylor—bass; Sonny Greer—drums; Billy Strayhorn—arranger.
Savoy Strut
Rent Party Blues
Dance of the Goon
Good Gal Blues

COOTIE WILLIAMS AND HIS RUG CUTTERS
21 JUNE 1939, NEW YORK CITY [VOCALION]

Cootie Williams—trumpet, vocal; Barney Bigard, Johnny Hodges, Harry Carney—reeds; Duke Ellington—piano; Billy Taylor—bass; Sonny Greer—drums.
Night Song

COOTIE WILLIAMS AND HIS RUG CUTTERS
22 JUNE 1939, NEW YORK CITY [VOCALION]

Cootie Williams—trumpet, vocal; Barney Bigard, Johnny Hodges, Harry Carney—reeds; Billy Strayhorn, Duke Ellington—piano; Billy Taylor—bass; Sonny Greer—drums.
Blues A Poppin'

Top and Bottom
Black Beauty

JOHNNY HODGES AND HIS ORCHESTRA
1 SEPTEMBER 1939, NEW YORK CITY [VOCALION]

Cootie Williams—trumpet; Lawrence Brown—trombone; Johnny Hodges, Harry Carney—reeds; Billy Strayhorn, Duke Ellington—piano; Billy Taylor—bass; Sonny Greer—drums.
　The Rabbit's Jump
　Moon Romance
　Truly Wonderful
　Dream Blues

COOTIE WILLIAMS AND HIS RUG CUTTERS
14 FEBRUARY 1940, CHICAGO [OKEH]

Cootie Williams—trumpet, vocal; Barney Bigard, Johnny Hodges, Harry Carney—reeds; Duke Ellington—piano; Jimmie Blanton—bass; Sonny Greer—drums.
　Mardi Gras Madness
　Watch the Birdie
　Black Butterfly
　Dry Long So (v—CW)
　Toasted Pickle
　Give It Up (Strayhorn replaces Ellington)

JOHNNY HODGES AND HIS ORCHESTRA
2 NOVEMBER 1940, CHICAGO [BLUEBIRD]

Cootie Williams—trumpet; Lawrence Brown—trombone; Johnny Hodges, Harry Carney—reeds; Duke Ellington—piano; Jimmie Blanton—bass; Sonny Greer—drums.
　Day Dream
　Good Queen Bess
　That's the Blues Old Man
　Junior Hop

METRONOME ALL STAR BAND
16 JANUARY 1941, NEW YORK CITY [VICTOR]

Cootie Williams, Harry James, Ziggy Elman—trumpet; Tommy Dorsey, J. C. Higginbotham—trombone; Benny Goodman—clarinet; Toots Mondello, Benny Carter—alto sax; Coleman Hawkins, Tex Beneke—tenor sax; Count Basie—piano; Charlie Christian—guitar; Art Bernstein—bass; Buddy Rich—drums.
    Bugle Call Rag
    One O'Clock Jump

COOTIE WILLIAMS
7 MAY 1941, NEW YORK CITY [OKEH]

Cootie Williams—trumpet; Lou McGarity—trombone; Les Robinson—alto sax; Skippy Martin—baritone sax; Johnny Guarnieri—piano; Artie Bernstein—bass; Jo Jones—drums.
    West End Blues
    Ain't Misbehavin'
    Blues In My Condition
    G-Men

JACK LEONARD
RECORDED DECEMBER 1941, NEW YORK CITY [OKEH]

Jack Leonard—vocal; Cootie Williams—trumpet; four strings; four saxes; piano; guitar; bass; drums. Conducted by Morty Palitz.
    Madeleine
    I'll Never Forget
    It Isn't a Dream Anymore
    Who Calls?

METRONOME ALL STAR BAND
31 DECEMBER 1941, NEW YORK CITY [COLUMBIA]

Cootie Williams, Roy Eldridge, Harry James—trumpet; J. C. Higginbotham, Lou McGarity—trombone; Benny Goodman—clarinet; Benny Carter, Toots Mondello—alto sax; Vido Musso, Tex Beneke—tenor sax; Count Basie—piano; Freddie Green—guitar; Doc Goldberg—bass; Gene Krupa—drums.
    Royal Flush
    Dear Old Southland

METRONOME ALL STAR LEADERS
16 JANUARY 1942, NEW YORK CITY [COLUMBIA]

Cootie Williams—trumpet; J. C. Higginbotham—trombone; Benny Goodman—clarinet; Benny Carter—alto sax; Charlie Barnet—tenor sax; Count Basie—piano; Alvino Rey—guitar; John Kirby—bass; Gene Krupa—drums.
I Got Rhythm

COOTIE WILLIAMS AND HIS ORCHESTRA
1 APRIL 1942, CHICAGO [OKEH]

Cootie Williams, Milton Fraser, Joe Guy, Milton Fletcher—trumpet; Louis Bacon—trumpet, vocal; Jonas Walker, Robert Horton, Sandy Williams—trombone; Charlie Holmes—alto sax; Eddie "Cleanhead" Vinson—alto sax, vocal; Bob Dorsey, Greely Walton—tenor sax; John Williams—baritone sax; Kenny Kersey—piano; Norman Keenan—bass; George "Butch" Ballard—drums.
Sleepy Valley
Marchita (v—LB)
When My Baby Left Me
Fly Right (Epistrophy)

PLATTERBRAINS
14 NOVEMBER 1942, NEW YORK CITY

Leonard Feather, host; Cootie Williams, Joe Sullivan, George Simon, Bob Bach, Barry Ulanov, guests.

NOTE—This item can be found in the Leonard Feather Jazz Collection, housed at the University of Idaho.

COOTIE WILLIAMS AND HIS ORCHESTRA
RECORDED JUNE 1943, MOVIETONE STUDIOS, NEW YORK CITY

Cootie Williams, Louis Bacon, Ermit V. Perry, Frank Humphries—trumpet; Ed Burke, Robert Horton, Jonas Walker (?)—trombone; Eddie "Cleanhead" Vinson, Charlie Holmes—alto sax; Sam "The Man" Taylor, Bob Dorsey—tenor sax; Greely Walton—baritone sax; Fletcher Smith—piano; Norman Keenan—bass; George "Butch" Ballard—drums, Eddie "Cleanhead" Vinson, Laurel Watson—vocals.
Get Hep

Things Ain't What They Used to Be (v—EV)
Unidentified Number
Giddap Mule (LW—vocal)
Let's Keep on Jumping

COLEMAN HAWKINS AND LEONARD FEATHER'S ESQUIRE ALL STARS
4 DECEMBER 1943, NEW YORK CITY [COMMODORE]

Cootie Williams—trumpet; Edmond Hall—clarinet; Coleman Hawkins—tenor sax; Art Tatum—piano; Al Casey—guitar; Oscar Pettiford—bass; Sid Catlett—drums.
Esquire Bounce
Boff Boff #2 (aka Mop Mop)
My Ideal
Esquire Blues

COOTIE WILLIAMS AND HIS ORCHESTRA
4 JANUARY 1944, NEW YORK CITY [HIT]

Cootie Williams—trumpet, vocal; Eddie "Cleanhead" Vinson—alto sax; Eddie "Lockjaw" Davis—tenor sax; Bud Powell—piano; Norman Keenan—bass; Sylvester "Vess" Payne—drums.
You Talk a Little Trash
Floogie Boo
I Don't Know
Do Some War Work, Baby (v—CW)

COOTIE WILLIAMS AND HIS ORCHESTRA
6 JANUARY 1944, NEW YORK CITY [HIT]

Cootie Williams—trumpet; Eddie "Cleanhead" Vinson—alto sax; Eddie "Lockjaw" Davis—tenor sax; Bud Powell—piano; Norman Keenan—bass; Sylvester "Vess" Payne—drums.
My Old Flame
Sweet Lorraine
Echoes of Harlem
Honeysuckle Rose

COOTIE WILLIAMS AND HIS ORCHESTRA
6 JANUARY 1944, NEW YORK CITY [HIT]

Cootie Williams, Ermit V. Perry, George Treadwell, Harold "Money" Johnson—trumpet; Ed Burke, George Stevenson, Robert Horton—trombone; Charlie Holmes, Eddie "Cleanhead" Vinson—alto sax; Eddie "Lockjaw" Davis, Lee Pope—tenor sax; Bud Powell—piano; Norman Keenan—bass; Sylvester "Vess" Payne—drums, Eddie "Cleanhead" Vinson, Pearl Bailey—vocal.
    Now I Know (v—PB)
    Tess's Torch Song (v—PB)
    Red Blues (v—EV)
    Things Ain't What They Used to Be (v—EV)

COOTIE WILLIAMS AND HIS ORCHESTRA
1 MAY 1944, HOLLYWOOD (SESSION FOR AFRS JUBILEE SHOW)

Cootie Williams, Ermit V. Perry, George Treadwell, Harold "Money" Johnson—trumpet; Ed Burke or George Stevenson, Robert Horton—trombone; Charlie Holmes, Eddie "Cleanhead" Vinson—alto sax; Sam Taylor, Lee Pope—tenor sax; Eddy DeVerteuil—baritone sax; Bud Powell—piano; Norman Keenan—bass; Sylvester "Vess" Payne—drums, Ella Fitzgerald, The Ink Spots—vocal.
    One O' Clock Jump
    Roll 'Em
    A-Tisket, A-Tasket (v—EF)
    Do Nothin' till You Hear from Me (v—EF)
    You Talk a Little Trash (mistitled "Let's Toot")
    If I Didn't Care (v—IS)
    Java Jive (v—IS)
    A Lovely Way to Spend an Evening (v—IS)
    Air Mail Special
    One O' Clock Jump

COOTIE WILLIAMS AND HIS ORCHESTRA
22 AUGUST 1944, NEW YORK CITY [HIT]

Cootie Williams, Ermit V. Perry, George Treadwell, Lamar Wright, Tommy Stevenson—trumpet; Ed Burke, Robert Horton, Ed Glover—trombone; Frank Powell, Eddie "Cleanhead" Vinson—alto sax; Sam Taylor, Lee Pope—tenor sax; Eddy DeVerteuil—baritone sax; Bud

Powell—piano; Leroy Kirkland—guitar; Carl Pruitt—bass; Sylvester "Vess" Payne—drums.
  Is You Is or Is You Ain't (v—EV)
  Somebody's Gotta Go (v—EV)
  'Round Midnight
  Blue Garden Blues (Royal Garden Blues)

COOTIE WILLIAMS AND HIS ORCHESTRA
UNKNOWN MONTH* 1944, NEW YORK CITY

Cootie Williams, Ermit V. Perry, George Treadwell, Lamar Wright, Tommy Stevenson—trumpet; Ed Burke, Robert Horton, Ed Glover—trombone; Frank Powell, Eddie "Cleanhead" Vinson—alto sax; Sam Taylor, Lee Pope—tenor sax; Eddy DeVerteuil—baritone sax; Bud Powell—piano; Leroy Kirkland—guitar; Carl Pruitt—bass; Sylvester "Vess" Payne—drums.
  Perdido
  When My Baby Left Me (v—EV)
  Royal Garden Blues

*Allegedly from the Apollo Theater and Savoy Ballroom and recorded between January and May 1944. This is not possible since Cootie Williams and his Orchestra was on tour with the Big Three Unit. For the venues to be correct, Williams was at the Savoy Ballroom in July and December 1944 and at the Apollo Theater in August 1944.

COOTIE WILLIAMS
4 JULY 1944, NEW YORK CITY, THE CANADA LEE SHOW, WAR DRIVE TRANSCRIPTION

  Spoken Introduction by Canada Lee and Cootie Williams
  West End Blues

TEDDY WILSON SEXTET
29 DECEMBER 1944, NEW YORK CITY, "MUSIC 'TIL MIDNIGHT," CBS BROADCAST

Cootie Williams—trumpet; Red Norvo—vibraphone; Teddy Wilson—piano; Remo Palmieri—guitar; Oscar Pettiford—bass; Specs Powell—drums.
  Tea for Two

COOTIE WILLIAMS AND HIS ORCHESTRA
5 FEBRUARY 1945, SAVOY BALLROOM, NEW YORK CITY, RADIO BROADCAST—"ONE NIGHT STAND"

Probable personnel: Cootie Williams, Ermit V. Perry, George Treadwell, Harold "Money" Johnson—trumpet; Ed Burke, Robert Horton—trombone; Charlie Parker, Frank Powell—alto sax; Lee Pope, Sam Taylor—tenor sax; Ed de Verteuil—baritone sax; Arnold Jarvis—piano; Leroy Kirkland—guitar; Carl Pruitt—bass; Sylvester "Vess" Payne—drums, Warren Evans—vocal.

    The Rhythm Is Jumping
    Don't Blame Me
    Perdido
    You Talk a Little Trash
    Royal Garden Blues
    'Round Midnight
    Birmingham Special
    Roll 'Em

COOTIE WILLIAMS AND HIS ORCHESTRA
12 FEBRUARY 1945, SAVOY BALLROOM, NEW YORK CITY, RADIO BROADCAST—"ONE NIGHT STAND"

Cootie Williams, Ermit V. Perry, George Treadwell, Harold "Money" Johnson—trumpet; Ed Burke, Robert Horton—trombone; Charlie Parker, Frank Powell—alto sax; Lee Pope, Sam Taylor—tenor sax; Ed de Verteuil—baritone sax; Arnold Jarvis—piano; Leroy Kirkland—guitar; Carl Pruitt—bass; Sylvester "Vess" Payne—drums, Warren Evans—vocal.

    'Round Midnight
    Roll 'em
    Do Nothin' till You Hear from Me
    Don't Blame Me
    Perdido
    Night Cap
    Saturday Night (Is the Loneliest Night of the Week)
    Floogie Boo
    St. Louis Blues

COOTIE WILLIAMS AND HIS ORCHESTRA
26 FEBRUARY 1945, NEW YORK CITY [MAJESTIC]

Cootie Williams, Ermit V. Perry, George Treadwell, Harold "Money" Johnson—trumpet; Ed Burke, Robert Horton—trombone; Rupert Cole, Frank Powell—alto sax; Lee Pope, Sam Taylor—tenor sax; Ed de Verteuil—baritone sax; Arnold Jarvis—piano; Leroy Kirkland—guitar; Carl Pruitt—bass; Sylvester "Vess" Payne—drums, Warren Evans (credited on the original release as Tony Warren)—vocal.
    Saturday Night (Is the Loneliest Night of the Week) (v—WE)
    I'm Beginning to See the Light (v—WE)
    Unknown Title 1
    Unknown Title 2

COOTIE WILLIAMS AND HIS ORCHESTRA
29 MAY 1945, NEW YORK CITY [CAPITOL]

Cootie Williams, Ermit V. Perry, George Treadwell, Billy Ford, Clarence "Gene" Redd—trumpet; Ed Burke, Robert Horton, Dan Logan—trombone; Rupert Cole, Eddie "Cleanhead" Vinson—alto sax; Lee Pope, Sam Taylor—tenor sax; George Favors—baritone sax; Arnold Jarvis—piano; Leroy Kirkland—guitar; Carl Pruitt—bass; Sylvester "Vess" Payne—drums.
    Mood for Coot
    Juice Head Baby (v—EV)
    Salt Lake City Bounce
    Jitterbug Serenade

COOTIE WILLIAMS AND HIS ORCHESTRA
19 JUNE 1945*, NEW YORK CITY [CAPITOL]

Cootie Williams, Ermit V. Perry, George Treadwell, Billy Ford, Clarence "Gene" Redd—trumpet; Ed Burke, Robert Horton, Dan Logan—trombone; Rupert Cole, Eddie "Cleanhead" Vinson—alto sax; Lee Pope, Sam Taylor—tenor sax; George Favors—baritone sax; Arnold Jarvis—piano; Leroy Kirkland—guitar; Jimmy Glover—bass; Sylvester "Vess" Payne—drums.
    House of Joy
    Mood for Coot
    When My Baby Left Me (v—EV)
    Everything But You

*Most discographies and references to this session have erroneously said it took place on 19 July. The Big Three group was in Minneapolis on 19 July. Scott Wenzel of Mosaic Records consulted the Capitol Records logs and reported that 19 June is the actual date.

METRONOME ALL-STAR BAND
15 JANUARY 1946, NEW YORK CITY [RCA VICTOR]

Sonny Berman, Pete Candoli, Harry Edison, Neal Hefti, Rex Stewart, Cootie Williams—trumpet; Will Bradley, Tommy Dorsey, Bill Harris, J.C. Higginbotham—trombone; Buddy DeFranco—clarinet; Herbie Fields, Johnny Hodges—alto sax; Georgie Auld, Flip Phillips—tenor sax; Harry Carney—baritone sax; Teddy Wilson—piano; Billy Bauer, Tiny Grimes—guitar; Chubby Jackson—bass; Dave Tough—drums; Sy Oliver—conductor.

Look Out

COOTIE WILLIAMS AND HIS ORCHESTRA
21 JANUARY 1946, WNEW BROADCAST (NBC NETWORK), "LET'S GO NIGHT CLUBBING," ZANZIBAR CAFE, NEW YORK CITY

Cootie Williams, Bob Merrill—trumpet, vocal; Ermit V. Perry, George Treadwell, Billy Ford, Clarence "Gene" Redd—trumpet; Ed Burke, Robert Horton, Edward Johnson—trombone; Rupert Cole, John Jackson—alto sax; Everett Gains, Sam Taylor—tenor sax; Bob Ashton—baritone sax; Arnold Jarvis—piano; Sam "Christopher" Allen—guitar; Jimmy Glover—bass; George "Butch" Ballard—drums; Ella Fitzgerald—vocal.

House of Joy
I've Found a New Baby
It's Only a Paper Moon (v—EF)
I'll Be Yours
You're the One for Me, Sweetheart (v—BM)
Blue
The Honey Dripper (v—EF)
Jumpin' at the Zanzibar (aka Jumping to Conclusions)
Piney Brown's Gone (v—BM)

COOTIE WILLIAMS AND HIS ORCHESTRA
22 JANUARY 1946, NEW YORK CITY [CAPITOL]

Cootie Williams, Bob Merrill—trumpet, vocal; Ermit V. Perry, George Treadwell, Billy Ford, Clarence "Gene" Redd—trumpet; Ed Burke, Robert Horton, Edward Johnson—trombone; Rupert Cole, John Jackson—alto sax; Everett Gains, Sam Taylor—tenor sax; Bob Ashton—baritone sax; Arnold Jarvis—piano; Sam "Christopher" Allen—guitar; Jimmy Glover—bass; George "Butch" Ballard—drums.
    Jumping to Conclusions (part one)
    Jumping to Conclusions (part two)
    Someone I Knew
    You're the One for Me, Sweetheart (v—BM)

COOTIE WILLIAMS AND HIS ORCHESTRA
29 JANUARY 1946, NEW YORK CITY [CAPITOL]

Cootie Williams, Bob Merrill—trumpet, vocal; Ermit V. Perry, George Treadwell, Billy Ford, Clarence "Gene" Redd—trumpet; Ed Burke, Robert Horton, Edward Johnson—trombone; Rupert Cole, John Jackson—alto sax; Everett Gains, Sam Taylor—tenor sax; Bob Ashton—baritone sax; Arnold Jarvis—piano; Sam "Christopher" Allen—guitar; Norm Keenan—bass; George "Butch" Ballard—drums, Johnny Mercer—vocal.
    Stingy Blues
    He Should'a Flip'd When He Flop'd (v—CW, JM)
    Echoes of Harlem
    That's the Lick

COOTIE WILLIAMS AND HIS ORCHESTRA
5 JULY 1946, NEW YORK CITY [CAPITOL]

Cootie Williams, Bob Merrill, Ermit V. Perry, Otis Gamble, Billy Ford, Clarence "Gene" Redd—trumpet; Ed Burke, Ed "Jack Raggs" Johnson, Julius "Hawkshaw" Watson—trombone; Rupert Cole, Daniel Williams—alto sax; Charles "Chuck" Clarke, Edwin Johnson—tenor sax; Bob Ashton—baritone sax; Arnold Jarvis—piano; William "Pee Wee" Tinney—guitar; Norman Keenan—bass; George "Butch" Ballard—drums.
    Wrong Neighborhood
    Piney Brown's Gone
    I May Be Easy, But I'm No Fool (v—BM)

Vibraphonia
Let's Do the Whole Thing or Nothing at All (v—CW)

COOTIE WILLIAMS AND HIS ORCHESTRA
11 SEPTEMBER 1946, NEW YORK CITY [CAPITOL]

Cootie Williams, Bob Merrill, Ermit V. Perry, Otis Gamble, Billy Ford, Clarence "Gene" Redd—trumpet; Ed Burke, Ed "Jack Raggs" Johnson, Julius "Hawkshaw" Watson—trombone; Rupert Cole, Daniel Williams—alto sax; Charles "Chuck" Clarke, Edwin Johnson—tenor sax; Bob Ashton—baritone sax; Arnold Jarvis—piano; Norman Keenan—bass; George "Butch" Ballard—drums.

Rhapsody In Bass
Ain't Got No Blues Today (v—BM)
Bring 'em Down Front (v—CW)

COOTIE WILLIAMS AND HIS ORCHESTRA
[EARLY APRIL] 1947, NEW YORK CITY [MAJESTIC]

Cootie Williams, Bob Merrill, Ermit V. Perry, Otis Gamble, Billy Ford, Clarence "Gene" Redd—trumpet; Ed Burke, Ed "Jack Raggs" Johnson, Julius "Hawkshaw" Watson—trombone; Rupert Cole, Daniel Williams—alto sax; Charles "Chuck" Clarke, Edwin Johnson—tenor sax; Bob Ashton—baritone sax; Arnold Jarvis—piano; Norman Keenan—bass; George "Butch" Ballard—drums; Billy Mathews, Bob Merrill—vocals.

I Can't Get Started
Inflation Blues (v—Bob Merrill)
I Want to Be Loved (But Only by You) (v—Billy Mathews)
Sound Track

COOTIE WILLIAMS AND HIS ORCHESTRA
24 JULY 1947, NEW YORK CITY [MAJESTIC]

Cootie Williams, Bob Merrill, Ermit V. Perry, Otis Gamble, Billy Ford, Clarence "Gene" Redd—trumpet; Ed Burke, Ed "Jack Raggs" Johnson, Julius "Hawkshaw" Watson—trombone; Rupert Cole, Daniel Williams—alto sax; Charles "Chuck" Clarke, Edwin Johnson—tenor sax; Bob Ashton—baritone sax; Arnold Jarvis—piano; Norman Keenan—bass; George "Butch" Ballard—drums; Cootie Williams, Billy Mathews, Bob Merrill—vocals.

Ooh La-La (v—Merrill and band)

Save the Bones for Henry Jones (v—CW, Merrill)
If It's True (v—Mathews)
I Should o' Been Thinkin' Instead of Drinkin' (v—Merrill)

COOTIE WILLIAMS AND HIS ORCHESTRA
6 AUGUST 1947, MIDNIGHT JAMBOREE RADIO BROADCAST, HOWARD THEATRE, WASHINGTON, DC

[Probable personnel] Cootie Williams, Bob Merrill, Ermit V. Perry, Otis Gamble, Billy Ford, Clarence "Gene" Redd—trumpet; Ed Burke, Ed "Jack Raggs" Johnson, Julius "Hawkshaw" Watson—trombone; Rupert Cole, Daniel Williams—alto sax; Charles "Chuck" Clarke, Edwin Johnson—tenor sax; Bob Ashton—baritone sax; Arnold Jarvis—piano; Norman Keenan—bass; George "Butch" Ballard—drums; Ella Fitzgerald—vocal.

Ooh La-La (v—BM and band)
I Should o' Been Thinkin' Instead of Drinkin' (v—BM)
Across the Alley from the Alamo (v—EF)
Bring 'em Down Front (v—CW)/*'Round Midnight*

COOTIE WILLIAMS AND HIS ORCHESTRA
27 DECEMBER 1947, NEW YORK CITY [MERCURY]

Cootie Williams, Bob Merrill—trumpet; Rupert Cole—alto sax; Bill "Weasel" Parker—tenor sax; Arnold Jarvis—piano; Mundell Lowe—guitar; Leonard "Heavy" Swain—bass; Sylvester "Vess" Payne—drums, Billy Mathews, The Balladeers—vocal.

You Talk a Little Trash
Typhoon
I Love You, Yes I Do (v—Billy Mathews, The Balladeers)
Smooth Sailing

DINAH WASHINGTON WITH COOTIE WILLIAMS AND HIS ORCHESTRA
30 DECEMBER 1947, NEW YORK CITY
[SOMETIMES ERRONEOUSLY REPORTED AS OCCURRING ON 16 JULY 1947] [MERCURY]

Dinah Washington—vocal; Cootie Williams, Robert Merrill—trumpet; Rupert Cole—alto sax; William "Weasel" Parker—tenor sax; Arnold Jarvis—piano; Mundell Lowe—guitar; Leonard "Heavy" Swain—bass; Sylvester "Vess" Payne—drums.

I'm Getting Old Before My Time (v—DW)
Record Ban Blues (v—DW)

Resolution Blues (v—DW)
I Want to Cry (v—DW)

[NOTE—In a Mercury session that has only been dated "Fall 1948," Dinah Washington recorded two songs, "It's Funny" and "Why Can't You Behave." The original 78 RPM credit reads "Dinah Washington with Orchestral Accompaniment." Some releases and discographies have added "Dinah Washington with possibly Cootie Williams Orchestra." (For example, "Mercury Records Discography: 1948," https://www.jazzdisco.org/mercury-records/discography-1948/#480900.) This is incorrect. The trumpet soloist doesn't sound like Williams and the instrumentation doesn't match what Williams had at that time. In the last part of 1948, Washington toured with George Hudson and his orchestra. Hudson was also a trumpeter. It's highly possible that it's his trumpet and orchestra that is heard on these sides.]

COOTIE WILLIAMS AND HIS ORCHESTRA
2 MARCH 1949, NEW YORK CITY [MERCURY]

Cootie Williams—trumpet; Bob Merrill—trumpet, vocal; Rupert Cole—alto sax; Willis Jackson—tenor sax; Lester Fauntleroy—piano; Leonard "Heavy" Swain—bass; Gus Johnson—drums.
Gator Tail, Part 1
Gator Tail, Part 2
Let 'Em Roll (v—CW, BM)
Slidin' and Glidin'

COOTIE WILLIAMS AND HIS ORCHESTRA
20 SEPTEMBER 1949, NEW YORK CITY [MERCURY]

Cootie Williams, Bob Merrill—trumpet; Rupert Cole—alto sax; Willis Jackson—tenor sax; Lester Fauntleroy—piano; Leonard "Heavy" Swain—bass; Gus Johnson—drums, Eddie Mack—vocal.
Mercenary Papa (v—EM)
You Got to Pay Those Dues (v—EM)
Doin' the Gator Tail

MACK EDMONDSON WITH COOTIE WILLIAMS AND HIS ORCHESTRA
RECORDED 1950 [DERBY]

Cootie Williams—trumpet; Rupert Cole—alto sax, clarinet; Willis Jackson—tenor sax; Arnold Jarvis—piano; Dick Fulbright—bass; Ed Thigpen—drums, Eddie Mack—vocal.
Shotgun Boogie (v—EM)
Divorce Me C.O.D. (v—EM)

Steam Roller Blues (v—EM)
Beauty Parlor Gossip (v—EM)

COOTIE WILLIAMS AND HIS ORCHESTRA
RECORDED FEBRUARY 1951, SAVOY BALLROOM, NEW YORK CITY (VOICE OF AMERICA RECORDING. JAZZ CLUB USA, PROGRAM #14) ORIGINAL BROADCAST DATE IS APRIL 1, 1951

Cootie Williams—trumpet; Rupert Cole—clarinet, alto sax; Bill "Weasel" Parker—tenor sax; Arnold Jarvis—piano; Leonard "Heavy" Swain—bass; Sylvester "Vess" Payne—drums, Eddie Mack—vocal.
Echoes of Harlem
Gator Tail
Things Ain't What They Used to Be (v—EM)
Soft Winds

DINAH WASHINGTON
RECORDED 27 JUNE 1952, NEW YORK CITY

Cootie Williams—trumpet; Dickie Harris—trombone; Arnett Cobb—tenor sax; George Rhodes—piano; Walter Buchanan—bass; Al Walker—drums; Dinah Washington—vocal.
I Got It Bad (v—DW)

COOTIE WILLIAMS
CA. 1954, PROBABLY NEW YORK CITY, AIRCHECK ACETATE (AUTHOR'S COLLECTION)

Cootie Williams—trumpet; unknown tenor sax, piano, bass, and drums.
Lean Baby
Perdido
You Are Too Beautiful

EDDIE VINSON AND HIS ORCHESTRA
CA. FEBRUARY 1954, NEW YORK CITY [KING]

Eddie "Cleanhead" Vinson—alto sax, vocal; Cootie Williams—trumpet; Arnett Cobb—tenor sax; unknown baritone sax, piano, guitar, bass, and drums.
Who is Whose (v—EV)
Old Man Boogie (v—EV)
You Can't Have My Love No More (v—EV)
I Need Your Love (v—EV)

COOTIE WILLIAMS
29 MARCH 1957, NEW YORK CITY [RCA VICTOR]

Cootie Williams—trumpet; Rupert Cole—alto sax; George Clarke—tenor sax; Elwyn Fraser—baritone sax; Preston Brown—organ; Larry Dale—guitar, vocal; Al Lucas—bass; Lester Jenkins—drums.
   Rinky Dink
   Please Give Your Love to Me
   Block Rock
   Percy Speaks

COOTIE WILLIAMS AND REX STEWART
30 APRIL 1957, NEW YORK CITY [JAZZTONE]

Rex Stewart—cornet; Cootie Williams—trumpet; Lawrence Brown, J. C. Higginbotham—trombone; Coleman Hawkins, Bud Freeman—tenor sax; Hank Jones—piano; Billy Bauer—guitar; Milt Hinton—bass; Gus Johnson—drums.
   I'm Beginning to See the Light
   Do Nothing till You Hear from Me
   Alphonse and Gaston

COOTIE WILLIAMS AND REX STEWART
7 MAY 1957, NEW YORK CITY [JAZZTONE]

Rex Stewart—cornet; Cootie Williams—trumpet; Lawrence Brown, J. C. Higginbotham—trombone; Coleman Hawkins, Bud Freeman—tenor sax; Hank Jones—piano; Billy Bauer—guitar; Milt Hinton—bass; Gus Johnson—drums.
   I Gotta Right to Sing the Blues
   Walkin' My Baby Back Home
   When Your Lover Has Gone
   I Knew You When

LARRY DALE WITH COOTIE WILLIAMS AND HIS ORCHESTRA
15 MAY 1957, NEW YORK CITY [RCA VICTOR]

Cootie Williams, Phil Barboza—trumpet; Rupert Cole, George Clarke, Al Sears, Elwyn Fraser—saxes; Eddie Wilcox—piano; Everett Barksdale, Larry Dale—guitar; Abe Baker—bass; Lester Jenkins—drums; Wini Brown, Larry Dale—vocals.
   Now That You've Loved Me

Blue Sunday (as Wini Brown with Cootie Williams)
Available Lover (as Wini Brown with Cootie Williams)
It's All in Your Mind (as Wini Brown and Larry Dale with Cootie Williams)

COOTIE WILLIAMS AND HIS ORCHESTRA
10 JULY 1957, NEW YORK CITY [RCA VICTOR]

Cootie Williams—trumpet; Rupert Cole, George Clarke, George Berg, Elwyn Fraser—saxes; Dave Martin—piano; Skeeter Best—guitar, Larry Dale—guitar, vocal; Abe Baker—bass; Lester Jenkins—drums.

It Hurts Me (as Larry Dale with Cootie Williams)
Rangoon
Boomerang

RONNIE GILBERT
8 AUGUST 1957, NEW YORK CITY [RCA VICTOR]

Ronnie Gilbert—vocal; Cootie Williams—trumpet; Bennie Morton—trombone; Buster Bailey—clarinet; Claude Hopkins—piano; Fred Hellerman, Steve Jordan—guitar; George Duvivier—bass; Osie Johnson—drums.

A Good Man Is Hard to Find
After You've Gone
Trombone Cholly
Yellow Dog Blues
Black Eye Blues
Cake Walking Babies

RONNIE GILBERT
9 AUGUST 1957, NEW YORK CITY [RCA VICTOR]

Ronnie Gilbert—vocal; Cootie Williams—trumpet; Bennie Morton—trombone; Buster Bailey—clarinet; Claude Hopkins—piano; Fred Hellerman, George Barnes—guitar; George Duvivier—bass; Osie Johnson—drums.

You've Been a Good Old Wagon
Weepin' Willow Blues
Gin House Blues
Nobody Knows When You Are Down and Out
Trouble In Mind
Empty Bed Blues

W. C. HANDY FUNERAL
2 APRIL 1958, NEW YORK CITY, BRITISH PATHE NEWSREEL

Cootie Williams—trumpet; unknown accompaniment
   Holy City (excerpt)

COOTIE WILLIAMS
5 MARCH 1958, NEW YORK CITY [RCA VICTOR]

Cootie Williams—trumpet; Billy Byers, Bobby Byrne, Lou McGarity—trombone; Dick Hixon—bass trombone; Phil Bodner, Elwyn Fraser, Nick Gaiazza, Romeo Penque, Boomie Richman—reeds; Lou Stein—piano; George Barnes—guitar; Eddie Safranski—bass; Don Lamond—drums.
   If I Could Be with You One Hour Tonight
   Caravan
   Contrasts
   New Concerto for Cootie

COOTIE WILLIAMS
25 MARCH 1958, NEW YORK CITY [RCA VICTOR]

Cootie Williams—trumpet; Billy Byers, Bobby Byrne, Lou McGarity—trombone; Dick Hixon—bass trombone; Phil Bodner, Elwyn Fraser, Nick Gaiazza, Romeo Penque, Boomie Richman—reeds; Hank Jones—piano; Tony Mottola—guitar; Eddie Safranski—bass; Don Lamond—drums.
   Air Mail Special
   My Old Flame
   Swingin' Down the Lane
   Just In Time

COOTIE WILLIAMS
8 APRIL 1958, NEW YORK CITY [RCA VICTOR]

Cootie Williams—trumpet; Billy Byers, Bobby Byrne, Chauncey Welch—trombone; Dick Hixon—bass trombone; Phil Bodner, Elwyn Fraser, Stan Webb, Romeo Penque, Boomie Richman—reeds; Henry Rowland—piano; Barry Galbraith—guitar; Eddie Safranski—bass; Osie Johnson—drums.
   Summit Ridge Drive
   On the Street Where You Live

I'll See You in My Dreams
Nevertheless, I'm In Love with You

REX STEWART AND THE DUKE ELLINGTON ALUMNI ALL STARS
RECORDED 3 JULY 1958, NEWPORT, RI

Rex Stewart—cornet; Cootie Williams—trumpet; Tyree Glenn—trombone; Hilton Jefferson—alto sax; Ben Webster—tenor sax; Billy Strayhorn—piano; Oscar Pettiford—bass; Sonny Greer—drums.

East St. Louis Toodle-oo
Rockin' in Rhythm
New Concerto for Cootie
C-Jam Blues
Le Grand Romp

ART FORD'S JAZZ PARTY
28 AUGUST 1958, WNTA-TV, NEW YORK CITY

Cootie Williams, Buck Clayton—trumpet; Rolf Kuhn—clarinet; Georgie Auld—tenor sax; Harry Sheppard—vibraphone; Roland Hanna—piano; Mundell Lowe—guitar; Vinnie Burke—bass; Roy Burnes—drums.

Airmail Special
Time on My Hands
How Deep Is the Ocean
Jumpin' at the Woodside
One O'Clock Jump

ART FORD'S JAZZ PARTY
16 OCTOBER 1958, WNTA-TV, NEW YORK CITY

Cootie Williams—trumpet; Nat Adderley—cornet; Kai Winding—trombone; Rolf Kuhn—clarinet; Julian "Cannonball" Adderley—alto sax; Coleman Hawkins—tenor sax; Harry Sheppard—vibraphone; Billy Taylor—piano; Roy Gaines—guitar; Vinnie Burke—bass; Bert Dahlander—drums; Lil Greenwood—vocal.

Fine and Dandy
Bill Bailey Won't You Please Come Home
Cootie's Blues (Cootie's Big Time Blues)
I Got It Bad and That Ain't Good
Airmail Special

Bugle Call Rag
Basin Street Blues

COOTIE WILLIAMS & REX STEWART
LATE 1958 [WARNER BROS.]

Cootie Williams, Al DeRisi, Bernie Glow, Ernie Royal, Joe Wilder—trumpet; Rex Stewart—cornet; Lawrence Brown, Eddie Bert, Urbie Green, Sonny Russo—trombone; Hilton Jefferson, Sid Cooper, Walt Levinsky—alto sax; Abraham "Boomie" Richman, Al Klink—tenor sax; Pinky Williams—baritone sax; Buddy Weed—piano; Barry Galbraith—guitar; Milt Hinton—bass; Don Lamond—drums; Joe Venuto—percussion; Jim Timmens—arranger, conductor; other musicians unidentified.

It Ain't Necessarily So
Bess, You Is My Woman
I Got Plenty o' Nuttin'
My Man's Gone Now
There's a Boat Dat's Leavin' Soon for New York
Summertime
A Red-Headed Woman
Oh Bess, Oh Where's My Bess
A Woman Is a Sometime Thing
Oh Lawd, I'm on My Way

COOTIE WILLIAMS
28 JANUARY 1959, MARS CLUB, PARIS

Cootie Williams—trumpet; George Clarke—tenor sax; Arnold Jarvis—piano; Larry Dale—guitar, vocal; Lester Jenkins—drums.
Echoes of Harlem

COOTIE WILLIAMS
31 JANUARY 1959, OLYMPIA THEATER, PARIS

Cootie Williams—trumpet; George Clarke—tenor sax; Arnold Jarvis—piano, organ; Larry Dale—guitar, vocal; Lester Jenkins—drums.
Night Train
Mood Indigo
Li'l Darlin'
Easy Swing

Three O'Clock in the Morning [*sic*—the correct title is "Chains of Love"]
Lester Leaps In
Echoes of Harlem
April in Paris
Alright, Okay, You Win
When the Saints Go Marching In
Caravan

COOTIE WILLIAMS
11 FEBRUARY 1959, PARIS

Cootie Williams, Nelson "Cadillac" Williams*—trumpet; George Clarke—tenor sax; Arnold Jarvis—piano, organ; Larry Dale—guitar, vocal; Guy Perderson—bass; Lester Jenkins—drums.
Sweet Lorraine (v—CW)
I Will Return to Paris
Lawdy Miss Claudy
Echoes of Harlem
I Know You Love Me
*We Remember Duke**
Hide And Go Seek
Perdido*

COOTIE WILLIAMS
11 JANUARY 1959, TV STUDIO, PARIS

Cootie Williams—trumpet; George Clarke—tenor sax; Arnold Jarvis—piano; Larry Dale—guitar, vocal; Lester Jenkins—drums.
Echoes of Harlem
Caravan
Royal Garden Blues
Air Mail Special
Rock a While
Night Train

COOTIE WILLIAMS & WINI BROWN
1959, NEW YORK CITY [JARO INTERNATIONAL]

Cootie Williams—trumpet, vocal; Wini Brown—vocal; Richard Harris—trombone; George Clarke—tenor sax; Arnold Jarvis—piano; Carl Lynch—guitar; George Duvivier—bass; James Johnson—drums; William Rodriguez—percussion; Quincy Jones—arranger.
    Lover (v—CW, WB)
    Gone Again (v—WB)
    You Got to Laugh (v—CW)
    I Surrender Dear/Sweet Lorraine (v—CW, WB)
    Goin' Around (v—CW, WB)
    Johnny with the Gentle Hands (v—WB, band)
    On the Sunny Side of the Street (v—CW)
    Around Midnight (v—WB)
    Bewitched (v—WB)
    That Old Feeling (v—CW)

COOTIE WILLIAMS
1960 [WARWICK]

Cootie Williams—trumpet, vocal; unidentified vibraphone, baritone sax, guitar, piano, bass, drums (two sessions?)
    Always
    Don't Get Around Much Anymore
    It Don't Mean a Thing If It Ain't Got That Swing
    I Found a New Baby
    Caravan
    When The Saints Go Marching In (v—CW, band)
    Do Nothing till You Hear from Me
    Drop Me Off in Harlem
    I Got It Bad and That Ain't Good
    There's No You
    Mack the Knife
    Blue Skies

BELLE BARTH
1961, THE ROUNDTABLE, NEW YORK CITY [ROULETTE]

Belle Barth—monologue, vocals; Cootie Williams—trumpet; unknown—piano; unknown—bass; unknown—drums.

BELLE BARTH
25 NOVEMBER 1961, CARNEGIE HALL, NEW YORK CITY [ROULETTE]

Belle Barth—monologue, vocals; Cootie Williams—trumpet; unknown—piano; unknown—bass; unknown—drums, Mercer Ellington—master of ceremonies.

NOTE—The *New York Daily News* reported that the Carnegie Hall performance would be recorded by Roulette Records and released as an album titled *The Belle Rings at Carnegie*. ("Record Review," Douglas Watt, *New York Daily News*, November 19, 1961, Section 2, 9.) The album has not been released as of this date. It is unknown if the tapes still (or ever did) exist.

COOTIE WILLIAMS
4 APRIL 1962, MIAMI [MOODSVILLE]

Cootie Williams—trumpet; Nat Jones—piano; Harold Dodson—bass; Bill Peeples—drums.
    Concerto for Cootie
    Sugar Blues
    You're Nobody 'Till Somebody Loves You
    Some of These Days
    Night Train
    Around the World in Eighty Days
    Liza
    Birmingham Blues

JOYA SHERRILL
12 JANUARY 1965, CHICAGO [20TH CENTURY FOX]

Cootie Williams—trumpet; Johnny Hodges—alto sax; Paul Gonsalves—tenor sax; Ernie Harper—piano; John Lamb—bass; Sam Woodyard—drums.
    Mood Indigo
    Sophisticated Lady
    Kissing Bug
    Duke's Place
    Things Ain't What They Used to Be
    Just Squeeze Me (But Please Don't Tease Me)

THE DUKE ELLINGTON ORCHESTRA, UNDER THE DIRECTION OF MERCER ELLINGTON
16-17 JULY 1974, NEW YORK [FANTASY]

Mercer Ellington—conductor; Cootie Williams, James "Buddy" Bolden, Harold "Money" Johnson, Barrie Lee Hall, Jr.—trumpet; Art Baron, Vince Prudente, Chuck Connors—trombone; Harold Minerve, James Spaulding, Maurice Simon, Harold Ashby, Harry Carney—reeds; Lloyd Mayers—piano; Larry Ridley—bass; Quentin "Rocky" White—drums.
   Drop Me Off in Harlem
   Blue Serge
   Wave

THE DUKE ELLINGTON ORCHESTRA, UNDER THE DIRECTION OF MERCER ELLINGTON
6-7 JANUARY 1975, CHICAGO [FANTASY]

Mercer Ellington—conductor; Cootie Williams, James "Buddy" Bolden, Harold "Money" Johnson, Barrie Lee Hall Jr., Calvin Ladner—trumpet; Art Baron, Vince Prudente, Chuck Connors—trombone; Harold Minerve, Maurice Simon, Harold Ashby, Ricky Ford, Anatole Gerasimov, Joe Temperley—reeds; Lloyd Mayers—piano; Edward Ellington II—guitar; J. J. Wiggins—bass; Freddie Waits—drums.
   Jump for Joy
   Black and Tan Fantasy
   Warm Valley
   All Too Soon
   Rock Skippin' at the Blue Note
   Jeep's Blues
   Ko-Ko
   Carney
   Blem
   Harlem Air Shaft
   Conga Brava

THE DUKE ELLINGTON ORCHESTRA, UNDER THE DIRECTION OF MERCER ELLINGTON
12 JANUARY 1975, SUPER BOWL IX HALF-TIME SHOW, NEW ORLEANS

Mercer Ellington—conductor; Cootie Williams, James "Buddy" Bolden, Harold "Money" Johnson, Barrie Lee Hall Jr., Calvin Ladner—trumpet; Art Baron, Vince Prudente, Chuck Connors—trombone; Harold Minerve, Maurice Simon, Harold Ashby, Ricky Ford, Joe Temperley—reeds; Lloyd Mayers—piano; Edward Ellington II—guitar; J. J. Wiggins—bass; Freddie Waits—drums; Anita Moore—vocal.

    Take the "A" Train
    Things Ain't What They Used to Be
    It Don't Mean a Thing (If It Ain't Got That Swing)
    C-Jam Blues

THE DUKE ELLINGTON ORCHESTRA, UNDER THE DIRECTION OF MERCER ELLINGTON
3 MARCH 1975, CAFÉ ATLANTIQUE, STOCKHOLM, SWEDEN

Mercer Ellington—conductor; Cootie Williams, James "Buddy" Bolden, Barrie Lee Hall Jr.—trumpet; Harold "Money" Johnson—trumpet, vocal; Art Baron, Vince Prudente, Chuck Connors—trombone; Harold Minerve, Maurice Simon, Harold Ashby, Ricky Ford, Joe Temperley—reeds; Lloyd Mayers—piano; Edward Ellington II—guitar; J. J. Wiggins—bass; Freddie Waits—drums; Anita Moore—vocal.

    Take the "A" Train
    Jump for Joy
    Just Squeeze Me
    Rock Skippin' at the Blue Note
    Unknown selection from "The New Orleans Suite"
    Sophisticated Lady
    Mack the Knife (v—MJ)
    Hello Dolly (v—MJ)
    The Shepherd Who Watches Over the Night Flock
    I Let a Song Go Out of My Heart
    It Don't Mean a Thing (If It Ain't Got That Swing)
    Just Squeeze Me
    Three Black Kings

THE DUKE ELLINGTON ORCHESTRA, UNDER THE DIRECTION OF MERCER ELLINGTON
12 MAY 1975, NEW YORK CITY [FANTASY]

Mercer Ellington—conductor; Cootie Williams, James "Buddy" Bolden, Willie Singleton, Barry Lee Hall Jr.—trumpet; Art Baron, Vince Prudente, Chuck Connors—trombone; Harold Minerve, Maurice Simon, Ricky Ford, Bill Easley, Percy Marion—reeds; Lloyd Mayers—piano; Edward Ellington II—guitar; J. J. Wiggins—bass; Quentin "Rocky" White—drums.

Happy-Go-Lucky Local

THE DUKE ELLINGTON ORCHESTRA, UNDER THE DIRECTION OF MERCER ELLINGTON
7-14 JUNE 1975, ABOARD THE SS ROTTERDAM FROM NEW YORK CITY TO NASSAU, BERMUDA, AS PART OF THE JAZZ AT SEA FESTIVAL SHOWBOAT 3. VIDEO FROM THIS VOYAGE BROADCAST ON THE BBC ON THE SHOW JAZZ SHIP.

Unknown numbers

THE DUKE ELLINGTON ORCHESTRA, UNDER THE DIRECTION OF MERCER ELLINGTON
THE MIKE DOUGLAS SHOW [EPISODE #15.31] PHILADELPHIA

Recorded ? Aired in Los Angeles TV on 8 July 1975
Ella Fitzgerald
Recorded (Date Unknown) Original Air Date—13 October 1975
  Black and Tan Fantasy
  Jeep's Blues
  Happy-Go-Lucky Local

COOTIE WILLIAMS
1 MAY 1976, WASHINGTON, DC

Cootie Williams Jazz Oral History Project interview conducted by Helen Oakley Dance

TED EASTON AND HIS JAZZ FRIENDS
13 MAY 1976, NEW ORLEANS JAZZ CLUB, SCHEVENINGEN, HOLLAND [RIFF RECORDS]

Cootie Williams—trumpet; Frits Kaatee, Dave Mitchell, Scat Nicholson—clarinet; Chris Smildiger—piano; Jacques Kingma—bass; Ted Easton—drums.
    Creole Love Call

NEWPORT JAZZ FESTIVAL ALL STARS
11 JULY 1976, MONTREUX JAZZ FESTIVAL, MONTREUX, SWITZERLAND

Cootie Williams, Joe Newman—trumpet, Vic Dickenson—trombone, Illinois Jacquet, Budd Johnson—tenor sax; George Wein—piano; George Duvivier—bass; Oliver Jackson—drums; Claude Nobs—harmonica.
    Session was videotaped and some portion was shown on the BBC2; titles are unknown at this time

COOTIE WILLIAMS
26-27 JULY 1976, BARCELONA, SPAIN [BLACK & BLUE]

Cootie Williams—trumpet; Booty Wood—trombone; Gerard Badini—tenor sax; Raymond Fol—piano; Michel Gaudry—bass; Sam Woodyard—drums.
    Caravan
    Blues
    In a Mellow Tone
    C Jam Blues
    Las Tres Senoras
    You Talk a Little Trash
    Finger Poppin' at the Popcorn

TERESA BREWER
5 APRIL 1978, CARNEGIE HALL, NEW YORK CITY [DOCTOR JAZZ]

Teresa Brewer—vocal; Cootie Williams, Marvin Stamm, Joe Newman, Jon Faddis, Chris Griffin—trumpet; Bob Alexander, Warren Covington, Al Grey—trombone; Babe Clarke, Lenny Hambro, Arnie Lawrence, Steven Marcus, Seldon Powell—reeds; Derek Smith—piano; Bucky Pizzarelli, Hiram Bullock—guitar; Wilbur Bascomb—bass;

Andy Newmark, Grady Tate—drums; Phil Kraus, Guillermo Franco, Ray Mantilla—percussion.

Mood Indigo

THE DUKE ELLINGTON ORCHESTRA, UNDER THE DIRECTION OF MERCER ELLINGTON
22 MARCH 1980, HARRY S TRUMAN HIGH SCHOOL, CO-OP CITY, BRONX, NY

Cootie Williams, Barrie Lee Hall, Johnny Longo, Yuzef Rakha—trumpet; Malcolm Taylor, Chuck Connors, Robert Farrell—trombone; Harold Minerve, Kenny Garrett, David Young, Courtney Winter, Marvin Holladay—reeds; Onzy Matthews—piano; David Eubanks—bass; Quentin "Rocky" White—drums.

The Shepherd Who Watches Over the Night Flock
Take the "A" Train
Things Ain't What They Used to Be
(Plus eighteen other selections that don't feature Williams)

COOTIE WILLIAMS
18 JUNE OR 1 JULY 1980, SYDNEY, AUSTRALIA

Cootie Williams interview for the *Joy-a-Jazz* radio show, broadcast on 23 July 1980 on 2MBS-FM.

UNKNOWN BRITISH DOCUMENTARY
1980, MERCER ELLINGTON'S APARTMENT, NEW YORK

Interview footage with Cootie Williams passing his trumpet to Barrie Lee Hall Jr.

THE COMPOSITIONS OF COOTIE WILLIAMS

The source for this information is the online ASCAP Repertory database, the Library of Congress copyrights, record labels and discographies.

Ain't Got No Blues Today (Clarence Redd—Katherine Redd—Cootie Williams)
Be Cool and Groovy for Me (Duke Ellington—Tony Bennett—Cootie Williams)
Beautiful Romance (Duke Ellington [music]—Cootie Williams [music]—Lupin Fien [words])
Birmingham Special (Cootie Williams)
Block Rock (Cootie Williams)
Blues a' Poppin' (Cootie Williams)
Blues In My Condition (Cootie Williams)
Boomerang (Cootie Williams—Elwyn Fraser)
Boudoir Benny (Duke Ellington—Cootie Williams)
Bring 'em Down Front (Edward Johnson—Cootie Williams [music]—Norman Keenan [words])
Chasin' Chippies (Duke Ellington—Cootie Williams)
Coffee Break (Cootie Williams—Elwyn Fraser)
Concerto for Cootie (Duke Ellington*)
Do Some War Work, Baby (Cootie Williams)
Doin' the Gator Tail (Willis Jackson—Cootie Williams)
Downtown Uproar (Duke Ellington—Cootie Williams)
The Duke Steps Out (Duke Ellington—Johnny Hodges—Cootie Williams)
Easy Swing (Cootie Williams)
Echoes of Harlem (Duke Ellington*)
Echoes of the Jungle (Cootie Williams—Irving Mills**)
Empty Ballroom Blues (Duke Ellington—Cootie Williams)
Fish for Supper (Joe Guy—Cootie Williams—Al Cooper)

Floogie Boo (Eddie Vinson—Cootie Williams)
Frolic Sam (Cootie Williams)
Gal-a-vantin' (Duke Ellington—Cootie Williams)
Gator Tail (Cootie Williams—Willis Jackson) Note—although the label of the original Mercury 78 RPM release credits Jackson as a cocomposer, the ASCAP database credits the composition solely to Williams.
Give It Up (Cootie Williams)
G-Men (Cootie Williams)
Hangin' Around (Horace Davis—Henry Cooper—Cootie Williams)
House of Joy (Cootie Williams—Bernie Hanighen)
I Don't Know (Cootie Williams—Eddie Vinson)
I May Be Easy, But I'm No Fool (Johnson, Cootie Williams, Alston)
I Should o' Been Thinkin' Instead of Drinkin' (Cootie Williams)
I Will Return to Paris (Cootie Williams)
It's Glory (Duke Ellington—Cootie Williams)
Jet Propelled Papa (Helen Humes—Cootie Williams)
Juice Head Baby (Cootie Williams—Holmes Daylie)
Jumping to Conclusions (Cootie Williams)
Let 'em Roll (Cootie Williams—Robert Merrill)
Let's Do the Whole Thing or Nothing at All (Cootie Williams—Johnson—Johnson)
Mobile Blues (Duke Ellington—Cootie Williams)
Mood for Coot (Cootie Williams)
New Concerto for Cootie (Cootie Williams—Elwyn Fraser)
Ooh La-La (Cootie Williams—Dyson—Ford—Williams—Jewell)
The Opener (Cootie Williams—Elwyn Fraser)
Rangoon (Cootie Williams—Elwyn Fraser)
Rhapsody in Bass (Cootie Williams)
Rinkey Dink (Jack Allen—Larry Dale—Cootie Williams)
'Round Midnight (Thelonious Monk—Cootie Williams—Bernie Hanighen)
She's Gone (Duke Ellington—Cootie Williams)
Sleepy Valley (Cootie Williams)
Slidin' and Glidin' (Cootie Williams)
Smooth Sailing (Cootie Williams—Clarence Redd)
Sound Track (Cootie Williams—Eddie Johnson)
Swing Pan Alley (Duke Ellington—Cootie Williams)
Takes a Good, Good Woman (Arthur Berman—Morey Davidson—Cootie Williams)
That's the Lick (Cootie Williams—Eddy De Verteuil)
Toasted Pickle (Cootie Williams)

Top and Bottom (Cootie Williams)
Typhoon (Cootie Williams—Clarence Redd)
Vibraphonia (Clarence Redd—Cootie Williams)
We Remember Duke (Cootie Williams)
When My Baby Left Me (Cootie Williams—Eddie Vinson)
You Talk a little Trash (Cootie Williams)
You're the One for Me, Sweetheart (Bob Merrill—Cootie Williams)
You've Got to Laugh (Cootie Williams)
You've Got to Pay Those Dues (Travis Edmonson—Leonard Swain—Cootie Williams)

*Although these compositions are credited to Duke Ellington, Cootie Williams has maintained that they were written by him.

**Irving Mills has no known musical contributions to any music his name is listed on. He added his name to the compositions of the musicians he managed in order to collect additional royalty payments for himself.

AWARDS AND HONORS

1940—*Down Beat*, All-American Swing Band, Trumpet, third
1941—*Down Beat*, All-American Swing Band, Trumpet, second
1941—*Metronome*, Hall of Fame
1941—*Metronome*, All-Stars, Hot Trumpet
1942—*Down Beat*, All-American Swing Band, Trumpet
1942—*Metronome*, All-Stars, Hot Trumpet
1943—Camp Shanks (Orangeburg, NJ), "King of Swing"
1944—*Esquire*, All-American Band, Trumpet, Silver
1945—*Esquire*, All-American Jazz Band, Trumpet, Gold
1945—*Metronome*, All-Stars, Hot Trumpet
1946—*Esquire*, All-American Jazz Award, Trumpet, Gold
1946—Southern University, Most Popular Band
1946—Southern University, Most Exciting Arrangement of the Year—"House of Joy"
1946—KECA (Los Angeles AM Radio), All-American Band
1946—Junior Jazz Foundation, Trumpeter of the Year
1946—Key to the City, Mobile, Alabama
1947—*Pittsburgh Courier*'s All-American Band, Trumpet, second
1960—Academie du Disque, Best Jazz Album of 1959, *Cootie*

BIBLIOGRAPHY

Allen, Walter C. *Hendersonia: The Music of Fletcher Henderson and his Musicians*. Walter C. Allen. 1973.
Bailey, Pearl. *The Raw Pearl*. Harcourt, Brace & World. 1968.
Balliett, Whitney. *Collected Works: A Journal of Jazz, 1954-2000*. St. Martin's Press. 2000.
Barnet, Charlie, with Stanley Dance. *Those Swinging Years: The Autobiography of Charlie Barnet*. Louisiana State University Press. 1984.
Bennett, Bryan Wendell. *Cootie Williams, Rex Stewart, and Ray Nance: Duke Ellington's trumpet soloists 1940-1942*. University of Iowa doctoral thesis. 2009.
Bied, Dan. *Dan Bied's Jazz Memories*. Craftsman Press. 1994.
Bigard, Barney, edited by Barry Martyn. *With Louis and the Duke*. Oxford University Press. 1980.
Brown, James, with Bruce Tucker. *James Brown: The Godfather of Soul*. Macmillan. 1986.
Bushell, Garvin, with Mark Tucker. *Jazz from the Beginning*. Da Capo Press. 1998.
Carlin, Richard, and Kinshasha Holman Conwill, editors. *Ain't Nothing Like the Real Thing: The Apollo Theater and American Entertainment*. Smithsonian Books. 2010.
Chambers, Jack. "Ellington the Composer: Caught in the Act." Unpublished manuscript.
Chapman, Con. *Rabbit's Blues: The Life and Times of Johnny Hodges*. Oxford University Press. 2019.
Chilton, John. *Ride, Red, Ride: The Life of Henry "Red" Allen*. Bloomsbury. 1999.
Chilton, John. *Roy Eldridge—Little Jazz Giant*. Continuum. 2002.
Clayton, Buck, assisted by Nancy Miller Elliott. *Buck Clayton's Jazz World*. Oxford University Press. 1986.
Cohodas, Nadine. *Queen: The Life and Music of Dinah Washington*. Pantheon Books. 2004.
Collier, James Lincoln. *Benny Goodman and the Swing Era*. Oxford University Press. 1989.
Collier, James Lincoln. *Duke Ellington*. Oxford University Press. 1987.
Connor, D. Russell, and Warren W Hicks. *BG—On the Record: A Bio-discography of Benny Goodman*. Arlington House. 1969.
Crease, Stephanie Stein. *Rhythm Man: Chick Webb and the Beat That Changed America*. Oxford University Press. 2023.
Crow, Bill. *Jazz Anecdotes Second Time Around*. Oxford University Press. 2005.
Dance, Helen Oakley. *Smithsonian Institution Oral History Interview of Cootie Williams*. 1976.
Dance, Stanley. *The World of Duke Ellington*. Charles Scribner's Sons. 1970.
Dance, Stanley. *The World of Earl Hines*. Da Capo Press. 1977.

Dance, Stanley. *The World of Swing*. Charles Scribner's Sons. 1974.
Daniels, Douglas Henry. *Lester Leaps In: The Life and Times of Lester "Pres" Young*. Beacon Press. 2002.
Davis-Horton, Paulette. *The Davis Avenue Story*. Horton. 1991.
Dexter, Dave Jr. *Playback*. Billboard Publications. 1976.
Dietrich, Kurt. *Duke's Bones: Ellington's Great Trombonists*. Advance Music. 1995.
Dunning, John. *The Encyclopedia of Old-Time Radio*. Oxford University Press. 1998.
Ellington, Duke. *Music Is My Mistress*. Da Capo. 1976.
Ellington, Mercer, with Stanley Dance. *Duke Ellington in Person*. Houghton Mifflin. 1978.
Feather, Leonard. *The Jazz Years: Earwitness to an Era*. DaCapo Press. 1987.
Firestone, Ross. *Swing, Swing, Swing: The Life and Times of Benny Goodman*. Norton. 1993.
Forrest, Helen, with Bill Libby. *I Had the Craziest Dream*. Coward, McCann and Geoghagan. 1982.
Gillespie, Dizzy, with Al Fraser. *To Be or Not to Bop*. Doubleday. 1999.
Goldberg, Marv. *More Than Words Can Say: The Ink Spots and Their Music*. Scarecrow Press. 1998.
Gordon, Claire P. *My Unforgettable Jazz Friends: Duke, Benny, Nat, Rex . . .* Phase V Press. 2004.
Green, Dr. Edward, ed. *The Cambridge Companion to Duke Ellington*. Cambridge University Press. 2014.
Haley, Alex. *The Autobiography of Malcolm X*. Random House. 1964.
Hammond, John, with Irving Townsend. *John Hammond on Record*. Ridge Press/Summit Books. 1977.
Hampton, Lionel, with James Haskins. *Hamp: An Autobiography*. Amistad Press. 1993.
Hancock, Jon. *Benny Goodman—The Famous 1938 Carnegie Hall Jazz Concert*. Prancing Phish Publishing. 2008.
Hasse, John Edward. *Beyond Category: The Life and Genius of Duke Ellington*. Da Capo Press. 1993.
Hershorn, Tad. *Norman Granz: The Man Who Used Jazz for Justice*. University of California Press. 2011.
Hodeir, Andre. *Jazz: Its Evolution and Essence*. Grove Press. 1961.
Jewell, Derek. *Duke: A Portrait of Duke Ellington*. W.W. Norton. 1977.
Johnson, John, Joel Selvin, and Dick Cami. *Peppermint Twist: The Mob, the Music, and the Most Famous Dance Club of the '60s*. St. Martin's. 2012.
Kelley, Robin D. G. *Thelonious Monk: The Life and Times of an American Original*. Free Press. 2009.
Kernfeld, Barry, ed. *The New Grove Dictionary of Jazz*. St. Martin's Press. 1994.
Kerouac, Jack. *On the Road*. Penguin. 1957.
Koch, Stephen. *Louis Jordan: Son of Arkansas, Father of R&B*. History Press. 2014.
Lambert, Eddie. *Duke Ellington: A Listener's Guide*. Scarecrow Press. 1999.
Levinson, Peter J. *Trumpet Blues, The Life of Harry James*. Oxford University Press. 1999.
Magee, Jeffrey. *The Uncrowned King of Swing: Fletcher Henderson and Big Band Jazz*. Oxford University Press. 2005.
Manning, Frankie, and Cynthia R. Millman. *Frankie Manning: Ambassador of Lindy Hop*. Temple University Press. 2007.
McCarthy, Albert. *Big Band Jazz*. Royce Publications. 1983.
Miller, Norma, and Evette Jensen. *Swingin' at the Savoy*. Temple University Press. 1996.

Nicholson, Stuart. *Ella Fitzgerald*. Charles Scribner's Sons. 1994.
Pullman, Peter. *Wail: The Life of Bud Powell*. Bop Changes. 2012.
Reig, Teddy, with Edward Berger. *Reminiscing in Tempo: The Life and Times of a Jazz Hustler*. Scarecrow Press. 1990.
Riccardi, Ricky. *Heart Full of Rhythm: The Big Band Years of Louis Armstrong*. Oxford University Press. 2020.
Rosenkrantz, Timme, and Frank Buchmann-Moller. *Is This to Be My Souvenir? Jazz Photos from the Timme Rosenkrantz Collection 1918–1969*. Odense University Press. 2000.
Rosenthal, George S., and Frank Zachary, eds. *Jazzways*. Greenberg Publishing. 1946.
Rust, B. A. L., and Walter C. Allen. *King Joe Oliver*. Jazz Book Club. 1957.
Schuller, Gunther. *The Swing Era: The Development of Jazz, 1930–1945*. Oxford University Press. 1989.
Serant, Claire. *Images of America: St. Albans*. Arcadia Publishing. 2020.
Smith, Jessie Carney, ed. *Notable Black Women: Book II*. Gale/Cengage Learning. 1995.
Smith, RJ. *The One: The Life and Music of James Brown*. Gotham Books. 2012.
Stewart, Rex, edited by Claire P. Gordon. *Boy Meets Horn*. University of Michigan Press. 1993.
Stratemann, Dr. Klaus. *Duke Ellington: Day by Day and Film by Film*. Jazz Media. 1992.
Tenot, Frank. *Frankly Speaking: Chroniques de Jazz de 1944 à 2004*. Editions du Layeur. 2004.
Terry, Clark, with Gwen Terry. *Clark: The Autobiography of Clark Terry*. University of California Press. 2011.
Timner, W. E. *Ellingtonia: The Recorded Music of Duke Ellington and His Sidemen*. Scarecrow Press. 1996.
Travis, Dempsey. *An Autobiography of Black Jazz*. Urban Research Institute. 1983.
Treadwell, Bill, ed. *The Big Book of Swing*. Cambridge House. 1946.
Tucker, Mark, ed. *The Duke Ellington Reader*. Oxford University Press. 1993.
Tucker, Mark. *Ellington: The Early Years*. University of Illinois Press. 1995.
Tye, Larry. *Satchel: The Life and Times of an American Legend*. Random House. 2009.
Ulanov, Barry. *Duke Ellington*. Da Capo. 1975.
Vail, Ken. *Duke's Diary: Part One, The Life of Duke Ellington 1927–1950*. Vail Publishing. 1999.
Vail, Ken. *Duke's Diary: Part Two, The Life of Duke Ellington 1950–1974*. Scarecrow Press. 2002.
Wein, George, with Nate Chinen. *Myself Among Others: A Life in Music*. Da Capo. 2003.
Wells, Dicky, as told to Stanley Dance. *The Night People*. Robert Hale & Company. 1971.
Weeks, Todd Bryant. *Luck's in My Corner: The Life and Music of Hot Lips Page*. Routledge. 2008.
Whitburn, Joel. *The Billboard Book of Top 40 R&B and Hip-Hop Hits*. Billboard Books. 2006.
Whitburn, Joel. *Pop Memories 1890–1954: The History of American Popular Music*. Record Research. 1986.
Wilmer, Val. *Mama Said There'd Be Days Like This*. Woman's Press. 1989.
Wright, Laurie, ed. *Storyville 1996/7*. L. Wright Publishing. 1997.
Historically Black newspapers such as *The Chicago Defender*, *The New York Age*, *The Pittsburgh Courier*, *The Los Angeles Sentinel*, *The Baltimore Afro-American*, *The Black Dispatch*, *The People's Voice*, *Cleveland Call and Post*, and others.
Smithsonian Institute Jazz Oral History Project was an invaluable resource in the preparation of this biography. I used the interviews with Cootie Williams, Barney Bigard, Lawrence Brown, Sonny Greer, Charlie Holmes, Jimmy Jones, Charlie Barnet, Arnett Cobb, and John Simmons. But there are many more available in the series and they provide a candid and fascinating insight into the world of jazz.

INDEX

Page numbers in **bold** indicate illustrations.

Abyssinian Baptist Church, 234
Academie du Disque, 243
"Across the Alley from the Alamo," 201
Adderley, Julian Carlo, 22, 237
Adderley, Julian Edwin "Cannonball," 22, 236
Adderley, Nat, 22, 236
Addisleigh Park, 190
"Ain't Got No Blues Today," 182
"Ain't Misbehavin,'" 82
Ain't Misbehavin' (show), 321
"Air Mail Special" / "Good Enough to Keep," 80, 95, 144, 147, 161, 237, 244
Alabama Jazz Hall of Fame, 315
Albee Theater, 144
Alcoholics Anonymous, 224
Alexander, Van, 218
Alexander, Willard, 95
Allen, Henry "Red," 30, 72, 98, 227, 228
Allen, Walter C., 30
Alonzo Ross's DeLuxe Syncopators, 22–25, **23**
"Alright, OK, You Win," 244
Altiere, James, 28
American Federation of Musicians (AFM), 116, 140, 209
American High School Jazz Festival, 315
Ammons, Gene, 74
Amos 'n' Andy, 42, 146
And His Mother Called Him Bill, 289
Anderson, Ernest, 174
Anderson, Ivie, 45, 60, 62, 63, 96
Anderson, Marion, 97, 149
Anderson, William "Cat," 53, 54, 82, 200, 254, 263–66, 270, 275, **279**, 280–81, 295, 296, 306; opinion of Cootie Williams, 265, 307

Anthony, Ray, 210, 318
Apollo Theater, 108, 113, 118, 130, 133, 136, 179, 182, 198, 201, 210, 216, 221, 224
Arban, Jean-Baptiste, 15
Arizona Sun, 222
Armed Forces Radio Service (AFRS), 147
Armstrong, Lil, 292
Armstrong, Louis, 9, 21, 27, 38, 44, 45, 50, 51, 58, 65, 69, 82, 126, 127, 151, 157, 172, 181, 198, 200, 201, 204, 221, 227, 231, 236, 250, 262, 266, 274, 308, 322; Cootie Williams's opinion of, 15–16, 30, 42; poll winner, 137, 161, 173–75; tributes, 292
Around Midnight, 250, **251**
Art Ford's Jazz Party, 236
ASCAP, 43, 154
Ash, Paul, 24
Ashby, Harold, 309
"Ask Me Now," 153
"A-Tisket, A-Tasket," 147
Atlanta University, 30
Attucks, Crispus, 184
Auld, George, **72**, 79, 80, **87**, 236
Australian Elizabethan Theatre Trust, 318
"Available Lover," 229

Bach, Bob, 128
Bach, Johann Sebastian, 124
Bacon, Louis, **47**, 51, 96, 98, 104, 105, 112, 118
Badini, Gerard, 314
Bailey, Bill, **47**
Bailey, Buster, **29**, 231
Bailey, Pearl, 110, 118, 122–23, 133, 142
Bakaleinikoff, Vladimir, 97

Baker, Dorothy, 157
Baker, Howard, 157
Baker, Josephine, 254
Baker, LaVern, 224
Balladeers, 208
Ballard, George "Butch," 94, 96, **160**
Balliett, Whitney, 263
Baltimore Afro-American, 42, 74, 88, 90, 172, 198, 220
Baltimore Sun, 82
Band Box, the, 27
Band Leader, 156
Bankhead, Tallulah, 227
Barksdale, Everett, **230**
Barnet, Charlie, 74, 86, 92, 95, 147
Baron, Art, 50, 285, 287
Barron, Blue, 111
Bart, Ben, 202, 254
Barth, Belle, 253–55, 257
Bascomb, Wilbur "Dud," 71
Basie, Katherine, 192
Basie, William "Count," 38, 44, 61, 72, 80, 81, 92, 95, 99, 105, 114, 115, 129, 145, 147, 161, 190, 192, 195, 197, 203, 204, 222, 244, 245, 262, 295, 314
Basie Brothers, 103
"Basin Street Blues," 57, 244
Battle of Shiloh, 183
Bauer, Billy, 231
BBC, 311
"Beauty Parlor Gossip," 220
Bechet, Sidney, 70, 173, 228, 237
Beiderbecke, Bix, 27, 127, 173, 198
Bell, Aaron, 284, 306
Belle Barth in Person, 253, **253**
Belle of the Nineties, 42
Bellson, Louie, 46, 295, 306
Belmont Park, 305
Benado, Fernando, 284
Beneke, Gordon "Tex," 318
Bennett, Tony, 324
"Benny Rides Again," 76
Berendt, Joachim-Ernst, 244
Berglas, Max, 192
Berigan, Bernard "Bunny," 85, 127, 173, 198
Berle, Milton, 187

Bernie, Ben, 24
Bernstein, Artie, 72, **87**
Bernstein, Leonard, 299
Berry, Bill, 54, 264, 306
Berry, Chu, 30, 59, 214
Beware, 157
Big Challenge, The, 231–32, 236
"Big Fat Mama," 216
Big Three Tour, 143, 157, 162, 169, 189, 197; and segregation, 148–49; success of, 150
Bigard, Barney, **37**, 42, 45, 49, 56, 57, 58, 61, 64, 121, 137, 310, 313
Billboard, The, 23, 70, 79, 90, 97, 115, 122, 136, 142, 154, 164, 169, 197, 198, 201, 229, 255
"Bird with Strings," 149
Birdland Club, 223
"Black, Brown, and Beige," 184, 262
"Black and Tan Fantasy," 40, 265, 280, 311
Black and Tan (movie short), 40
Blackman, Elaine, 180
Blackwell, Otis, 229
Blake, Eubie, 321
Blanton, Jimmie, 63, 65, 227, 264, 317
"Block Rock," 229–30
"Blue Garden Blues," 152, 161
"Blue Mood," 57
"Blue Reverie," 58, 61
Blue Steele, 24
"Blue Sunday," 229
"Blues in my Condition," 82
"Boff Boff," 139
Bolden, Charles "Buddy," 196
"Boomerang," 229
Bostic, Earl, 203
Bostic, Joe, 178, 212
Boston Globe, The, 283
Boston Globe Jazz Festival, 283
"Boy Meets Horn," 64
Boy Meets Horn (book), 30, 54
Bradshaw, Tiny, 195
Braff, Ruby, 250
Brandenburg Concerto, 124
Braud, Wellman, **37**, **47**, 291
Brewer, Teresa, 316
Brice, Carol, 187
Briggs, Bunny, 95

"Bring 'em Down Front," 182
British Pathé, 234
Brooks, Randy, 181, 200
Brooks, Sidney Johnstone, Jr., 183
Brooks Field, 183
Brown, Clifford, 214, 322
Brown, "Fabulous" Preston, 222, 229
Brown, James, 254
Brown, Lawrence, 38, **47**, 54, 57, 59, 90, 128, 231, 236, 262–63, 283, 288–89, 290, 296, 304, 322
Brown, Ralph, 139, 178
Brown, Ray, 150
Brown, W. Abner, 40
Brown, Winifred "Wini," 223, 229, 250, 252, 317
Brubeck, Dave, 274, 311, 320
Bruce, Spider, 182
Buchanan, Charlie, 119, 179, 189, 225, 226
"Bugle Call Rag," 44, 81
Burke, Vinnie, 236
Burns, Roy, 236
Burrell, Kenny, 229
Burrowes, Roy, 264
Burrs, Glenn, 75
Busch, Adolph, 124
Byard, Jaki, 298
"Bye Bye Baby Blues," 213
Byrne, Bobby, 131

Cabin in the Sky, 157
Cafe Zanzibar, 177, **178**, 179
California Eagle, 180
Calloway, Cab, 43, 45, 59, 114, 115, 117, 133, 146, 150, 157, 187, 203, 204, 207, 208, 219, 262
Cambridge Companion to Duke Ellington, The, 65
Camp Edison, 117
Camp Gruber, 177
Camp Shanks, 117
Campanella, Roy, 192
Campbell, Flea, 261
Cantor, Mark, 131–32
Capitol News, 169
Capitol Records, 164–68, 169, 177, 180, 181, 182, 197

Capitol Theatre, 319–20
Capone, Al, 103
"Caravan," 280
"Carelessly," 59
Carmichael, Hoagy, 43
Carnegie Hall, 61, 69, 181, 254, 262, 280, 312, 316
Carney, Dorothy, 151, 190
Carney, Harry, **37**, **47**, 54, 56, 58, 59, 61, 94, 128, 151, 169, 190, 226, 227, 262, 264, 269, 270, **270**, 288–89, 294, 295, 298, 302, 310, 317, 322; death of, 306; illness, 290, 296–97, 298
Carter, Benny, **29**, 30, 59, 81, 150
Casey, Al, **138**, 139, 150
Cash Box, 219
Castleman, Jeff, 269, 284–85, 286, 289–90
Catamaran Hotel, 318
Catholic University of America, 85
Catlett, Sidney "Big Sid," 85, 86, 88, 90, 94, **138**, 150
"Cavalcade of Jazz, A," 184
CBS, 115–16, 295
Celebrity Club, 221
Celley, Al, 288
Central High Register, 145
Chambers, Jack, 292
Chambers, Jordan, 208
Champlin, Charles, 54
Charles, Ray, 295
"Charleston," 27
Charleston Bearcats, 120
"Chasin' Chippies," 76, 85
Cheatham, Doc, 312
Checkers, 224
"Chicago Blues," 28
Chicago Defender, 22, 23, 24, 86, 95, 103, 105, 159, 178, 181, 189, 237
Christian, Charlie, 59, **72**, 77, 80, 81, 85, 86, **87**, 90, **98**, 317; illness, 88, 99
Churchill, Savannah, 163
"C-Jam Blues," 308–9, 314
"Clarinet Concerto," 88
"Clarinet Lament" / "Barney's Concerto," 56
Clarke, George, 229, 239–48, **241**
Clarke, Kenny, 106
Classic Capitol Jazz Sessions, 167

Clayton, Wilbur "Buck," 44, 61, 80, 236
Cleveland Call and Post, 180, 236
Cleveland Orchestra, 96
Clooney, Rosemary, 219
Cloud, Robert, 22, 24
Club Bengazi, 209
Club Riviera, 176, 208
Club Zanzibar, 173
Cobb, Arnett, 92, 210, 297
Coda, 279
Coin, Son, 22
Cole, Cozy, 59
Cole, Nat "King," 18, 150, 170, 187, 192
Cole, Rupert, 214, 229
Coleman, Marcus, 214
Coleman, Ornette, 292
Coles, Johnny, 169
Colgate University, 115
Collier, Ron, 292–93
Coltrane, John, 169, 190, 262, 264, 268
Columbia Records, 140, 143, 147, 266
Columbia Studios, 131
Commodore Records, 137
"Concerto for Clarinet," 97
"Concerto for Cootie," 56, 63–65, 69, 79, 80, 88, 97, 147, 213, 256, 282, **380**
Condoli, Pete, 172, 181
Condon, Eddie, 106, 174, 188, 208, 237
"Conga Brava," 63
Congaroos, 200
Conn trumpets, 126, 321
Conn, Billy, 195
Connors, Chuck, 280, 316
Cons, Carl, 75
Constitution Hall, 97, 184
Continuum, 310, **310**, 319
Cooper, Al, 135
Cooper, Eddie, 22
Cooper, George "Buster," 263, 270–72, 275–76, **279**, 281–82, 293, 306
Cooper, Ralph, 183
"Cootie Williams and the Newport All Stars," 314
Cootie Williams in Hi-Fi / *Cootie Williams in Stereo*, **232**, 314
"Cootie's Beauty," 198

"Cootie's Big Time Blues," 237
Copa City, 254–55, 257
Costello, William, 125–26, **125**, 322
Cotton Club (Harlem), 35, 36, 40, 81, 170–71, 235, 281
Cotton Club (Los Angeles), 42
"Cowpox Boogie," 188
Craft, Mortie, 252
"Creole Love Call," 280, 287, 314
Crescendo, 270
Crosby, Israel, 262
Cuba, 23
Cugat, Xavier, 111, 146
Cummings' Guest House, 151

Daily News, 162, 323
Daily Times, 87
Dale, Larry (Ennis Lowery), 229, 239–48
Dance, Helen Oakley, 58, 277
Dance, Stanley, 261, 318
Dandridge, Dorothy, 235
Daniels, Douglas Henry, 18
Daughters of the American Revolution (DAR), 97, 107, 184–85
Davies, Russell, 284
Davis, Eddie "Lockjaw," 106, 129, 140, 143, 151, 156
Davis, Miles, 127, 173, 174, 175, 227, 236, 322, 324
Davis, Sammy, Jr., 236, 295
Davis Avenue (Mobile, Alabama), 12, 14
Daylie, Holmes, 166
Daytona Beach, Florida, 23
"Dear Old Southland," 88
Decca Records, 140, 144, 243
"Deep River," 88, 97
Della Robia Garden, 23, 24
DeParis, Sidney, 71
Derby Records, 219
DeSilva, Buddy, 165
Destombes, Aris, 242
Detroit Tribune, 86
DiFabio, Frank, 255
"Diga Diga Doo," 58
"Dinah," 45
"Ding Dong Daddy from Dumas," 42

"Divorce Me, C.O.D.," 219
"Do Nothing 'Til You Hear From Me," 147, 250, 256, 282, 295
Do Nothing Till You Hear From . . . Cootie Williams, **251**, 252
Dodson, Harold, 256
Doggett, Bill, 99, 150, 155
Dominoes, 221
"Don't Be That Way," 88
Donte's, 307
Dorsey, Bob, 96, 98
Dorsey, Jimmy, 27, 73, 132
Dorsey, Tommy, 27, 95, 114
Douglas, Al, 132
Douglas, Bob, 167
Douglas, Freddie, 132
Douglas Brothers, 132
Dowell, Saxie, 131
Down Beat, 56, 65, 73–74, 77, 81, 82, 96, 99, 105, 107, 126, 139, 144, 174, 182, 198, 211, 220, 226, 228, 230, 231, 232, 235, 250, 257, 262, 289, 294, 298
Down Beat Hall of Fame, 154, 315
"Downtown Uproar," 58
Drifters, 224
"Drop Me Off in Harlem," 306
Du Bois, W. E. B., 184
"Ducky Wucky," 48
Duke Ellington, We Love You Madly, 295
"Duke Ellington Week," 294
Duke Ellington's 70th Birthday Concert, 291
Dunbar Hotel, 209
Duncan, Direction, 120
Dunn, Johnny, 38

Earle Theatre, 150, 163, 180
Easley, Bill, 310
"East St. Louis Toodle-oo," 235, 317
Easton, Ted, 314
"Echoes of Harlem," 56–57, 141, 179, 199, 207, 220, 242, 273–74, 323
Echoes of Harlem (album), **141**, 161
"Echoes of the Jungle," 43, 45
Eckstine, Billy, 161
Eddie Condon Floor Show, The, 237
Edmonds, Shepard, 184

Eisenhower, Dwight D., 227
Eldridge, Roy, 30, 51, 65, 71, 86, 90, 96, 126, 127, 133, 161, 172, **173**, 253, 324; on racial attitudes, 84; summing up his career, 262
Ellington, Edward Kennedy, II, 190
Ellington, Edward Kennedy "Duke," 11, 19, 27, 28, 35–37, 42–45, **47**, 54, 55, 57–59, **58**, 61, 77, 78, 80, 82, 93–96, 104, 107, 115, 126, 147, 150, 151, 161, 167, 169, 174, 177, 182, 183, 204, 207, 209, 213, 221, 226, 227, 229, 231, 232, 234–35, 252, 254, 256, 261, 262, 270, 277, 282, **282**, 283, 289, 314, 316, 322, 324; 1939 European tour, 238; 1963 European tour, 273; 1963 State Department tour, 274–78; 1971 European tour, 294; 1973 European tour, 296; affairs, 285; appetite, 103; band battle with Cootie Williams, 129–30; band battle with Jimmie Lunceford, 121; band bus seating arrangements, 269; band intonation, 269, 271; death of, 299; discipline, 79, 267; and the FBI, 186; illness, 295–96, 297–98; investment in Cootie Williams's orchestra, 92; loss of Cootie Williams in band, 73; negotiations with Goodman, 69; opinion of Cootie Williams, 265; on personnel, 89; Pullman cars, 84, 114; relationship with Cootie Williams, 293, 296–97; the "stockpile," 262; tributes, 298–99, 306, 308–9, 312; vacation, 292; writing style, 52
Ellington, Gay, 190
Ellington, Mercer, 38, 180, 190, 204, 270, 274, 276, 280, 287, 293, 294, 302, 308–9, 314, 316, 321, 323; arranger, 254; critical evaluations of, 320; disk jockey, 254; on the legacy of Duke Ellington, 303, 304, 306, 310–11; rebuilding the Duke Ellington orchestra, 303–4; recording sessions, 306; relationship to Cootie Williams, 190; road manager, 112, 288–89; solo responsibility rules, 282
Ellington Fresh Up, 314
Ellington the Composer: Caught in the Act, 292
Elman, Ziggy, 81, 85, 96
Encyclopedia Yearbook of Jazz, The, 226–27
"Epistrophy" / "Fly Right," 106, 128, 143, 152

Ericson, Rolf, 267
Esquire, 137, 161, 172, 174
"Esquire Blues," 139
"Esquire Bounce," 137
Essentially Ellington program, 324
Eubie!, 321
Evans, Earl, 22
Evans, Gil, 236
Evans, Herschel, 92
Evans, Warren, 161
Evening Star, 97
"Everything But You," 166, 169
"Evil Gal Blues," 208
"Evil Woman Blues," 216
Excelsior Band, 20

Faddis, Jon, 312
Faggen, Jay, 24, 25
Fair Employment Practices Committee (FEPC), 185
Fauntleroy, Lester, 214
FCC, 170
Feather, Leonard, 60, 128, 137, **138**, 174, 220, 226, 303, 304, 318
Ferguson, Maynard, 227
Fess Williams's Royal Flush Orchestra, 120
Fields, Shep, 74
"Fiesta in Blue" / "Cootie Growls," 79–80
Fila, Alec, 76
Filipacchi, Daniel, 238
Film Vodvil, 131–33, 143
"Fine and Dandy," 59, 237
"Finger Poppin' at the Popcorn," 314
Fitch Bandwagon, 81
Fitzgerald, Ella, 74, 119, 122, 139, 140, 142, 144, 145, **148**, 150, 162, 163, **164**, 174, 176, 177, 178, 182, 190, 197, 199, 201, 222, 227, 228, 236, 283
Flanagan, Jimmy, 181
Fletcher, Clinton "Dusty," 209
"Floogie Boo," 159
"Flying Home," 89
Fol, Raymond, 314
Ford, Arthur, 26, 236
Ford, Ricky, 304–6, 311, 313
Ford, Tennessee Ernie, 219

Forrest, Helen, 77
Fort Polk, 183
Forum, 318
Fox, Ed, 103
Frankie Manning, Ambassador of Lindy Hop, 218
Franklin, Aretha, 295
Franklin, Art, 149, 226
Frankly Speaking, 239
Fraser, Elwyn, 229
Frazier, George, 77, 115
Freedom of Information Act (FOIA), 186
Freedomland USA, 261
Freeman, Bud, 16, 111, 231, 314
Fritz, Roscoe, 98–99
From Harlem to Hollywood—My Life in Music, 218
Front Page Ball, 188
Frost, Agnes (aunt), 16
Frost, Alma Lue (aunt), 144
Frost, Baalam, Jr. (uncle), 144
Frost, Baalam A. (grandfather), 12
Frost, Gillbert (great uncle), 11
Frost, Granville (great-grandfather), 11–12
Frost, Mary Huckabee (great-grandmother), 11
Fulbright, Richard, **23**, 221
Fuqua, Charlie, 222

Gaines, Roy, 237
Gale, Charles, 119
Gale, Moe, 114, 139, 143, 144, 149, 150, 177, 189, 201–3
Gale, Tim, 121
Gale Agency, 149, 168, 177, 199, 201–3, 213
Gant, Cecil, 219
Gardner, Ava, 285
Garland, Red, 169
Garner, Erroll, 221
Garrett, Kenny, 319
Gaskill, Clarence, 58
"Gator Tail," 213, 220
Genzel, John, 323
Gershwin, George, 235
"Get Hep" / "Wild Fire," 132
Gibbs, Terry, 227

Gibson, Margie, 82
"Giddup Mule," 132, 143
Gilbert, Ronnie, 231
Gillespie, John Birks "Dizzy," 59, 127, 132, 161, 172, 173, 175, 195, 200, 201, 227, 267, 274, 280, 311, 314, 322
"Girl of my Dreams," 24
"Git It," 122
Glaser, Joe, 114, 150
Gleason, Ralph J., 231, 264
Glenn, Tyree, 234, 236; death of, 299
Glover, Jimmy, 182
"G-Men," 82
Goffin, Robert, 137
Golden Gate Ballroom, 140
"Gone Again," 250
Gonsalves, Paul, 234, 263, 271, 276–77, 281, 290, 291, 294, 295, 296, 298, 304; death of, 299
Goodman, Alice Hammond Duckworth, 69
Goodman, Benny, 16, 18, 28, 59, 69–75, **72, 73**, 77–83, **87, 89**, 90, 93, 95, 96, 99, 107, 113, 114, 135, 137, 139, 154, 155, 172, 177, 183, 212, 227, 257, 261–62, 263, 274, 275, 297, 316, 323; assistance to Cootie Williams, 91; and Carnegie Hall, 61; classical and jazz concerts, 88, 96–97; evaluation of Cootie Williams's orchestra, 104; integration, 86, 98; opinion of Cootie Williams, 85, 283; personality, 77–79, 283
Goodman, Gene, 69
Goodman, Harry, 69
Goodman, Irving, 69, 76, 82
Gordon, Claire P., 54
Gordon, Dexter, 30
"Got to do some war work, baby," 143
Gotham Stompers, 59
Graham, Shirley, 184
Grambling State University, 308–9
Grand Terrace Cafe, 103–8, 144, 170
Grant Park, 88
Granz, Norman, 149, 174
Great Paris Concert, The, 273
Green, Charlie "Big," 29–31, **29**, 261
Green, Edward, 65

Greer, William "Sonny," 37, 45, **47**, 54, 62, 90, 190, 234–35, 236, 264, 306, 313, 324
Grey, Al, 38, 316
Greystone Ballroom, 108
Guide to After Dark Miami, 254
Guy, Fred, **37, 47**
Guy, Joe, 96, 98, 150

Hackett, Bobby, 172, 237
Haley, Bill, 242
Hall, Barrie Lee, Jr., 297, 304, 307, 308, 315, 317, 321–22, 323
Hall, Edmond, 21–26, **23**, 137, **138**, 139
Hall, Jack, 70
Hamilton, Jimmy, 263, **270**, 271, 296, 310
Hammond, John, 54–55, 69, 75, 112, 117, 167, 174, 211, 226, 228, 230; on Cootie Williams's talent, 124; investment in Cootie Williams's orchestra, 92
Hampton, Lionel, 18, 56, 59, 83, 89, 91, 176, 187, 204, 208, 211, 217, 220, 229, 250, 281, 311, 324
Hancock, Herbie, 154
Handy, W. C., 187, 199, 234–35, 324
Hanighen, Bernie, **153**, 167
Hanna, Roland, 236
"Happy-Go-Lucky Local," 256, 310, 311
Happyland Ballroom, 26, 27
Hardwick, Otto, 39, **47**, 84, 128, 203
"Harlem Air Shaft," 65, 311
"Harlem Flat Blues," 38
"Harlem Hit Parade," 142
"Harmony in Harlem," 82
Harold's Club, 290
Harper, Ernie, 281
Harrah's, 290
Harris, Barry, 153
Harris, Franco, 309
Harrison, Charlie, 315
Harrison, Jimmy, **29**
Hawkins, Coleman, **29**, 30, 35, 81, 93, 137, **138**, 139, 154, 226, 228, 231, 236, 324
Hawkins, Erskine, 111, 119, 130, 132, 151, 170, 177, 181, 187, 200, 201, 204, 218, 220, 227, 266, 281
Hawkins, Florence, 181

Hayes, Roland, 98
Haymes, Dick, 113
"He Should'a Flip'd When He Flop'd," 180
Henderson, Fletcher, 15, 16, 28, **29**, 30, 35, 43, 52, 76, 77, 81, 85, 120, 132, 261
Henderson, Rick, 311
Hendersonia, 30
Henry, Ann, 292–93
Hentoff, Nat, 228, 230
Herman, Woody, 74
Herndon, Coy, 22
Higginbotham, J. C., 75, **173**, 231
Hill, Connie, 133
Hines, Earl "Fatha," 95, 103, 120, 226, 227, 292, 311
Hinton, Milt, 231
"Hip, Hip, Hooray," 122
Hit Records, 140, 143, 152, 161, 164, 167, 169, 197, 199, 208
Hodeir, Andre, 65
Hodges, Johnny, 35, **37**, 45, **47**, 49, 54, 56, 57, 59, 61, 63, 70, 71, 80, 89, 94, 226, 227, 262–63, 271, 281, 284, 285, 288–89, 290, 317, 322; death of, 291
Holiday, Billie, 19, 59, 106, 150, 174, 187
Holiday, Clarence, **29**
Holley, Major, 46
Hollywood Reporter, 199, 201
Holman, Nathaniel T., 20
Holmes, Charlie, 28, 94, 96, 98, 129–30, 145, 150, 169, 275; opinion of Cootie Williams's orchestra, 105; on quitting Cootie Williams's band, 151
Holmes, Wally, 181–82
"Holy City, The," 234
"Honeysuckle Rose," 61, 141
Honi and Brown, 182
Hopkins, Claude, 27, 231
Horne, Lena, 86, 147, 157, 186, 190
Horton, R. H., 98, 167
"Hot Feet," 38
Hot-Revue, 49
"House of Joy," 50, 166, 176, 183, 207, 209
Houston, Frank, 23
Howard Theater, 163, 201, 210

Hues Corporation, 182
Hughes, Franklin, 254
Hurricane, 130

"I Can't Believe That You're in Love with Me," 58
"I Can't Get Started," 198
"I Got Plenty of Nothin'," 236
"I Got Rhythm," 82, 167, 208
I Had the Craziest Dream, 77
"I Like the Sunrise," 289
"I Love You, Yes I Do," 208
"I May Be Easy, But I'm No Fool," 181
"I Should o' Been Thinkin' Instead of Drinkin'," 201
"I Want to be a Rug Cutter," 60
"I Want to Be Loved (But Only By You)," 198
"If It's True," 201
"If You Were In My Place," 60
"I'll Be Satisfied," 252
"I'm Beginning to See the Light," 161
Imitation of Life, 42
Impulse! Records, 262
"In a Mellotone" / "In a Mellow Tone," 65, 80, 284
"Indian Summer," 290
Indianapolis 500, 216
"Inflation Blues," 198
Ink Spots, 119, 120, 135, 139, 140, 144, 146, 147, **148**, 150, 162, 177, 178, 197, 202, 203, 222
Inspired Abandon, 57
"Is You Is or Is You Ain't," 152
"It Don't Mean a Thing (If It Ain't Got That Swing)," 45
"It Hurts Me," 229
Ives, Burl, 231

Jackson, Benjamin "Bull Moose," 208
Jackson, Franz, 93, 99
Jackson, Mahalia, 291
Jackson, Quentin, 38, 306
Jackson, Willis "Gator," 212, 214, 217, 220, 221
Jacquet, Illinois, 89, 92, 190, 199, 212
Jaegar, Harry, 72

James, Harry, 59, 61, 80, 81, 82, 85, 96, 137, 139, 147, 151, 167, 172, 173, 181, 200, 290, 322
James, Leon, 133, 144
James, Stephen, 70
Jaro International Records, 250, 251
Jarvis, Arnold, 182, 195, 239–48
Jazz Book, 174
Jazz Club U.S.A., 220
"Jazz Convulsions," 39
Jazz Hot, 242
Jazz Information, 71
Jazz: Its Evolution and Essence, 65
Jazz Magazine, 239, 245
Jazz Odyssey, The Sound of Harlem, 143
Jazz Oral History Project, 203, 250, 277, 296
Jazz Podium, 322
Jazz Ship, 311
Jazz Tango Dancing, 49
"Jeep's Blues," 311, 319
Jefferson, Hilton, 234, 236
Jenkins, Freddie, **37**, 38, 42, **47**, 48, 49, 52
Jenkins, Lester, 225, 229, 239–48, **241**
Jenkins Orphanage, 265
Jet, 216, 276
Jewish Floridian, The, 255
Johnson, Albert Sidney, 183
Johnson, Buddy, 161, 220, 262
Johnson, Bunk, 172
Johnson, Dottie Mae, 133
Johnson, Frank, 211
Johnson, Gus, 231
Johnson, Harold "Money," 315
Johnson, James P., 28, 106
Johnson, John, 307
Johnson, Pete, 142
Johnson Publishing, 307
Jones, Elvin, 268
Jones, Hank, 231
Jones, Herbie, 276
Jones, Heywood, 200
Jones, Isham, 24
Jones, Jimmy, 280–81
Jones, Jonah, 84, 86, 257
Jones, LeRoi (Amiri Baraka), 256
Jones, Muriel, 103
Jones, Nat, 256

Jones, Quincy, 295, 299
Jones, Richard "Jonesy," 62
Jones, Wallace, 267
Jordan, Louis, 152, 157, 187, 197, 201, 221
Jordan, Taft, 71, 130
Joya Sherrill Sings Duke, 281
Juarez, Gregg, 216
Jubilee, 147
"Juice Head Baby," 166, 224
"Jumping to Conclusions," 179

Kapp, Dave, 144
Kaye, Danny, 142
KBCA, 311
Keenan, Norman, 132, 143, **160**, 182
Kelley, Robin D. G., 154
Kennedy, John F., 278
Kenny, Bill, 139, 252; on Gale management fees, 120
Kenton, Stan, 147, 232
Kerouac, Jack, 213
Kersey, Ken, 96, 98, 116
Keys, Gary, 316
"Kidney Stew Blues," 180, 224
Killian, Al, 95
Kimbrough, Frank, 154
King of American Jazz, The—Duke Ellington and his Orchestra, 277
Kirby, John, 95, 111
Kirk, Andy, 92, 103, 116, 132, 151, 189
Kirkpatrick, Don, 99, 106
Krupa, Gene, 74, 83, 84, 86, 111, **173**, 237
Kuhn, Rolf, 236

Lachman and Carson Circus, 18
Ladnier, Tommy, 50
"Lady Mine," 24
LaFaro, Scott, 214
Laine, Frankie, 208
Lamb, John, 50, 281, 285, 306
Lambert, Eddie, 43, 286
Lambert, Hendricks, and Ross, 80
Lane, Lovey, 103
Larkin, Milton, 92
"Las Tres Senoras," 314
Lasker, Steven, 59

Lawrence, Robert, 124
Le Grand Romp, 235
Le Roi du Jazz Americain—Duke Ellington et son Orchestre, 277
Lee, Canada, 189
Lee, Peggy, 96, 97, 295
Left Bank Jazz Society, 310
Legend of Bessie Smith, The, 231
Leighton, Bernie, **87**
Leonard, Jack, 95
"Let the Door Knob Hitcha," 81–82
"Let the Good Times Roll," 213
"Let's Dance," 155
"Let's Do the Whole Thing or Nothing At All," 181, 182
Let's Go Night Clubbing, 179
"Let's Keep on Jumping," 133
Levy, Morris, 252
Lewis, Alma, 304
Lewis, Ted, 122
Lewisohn Stadium, 88, 187
"Liberian Suite," 289
Lieberman, Harold, 261
Lincoln Garden, 16
Lincoln Memorial, 97
Lipscomb, Charles Bridget "Charlie," 14–15, 19, 29, 92, 125, 183–84, 322
Lipscomb, Perico, 14
Little, Malcolm (Malcolm X), 142
Little, Steve, 284
Little Orpheus, 157
Live in Tokyo, 153
Lock, Bob, 105
Logan, Arthur, 209
Lombardo, Guy, 151
Long Island, 189, 211
Long Island Jewish Hillside Medical Center, 322
Look, 172, 181
Los Angeles, 42
Los Angeles Examiner, 146
Los Angeles Times, 54, 265, 318
Louis, Joe, 99, 187, 189, 192, 195, 227
"Lover," 250
Lowe, Mundell, 236
Lucas, Al, 229

Lunceford, Jimmie, 121, 147, 313
Luper, William "Billy," 92
"Lush Life," 278
Lynch, Dorothy, 189
Lynch, Walter J., 189

Mack, Eddie (Matthews Mack Edmonson), 216, 219, 220, 250
"Madeleine," 95
Majestic Records, 197–99, 201, 207–8
Mann, Herbie, 283
Manning, Frankie, 119, 218
"Marcheta," 106
Maritime Strike of 1946, 186
Marshall, Kaiser, **29**
"Mary Bell," 24
Mason, Robert "Cookie," 24
Masse, Jean-Marie, 240
Master Records, 57
Mathews, Billy, 198, 201, 208
"Matinee at Meadowbrook," 88
Matthews, Onzy, 318
Maxwell, Jimmy, 69, 76, 78, 82, 83, 90
May, Billy, 289–90
Mayflower Hotel, 82
McCarthy, Jim, 212
McCoy, Clyde, 219, 257
McGarity, Lou, **173**
McGhee, Howard, 95
McHugh, Jimmy, 58
McKay, Cliff, 249
McKinley, Ray, 207
McPartland, Jimmy, 16
McRae, Bob, 106
McRae, Carmen, 236, 311
McShann, Jay, 159
McVea, Jack, 197
"Me and You," 63, 65
Meadowbrook Club, 88–89
Melody Maker, 228, 273
Memories of Duke, 316
Mercer, Johnny, 165, 167, 180
Merchant Marines, 186
Mercury Records, 208, 224
Merrill, Bob, **168**, 170, 179, 180, 181, 182, 189, 197, 199, 201, 208, 211, 213, 214, 250

Merrill, Robert, Jr., 170
Metronome, 57, 60, 62, 72–73, 81, 89, 96, 106, 109, 121, 125, 126, 128, 130, 136, 141, 146, 201, 208, 230, 233, 235, 236, 253
Metropole Cafe, 252
Metropolitan Opera Company, 86
Mezzrow, Mezz, 228
Michels, Lloyd, 292
Mike Douglas Show, 311
Milano, Bobby, 255
Miley, James "Bubber," 36, 38, 39, 49, 254, 287
Miller, Glenn, 45
Miller, Irving, 119
Miller, Norma, 218
Millinder, Lucky, 119, 170, 177, 187, 195, 225
Mills, Irving, 43, 57
Mills Brothers, 108, **109**
Milt Hinton Place, 190
Minerve, Harold, 294, 316, 318
Mingus, Charles, 264, 305–6
Minnesota Vikings, 308–9
Mississippi Enterprise, 183
Mitchell, William P., 177
Mobile Music Award, 315
Mobile Register, 315
Moke and Poke, 139, 144
Money Jungle, 264
Monk, Thelonious, 106, 152, 154
Monk! Thelonious, Pannonica, and the Friendship Behind a Musical Revolution, 154
Monroe, Al, 105
Monroe, Vaughn, 95
Montreux Jazz Festival, 314
"Mooche, The," 265, 280, 287, 297
"Mood for Coot," 166–67, 182
"Mood Indigo," 64, 242, 281, 315, 316, 317
Moodsville, 255–56
Mooney, Art, 131
Moore, Anita, 309, 317, 318, 323
Moore, Gatemouth, 203
Moreland, Mantan, 200
Morgan, Rose, 192
Morton, Bennie, 231
Morton, Jelly Roll, 228
Morton, Tommy, 25

Mosaic Records, 59
Mount Angel Benedictine Abbey, 292–93
"Mournful Tho'ts," 28
Movietone Studios, 131
Mück, Rudy, 126
Muppet Show, The, 236
Murder at the Vanities, 42
Murphy, Mark, 80
Music and Rhythm, 75, 85, 110–11, 114, 127, 129, 322
Music Is My Mistress, 27, 278
Musical Chairs, 252
Mutual Broadcasting System (MBS), 123
"My Ideal," 139
"My Old Flame," 42
Myers, Eric, 320

NAACP, 117
Nance, Gloria, 275
Nance, Ray, 38, 71, 89, 254, 264, 265, 266, 273, 275–78, 280, 282, 298, 309, 315
Nanton, Joe "Tricky Sam," 36–39, **37**, 44, **47**, 49, 54, 264, 313, 317
NASCAR, 216
National Register of Historic Places, 151
NBC Orchestra, 119
New Orleans Suite, 291
New Orleans Superdome, 308
New York Age, 86, 98, 120
New York Amsterdam News, 91, 228
New York Herald, 124
New York Jazz Repertory Company, 312
New York Newspaper Guild, 188
New York Times, 62, 192, 303, 307
New Yorker Hotel, 86, 89, 90, 108
Newman, Joe, 196, 312, 323
Newport All Stars, 314
Newport Jazz Festival, 234, 313–14
Newton, Frankie, 95
Nice Festival, 320
Nicholas, Fayard, 132
Nicholas Brothers, 132
Nichols, Red, 127
"Night Train," 255, 256
Nightingale, Billy, 103
"Nightmare," 155

Nixon, Richard, 291
North Sea Jazz Festival, 314
"Now I Know," 142
"Now That You've Loved Me," 229
NYC Landmarks Preservation Commission, 190

Oberstein, Eli, 59, 140, 161, 166, 167, 198, 199
Ocean Forest Hotel, 186
Office of Defense Transportation (ODT), 113, 129
Office of Facts and Figures (OFF), 116
Ohio University, 87
Okazaki, Miles, 154
Okeh Records, 59, 106, 107, 143, 144, 166
"Old Maid Boogie," 224
"Old Man Blues," 42
"Old Man River," 213
Oliver, Joe "King," 16, 38, 245
"On the Road," 213
"On the Sunny Side of the Street," 250
One Night Stand, 159
"One O'Clock Jump," 81, 147
"Ooh-La-La," 201
"Open the Door, Richard," 197, 209
Orioles, 220, 223
Orodenker, Maurie, 79
Orpheum Theater (Los Angeles), 146
Orpheum Theater (Omaha), 145
"Outskirts of Town," 110
Overbea, Danny, 224

Pack, Lorenzo, 180
"Paducah," 38
Page, Leroy "Satchel," 9, 12
Page, Oran "Hot Lips," 84, 200
Palace Theater, 144
Palms, 23
Panassie, Hugues, 48–50, 213
Paradise Theater, 184
Paramount Theatre, 125, 162, 197, 200
Parker, Bill "Weasel," 208, 217, 220
Parker, Charlie "Bird," 149, 173, 292, 317; with Cootie Williams, 159–60
Payne, Sylvester "Vess," 136, 143, 144, 156
PBS American Masters, 154
"Peckin'," 80

Peeples, Bill, 256
People's Voice, The, 90, 92, 114, 119, 121, 128, 135, 139, 147–48, 181
Pensacola Jazz Band, 21
Pepper, Art, 320
"Percy Speaks," 229
"Perdido," 242
Peterson, Chuck, 117
Pettiford, Oscar, 74, 95, 138, 234
Philadelphia Symphony Orchestra, 125
Philadelphia Theater, 213
Philadelphia Tribune, 115
Pier Casino ballroom, 151
Pittsburgh Courier, 57, 62, 71, 75, 90, 93, 165, 201, 242
Pittsburgh Post Gazette, 97
Pittsburgh Press, 95, 162
Pittsburgh Steelers, 308–9
Pittsburgh Sun-Telegraph, 97
Pittsburgh Symphony Orchestra, 96
Pla-Mor, 187
Platterbrains, 128
"Please Give Your Love to Me," 229
PM, 172
Poitier, Sidney, 235
Pollock, Ben, 80
Pope, John A., 20
Pope, John C. "Johnny," 20
Popular Duke Ellington, The, 287
Porgy and Bess, 235
Porgy and Bess Revisited, 236
Porter, Cole, 143
"Portrait of Louis Armstrong," 291
"Portrait of Sidney Bechet," 291
Powell, Adam Clayton, Jr., 234
Powell, Earl "Bud," 136, 140, 143, 145, 147, 152, 155–57, 159, 317
Powell, Mel, 116
Powerhouse, 116
"Prelude in C# Minor," 155
Preminger, Otto, 235
Preservation Hall Jazz Band, 314
Presley, Elvis, 228, 230
Prestige Records, 256
Preston, Eddie, 290
Price, Sammy, 161
Priester, Julian, 268

Prima, Louis, 250
Procope, Russell, 30, 266, 292, 294, 295, 302, 306, 310, 316
Prudente, Vince, 50, 287, 295, 307, 308–9; on Ellington-Williams relationship, 293–94, 307
Prysock, Arthur, 221
Prysock, Wilburt "Red," 221
Pulitzer Prize, 154

Quinichette, Paul, 304

Ra, Sun, 292
Racette, Frank, 269, 281
Rachmaninoff, Sergei, 155
Radzitzky, Carlos de (Baron Radzitzky of Ostrowick), 240, 242
Rainbow Grill, 292
Rainey, Ma, 217
"Rangoon," 229–30
Ravens, 213, 214, 220, 221
Ravinia Festival, 306
Ravinia Highland Park, 261
RCA Victor, 59, 63, 140, 169, 198, 228, 229, 230, 231, 292, 314
Reader's Digest, 292
Reardon, Casper, 74
Recollections of the Big Band Era, 266
"Red Blues" / "Cherry Red Blues," 109, 110, 122, 142–43, 166, 181, 203, 224
Redd, Freddie, 305
Redick, "Kid," 177
Redman, Don, 99, 133, 142
"Reflections," 153
Regal Theater, 224
Renaissance Ballroom, 93, 140, 167, 181
"Rent Party Blues," 38
Reprise Records, 266
Reuss, Allan, 59
Revere, Paul, 184
"Rhapsody in Bass," 182
Rich, Buddy, 81
Richmond, June, 150
"Rinky Dink," 229
Rivers, Fletcher, 144
RKO Theatre, 145

Roach, Max, 264
Robeson, Paul, 88, 149
Robin Hood Dell, 88
Robinson, Bill "Bojangles," 180–81, 234
Robinson, Jackie, 83, 190
Robinson, "Sugar" Ray, 170
"Rock Skippin' at the Blue Note," 289
"Rock the Boat," 182
"Rockin' in Rhythm," 80
Rodzinski, Artur, 96
"Roll 'Em," 105, 122, 147, 161
Roosevelt, Eleanor, 82, 97, 227
Roosevelt, Franklin D., 82
"Rose Room," 121, 285
Roseland Ballroom, 15, 24, 30
Rosemont Ballroom, 24, 25
Rosenkrantz, Timme, **270**
Ross, Alonzo, 10, 22, **23**, 26
"'Round Midnight," 152–55, **153**, 161, 321, 323
'Round Midnight (movie), 157
Roundtable, The, 252, 255
Rowe, Billy, 75, 165, 201
"Royal Garden Blues," 152
Royal Theater, 123, 169
Rubinstein, Helena, 192
"Rumpus in Richmond," 65
Russell, Pee Wee, 236, 237
Russell, Rosalind, 148

"Salt Lake City Bounce," 166
"Salty Papa Blues," 208
Salute to Duke Ellington, 314
Sampson, Edgar, 154
San Jacinto Medical Center, 296
San Stefan's Keller, 244
"Satin Doll," 315
Saturday Evening Post, 149
"Saturday Night (Is the Loneliest Night of the Week)," 161
Sauter, Eddie, 79
Savannah, Georgia, 24
"Save the Bones for Henry Jones," 201
Savoy Ballroom, 40, 106, 114, 119, 136, 139, 140, 151, 152, 159, **160**, 167, 169, 179, 189, 196, 200, 203, 209, 211, 212, 214, **218**, 220, 222, 225, 227, 230, 252–53, 254; closure for

Vice charges, 130; final closure, 203, 238; history, 120; reopening, 135
Savoy Sultans, 135, 225
Schiffman, Frank, 224
Schuller, Gunther, 204
Scott, Hazel, 149
Scott, Raymond, 70, 115–16, 119, 122
Seafarers International Union, 186
Sears, Al, 229, 267, 321
Sebastian, Frank, 42
"Second Line," 291
Serkin, Rudolph, 124
Sesame Street, 236
Shamrock Hotel, 295
Shaughnessy, Ed, 262
Shavers, Charlie, 84, 172, 236
Shaw, Artie, 74, 82, 84, 92, 155, 161, 172
"Shepherd (Who Watches Over the Night Flock), The," 50, 283–84, 311, 317, 320, 323
Shepp, Archie, 292
Sheppard, Harry, 236, 237
Sherman Hotel, 86, 114
Sherrill, Joya, 169, 281–82, **282**
Shields, Calvin "Eagle Eye," 21, 22, 23, 237
Sholes, Steve, 228
Shoobe, Louis, 116
Shore, Dinah, 142
Short, Casey, 26
Shorter, Howard "Bud," 214
"Shotgun Boogie," 219
Simmons, John, 85, 86, 90, 93
Simon, George, 61, 128, 231, 236
Simons, Tom, 274–78
Sinatra, Frank, 266, 289–90, 299
Singleton, Elvira, 196
Singleton, Zutty, 292
Sir John Hotel, 255
"Sixty Minute Man," 221
"Skrontch," 60
"Sleepy Valley," 106
"Slicing the Beat: Jazz Eighth-Notes as Expression Microrhythm," 284
Slide Trombone, 57
"Sliding and Gliding," 213
Small's Paradise, 160

Smith, Bessie, 214, 217, 231
Smith, Cladys "Jabbo," 27
Smith, Clara, 217
Smith, Fletcher, 132, **160**
Smith, Jimmy, 262
Smith, Keely, 250, 252
Smith, Russell "Pop," 29, 35
Smith, Willie "The Lion," 236
"Snibor," 289
Solid Trumpet of Cootie Williams, The, 255–56, **256**
"Solitude," 52, 315
"Somebody's Gotta Go," 152, 154, 224
"Someone I Knew," 179
Sophisticated Ladies, 321
"Sophisticated Lady," 281
"Sound Track," 198
Southern University, 183
Southway Hotel, 103
Spanier, "Muggsy," 28, 81
"Spanish Flea," 292
Spivak, Charlie, 139, 200
"St. Louis Blues," 121, 122, 161, 234
St. Peter's Church, 323
Stacy, Jess, 59, 78
Stark, Bobby, **29**, 30
"Steam Roller Blues," 220
Stegmeyer, Bill, 232
Stern, Edgar, 192
Stevenson, Adlai, 227
Stewart, Rex, **29**, 30, 51, 52–55, **53**, 57, 64, 70, 75, 153–54, 172, 195, 226, 231, 234, 236, 266, 267, 317
"Stingy Blues," 179–80
"Stompin' at the Savoy," 153–54
"Stompology," 59
"Stormy Weather," 81
Stormy Weather (movie), 157
Stovall, Don, 98
Straight, No Chaser, 154
"Strange As It Seems," **146**
Strayhorn, Billy, 64, 71, 89, 95, 234, 265, 275, 278, 289, 324
Südwestfunk, 244
"Sugar Blues," 257

Sugar Hill, 189
Sullivan, Ed, 212
Sullivan, Joe, 128
Sunset Royals Orchestra, 130
Super Bowl IX, 308–9
"Superman," 79, 88, 89
Swing Era, The, 204
Swingin' at the Savoy, 218
Sydney Opera House, 318
Syria Mosque concert hall, 97

"Take the 'A' Train," 89, 155, 278, 280, 282, 287, 291, 296, 297, 305, 308–9, 315, 317
Talmadge, Mrs. Julius, 184
"Taste of Honey, A," 292
Tate, Buddy, 92, 218
Tatum, Art, 137, **138**, 139, 149
Taylor, Billy (bassist), 59, 116
Taylor, Billy (pianist), 237, 303
Taylor, Sam "The Man," 132, **160**, 169, 242
Teagarden, Jack, 111, 176
Tempo (American magazine), 57, 74
Tempo (Australian magazine), 211
Tenot, Frank, 239–48, **239**
Terry, Clark, 95, 267, 295, 305, 306, 324
"Tess's Torch Song," 142
Texas Christian University, 297
"That Old Black Magic," 250
"That's the Lick," 180
Thelonious Monk Institute of Jazz, 154
Thelonious Monk: The Life and Times of an American Original, 154
Thiele, Bob, 262, 316
"Things Ain't What They Used to Be," 132, 309, 317, 318
Third Sacred Concert, 296, 307
Thomas, Joe, 231
"Three Black Kings, The," 287
Three Loose Nuts, 103
Thurmond, Strom, 186
Tic Toc Club, 115
"Tiger Rag," 58, 121
Til, Sonny, 220
Timmens, Jim, 236
Tin Pan Alley, 280
Titus, Horace, 192

Tizol, Juan, 36, **37**, 42, **47**, 56, 62, 297, 322
Tizol, Rose, **37**
To Be or Not to Bop, 267
"Tootin' Through the Roof," 54
Tough, Dave, **87**, 106
Towie, Casker, 22
Town Hall, 106, 124
Travis, Merle, 219
Treadwell, George, 155–56
Trianon, 114
Trifton, George, 261
"Trumpet Concerto, A," 184
Tucker, Earl "Snakehips," **47**
Tulane Stadium, 308
Tunnell, George "Bon Bon," 99
Turner, "Big" Joe, 142
Turney, Norris, 295
Tuskegee Army Air Field, 149
"Tutti for Cootie" / "Tootie for Cootie," 80, 257, 263, 277, 291
"Tuxedo Junction," 266
"Twitch, The," 287
"Typhoon," 207

Udkoff, Bob, 305
Ulanov, Barry, 59, 110, 121, 128, 174
United Service Organizations (USO), 117
Universal Attractions, 202, 213, 254
University of Idaho, 128
University of Wisconsin, 294
Up In Arms, 142

Vagabonds, 182
Vance, Dick, 238
Vanderbilt, Cornelius, 55
Variety, 85, 90, 108, 110, 133, 135, 140, 162, 207, 216, 221, 223, 229, 250, 254
Vaughan, Sarah, 306, 314
Victor Talking Machine Company, 24
Vinson, Eddie Lee "Cleanhead," Jr., 92, 98, 104, 106, 112, 116, 118, 122, 129, 136, 142, 143, 151, 152, **160**, 161, 167–70, **168**, 180, 201, 203, 208, 224; critical evaluations of, 105; drinking, 169, 224; *Film Vodvil*, 132–33; joining Cootie Williams, 93, 94;

return to Cootie Williams's band, 166; reunion with Cootie Williams, 224
Voice of America, 220

W. C. Handy Theatre, 199
Wade, Adam, 252
Wagner, Robert, 227
Walcott, "Jersey" Joe, 195
Walker, Aaron "T Bone," 229
Walker, Jimmy, 198
Walker, Jonas, 98
Waller, Thomas "Fats," 28, 43, 82, 141, 157, 190, 321
Wallichs, Glenn, 165, 167
Walton, Greely, 96, 98
War Mobilization Department, 162
Ward, Billy, 221
Warick Records, 251
Warren, Tony, 161
Washington, Dinah, 203, 208, 209, 213, 214, 221, 222, 224, 317
Washington, Fredi, 41, 42, 128, 148, **215**
Washington, George, 184
Washington, James, 196
Wassing, Robert, 192
Watkins, Toney, 269
Watson, Laurel, 132
WBBC, 25
We, The People, 77
"We Remember Duke," 242
Weavers, 231
Webb, William "Chick," 27, 28, 29, 35, 43, 59, 63, 120, 140, 144, 154, 212, 218, 234, 317
Webster, Ben, 19, 30, 63, 234, 264, 317
Wein, George, 312–14, 320
Welles, Orson, 187
Wells, Dicky, 225
WERD, 170
"West End Blues," 82, 122, 146
"When Cootie Left the Duke," 70
"When it's Sleepy Time Down South," 266
"When My Baby Left Me," 106, 166
"When the Saints Go Marching In," 244, 255
Whetsel, Arthur, **37**, 42, **47**, 52, **53**, 324
White, Walter, 117
Whiteman, Paul, 111

Whitman, Ernie "Bubbles," 147
Wilkins, Ernie, 231
Wilkins, Lucille, 103
Will the Big Bands Ever Come Back?, 266
William Morris Agency, 95, 116, 119
Williams, Catherine Henrietta Smith (wife), 40, **41**, 140, 181–82, **191**, **215**, 232, 238, 248, 305, 321, 322, **324**; Addisleigh Park home, 189–90; death of, 324; domestic life, 216; financial impact of keeping orchestra, 203; godmother to Ellington children, 190; on money, 91, 93, 135; nickname, 216; retirement, 311; St. Albans neighbors, 192; Sugar Hill apartment, 189; television, 223; touring with Cootie, 145, 147–48; vacation, 85, 151
Williams, Charles Melvin "Cootie:" 1933 tour with Ellington, 47–48; 1959 European tour, 238–48, 273; 1963 European tour, 273; accommodations at the Ocean Forest Hotel, 186; acting, 157; Addisleigh Park home, 189–90; Adler Shoe advertisement, **174**; affair with Ivie Anderson, 62; affairs, 285; and alcohol, 190–92, 194, 201, 209, 228; altercation with Bill Kenny, 162; Armstrong influence on, 43; arrival in New York, 25; assault of Eddie "Cleanhead" Vinson, 159; assault of pianist, 305; assault of Ray Nance, 275–78; assault of Rex Stewart, 30; awards, 181, 306, 315; badge, 200; band battle with Ellington, 129; band bus, 213; band fine system, 189; band leading strategy, 108; band personnel, 96; on being a band leader, 264; with Belle Barth, 253–55; and "Big" Green, 30; Big Three Tour, 139–40, 143–50, 157, 162, 189; on Bud Powell, 160; bus accident, 214; with Capitol Records, 164–69; car telephone, 170; and Carnegie Hall, 61; cars, 216; and Cat Anderson, 267, 271, 280, 307; on Charlie Parker, 160; on Chick Webb, 63; civil rights, 98, 184–85; comparison to Thelonious Monk's career, 154; compositions, 106, 179, 181, 182, 184, 201, 208; contract with Goodman, 76, 85, 89,

91; Cootie Williams Orchestra style, 96; critical evaluations of, 48–50, 96, 97, 107, 109–11, 121, 122, 130, 133, 135, 136, 139, 141, 143–46, 150, 154, 158, 162, 169, 172, 178, 182, 198, 199, 200, 204, 207, 210, 211, 213, 216, 220, 221, 223, 229–30, 231, 232, 235, 236, 242, 253, 257, 265, 280, 290, 297–98, 303, 307, 309, 311, 312–13, 317, 318, 320, 322; critical expectations with Goodman, 77; date of birth, 9; death of, 322; departure of Eddie "Cleanhead" Vinson, 170; Derby Records, **219**; "The Diplomat" drawing, **247**; disbanding, 115–16, 207, 217; discipline, 70, 79, 82, 189, 266; on domestic life, 211, 214–16; on *Down Beat*, 164; drums, 13; on Duke Ellington's band, 35; Edmond Hall guardianship, 21; on the Ellington band's lack of discipline, 45–46; on Ellington's trumpet section, 52; estrangement from father, 194; on European jazz fans, 48; fight with Dusty Fletcher, 209; on film, 40–42; *Film Vodvil*, 131–33; financial impact of keeping orchestra, 203; first trumpet lessons, 14–15; and food, 239–48, 285; freelance work with Goodman, 96, 113; friendship with Joe Louis, 192–93; funeral of, 323; on the future of big bands, 114–15; gambling, 195; genealogy of, 10–11; Goodman hiring, 69–70; Goodman salary, 75, 135; Goodman small group session, 82; hand injury, 209, 210; health, 286; hiring by Ellington, 35; on his musical style, 76, 80; and his Rug Cutters, 57–58, 61, 76; Hit Records, 140; and horse racing, 195, 305, 321, 322; house band leader at the Savoy, 225–26; ideas for band versatility, 222; illness, 178, 243, 290, 296, 311, 318, 319, 322; improvisation methods, 65–66, 286; incorporation, 199; and insurance, 210; issues with Bud Powell, 156; and Jim Crow, 186–87; "King of the Trumpet" cartoon, 152; knee injury, 162; on lack of crossover, 135, 142; last Ellington session, 310; lawsuits against, 196; lead trumpet with Goodman, 79, 82; leadership, 93; on leaving the music business, 203, 211; legacy, 322; letter to the DAR, 184–85; on life as a musician, 274; listening habits, 174; management, 119; military draft, 117; and Moe Gale, 119–20, 149; musical director for Belle Barth, 255; musical style, 80; nightclub ownership proposals, 170; onstage fire incident, 199; open letter regarding FEPC, 185–86; opinion of "be-bop," 173–74; opinion of Benny Goodman, 79, 85, 261, 283; opinion of Charlie Parker, 292; opinion of Duke Ellington, 265, 299, 303, 307, 312, 317; opinion of Eddie "Cleanhead" Vinson, 170; opinion of Ike Williams, 193; opinion of Louis Armstrong, 42, 227, 292; opinion of Mercer Ellington, 302–3, 320; opinion of Mercer Ellington's new musicians, 304; opinion of Paul Gonsalves, 277; Oral Jazz History Project interview, 11, 194, 203, 250, 262, 277, 296; orchestra debut, 103–4; orchestra recording debut, 106; origin of nickname, 10; and Pearl Bailey, 122–23; personality, 48–49, 93, 121, 122, 128, 140, 144, 151, 172, 176, 195, 228, 237, 244, 267–68, 271, 275, 281, 282, 284–87, 293, 305, 309–10; photograph of, **41**, **47**, **53**, **72**, **87**, **89**, **98**, **104**, **109**, **111**, **118**, **126**, **131**, **134**, **138**, **148**, **152**, **155**, **160**, **164**, **165**, **166**, **173**, **179**, **181**, **191**, **202**, **215**, **230**, **235**, **239**, **241**, **270**, **279**, **282**, **313**, **323**, **324**; plans for the future, 314; Platterbrains radio show, 128; playing Bach's Brandenburg Concertos, 124; playing style, 284; political views, 187, 227; poll winner, 81, 96, 105, 137, 161, 172, 174, 183, 210; popularity, 146, 174, 177, 189, 197, 204, 209, 210, 222, 224, 226, 244, 248, 262, 271, 284–85; racial barrier broken, 183, 188, 221; racial implications of Goodman hire, 72–75; radio broadcast, 179, 223; radio station partnership, 170; and Raymond Scott, 115–16; RCA recording contract, 228, 233; reasons for orchestra failure, 204; recording debut with James P. Johnson, 7; relationship with Duke Ellington, 292–93, 296–97, 298; relationship with Johnny Hodges, 291; relationship with Mercer Ellington, 302; resistance to downsizing orchestra, 201–2; retirement, 311–12, 316, 321–22; on the return of the blues, 217; return to Goodman, 261–62; return to Ellington, 263; return to Mobile, 183; reunion with Charlie Lipscomb, 183; reunion with Eddie "Cleanhead" Vinson, 224; and rhythm and blues, 242; and rock and roll, 226, 242; rooming with Jimmy Maxwell, 83; and "'Round Midnight," 152–55; sale of St. Albans home, 254; Savoy Ballroom, 128, 129, 130, 218; Savoy Ballroom battle with Duke Ellington, 121; Savoy Ballroom battle with Earl "Fatha" Hines, 121; Savoy Ballroom record, 218; and the Seafarers International Union, 186; and the second Ellington European tour, 62; sense of humor, 176, 287; "the show must go on" attitude, 162, 188, 214, 243; the small groups, 57–59; smallpox vaccine, 188; on song authorship, 56; St. Albans house, 211; St. Albans neighbors, 192, 234; stage presence, 97, 106, 109, 110, 133, 169, 306; starting his orchestra, 90, 91, 95, 96, 98, 99; stolen trumpet, 200; "Strange As It Seems," 146; Sugar Hill apartment, 189; talent scout, 105, 110, 150, 156, 216; television, 223, 236–37, 311; thoughts on leading a band, 107; thoughts on music, 325; thoughts on teaching, 294, 307; thoughts on Universal Attractions, 203; tours, 134, 157, 182–83, 199, 200, 210, 211, 221; trombone, 60; trumpet brand, 126, 321; trumpet sound of, 50, 277, 324; trumpet studies, 125, 127; union card problems, 28; vacation, 151, 210, 292; versatility, 48; virtuosity, 44, 50–51, 124; vocalist, 37, 45, 81–82, 143, 181, 182, 250, 318; and W. C. Handy, 234–35; war restrictions, 113–14, 115; wedding, 40; work as a single, 249–50; Young family circus job, 18–20

Williams, Clinton (uncle), 17
Williams, Elbert (brother), 12, 16, 18, 193
Williams, Isaac "Ike," Jr. (brother), 12, 16, 71, 144
Williams, Isaac "Ike," Sr. (father), 9, 11–12; death of, 194; discipline, 20; loss of money, 26; marriage, 16; permission for Cootie to move to Jacksonville, 21; visit to Cootie's home, 193–94
Williams, Joe, 283, 295, 320
Williams, Leroy Barney (brother), 16, 92, 193–94, 323
Williams, Luvenia (Lucy) (great-grandmother), 10
Williams, Maggie Sam (grandmother), 11
Williams, Mary Lou, 99, 147
Williams, Melvina Frost (mother), 9, 12; death, 16; marriage, 16
Williams, Nelson "Cadillac," 242
Williams, Pinky, 236
Williams, Richard, 268
Williams, Russell, 133
Williams, S. Walter, 28
Williams, Samuel (great-grandfather), 10
Williams, Sandy, 96, 98, 105, 149
Williams, Stephen (Steve) (grandfather), 10
Williams, Trudy Clabon (stepmother), 193
Wilmer, Valerie "Val," 273
Wilson, Derby, 47
Wilson, Gerald, 311
Wilson, Jackie, 252
Wilson, John S., 303
Wilson, Teddy, 59, 74, 83, 85, 91, 227, 237, 261
Winchell, Walter, 147
Winters, Shelly, 227
WLIB, 170, 254
WMCA, 25, 165–66
WOID (Miami), 24
Wood, Mitchell "Booty," 314
Woodard, Isaac, 187
Woodlawn Cemetery, 324
Woodman, Britt, 306, 316
Woodyard, Sam, 281, 290, 306, 314
World War II, 103, 113
World's Greatest Jazz Band, 311

Wright, Lammar, 126
"Write Me a Letter," 213
"Wrong Neighborhood," 181

York, Alvin, 176
"You Can't Have My Love No More," 224
"You Talk a Little Trash" / "Let's Toot," 147, 159, 208, 314
Young, Ben, 292
Young, Irma, 18, 19
Young, James "Trummy," 22, 313–14
Young, Lee, 18, 19
Young, Lester, 18, 19, 30, 61, 223, 226, 236
Young, Willis "Billy," 18–20
Young Man with a Horn, 157
Your Hit Parade, 147
"You're the One for Me Sweetheart," 179

ABOUT THE AUTHOR

Photo credits: Lyd & Mo Photography, Pasadena

Steve Bowie is a retired aerospace engineer who curates and hosts the Duke Ellington–themed podcast *Ellington Reflections*. He has presented papers on Cootie Williams and Kenny Burrell for conferences held by the Duke Ellington Society of Sweden. He plays saxophone and lives in Pasadena, California, with his wife, Julie Swayze, and their barely legal number of cats. He can be contacted at steve@cootiewilliams.com.

www.ingramcontent.com/pod-product-compliance
Lightning Source LLC
Chambersburg PA
CBHW030601230426
43661CB00053B/1790